Counter-Tradition

COUNTER-TRADITION

A Reader in the Literature of

Dissent and Alternatives / *Edited by*

SHEILA DELANY *With a Foreword*

by LOUIS KAMPF / *Basic Books, Inc.,*

Publishers NEW YORK/LONDON

1971 by Basic Books, Inc.
Library of Congress Catalog Card Number: 73–147018
SBN 465–01430–5
Manufactured in the United States of America
Designed by Vincent Torre

ACKNOWLEDGEMENTS

The Scripture quotations (Amos) in this publication are from the Revised Standard Version of the Bible, copyrighted 1946 and 1952 by the Division of Christian Education of the National Council of the Churches of Christ in the U.S.A. and used by permission.

Thucydides selection from *The Peloponnesian War*, translated by Rex Warner. Penguin Books edition (1954).

Lucius Annaeus Florus selection from *Epitome of Roman History*, translated by E. S. Forster. Loeb Classical Library edition, Harvard University Press.

"Henry at Le Mans" (anon.), "The Origins of the Waldensian Heresy" (anon.), "The Waldenses" by Walter Map, and "Prologue" to *A Treatise Against the Waldenses* by Bernard de Fontcaude reprinted from *Heresies of the High Middle Ages*, edited by Walter L. Wakefield & Austin P. Evans. New York: Columbia University Press, 1969, pp. 108–115, 200–202, 203–204, and 211–213.

"Twelve Articles," from *Luther's Works*, vol. 46. Reprinted by permission of Fortress Press, Philadelphia.

"Thomas Müntzer's Last Tract against Martin Luther," translated by Hans J. Hillerbrand, *The Mennonite Quarterly Review*, 38 (1964), 24–36.

Selections from *The Mechanical Bride* by Marshall McLuhan reprinted by permission of the publisher, The Vanguard Press. Copyright, 1951, by Herbert Marshall McLuhan.

Malcolm X selection from *Malcolm X Speaks*. Copyright © 1965 by Merit Publishers and Betty Shabazz.

R. D. Laing selection reprinted from *Journal of Existentialism*, vol. V (1965), pp. 417–422. Copyright, Libra Publishers, Inc., Roslyn Heights, L.I., N.Y.

Wilfred Pelletier, "Childhood in an Indian Village," reprinted by permission of Neewin Publishing Company, Toronto, Ontario, Canada.

Christopher Caudwell selection "Liberty: A Study on Bourgeois Illusion," from *Studies and Further Studies in a Dying Culture* by Christopher Caudwell. Reprinted by permission of Monthly Review Press, New York. (Condensed from the original.)

"Camilo," reprinted from Che Guevara, *Che Guevara Speaks*. Reprinted by permission of Pathfinder Press, Inc. Copyright © 1967 by Merit Publishers, New York.

"Their Morals and Ours" by Leon Trotsky, reprinted by permission of Pathfinder Press, Inc., New York, N.Y. Copyright © 1969 by Merit Publishers.

Jean Froissart's selections reprinted from *The Chronicles of Jean Froissart*. In Lord Berners' Translation. Selected, edited and introduced by Gillian and William Anderson (Centaur Classics Edition). Copyright © 1963 by Centaur Press Ltd. Reprinted by permission of Centaur Press Ltd. and Southern Illinois University Press.

E. M. Forster selection reprinted from *Abinger Harvest* by E. M. Forster. Copyright, 1936, renewed, 1964, by E. M. Forster. Reprinted by permission of Harcourt Brace Jovanovich, Inc. and Edward Arnold (Publishers) Ltd., London, England.

Roland Barthes selection reprinted from *Writing Degree Zero* by Roland Barthes. Translated from the French *Le Degré Zero de L'Ecriture* © 1953 by Editions du Seuil. Translation © 1967 by Jonathan Cape, Ltd. Preface Copyright © 1968 by Susan Sontag. Reprinted by permission of Hill & Wang, Inc.

Robert Jungk selection reprinted from *Brighter than a Thousand Suns* by Robert Jungk © 1958 by Harcourt Brace Jovanovich, Inc. and reprinted with their permission and with the permission of Victor Gollancz, Ltd., London, England.

FOREWORD

When I was a freshman, I took one look at the anthology the clerk in the bookstore handed me and knew that I couldn't possibly get through the year. I remember some of the names: Addison and Steele, Charles Lamb, Cardinal Newman, and those representative moderns—Franklin P. Adams and James Thurber. Miraculously, my teacher managed to ignore the oversized, overpriced, and irrelevant book for most of the semester.

But most teachers in composition or core humanities programs find themselves trapped by the social and political function of the courses they teach— and by the books they must use in them. Freshman courses and textbooks are usually an introduction to the dominant culture, to the standard language, and to the going ideologies masking the society's real concerns. The mysteries of style (which are to be unveiled in the works of certain "masters") allegedly contain the key to getting on in the great race for preferment. "Read Addison and Steele and learn to write like them," another English teacher told me. My answer was to forget about his (and the anthology's) version of the past. But the answer of most students was (and is) to accept the inevitability of their ignorance and to resign themselves to their incapacity to learn. One function of education as we misunderstand it today is to convince students that they have every opportunity to become "civilized" and to transcend their class origins; failure indicates that they have not measured up. "Too bad for them" says the system.

What do most textbooks full of exemplary specimens of style have to do with the possibilities of almost any student's life? What do all those minor classics have to do with the experience of someone beginning college? One consequence of most freshman curricula is that students find it difficult to believe that events in the past might have anything to do with the world they know.

The official literary tradition, as Sheila Delany points out in her Introduction to *Counter-Tradition,* has been established to serve the social objectives of elites. So we teach our students to absorb Matthew Arnold's attitudes toward the "populace" as literature, but we rarely encourage them to read Marx and Engels, who spoke so much more directly on behalf of the oppressed. *Culture and Anarchy* is literature; *The Communist Manifesto* is not. Here, finally, in Sheila Delany's *Counter-Tradition,* is a long overdue and invigorating alternative to the official (and deadening) version of the past which still dominates freshman studies in our colleges. This collection invites us to get into the habit of studying what really matters *to us*—and that is the beginning of a real education.

Yet how many will have the opportunity to use this book, or others like it? English in the academy mirrors the conservative nature of the institution. Yet if the study of verbal expression—of literature, writing, rhetoric—is to be anything more than an academic obstacle, we will have to engage in those struggles which will allow us to explore the past with quite different ends in mind.

LOUIS KAMPF
Massachusetts Institute
of Technology

November 1970

CONTENTS

Counter-Tradition

INTRODUCTION

The rationale for this anthology is that many teachers and students find the dominant values of our culture irreconcilable with their personal lives and political convictions. Some of these values are social hierarchy, the sanctity of private property, strongly differentiated sex roles, absolute morality, undiscriminating respect for law, and the wisdom of resignation to society as it is. They are conveyed in many ways, both overt and implicit in the structure of our political and educational institutions, in advertising, in family life and social relations, in the presentation of news by television, radio, and newspapers. So pervasive are these values that they may be said to constitute an official culture; and in general they are supported also by the European-American literary and critical tradition which we tend to accept as *the* tradition. To teach composition has usually meant, therefore, to teach essays that exemplify official values while they illustrate the art of writing. Francis Bacon, Thomas Browne, Samuel Johnson, Thomas Macaulay, John Henry Newman, Ralph Waldo Emerson, T. S. Eliot, Alfred North Whitehead —these are some of the names that appear in books of classic essays.

In order to compensate for the ideological uniformity of classic essays, another type of anthology has recently become popular: the collection of "relevant" writing, consisting of contemporary pieces on contemporary problems. The difficulty here for the teacher of composition is that contemporary prose offers little instruction in the art of writing: if it does not serve as a negative example, it is likely to be without much distinction at all. Further, that contemporary relevance is achieved only (or best) in contemporary writing is a solipsistic notion; it implies that our society sprang phoenix-like from the ashes of dead civilizations and that, being unique, it cannot be understood through history. The late scholar and critic C. S. Lewis wrote, "Humanity does not pass through phases as a train passes through stations: being alive, it has the privilege of always moving yet never leaving anything behind. Whatever we have been, in some sort we are still." Logically extended, the confusion of relevance with up-to-the-minute modernity generates absurd slogans ("Don't trust anyone over thirty") and absurd fables (the "generation gap"). These, carefully nurtured by establishment media, not only reassure us that our crises are without historical roots; not only divert our attention from their real causes; but cut us off from what help can be found in the revolutionary past. And in doing all this, the striving for "relevance" paradoxically shows itself to be of a piece, after all, with the conservative past.

There is, though, a tradition of opposition to the values of official culture. What makes such opposition traditional is not only direct influence, like that of the Old Testament prophets upon Blake and Carlyle, or of Marx upon

William Morris and Mao Tse-Tung; nor only common sources, such as the New Testament, which influenced medieval heretics, fifteenth-century revolutionaries, and the Digger Gerrard Winstanley. It is traditional simply as a habit of mind and a social force constantly present in history, always with us (as Jesus said of the poor) and (like the poor) revolutionary in its implications if not always in its outright statements. The impulse to oppose cultural norms appears as inarticulate revolt, as social criticism, as vision, as ideology, as completed revolution; it may spring from logic, disillusionment, or the experience of oppression. In short, it is part of the continuing dialectic of history, as much our cultural heritage as what it opposes. What I mean, then, by "counter-tradition" is not "that which opposes tradition," but "the tradition which opposes."

Besides constituting an intellectual tradition, the pieces in this volume also form a literary corpus of excellence and rhetorical variety. Not surprisingly, most of the prose included is recognizably "traditional" in its range of style, for rhetoric—nearly as versatile as religion in lending itself to opposite causes—does not confer meaning but receives it. No technique, no "know-how" (to borrow McLuhan's phrase) is entirely value-free, for no technique exists outside of history; and it is history that confers meaning. George Orwell reversed the causal order when he stated, in a famous essay, that "the present political chaos is connected with the decay of language, and one can probably bring about some improvement by starting at the verbal end." Who, after hearing the quite simple statements of modern politicians, can believe with Orwell that "if you simplify your language, you are freed from the worst follies of orthodoxy"? Style itself cannot always certify intention or value, since the meaning of a style shifts with events.

A case in point: the grandiloquence of eighteenth-century French revolutionary writing was justified, as Roland Barthes points out, by two facts: that it accurately reflected the enormity of events, and that—in not really altering the classical style—it accurately represented the limited aims of bourgeois revolution. As antagonists within a common culture, eighteenth-century revolutionaries and eighteenth-century reactionaries clothed their ideas in similar style. Yet that same style is compromised when used by a twentieth-century communist revolutionary like Ho Chi Minh. It is compromised not only by its association with bourgeois revolution, but by the weight of historical testimony as to the practical uses—the "real meaning"—of that style: testimony connecting the style with attitudes and actions which the contemporary revolutionary must reject. As the style accumulates meaning through history, its range of possibilities contracts. The lofty rhetoric of "law and order," based on the notion of God-given natural rights, served progressive ends in 1776 and 1789; but, as Kropotkin shows, it can no longer do so once the class interests it represents cease to be progressive. The rhetoric of "liberty," Christopher Caudwell argues, has similarly altered in function. These two essays, among others in the volume, indicate that abstract concepts like law, freedom, and democracy are constantly to be redefined in the light of history. And it would seem that this process of redefinition includes corresponding changes in language, insofar as the conceptual redefinition involves a change in audience, in the writer's relation to that audience, in the writer's background, and in his sense of how he relates to society.

It is a question, then, of assimilating what is valuable from the past and adapting it critically to the present. So that Malcolm X makes an illuminating change in the well-known slogan of the American bourgeois revolutionary Patrick Henry. Instead of "Give me liberty or give me death," Malcolm says, "It'll be liberty or it'll be death"; that is, liberty for everyone or else death for those who deny it. It is a change that says a good deal about the differences between the first American revolution and the American revolution that is implicit in Malcolm's analysis. Patrick Henry asks for liberty to be given, Malcolm will take it; Henry is prepared to die, Malcolm to win; Henry's attitude is self-sacrifice, Malcolm's is self-defense; Henry's liberty is centered (syntactically and politically) on himself, Malcolm's is a general condition; Henry's sentence has ceremonial balance and no deviant usage, Malcolm's, though balanced, includes the contraction that brings it back to the ordinary speech of ordinary men. To which one may add the extraliterary (but equally relevant) facts that Patrick Henry was a slaveholding white lawyer opposed to abolition, and Malcolm the descendant of slaves.

Style, then, is no absolute. Since many of the authors in this volume were writing for and from the same society as their opponents, and since—as Barthes has noted—the writer "cannot modify in any way the objective data which govern the consumption of literature," it follows that most of these authors used available and accepted techniques to express the consciousness that would (and will) eventually be fleshed out in social form.

A glance at the contents will show that these remarks on style and content do not apply equally to all the writers represented in this volume, some of whom (like Plutarch, Froissart, Swift, Muir, Jungk, and others) are neither revolutionary nor—despite their interest in reform—very deeply dissatisfied with the structure of their society. Their work has been included for two reasons. First, the primary sources for early reform or revolutionary movements (for example, Spartacus' revolt, the Waldensian heresy, the English rebellion of 1381) are scarce, if available at all. These movements have had to be represented by historians, who—because of class loyalty and privileged position—are often radically out of sympathy with the events they relate. Although such historical accounts cannot be used to study early revolutionary rhetoric, the material does raise its own special problems, which are equally valuable in a writing course: the function and meaning of objectivity, for instance, or the purpose of writing history, or the role of rhetoric in historiography. Second, many of the reformers included here focus on problems which —even if they are not treated from a revolutionary point of view—do have revolutionary implications. Family life, sex roles, conservation, disfranchisement, war atrocities—these are some areas of life in which the practical consequences of a social philosophy become apparent; they are like the visible portion of an iceberg, alerting us to the larger structure.

Probably the best guide to the use of any anthology is the interest and need of each group of students. The ways in which this anthology can be used will vary accordingly. It includes history, social criticism, and ideology. As examples of form it offers narrative, dialogue, nature description, polemic, scholarly tract, satire, eulogy, personal reminiscence, apocalyptic vision. As for style, it has more or less the range one would expect in a collection extending from biblical times to the present. A selective bibliography will provide the student with at least a toehold on the mass of material available for term-paper research, and the headnote that precedes each piece gives a brief historical background. In most of the headnotes I have suggested an approach to style and have sometimes referred to other material in the book which offers an interesting thematic or stylistic perspective.

Few of the pieces included here have been taught in colleges at all, far less as part of a course in English composition. Our cultural and literary tradition, having been defined through the work of its more conservative practitioners, usually stresses the importance of balanced impartiality—a quality noticeably lacking in this book. What is required, we are taught, is the dispassionate consideration of all issues: objectivity. We are confronted with such critical dicta as "literature and propaganda have nothing in common," or "work of literary value moves us to contemplation, not to action," or "art imposes a framework which takes the statement of the work out of the world of reality." Yet it is important to remember that "objectivity"—like "law" or "liberty"—may be used for specific ends, and that its meaning is not absolutely constant. Recently it seems to have acquired the meaning "apolitical," and to have become a synonym for "nonpartisan." That definition is in itself anything but objective, just as the demand for impartiality in literature is anything but impartial. To reject politics, for instance, is a deeply political gesture, since he who refuses to support or oppose, in fact acquiesces in the exercise of power. (Robert Jungk's study of the atomic scientists shows the hideous consequences of such false objectivity.) The writer who advocates and displays disengagement, has already committed himself. The mildest reformer, in refusing to be anything but that, already supports the status quo. So that what passes for objectivity is often intensely partisan in fact, and what is openly partisan may be wholly objective. It argues a sadly fragmented view of human nature to deny that analysis can lead to and justify the most violent partisanship, or to deny that objectivity and passion may point to the same goal.

Given the breadth of what I have called the counter-tradition, this anthology can provide only a sampling of it. I have chosen material that will represent the main currents of oppositional thought and at the same time offer a wide variety of form and style. In giving these examples of what others have thought before us and how others have written, the anthology attempts to fulfill the best aim of a freshman composition course: to provide the student with that sense of alternate opinions and styles which his previous educational experience may have omitted. It shows that clear thinking often leads to conclusions other than those acceptable to official culture, and that effective expression takes other forms than those traditionally taught. Although the book contains nothing that is historically new, it has a good deal, I hope, that is useful. And though much in the book will be new to those who use it, its purpose is not so much to discover the history of others, as it is to recover our own.

AMOS (about 755 B.C.) *Chapters 2, 4, 6*

*In a theocratic society, where nation and congregation are one, the prophet,
speaking by inspiration, is at once poet, visionary, and professional social
critic. The Old Testament prophet (and there were many more than the
dozen whose utterances survive) was often an important adviser to the
royal administration. Amos addresses himself to two related "transgressions." First, the Jews had begun to indulge in such foreign cultic practices
as astrology, idolatry, ritual fornication, and other fertility rites. Second,
the recent development of Israel's international commerce, cities, and government bureaucracy had generated sharp class distinctions: enormous luxury for a few, grinding poverty for many, the profit motive, bribery, and
miscarriage of justice in the courts. The prophet, therefore, laments lost
communal values as well as orthodoxy betrayed. His task is to warn his
countrymen of impending punishment and to exhort them to social and
spiritual reform.*
*The prophetic mode recurs often in the history of Western social criticism. It
is represented in this volume by the selections from Carlyle which, beside
recreating the prophetic warning to the ruling class, display the intense
emotional tone of Hebrew poetry and some of its characteristic devices:
syntactic parallelism, formulaic repetition, and sharply detailed visual
imagery.*

1 The words of Amos, who was among the shepherds of Tekoa, which he
saw concerning Israel in the days of Uzziah king of Judah [1] and in the days
of Jeroboam the son of Joash, king of Israel, two years before the earthquake. And he said:

The LORD roars from Zion, and utters his voice from Jerusalem; the pastures of
the shepherds mourn, and the top of Carmel withers. . . .

2 Thus says the LORD: "For three transgressions of Moab,[2] and for four, I
will not revoke the punishment; because he burned to lime the bones of the
king of Edom.

---

1. Judah and Israel: the southern and northern kindoms of Israel, which split after
the death of Solomon in the late tenth century B.C., probably over the issue of forced
labor. Amos was from the northern kingdom.
2. Moab: a territory east of the Dead Sea and bordering on Edom to the south; the
two kingdoms were often at war. To burn a king's corpse would make proper royal
burial impossible, and would thus be sacrilegious. Kerioth was the principal city of
Moab.

So I will send a fire upon Moab, and it shall devour the strongholds of Kerioth, and Moab shall die amid uproar, amid shouting and the sound of the trumpet;

I will cut off the ruler from its midst, and will slay all its princes with him," says the LORD.

Thus says the LORD: "For three transgressions of Judah, and for four, I will not revoke the punishment; because they have rejected the law of the LORD, and have not kept his statutes, but their lies have led them astray, after which their fathers walked.

So I will send a fire upon Judah, and it shall devour the strongholds of Jerusalem."

Thus says the LORD: "For three transgressions of Israel, and for four, I will not revoke the punishment; because they sell the righteous [3] for silver, and the needy for a pair of shoes—

they trample the head of the poor into the dust of the earth, and turn aside the way of the afflicted; a man and his father go in to the same maiden, [4] so that my holy name is profaned;

they lay themselves down beside every altar upon garments taken in pledge; and in the house of their God they drink the wine of those who have been fined.

"Yet I destroyed the Amorite [5] before them, whose height was like the height of the cedars, and who was as strong as the oaks; I destroyed his fruit above, and his roots beneath.

Also I brought you up out of the land of Egypt, and led you forty years in the wilderness, to possess the land of the Amorite.

And I raised up some of your sons for prophets, and some of your young men for Nazirites. [6] Is it not indeed so, O people of Israel?" says the LORD.

"But you made the Nazirites drink wine, and commanded the prophets, saying, 'You shall not prophesy.' "

"Behold, I will press you down in your place, as a cart full of sheaves presses down.

Flight shall perish from the swift, and the strong shall not retain his strength, nor shall the mighty save his life;

he who handles the bow shall not stand, and he who is swift of foot shall not save himself, nor shall he who rides the horse save his life;

and he who is stout of heart among the mighty shall flee away naked in that day," says the LORD.

---

3. Sell the righteous: that is, into slavery, which was a creditor's prerogative.
4. Maiden: probably a cultic prostitute.
5. The Amorite: early inhabitants of Canaan, displaced by the Hebrews.
6. Nazirites: a sect of holy warriors who marked their consecration by growing their hair long and by abstaining from wine. Samson was a Nazirite.

4 "Hear this word, you cows of Bashan,[7] who are in the mountains of Samaria,[8] who oppress the poor, who crush the needy, who say to their husbands, 'Bring, that we may drink!'

The Lord GOD has sworn by his holiness that, behold, the days are coming upon you, when they shall take you away with hooks, even the last of you with fishhooks.

And you shall go out through the breaches, every one straight before her; and you shall be cast forth into Harmon," says the LORD.

"Come to Bethel,[9] and transgress; to Gilgal, and multiply transgression; bring your sacrifices every morning, your tithes every three days;

offer a sacrifice of thanksgiving of that which is leavened, and proclaim freewill offerings, publish them; for so you love to do, O people of Israel!" says the Lord GOD.

"I gave you cleanness of teeth in all your cities, and lack of bread in all your places, yet you did not return to me," says the LORD.

"And I also withheld the rain from you when there were yet three months to the harvest: I would send rain upon one city, and send no rain upon another city; one field would be rained upon, and the field upon which it did not rain withered;

so two or three cities wandered to one city to drink water, and were not satisfied; yet you did not return to me," says the LORD.

"I smote you with blight and mildew; I laid waste your gardens and your vineyards; your fig trees and your olive trees the locust devoured; yet you did not return to me," says the LORD.

"I sent among you a pestilence after the manner of Egypt; I slew your young men with the sword; I carried away your horses; and I made the stench of your camp go up into your nostrils; yet you did not return to me," says the LORD.

"Therefore thus I will do to you, O Israel; because I will do this to you, prepare to meet your God, O Israel!"

For lo, he who forms the mountains, and creates the wind, and declares to man what is his thought; who makes the morning darkness, and treads on the heights of the earth—the LORD, the God of hosts, is his name!

6 "Woe to those who are at ease in Zion, and to those who feel secure on the mountain of Samaria, the notable men of the first of the nations, to whom the house of Israel come! . . .

---

7. Bashan: an area of fertile pastures, known for its prime livestock.
8. Samaria: capital of the northern kingdom; royal residence and administrative center.
9. Bethel and Gilgal: important state sanctuaries. The tone here is bitterly ironic, parodying the traditional hortatory formula.

Woe to those who lie upon beds of ivory, and stretch themselves upon their couches, and eat lambs from the flock, and calves from the midst of the stall;

who sing idle songs to the sound of the harp, and like David invent for themselves instruments of music;

who drink wine in bowls, and anoint themselves with the finest oils, but are not grieved over the ruin of Joseph!

Therefore they shall now be the first of those to go into exile, and the revelry of those who stretch themselves shall pass away."

The Lord GOD has sworn by himself (says the LORD, the God of hosts): "I abhor the pride of Jacob, and hate his strongholds; and I will deliver up the city and all that is in it." . . .

For behold, the LORD commands, and the great house shall be smitten into fragments, and the little house into bits.

Do horses run upon rocks? Does one plow the sea with oxen? But you have turned justice into poison and the fruit of righteousness into wormwood—

you who rejoice in Lo-debar,[10] who say, "Have we not by our own strength taken Karnaim for ourselves?"

"For behold, I will raise up against you a nation, O house of Israel," says the LORD, the God of hosts; "and they shall oppress you from the entrance of Hamath [11] to the Brook of the Arabah."

---

10. Lo-debar, Karnaim: place names, which also mean respectively "a thing of nought" and "horns."

11. Hamath, Arabah: frontiers of Israel's territory.

THUCYDIDES (460–400 B.C.), *The Melian Dialogue,* from *The Peloponnesian War*

The debate between Athens, the great imperialist power, and Melos, the island colony clinging quixotically to independence, illustrates some classic arguments in the politics of self-interest—arguments that are not without their contemporary spokesmen. For the Athenians, the Peloponnesian War, during which the Melian episode occurred, was the third major war of the century. A united Greek effort between 490 and 468 B.C. had repelled several Persian invasions. With the defeat of their common enemy, the two leading allies—Athens and Sparta—became rivals for power in the Aegean basin and warred sporadically for more than ten years. After a short, uneasy peace, hostilities erupted again and the Peloponnesian War began in 431 B.C.: it would continue for twenty-seven years. During this period of empire-building, internal reforms were made at Athens which, relative to what preceded, were called "democratic." The economy still depended on slave labor; the poor owned no land and had no political rights; office was restricted by property and income qualifications. It was, as Plutarch notes in his life of Pericles, "an aristocratical government, that went by the name of a democracy, but was, indeed, the supremacy of a single great man."

But history is only the raw material of historiography, and Thucydides, himself an Athenian general in the war, records not only events but attitudes. His dramatic dialogue is no literal record of the confrontation between Athenian and Melian diplomats, but an imaginative reconstruction which exposes both the underlying political issues, and the author's disillusioned view of the war.

Next summer [1] Alcibiades sailed to Argos with twenty ships and seized 300 Argive citizens who were still suspected of being pro-Spartan. These were put by the Athenians into the nearby islands under Athenian control.

The Athenians also made an expedition against the island of Melos. They had thirty of their own ships, six from Chios, and two from Lesbos; 1,200 hoplites, 300 archers, and twenty mounted archers, all from Athens; and about 1,500 hoplites from the allies and the islanders.

The Melians are a colony from Sparta. They had refused to join the Athenian empire like the other islanders, and at first had remained neutral with-

---

1. Next summer: during the sixteenth year of the war.

out helping either side; but afterwards, when the Athenians had brought force to bear on them by laying waste their land, they had become open enemies of Athens.

Now the generals Cleomedes, the son of Lycomedes, and Tisias, the son of Tisimachus, encamped with the above force in Melian territory and, before doing any harm to the land, first of all sent representatives to negotiate. The Melians did not invite these representatives to speak before the people, but asked them to make the statement for which they had come in front of the governing body and the few. The Athenian representatives then spoke as follows:

Athenians: So we are not to speak before the people, no doubt in case the mass of the people should hear once and for all and without interruption an argument from us which is both persuasive and incontrovertible, and should so be led astray. This, we realize, is your motive in bringing us here to speak before the few. Now suppose that you who sit here should make assurance doubly sure. Suppose that you, too, should refrain from dealing with every point in detail in a set speech, and should instead interrupt us whenever we say something controversial and deal with that before going on to the next point? Tell us first whether you approve of this suggestion of ours.

The Council of the Melians replied as follows:

Melians: No one can object to each of us putting forward our own views in a calm atmosphere. That is perfectly reasonable. What is scarcely consistent with such a proposal is the present threat, indeed the certainty, of your making war on us. We see that you have come prepared to judge the argument yourselves, and that the likely end of it all will be either war, if we prove that we are in the right, and so refuse to surrender, or else slavery.

Athenians: If you are going to spend the time in enumerating your suspicions about the future, or if you have met here for any other reason except to look the facts in the face and on the basis of these facts to consider how you can save your city from destruction, there is no point in our going on with this discussion. If, however, you will do as we suggest, then we will speak on.

Melians: It is natural and understandable that people who are placed as we are should have recourse to all kinds of arguments and different points of view. However, you are right in saying that we are met together here to discuss the safety of our country and, if you will have it so, the discussion shall proceed on the lines that you have laid down.

Athenians: Then we on our side will use no fine phrases saying, for example, that we have a right to our empire because we defeated the Persians, or that we have come against you now because of the injuries you have done us —a great mass of words that nobody would believe. And we ask you on your side not to imagine that you will influence us by saying that you, though a colony of Sparta, have not joined Sparta in the war, or that you have never done us any harm. Instead we recommend that you should try to get what it is possible for you to get, taking into consideration what we both really do think; since you know as well as we do that, when these matters are discussed by practical people, the standard of justice depends on the equality of power to compel and that in fact the strong do what they have the power to do and the weak accept what they have to accept.

Melians: Then in our view (since you force us to leave justice out of account and to confine ourselves to self-interest)—in our view it is at any rate useful that you should not destroy a principle that is to the general good of all men—namely, that in the case of all who fall into danger there should be such a thing as fair play and just dealing, and that such people should be allowed to use and to profit by arguments that fall short of a mathematical accuracy. And this is a principle which affects you as much as anybody, since your own fall would be visited by the most terrible vengeance and would be an example to the world.

Athenians: As for us, even assuming that our empire does come to an end, we are not despondent about what would happen next. One is not so much frightened of being conquered by a power which rules over others, as Sparta does (not that we are concerned with Sparta now), as of what would happen if a ruling power is attacked and defeated by its own subjects. So far as this point is concerned, you can leave it to us to face the risks involved. What we shall do now is to show you that it is for the good of our own empire that we are here and that it is for the preservation of your city that we shall say what we are going to say. We do not want any trouble in bringing you into our empire, and we want you to be spared for the good both of yourselves and of ourselves.

Melians: And how could it be just as good for us to be the slaves as for you to be the masters?

Athenians: You, by giving in, would save yourselves from disaster; we, by not destroying you, would be able to profit from you.

Melians: So you would not agree to our being neutral, friends instead of enemies, but allies of neither side?

Athenians: No, because it is not so much your hostility that injures us; it is rather the case that, if we were on friendly terms with you, our subjects would regard that as a sign of weakness in us, whereas your hatred is evidence of our power.

Melians: Is that your subjects' idea of fair play—that no distinction should be made between people who are quite unconnected with you and people who are mostly your own colonists or else rebels whom you have conquered?

Athenians: So far as right and wrong are concerned they think that there is no difference between the two, that those who still preserve their independence do so because they are strong, and that if we fail to attack them it is because we are afraid. So that by conquering you we shall increase not only the size but the security of our empire. We rule the sea and you are islanders, and weaker islanders too than the others; it is therefore particularly important that you should not escape.

Melians: But do you think there is no security for you in what we suggest? For here again, since you will not let us mention justice, but tell us to give in to your interests, we, too, must tell you what our interests are and, if yours and ours happen to coincide, we must try to persuade you of the fact. Is it not certain that you will make enemies of all states who are at present neutral, when they see what is happening here and naturally conclude that in course of time you will attack them too? Does not this mean that you are strengthening the enemies you have already and are forcing others to become your enemies even against their intentions and their inclinations?

Athenians: As a matter of fact we are not so much frightened of states on the continent. They have their liberty, and this means that it will be a long time before they begin to take precautions against us. We are more concerned about islanders like yourselves, who are still unsubdued, or subjects who have already become embittered by the constraint which our empire imposes on them. These are the people who are most likely to act in a reckless manner and to bring themselves and us, too, into the most obvious danger.

Melians: Then surely, if such hazards are taken by you to keep your empire and by your subjects to escape from it, we who are still free would show ourselves great cowards and weaklings if we failed to face everything that comes rather than submit to slavery.

Athenians: No, not if you are sensible. This is no fair fight, with honour on one side and shame on the other. It is rather a question of saving your lives and not resisting those who are far too strong for you.

Melians: Yet we know that in war fortune sometimes makes the odds more level than could be expected from the difference in numbers of the two sides. And if we surrender, then all our hope is lost at once, whereas, so long as we remain in action, there is still a hope that we may yet stand upright.

Athenians: Hope, that comforter in danger! If one already has solid advantages to fall back upon, one can indulge in hope. It may do harm, but will not destroy one. But hope is by nature an expensive commodity, and those who are risking their all on one cast find out what it means only when they are already ruined; it never fails them in the period when such a knowledge would enable them to take precautions. Do not let this happen to you, you who are weak and whose fate depends on a single movement of the scale. And do not be like those people who, as so commonly happens, miss the chance of saving themselves in a human and practical way, and, when every clear and distinct hope has left them in their adversity, turn to what is blind and vague, to prophecies and oracles and such things which by encouraging hope lead men to ruin.

Melians: It is difficult, and you may be sure that we know it, for us to oppose your power and fortune, unless the terms be equal. Nevertheless we trust that the gods will give us fortune as good as yours, because we are standing for what is right against what is wrong; and as for what we lack in power, we trust that it will be made up for by our alliance with the Spartans, who are bound, if for no other reason, then for honour's sake, and because we are their kinsmen, to come to our help. Our confidence, therefore, is not so entirely irrational as you think.

Athenians: So far as the favour of the gods is concerned, we think we have as much right to that as you have. Our aims and our actions are perfectly consistent with the beliefs men hold about the gods and with the principles which govern their own conduct. Our opinion of the gods and our knowledge of men lead us to conclude that it is a general and necessary law of nature to rule wherever one can. This is not a law that we made ourselves, nor were we the first to act upon it when it was made. We found it already in existence, and we shall leave it to exist for ever among those who come after us. We are merely acting in accordance with it, and we know that you or anybody else with the same power as ours would be acting in precisely the same way. And therefore, so far as the gods are concerned, we see no good reason why we should fear to be at a disadvantage. But with regard to your views about Sparta and your confidence that she, out of a sense of honour, will come to your aid, we must say that we congratulate you on your simplicity but do not envy you your folly. In matters that concern themselves or their own constitution the Spartans are quite remarkably good; as for their relations with others, that is a long story, but it can be expressed shortly and clearly by saying that of all people we know the Spartans are most conspicuous for believing that what they like doing is honourable and what suits their interests is just. And this kind of attitude is not going to be of much help to you in your absurd quest for safety at the moment.

Melians: But this is the very point where we can feel most sure. Their own self-interest will make them refuse to betray their own colonists, the Melians, for that would mean losing the confidence of their friends among the Hellenes and doing good to their enemies.

Athenians: You seem to forget that if one follows one's self-interest one wants to be safe, whereas the path of justice and honour involves one in danger. And, where danger is concerned, the Spartans are not, as a rule, very venturesome.

Melians: But we think that they would even endanger themselves for our sake and count the risk more worth taking than in the case of others, because we are so close to the Peloponnese that they could operate more easily, and because they can depend on us more than on others, since we are of the same race and share the same feelings.

Athenians: Goodwill shown by the party that is asking for help does not mean security for the prospective ally. What is looked for is a positive preponderance of power in action. And the Spartans pay attention to this point even more than others do. Certainly they distrust their own native resources so much that when they attack a neighbour they bring a great army of allies with them. It is hardly likely therefore that, while we are in control of the sea, they will cross over to an island.

Melians: But they still might send others. The Cretan sea is a wide one, and it is harder for those who control it to intercept others than for those who want to slip through to do so safely. And even if they were to fail in this, they would turn against your own land and against those of your allies left unvisited by Brasidas.[2] So, instead of troubling about a country which has nothing to do with you, you will find trouble nearer home, among your allies, and in your own country.

Athenians: It is a possibility, something that has in fact happened before. It may happen in your case, but you are well aware that the Athenians have never yet relinquished a single siege operation through fear of others. But we are somewhat shocked to find that, though you announced your intention of discussing how you could preserve yourselves, in all this talk you have said absolutely nothing which could justify a man in thinking that he could be preserved. Your chief points are concerned with what you hope may happen in the future, while your actual resources are too scanty to give you a chance of survival against the forces that are opposed to you at this moment. You will therefore be showing an extraordinary lack of common sense if, after you

---

2. Brasidas: a Spartan general.

have asked us to retire from this meeting, you still fail to reach a conclusion wiser than anything you have mentioned so far. Do not be led astray by a false sense of honour—a thing which often brings men to ruin when they are faced with an obvious danger that somehow affects their pride. For in many cases men have still been able to see the dangers ahead of them, but this thing called dishonour, this word, by its own force of seduction, has drawn them into a state where they have surrendered to an idea, while in fact they have fallen voluntarily into irrevocable disaster, in dishonour that is all the more dishonourable because it has come to them from their own folly rather than their misfortune. You, if you take the right view, will be careful to avoid this. You will see that there is nothing disgraceful in giving way to the greatest city in Hellas when she is offering you such reasonable terms—alliance on a tribute-paying basis and liberty to enjoy your own property. And, when you are allowed to choose between war and safety, you will not be so insensitively arrogant as to make the wrong choice. This is the safe rule—to stand up to one's equals, to behave with deference towards one's superiors, and to treat one's inferiors with moderation. Think it over again, then, when we have withdrawn from the meeting, and let this be a point that constantly recurs to your minds—that you are discussing the fate of your country, that you have only one country, and that its future for good or ill depends on this one single decision which you are going to make.

The Athenians then withdrew from the discussion. The Melians, left to themselves, reached a conclusion which was much the same as they had indicated in their previous replies. Their answer was as follows:

Melians: Our decision, Athenians, is just the same as it was at first. We are not prepared to give up in a short moment the liberty which our city has enjoyed from its foundation for 700 years. We put our trust in the fortune that the gods will send and which has saved us up to now, and in the help of men—that is, of the Spartans; and so we shall try to save ourselves. But we invite you to allow us to be friends of yours and enemies to neither side, to make a treaty which shall be agreeable to both you and us, and so to leave our country.

The Melians made this reply, and the Athenians, just as they were breaking off the discussion, said:

Athenians: Well, at any rate, judging from this decision of yours, you seem to us quite unique in your ability to consider the future as something more certain than what is before your eyes, and to see uncertainties as realities, simply because you would like them to be so. As you have staked most on and trusted most in Spartans, luck, and hopes, so in all these you will find yourselves most completely deluded.

The Athenian representatives then went back to the army, and the Athenian generals, finding that the Melians would not submit, immediately commenced hostilities and built a wall completely round the city of Melos, dividing the work out among the various states. Later they left behind a garrison of some of their own and some allied troops to blockade the place by land and sea, and with the greater part of their army returned home. The force left behind stayed on and continued with the siege. . . .

Meanwhile the Melians made a night attack and captured the part of the Athenian lines opposite the market-place. They killed some of the troops, and then, after bringing in corn and everything else useful that they could lay their hands on, retired again and made no further move, while the Athenians took measures to make their blockade more efficient in future. So the summer came to an end.

In the following winter the Spartans planned to invade the territory of Argos, but when the sacrifices for crossing the frontier turned out unfavourably, they gave up the expedition. The fact that they had intended to invade made the Argives suspect certain people in their city, some of whom they arrested, though others succeeded in escaping.

About this same time the Melians again captured another part of the Athenian lines where there were only a few of the garrison on guard. As a result of this, another force came out afterwards from Athens under the command of Philocrates, the son of Demeas. Siege operations were now carried on vigorously and, as there was also some treachery from inside, the Melians surrendered unconditionally to the Athenians, who put to death all the men of military age whom they took, and sold the women and children as slaves. Melos itself they took over for themselves, sending out later a colony of 500 men.

PLUTARCH (about 45–120), *On Spartacus*, from
Life of Crassus

LUCIUS ANNAEUS FLORUS (about 140), *The War
Against Spartacus*, from *Epitome of Roman History*

The Roman slave revolt that began in 73 B.C. *under the leadership of Spartacus was not the only important rising of the period, but it was the largest.
Spartacus himself, a freeborn Greek, had been sent as a prisoner of war to
the gladiatorial school at Capua. His army of slaves and unemployed
workers grew to 70,000, several times defeated the imperial army, took
possession of southern Italy, and survived for two years. The "Slave
Army" seems to have had no program beyond escape from Italy but the
scarcity of historical sources makes it difficult to know whether it had any
revolutionary aims. After Spartacus' defeat, 3,000 Roman prisoners of war
were found unharmed in his camp; of the captured rebels, 6,000 were crucified along the highway from Capua to Rome.*

*In style and in sympathies, the accounts given below form a contrasting pair.
Plutarch, the Greek moralist and biographer, presents a detailed, expansive
portrait of Spartacus, using narrative action, anecdote, and analysis of character. The private virtues of public men interest him because, as he remarks elsewhere in the* Lives, *"men's calamities are not to be wholly imputed to fortune, but refer themselves to differences in character." The
prudence and judicious generosity that Plutarch praises in his subjects are
displayed in his own writing. Florus, about whose life little is known,
makes no attempt to conceal his disdain for the rebels, for his purpose in
writing is to "contribute something to the admiration in which this illustrious people [the Romans] is held by displaying their greatness all at
once in a single view." The compact elegance of Florus' style is well-
suited to this propagandistic aim, though it conveys little sense of the per-
sonalities or issues of the servile rebellions.*

*

PLUTARCH

On Spartacus

The insurrection of the gladiators and the devastation of Italy, commonly called the war of Spartacus, began upon this occasion. One Lentulus Batiates trained up a great many gladiators in Capua, most of them Gauls and Thracians, who, not for any fault by them committed, but simply through the cruelty of their master, were kept in confinement for this object of fighting one with another. Two hundred of these formed a plan to escape, but being discovered, those of them who became aware of it in time to anticipate their master, being seventy-eight, got out of a cook's shop chopping-knives and spits, and made their way through the city, and lighting by the way on several waggons that were carrying gladiators' arms to another city, they seized upon them and armed themselves. And seizing upon a defensible place, they chose three captains, of whom Spartacus was chief, a Thracian of one of the nomad tribes, and a man not only of high spirit and valiant, but in understanding, also, and in gentleness superior to his condition, and more of a Grecian than the people of his country usually are. When he first came to be sold at Rome, they say a snake coiled itself upon his face as he lay asleep, and his wife, who at this latter time also accompanied him in his flight, his countrywoman, a kind of prophetess, and one of those possessed with the bacchanal frenzy, declared that it was a sign portending great and formidable power to him with no happy event.

First, then, routing those that came out of Capua against them, and thus procuring a quantity of proper soldiers' arms, they gladly threw away their own as barbarous and dishonourable. Afterwards Clodius, the praetor,[1] took the command against them with a body of three thousand men from Rome, and besieged them within a mountain, accessible only by one narrow and difficult passage, which Clodius kept guarded, encompassed on all other sides with steep and slippery precipices. Upon the top, however, grew a great many wild vines, and cutting down as many of their boughs as they had need of, they [the rebels] twisted them into strong ladders long enough to reach from thence to the bottom, by which, without any danger, they got down all but one, who stayed there to throw them down their arms, and after this succeeded in saving himself. The Romans were ignorant of all this, and, therefore, coming upon them in the rear, they [the rebels] assaulted them unawares and took their camp. Several, also, of the shepherds and herdsmen that were there, stout and nimble fellows, revolted over to them, to some of whom they gave complete arms, and made use of others as scouts and light-armed soldiers. Publius Varinus, the praetor, was now sent against them, whose lieutenant, Furius, whose two thousand men, they fought and routed. Then Cossinius was sent with considerable forces, to give his assistance and advice, and

---

1. Praetor: an elected magistrate.

him Spartacus missed but very little of capturing in person, as he was bathing at Salinae; for he with great difficulty made his escape, while Spartacus possessed himself of his baggage, and following the chase with a great slaughter, stormed his camp and took it, where Cossinius himself was slain. After many successful skirmishes with the praetor himself, in one of which he took his lictors [2] and his own horse, he began to be great and terrible; but wisely considering that he was not to expect to match the force of the empire, he marched his army towards the Alps, intending, when he had passed them, that every man should go to his own home, some to Thrace, some to Gaul. But they, grown confident in their numbers, and puffed up with their success, would give no obedience to him, but went about and ravaged Italy; so that now the senate was not only moved at the indignity and baseness, both of the enemy and of the insurrection, but, looking upon it as a matter of alarm and of dangerous consequence, sent out both the consuls [3] to it, as to a great and difficult enterprise. The consul Gellius, falling suddenly upon a party of Germans, who through contempt and confidence had straggled from Spartacus, cut them all to pieces. But when Lentulus with a large army besieged Spartacus, he [Spartacus] sallied out upon him, and, joining battle, defeated his chief officers, and captured all his baggage. As he made toward the Alps, Cassius, who was praetor of that part of Gaul that lies about the Po, met him with ten thousand men, but being overcome in the battle, he had much ado to escape himself, with the loss of a great many of his men.

When the senate understood this, they were displeased at the consuls, and ordering them to meddle no further, they appointed Crassus general of the war, and a great many of the nobility went volunteers with him, partly out of friendship, and partly to get honour. He stayed himself on the borders of Picenum, expecting Spartacus would come that way, and sent his lieutenant, Mummius, with two legions, to wheel about and observe the enemy's motions, but upon no account to engage or skirmish. But he, upon the first opportunity, joined battle, and was routed, having a great many of his men slain, and a great many only saving their lives with the loss of their arms. Crassus rebuked Mummius severely, and arming the soldiers again, he made them find sureties for their arms, that they would part with them no more, and five hundred that were the beginners of the flight he divided into fifty tens, and one of each was to die by lot, thus reviving the ancient Roman punishment of decimation, where ignominy is added to the penalty of death, with a variety of appalling and terrible circumstances, presented before the eyes of the whole army, assembled as spectators. When he had thus reclaimed his men, he led them against the enemy; but Spartacus retreated through Lucania toward the sea, and in the straits meeting with some Cilician pirate ships, he had thoughts of attempting Sicily, where, by landing two thousand men, he hoped to new kindle the war of the slaves, which was but lately extinguished, and seemed to need but little fuel to set it burning again. But after the pirates had struck a bargain with him, and received his earnest, they deceived him and sailed away. He thereupon retired again from the sea, and established his army in the peninsula of Rhegium; there Crassus came upon him, and considering the nature of the place, which of itself suggested the undertaking, he set

2. Lictors: attendants.
3. Consuls: military commanders.

to work to build a wall across the isthmus; thus keeping his soldiers at once from idleness and his foes from forage. This great and difficult work he perfected in a space of time short beyond all expectation, making a ditch from one sea to the other, over the neck of land, three hundred furlongs long, fifteen feet broad, and as much in depth, and above it built a wonderfully high and strong wall. All which Spartacus at first slighted and despised, but when provisions began to fail, and on his proposing to pass further, he found he was walled in, and no more was to be had in the peninsula, taking the opportunity of a snowy, stormy night, he filled up part of the ditch with earth and boughs of trees, and so passed the third part of his army over.

Crassus was afraid lest he should march directly to Rome, but was soon eased of that fear when he saw many of his men break out in a mutiny and quit him, and encamped by themselves upon the Lucanian lake. This lake they say changes at intervals of time, and is sometimes sweet, and sometimes so salt that it cannot be drunk. Crassus falling upon these beat them from the lake, but he could not pursue the slaughter, because of Spartacus suddenly coming up and checking the flight. Now he began to repent that he had previously written to the senate to call Lucullus out of Thrace, and Pompey out of Spain; so that he did all he could to finish the war before they came, knowing that the honour of the action would redound to him that came to his assistance. Resolving, therefore, first to set upon those that had mutinied and encamped apart, whom Caius Cannicius and Castus commanded, he sent six thousand men before to secure a little eminence, and to do it as privately as possible, which that they might do they covered their helmets, but being discovered by two women that were sacrificing for the enemy, they had been in great hazard, had not Crassus immediately appeared, and engaged in a battle which proved a most bloody one. Of twelve thousand three hundred whom he killed, two only were found wounded in their backs, the rest all having died standing in their ranks and fighting bravely. Spartacus, after this discomfiture, retired to the mountains of Petelia, but Quintius, one of Crassus's officers, and Scrofa, the quaestor,[4] pursued and overtook him. But when Spartacus rallied and faced them, they were utterly routed and fled, and had much ado to carry off their quaestor, who was wounded. This success, however, ruined Spartacus, because it encouraged the slaves, who now disdained any longer to avoid fighting, or to obey their officers, but as they were upon the march, they came to them with their swords in their hands, and compelled them to lead them back again through Lucania, against the Romans, the very thing which Crassus was eager for. For news was already brought that Pompey was at hand; and people began to talk openly that the honour of this war was reserved to him, who would come and at once oblige the enemy to fight and put an end to the war. Crassus, therefore, eager to fight a decisive battle, encamped very near the enemy, and began to make lines of circumvallation; but the slaves made a sally and attacked the pioneers. As fresh supplies came in on either side, Spartacus, seeing there was no avoiding it, set all his army in array, and when his horse was brought him, he drew out his sword and killed him, saying, if he got the day he should have a great many better horses of the enemies', and if he lost it he should have no need of this. And so making directly towards Crassus himself, through the midst of arms and wounds, he

---

4. Quaestor: collector of revenue.

missed him, but slew two centurions that fell upon him together. At last being deserted by those that were about him, he himself stood his ground, and, surrounded by the enemy, bravely defending himself, was cut in pieces. But though Crassus had good fortune, and not only did the part of a good general, but gallantly exposed his person, yet Pompey had much of the credit of the action.

*

LUCIUS ANNAEUS FLORUS

The War Against Spartacus

One can tolerate, indeed, even the disgrace of a war against slaves; for although, by force of circumstances, they are liable to any kind of treatment, yet they form as it were a class (though an inferior class) of human beings and can be admitted [1] to the blessings of liberty which we enjoy. But I know not what name to give to the war which was stirred up at the instigation of Spartacus; for the common soldiers being slaves and their leaders being gladiators—the former men of the humblest, the latter men of the worse, class—added insult to the injury which they inflicted upon Rome.

Spartacus, Crixus and Oenomaus, breaking out of the gladiatorial school of Lentulus with thirty or rather more men of the same occupation, escaped from Capua. When, by summoning the slaves to their standard, they had quickly collected more than 10,000 adherents, these men, who had been originally content merely to have escaped, soon began to wish to take their revenge also. The first position which attracted them (a suitable one for such ravening monsters) was Mt. Vesuvius. Being besieged here by Clodius Glabrus, they slid by means of ropes made of vine-twigs through a passage in the hollow of the mountain down into its very depths, and issuing forth by a hidden exit, seized the camp of the general by a sudden attack which he never expected. They then attacked other camps, that of Varenius and afterwards that of Thoranus; and they ranged over the whole of Campania. Not content with the plundering of country houses and villages, they laid waste Nola, Nuceria, Thurii and Metapontum with terrible destruction. Becoming a regular army by the daily arrival of fresh forces, they made themselves rude shields of wicker-work and the skins of animals, and swords and other weapons by melting down the iron in the slave-prisons. That nothing might be lacking which was proper to a regular army, cavalry was procured by breaking in herds of horses which they encountered, and his men brought to their leader the insignia and fasces [2] captured from the praetors,[3] nor were they refused by the man who, from being a Thracian mercenary, had become a soldier, and from a soldier a deserter, then a highwayman, and finally, thanks to his strength, a gladiator. He also celebrated the obsequies of his officers who had

---

1. By manumission.
2. Fasces: a bundle of wooden rods, bound together and enclosing an axe. It was the symbol of Roman authority.
3. Praetor: an elected magistrate.

fallen in battle with funerals like those of Roman generals, and ordered his captives to fight at their pyres, just as though he wished to wipe out all his past dishonour by having become, instead of a gladiator, a giver of gladiatorial shows. Next, actually attacking generals of consular rank, he inflicted defeat on the army of Lentulus in the Apennines and destroyed the camp of Publius Cassius at Mutina. Elated by these victories he entertained the project—in itself a sufficient disgrace to us—of attacking the city of Rome. At last a combined effort was made, supported by all the resources of the empire, against this gladiator, and Licinius Crassus vindicated the honour of Rome. Routed and put to flight by him, our enemies—I am ashamed to give them this title—took refuge in the furthest extremities of Italy. Here, being cut off in the angle of Bruttium and preparing to escape to Sicily, but being unable to obtain ships, they tried to launch rafts of beams and casks bound together with withies on the swift waters of the straits. Failing in this attempt, they finally made a sally and met a death worthy of men, fighting to the death as became those who were commanded by a gladiator. Spartacus himself fell, as became a general, fighting most bravely in the front rank.

ANONYMOUS, *Henry at Le Mans*

ANONYMOUS, *The Origins of the Waldensian Heresy*

WALTER MAP (1140–1209), *The Waldenses,* from *De Nugis Curialium*

BERNARD OF FONTCAUDE (died 1192), Prologue to *A Treatise Against the Waldenses*

Speculative heresy, or intellectual dissent from points of theology, had been a constant concern of the Catholic Church since its earliest years; but popular heresy, involving social and ecclesiastic reform as well as matters of belief, developed only from the eleventh century. It spread quickly from commercial and industrial centers, attracting large numbers of merchants, professional men, and artisans. Since most early heretical writings were destroyed by the Inquisition, the movement is known mainly through the testimony of its critics and persecutors. Nonetheless it is clear that many sects began in protest against clerical wealth, corruption, and political influence; many of them advocated apostolic poverty, communal property, the right of women and laymen to preach, and obedience to good prelates only.

The first two narratives below are from twelfth-century chronicles. Henry of Lausanne, monk turned wandering preacher, spoke throughout France over a period of some thirty years with immense success. His first appearance (1115) in the city of Le Mans is recorded in a chronicle of the deeds of Bishop Hildebert, whose duty it was to deal with Henry. The document presents an extraordinarily lively account of the charismatic heretic, in the flamboyant style characteristic of much medieval clerical writing.

From its modest beginning in a moneylender's repentance, the Waldensian movement (the subject of the last three selections) grew to be one of the most widespread and enduring in Europe; after the Reformation it became a Protestant sect and its American branch is included in the Presbyterian Order. Walter Map, an English courtier and ecclesiastic, describes the humiliation of the Waldenses at the Third Lateran Council (1179), at which they were forbidden to preach. The injunction was disobeyed; the Poor of Lyons (as the Waldenses were known) were expelled from that city but continued to preach elsewhere. Of Bernard of Fontcaude, author of the treatise (1190) whose prologue is given below, little is known.

Between them the four pieces suggest the versatility of medieval prose, ranging as they do from the charming narrative of Waldes' conversion, to Ber-

nard's hyperbolic polemics; from clear simplicity to scholarly opacity with
its biblical and classical references, rhetorical questions, exclamations, and
elaborate metaphors.

*

ANONYMOUS

Henry at Le Mans

About the same time [ca. 1115], in nearby districts there appeared a certain
charlatan whose personal conduct, evil habits, and detestable doctrine testi-
fied that he deserved flogging and the punishments of a murderer. He hid the
madness of a ravening wolf under sheep's clothing; the driving power in his
countenance and glance was like that of the cruel sea. Hair cropped, beard
untrimmed, tall of stature, quick of pace, he glided along the ground barefoot
as winter raged; easy of address, awe-inspiring in voice, young in years,
scornful of ornate dress; his unconventional way of life was on the surface
unlike that of ordinary folk—shelter in the houses of burghers, a night's lodging as a transient, a meal, a bed in a garret (not at all in keeping with the
prophet Daniel but in accord with that verse which reads, "For death is come
up through our windows").[1] What more can be said? For everywhere he
gained an increasing reputation for astonishing holiness and wisdom; not by
merit, but by deceit; not by truth, but by appearance; not in character nor
habits nor piety, but by mere hearsay. Matrons and adolescent boys (for he
enjoyed the pandering of both sexes), attending him at different times,
avowed openly their aberrations and increased them, caressed his feet, his
buttocks, his groin, with tender hands. Completely carried away by this fellow's wantonness and by the enormity of adultery, they publicly proclaimed
that they had never touched a man of such strength, such humanity, such
power. By his speech even a heart of stone could be moved to repentance;
monks, anchorites, and all the cloistered clergy could well imitate his piety
and celibate life. Indeed, they declared, the Lord God had bestowed upon
him the ancient and veritable blessing and spirit of the prophets, through
which, by only scanning their faces, he might know and declare the sins of
mortal men which they hid from others.

When rumors of this sort floated into our district, the people, applauding
their own destruction with their peculiar fickleness, daily and every day
longed to be beguiled by his discourse, longed for his advent, by which they
might the more quickly become intimates and participants in his heresy. For
it often happens that those things are the more welcome to the masses which
are the worse for them. Indeed, the cycle of the days brought still more! The
man, determined on the infection of our fellow-citizens with his venomous
breath, in imitation of the Savior dispatched before him to the bishop two of
his disciples, like him in life and character. When they entered the outskirts
of our city on Ash Wednesday, the whole population, eager for the wickedness offered them, received them as angels of the Lord of all. As teachers do,

---

1. Jeremiah, 9:21.

they carried staves, to the tips of which a standard like a cross, made of iron, was fastened; in outward appearance and in speech they put on the appearance of penitents. The pontiff [Hildebert], a man of the greatest piety, little suspecting the deceits of a Trojan horse, received them courteously and in good faith and turned upon them a gracious and friendly countenance. Although he had undertaken to go to Rome, he instructed his archdeacons, among other things, to grant to the pseudohermit Henry (for that was the heretic's name), peaceful entry and license to preach to the people.

Henry entered within the city walls, and the populace, as usual, applauded novelty, as we have said, and were more interested in an unknown character than in one of proven worth. How strange! They thought his virtues exceeded his reputation, and, as usual, gossip had made full use of its frequent repetition and inflated it still further. Some of the clergy, led astray in his schism by quarrels and private donations, encouraged the rabble by their ranting and prepared a platform from which that demagogue might harangue the crowds of people who hung on his lips. Furthermore, when he addressed the people, these clerics sat weeping at his feet as he roared pronouncements like an oracle. It was as if legions of demons were all making their noise in one blast through his mouth. Nevertheless, he was remarkably fluent. When his speech entered the ears of the mob, it stuck in their minds. Like a potent poison, it penetrated to the inner organs, vented an inexorable hatred on life. Ever more eagerly it changes its form and renews its attacks. By this heresy the people were so charged with hatred for the clergy that they threatened their servants with torture and sought to allow no one to sell anything to them or to buy from them. Indeed, they treated them like heathen and publicans. Furthermore, they had resolved not only to tear down their dwellings and pillage their goods, but to stone them or hang them from the gibbet as well [and would have done so] had not the count [2] and his vassals learned of the wickedness of these people and prevented their abominable attempts by force rather than by argument, for beasts hearken not to reason.

Some of the clergy who lived in the city, namely Hugh Bird, William Drinknowater, and Pagan Aldric, approached Henry one day, intending to debate with him, and were violently assaulted and abusively tumbled and fouled with mud and filth in the gutters and barely escaped from the attack of the furious crowd with their lives; indeed, once they were out of immediate danger their retreat seemed like flight. Surrounded by the mob, they would never have escaped the peril, had not the protection of the count and his vassals permitted them to reach shelter. For, as we said, the lord of the city opposed the folly of those people and was resolved never to abandon the defense of the clergy.

The clergy did not dare to speak to the charlatan personally so they sent a letter by one of the canons, couched in the following terms:

"In peace and respect our Church received you and your companions, who came in sheep's clothing but who inwardly devised the wiles of ravening wolves. It likewise displayed toward you the promise and performance of brotherly love, believing that you would honestly admonish the people for the salvation of their souls and would faithfully sow the seed of the word of God

---

2. The count: Fulk V, count of Anjou and Maine.

in their hearts. But you took upon yourself to give in return the very opposite of what you should—wrath for peace, disgrace for honor, hatred for love, a curse for a blessing—and to disturb the Church of God by your knavery. You have sown discord between clergy and people, and by treachery ten times repeated you have moved the mass of unruly people with swords and cudgels against Mother Church. You have proffered us the kiss of Judas; you have, as a public insult, called us and the whole clergy heretics. Above all— and what is worse—you have banefully and perfidiously uttered much that is contrary to the Catholic faith, which a faithful Christian trembles to recapitulate. Therefore, by the authority of the high and indivisible Trinity, of the whole orthodox Church, of Mary, Holy Mother of God, of St. Peter, prince of the apostles, and of his vicar, our reverend father, Pope Paschal, and of our bishop, Hildebert, we altogether forbid you and the companions who so wickedly and damnably associate themselves with your error to preach further in the entire diocese of Le Mans, privately or publicly; nor shall you dare to disseminate the absurdities of your wicked doctrines. If, however, you assert yourself against such authority and open wide your jaws again to spew out poison, we, buttressed by this authority and its prerogative, excommunicate you and all your accomplices, supporters, and assistants; and He, whose divinity you unceasingly oppose, shall cause you to be delivered to eternal malediction on the day of stern judgment."

The fellow, however, refused to accept the letter, so William Muscha read it aloud, phrase by phrase, in his presence. To William the bystanders threatened bodily injury, for it seemed to them that he had publicly and rudely put Henry to shame. The latter, at each phrase of the letter, shook his head and kept repeating, "You lie." Surely, if the count's steward, under whose protection William had undertaken the mission, had not been there, William would never have returned to Mother Church alive.

After these events, Henry nonetheless held sacrilegious meetings even at Saint-Germain and Saint-Vincent,[3] where he proclaimed a new doctrine: that women who had lived unchastely should, all unclothed, burn their garments, together with their hair, in the sight of everyone; that no one in the future should receive gold, silver, property, or betrothal gifts with his wife, nor should she bring him a dowry, but the naked should marry the nude, the ailing the sick, the pauper the destitute. Nor was he concerned whether the chaste or the unchaste married.

While they behaved as the charlatan suggested, the fellow admired the beautiful features of individual women, how one surpassed the other in whiteness, while another was more attractive for plumpness of body. The whole behavior and mood of the people hung upon his dictate. What a shower of gold and silver he might have reveled in, had he wished, but he restrained his avarice for fear of being thought too greedy. In reality, while keeping much for himself, he did devote a little to replacing the clothing which, as we have recorded, had been burned. Also, at his behest many young men took in marriage women of the streets, for whom Henry bought clothing worth four shillings, scarcely sufficient to cover their nakedness.

But the Just Judge destroyed the works of the heretic and revealed to oth-

---

3. Saint-Germain and Saint-Vincent: monasteries in Le Mans.

ers what sort of tree this was: one which bears leaves but no fruit, which monopolizes the ground and chokes out everything that sprouts nearby, one which cannot endure until the rainy season, but withers and dies in summer. For after a short lapse of time, the young men who had taken wives according to his wicked advice ran away to other parts, driven thereto either by hunger or by the debauchery of the women, and left their wives totally destitute of support. And so the men took other women to themselves in adultery; the women, though their husbands were still alive, sought illicit union with other men. Although they were many, no man or woman of those who entered into matrimony at this man's urging ever displayed faithfulness or respect to wife or husband. Nor could any other woman who by oath renounced fornication and the pleasures of dress restrain herself, but within a matter of days, as her misdeeds increased, she would lapse into worse habits.

As this publican was constantly engaged in such acts and many others like them, he learned of the return of the bishop, who, as we have already indicated, had set out for Rome. He withdrew to the village of Saint-Calais and lived there and in places nearby. He was far from abandoning his career; on the contrary, he steadily introduced worse innovations. For on the most sacred day of Pentecost, when faithful children, indeed, are wont devoutly to attend divine service, this lowest of men attached to himself a certain very young cleric (by whose report so much of the sensuality of the man was later exposed) and set out stealthily and in the solitary quiet of the night for the house of a certain knight and there lay wantonly in bed with the matron of the house until midday. Thus, neither out of holy fear or for shame before men would he moderate his lewdness, until he had displayed the enormity of his villainy to people near and far.

While these things were going on, the bishop already mentioned approached the outskirts of the city, accompanied by a great and mighty throng of his clergy. When with fatherly kindness he bestowed the blessing of the living God by word and sign upon the people, they were stirred in animosity of thought and speech to disparagement of the Creator. Spurning his sign of the Cross and the episcopal blessing, they cried out, "We want no knowledge of your ways! We don't want your blessing! Bless filth! Consecrate filth! We have a father, we have a pontiff, we have an advocate who surpasses you in authority; he exceeds you in probity and knowledge. The wicked clergy, your clergy, oppose him. They gainsay his teaching. They despise and reject him as guilty of sacrilege, fearing that by prophetic insight he would expose their crimes. They condemned his heresy and incontinence behind the prerogative of a letter, but all these things shall fall back at once upon the heads of those who have presumed by unimaginably overweening audacity to forbid to the holy man of God the word of heavenly preaching."

The bishop had compassion on their error and stupidity and patiently bore the insults which they heaped upon him, praying without cease to the God of Majesty that He would restrain popular delusion compounded with pride, lest they succeed in creating a schism in His Church. But in accordance with the words of the Psalmist pleading for the salvation of transgressors, "Fill their faces with shame and they shall seek thy name, O Lord," [4] the same Lord God allowed the major part of the city's suburbs to be burned by a sudden

---

4. Psalms 83:16.

conflagration, that by the loss of worldly goods at least, they might abandon their evil way of life and call upon the sacred name, the name of the living God. Indeed, the pontiff (echoing the words of the prophet, "O how great is the multitude of thy sweetness, O Lord, which thou hast hidden for them that fear thee") [5] a few days later sought out the seducer and put a stop to his irreverence by divine authority. For when they met in parley the bishop inquired on the basis of what special fitness the man had chosen his vocation. He was mute, not understanding what "vocation" meant. The bishop tried again, inquiring what office the man exercised. "I am a deacon," said he. Then said the bishop, "Tell me, now, did you go to Mass today?" "No." "Then let us sing the morning hymns unto God." But when they began to do so, Henry acknowledged that he did not know the order of service for the day. Still the bishop, wishing to disclose to the full the fellow's lack of knowledge, began to sing the customary hymns to the Mother of God. Of these the man knew neither the words nor the sequence. And so, covered with shame, he acknowledged his life, his way of preaching, his presumption. In reality he was a camp-follower, completely untaught, and wholly given over to sensuality, yet he had gained notoriety by haranguing the people and throwing dice. Of such is it written: "True glory takes root and grows; all shams quickly pass away and wither like flowers, nor can anything which is based on pretense be long lasting." [6]

So the bishop, because he recognized the shallowness and irreverence of Henry, by apostolic authority ordered him to tarry no longer in his diocese but to make his way elsewhere and spare our people. Indeed, the man was overcome by the pontiff's persistence and fled secretly, and (if the report be valid) disturbed other regions in the same fashion and spread infection by his poisonous breath. I have recorded these facts about Henry and recounted the deeds of Hildebert for the convenience and instruction of posterity, that care may be taken lest the Church of Christ be disturbed at some other time by a delusion of this sort.

Thereafter, the same Hildebert arranged in various ways, by persuasion and humility in equal parts, to calm the madness of the people whom Henry had so seditiously incited against the clergy. Henry had so won them over to himself that even now it is scarcely possible to destroy his memory and to drive affection for him from their hearts.

*

ANONYMOUS

The Origins of the Waldensian Heresy

In the course of the same year (that is, 1173) of our Lord's incarnation, there was at Lyons in Gaul a certain citizen named Waldes, who had amassed a great fortune through the wicked practice of lending at interest. One Sunday he had been attracted by the crowd gathered around a minstrel and had been touched by the latter's words. Wishing to talk to him more fully, he took him

---

5. Psalms 31:19.
6. Cicero, *De officiis.*

to his home, for the minstrel was at a place in his narrative [1] in which Alexis had come peacefully to a happy end in his father's house.

On the following morning, the said citizen hastened to the school of theology to seek counsel for his soul's welfare and, when he had been instructed in the many ways of attaining to God, asked the master which was the most sure and perfect way of all. The master replied to him in the words of the Lord: "If thou wilt be perfect, go sell what thou hast," and so on. Waldes came to his wife and offered her the choice of keeping for herself all his property in either movable goods or real estate, that is, in lands, waters, woods, meadows, houses, rents, vineyards, mills, and ovens. Though greatly saddened by the necessity, she chose the real estate. From his movable goods, he made restitution to those from whom he had profited unjustly; another considerable portion of his wealth he bestowed upon his two small daughters, whom without their mother's knowledge he confided to the order of Fontevrault; but the greatest part he disbursed for the needs of the poor.

Now, a very severe famine was then raging throughout all Gaul and Germany. Wherefore Waldes, the citizen mentioned above, on three days a week from Pentecost to St. Peter in Chains [2] gave bountifully of bread, vegetables, and meat to all who came to him. On the feast of the Assumption of the Blessed Virgin,[3] as he was in the streets distributing an appreciable sum of money among the poor, he cried out, "No man can serve two masters, God and mammon." Then all the citizens hurried to him, supposing that he had lost his senses, but he climbed to a commanding spot and addressed them thus: "My friends and fellow townsmen! Indeed, I am not, as you think, insane, but I have taken vengeance on my enemies who held me in bondage to them, so that I was always more anxious about money than about God and served the creature more than the Creator. I know that a great many find fault with me for having done this publicly. But I did it for myself and also for you: for myself, so that they who may henceforth see me in possession of money may think I am mad; in part also for you, so that you may learn to fix your hope in God and to trust not in riches."

As he was leaving the church on the following day, he asked a certain citizen, one of his former associates, to give him food for the love of God. The latter took him to his home and said, "As long as I live I will give you the necessities of life." His wife, on learning of this incident, was no little saddened. Like one beside herself, she rushed into the presence of the archbishop of the city to complain that her husband had begged his bread from another rather than from her. This situation moved all who were present to tears, including the archbishop himself. At the archbishop's bidding, the citizen brought his guest [Waldes] with him into his presence, whereupon the woman, clinging to her husband's garments, cried, "Is it not better, O my husband, that I, rather than strangers, should atone for my sins through alms to you?" And from that time forth, by command of the archbishop, he was not permitted in that city to take food with others than his wife.

---

1. Narrative: "The Life of St. Alexis," a French poem written about 1040, and a favorite recitation of wandering singers. Born in the fourth century into the Roman nobility, Alexis renounced wealth and family for a mendicant life as a Christian.

2. Pentecost, etc.: May 27–August 1.

3. Assumption: August 15.

*

WALTER MAP

The Waldenses

At the Roman council held under Pope Alexander III, I saw simple and illiterate men called Waldenses, after their leader, Waldes, who was a citizen of Lyons on the Rhone. They presented to the lord pope a book written in French which contained the text and a gloss of the Psalms and many of the books of both Testaments. They most urgently requested him to authorize them to preach because they saw themselves as experienced persons, although they were nothing more than dabblers. It was the way of birds who see not the fine snares or the nets to suppose that everywhere there is free passage. Do not men who engage in sophistical discourse all their lives, who can trap and only with difficulty be trapped, who are probers of the most profound depths, do not they, for fear of giving offense, speak with reverence all the thoughts which they reveal about God, whose state is so exalted that no praises or powers of prayer can mount thereto except as mercy may draw them? In every letter of the sacred page, so many precepts fly on wings of virtue, such riches of wisdom are accumulated, that anyone to whom God has granted the means may draw from its fullness. Shall pearls, then, be cast before swine? [1] Shall the Word be given to the ignorant, whom we know to be incapable of receiving it, much less of giving in their turn what they have received? Away with this, erase it! Let the precious ointment on the head run down upon the beard, and thence down to the skirt of the garment.[2] Let waters be drawn from the fountain, not from puddles in the streets.

I, the least among the many thousands who were summoned, was scoffing at the Waldenses [and expressing surprise] that there should be any consultation or delay in deciding their request, when I was summoned by a certain great prelate to whom the supreme pontiff had entrusted the charge of confessions. A target for shafts, I took my seat. When many lawyers and men of learning had assembled, two Waldenses who seemed the leaders of their group were brought before me to argue about the faith, not for love of seeking the truth but hoping that when I had been refuted my mouth might be stopped like one speaking wicked things. I confess that I sat in fear lest in punishment for my sins the gift of speech might be denied me before so great a gathering. The bishop commanded me, who was preparing to answer, to test my skill against them. First, then, knowing that the lips of an ass which eats thistles find lettuce unworthy of them, I put very easy questions of which no one could be ignorant. "Do you believe in God the Father?" They replied, "We do." "And in the Son?" They answered, "We do." "And in the Holy Spirit?" They answered, "We do." I went on, "And in the mother of Christ?"

---

1. Swine: Matthew 7:6.
2. Garment: in Psalms 133:2, the unity of brothers is compared to the holy oil.

They again, "We do." They were answered with derisive laughter [3] from everyone present and withdrew in confusion; deservedly, for, like Phaëthon, who did not even know the names of his horses, they who were taught by none sought to become teachers.

They have no fixed habitations. They go about two by two, barefoot, clad in woolen garments, owning nothing, holding all things common like the apostles, naked, following a naked Christ. They are making their first moves now in the humblest manner because they cannot launch an attack. If we admit them, we shall be driven out.

*

BERNARD OF FONTCAUDE

Prologue to *A Treatise Against the Waldenses*

1. At the time when Lord Lucius [1] of glorious memory presided over the Holy Roman Church, new heretics suddenly raised their head who, choosing by chance a name with a forecast of the future, were called Waldenses, a name surely derived from "dense vale" (*valle densa*), inasmuch as they were enveloped in the deep, dense darkness of error. Although condemned by the aforesaid highest pontiff, they spewed the poison of their unbelief far and wide with rash impudence.

2. Because of this, Lord Bernard, archbishop of Narbonne, renowned for piety and integrity before God, an ardent lover of God's law, set himself as a strong wall against them and, therefore, convening many clerics and laymen, monks and secular clergy, he summoned them to judgment. What more is there to say? After the case was considered with the greatest care, they were condemned.

3. Nevertheless, they dared thereafter to sow the seed of their wickedness privately and publicly. And so again, although it was more than was required, they were invited to a discussion with certain persons, both clerics and laymen. So that the argument would not drag on too long, a certain priest, Raymond of Deventer, a man, indeed, devout and God-fearing, noble by birth, nobler in conduct, was chosen by both parties as a judge.

4. So when the day set for the debate arrived and both parties assembled, together with many other clerics and laymen, they [the Waldenses] were called to account by the true Catholics for certain matters on which their views were erroneous. As they replied to each charge, the argument was pursued at length, now by one side, now by the other, and many biblical texts were advanced by each party. When he had heard the statements of both sides, the aforementioned judge rendered a definitive verdict in writing and pronounced the Waldenses heretics on the points of which they had been accused.

---

3. Laughter: that is, the Waldenses' answer appeared to give the Virgin equal importance with the Trinity—an obvious doctrinal error.

---

1. Lucius: Pope Lucius III (1181–1185).

5. In the present little tract we describe the texts and arguments by which they defended their stand and the reply to them by us Catholics, with the scriptural texts by which the Catholic faith was defended; and we add certain other passages against other heresies. All this we have done particularly to instruct or encourage some of the clergy, who, either because they are burdened by inexperience or for want of books, become an offense and a scandal to the faithful under their charge by their failure to stand against the enemies of the truth; for they neither confirm [their parishioners] in the Catholic faith nor refresh them with the nourishment of the Holy Scriptures, wherefore they languish like starvelings on the journey through this world, deprived of spiritual powers and unable to find their way again to the homeland, that is, to paradise. This, indeed, is the real cause of the greater evil we have described: that the ravening wolves, to wit, the demon-heretics and tyrants, are not being driven out of the folds of Christ's sheep either by the word of preaching or by the rod of discipline or strictness.

6. Wherefore, may it please [such clerics] to accept from our humble self the little gift of this tract. Let them commit the texts of the Holy Fathers to memory, so that by God's mercy they may have invincible weapons against the masters of darkness, against the spinners of lies, against the worshipers of perverse dogmas who are the demon-heretics, to the end that, guided by the grace of God, they may win triumph over them and may be worthy to receive from the Highest Shepherd "a never-fading crown of glory" [2] for the governance and instruction of those under their charge.

---

2. I Peter 5:4.

JOHN BALL (died 1381), *Messages*

JEAN FROISSART (1337–1405), *The Rebellion of 1381*, from *The Chronicles*

Throughout Europe, the fourteenth century was a period of rapid social change and violent disorder. England and France were at war from 1337, and the Black Plague (which periodically swept Europe after 1348) provided frequent scenes of horror. Corruption and internal conflict had weakened the Church; the spectacle of the Great Schism (1373–1417), in which rival popes regularly excommunicated one another, showed that the Church was as deeply concerned with political influence as with the spiritual well-being of its flock. Industrial development, especially in textiles, had generated a large class of urban artisans. Since riots, strikes, and insurrections were occurring everywhere, the English rebellion of 1381 was not in itself unusual, though its aims were far more ambitious than most.
Partly as a result of the labor shortage created by the plague, English agricultural workers were becoming acutely conscious of their exploitation under the feudal system. To these men John Ball, an itinerant preacher, addressed his messages. Short sentences, simple diction, proverbial phrases, and internal rhyme made them easy to remember and easy to pass on by word of mouth. Ball's role in the rebellion is described by Jean Froissart, French poet, chronicler, courtier, and diplomat, from whom a fully sympathetic account is scarcely to be expected. Yet Froissart's aristocratic bias —unlike that of Florus in describing Spartacus' revolt—does not prevent him from giving a clear summary of the rebels' suffering, their arguments, and their effect. Indeed, so well does Froissart succeed that occasionally he fails. The material tends to escape its ideological frame, so that by the end of his account the rebels emerge as heroes of the drama, and the young King Richard an arrogant, treacherous lord. The Berners translation (1525) of Froissart retains the directness and elegance of its original.

*

JOHN BALL
Messages

John Schep, some time Saint Mary's priest of York, and now of Colchester, greeteth well John Nameless and John the Miller and John Carter, and biddeth them that they beware of guile in borough, and stand together in God's name, and biddeth Piers Plowman go to his work and chastise well Hob the

Robber,[1] and take with you John Trueman and all his fellows and no mo; and look sharp you to one-head and no mo.

> *John the Miller hath yground small, small, small.*
> *The King's son of heaven shall pay for all.*
> *Be ware or* [2] *ye be wo.*
> *Know your friend from your foe.*
> *Have enough and say "ho"!*
> *And do well and better and flee sin,*
> *And seek peace and hold therein.*
> *And so bid John Trueman and all his fellows.*

JOHN BALL'S RHYMING LETTER

John Ball greeteth you well all, and doth you to understand that he hath rungen your bell. Now right and might, will and skill. Now God haste you in every thing. Time it is that Our Lady help you with Jesus her son, and the Son with the Father, to make in the name of the Holy Trinity a good end to what has been begun. Amen, amen, for charity Amen.

*

JEAN FROISSART
The Rebellion of 1381

HOW THE COMMONS OF ENGLAND REBELLED AGAINST THE NOBLEMEN (1381)

. . . In the mean season while this treaty was, there fell in England great mischief and rebellion of moving of the common people, by which deed England was at a point to have been lost without recovery. There was never realm nor country in so great adventure [1] as it was in that time, and all because of the ease and riches that the common people were of which moved them to this rebellion; as sometime they did in France, the which did much hurt, for by such incidents the realm of France hath been greatly grieved. It was a marvellous thing and of poor foundation that this mischief began in England, and to give ensample to all manner of people, I will speak thereof as it was done, as I was informed, and of the incidents thereof.

There was a usage in England and yet is in divers countries, that the noblemen hath great franchises over the commons and keepeth them in service, that is to say, their tenants ought by custom to labour the lords' lands, to gather and bring home their corns, and some to thresh and to fan, and by servage to make their hay, and to hew their wood and bring it home. All these

---

1. Hob the Robber: Robert Hales, the king's treasurer.
2. Or: ere, before.

---

1. Adventure: peril, risk of loss.

things they ought to do by servage, and there be more of these people in England than in any other realm. Thus the noblemen and prelates are served by them and specially in the counties of Kent, Essex, Sussex and Bedford. These unhappy [2] people of these said countries began to stir, because they said they were kept in great servage, and in the beginning of the world they said there were no bondmen, wherefore they maintained that none ought to be bond, without he did treason to his lord, as Lucifer did to God. But they said . . . they were neither angels nor spirits, but men formed to the similitude of their lords, saying, why should they then be kept so under like beasts, the which they said they would no longer suffer, for they would be all one; and if they laboured or did anything for their lords, they would have wages therefor as well as other. And of this imagination was a foolish priest in the country of Kent, called John Ball, for the which foolish words he had been three times in the Bishop of Canterbury's prison. For this priest used oftentimes on the Sundays after mass, when the people were going out of the minister, to go into the cloister and preach and made the people to assemble about him, and would say thus, "Ah! ye good people, the matters goeth not well to pass in England, nor shall not do till everything be common, and that there be no villeins nor gentlemen, but that we may be all united together, and that the lords be no greater masters than we be. What have we deserved, or why should we be kept thus in servage? We be all come from one father and one mother, Adam and Eve: whereby can they say or show that they be greater lords than we be, saying by that they cause us to win and labour for that they dispend? They are clothed in velvet and camlet furred with grise, and we be vestured with poor cloth. They have their wines, spices and good bread, and we have the drawing out of the chaff, and drink water. They dwell in fair houses, and we have the pain and travail, rain and wind in the fields; and by that that cometh of our labours they keep and maintain their estates. We be called their bondmen, and without we do readily them service, we be beaten; and we have no sovereign to whom we may complain, nor that will hear us nor do us right. Let us go to the king, he is young, and show him what servage we be in, and show him how we will have it otherwise, or else we will provide us of some remedy. And if we go together all manner of people that be now in any bondage will follow us, to the intent to be made free, and when the king seeth us we shall have some remedy, either by fairness or otherwise." Thus John Ball said on Sundays when the people issued out of the churches in the villages, wherefore many of the mean people loved him, and such as intended to no goodness said how he said truth. And so they would murmur one with another in the fields and in the ways as they went together, affirming how John Ball said truth.

The Archbishop of Canterbury, who was informed of the saying of this John Ball, caused him to be taken and put in prison a two or three months to chastise him. Howbeit it had been much better at the beginning that he had been condemned to perpetual prison, or else to have died, rather than to have suffered him to have been again delivered out of prison: but the bishop had conscience to let him die. And when this John Ball was out of prison, he returned again to his error as he did before. Of his words and deeds there were

2. Unhappy: ill-fated, wretched, causing trouble.

much people in London informed, such as had great envy at them that were rich and such as were noble. And then they began to speak among them and said how the realm of England was right evil governed, and how that gold and silver was taken from them by them that were named noblemen. So thus these unhappy men of London began to rebel and assembled together, and sent word to the foresaid countries that they should come to London, and bring their people with them, promising how they should find London open to receive them and the commons of the city to be of the same accord, saying how they would do so much to the king that there should not be one bondman in all England.

This promise moved so them of Kent, of Essex, of Sussex, of Bedford, and of the countries about, that they rose and came towards London to the number of sixty thousand. And they had a captain called Water [3] Tyler and with him in company was Jack Straw and John Ball. These three were chief sovereign captains, but the head of all was Water Tyler and he was indeed a tiler of houses, an ungracious patron.

When these unhappy men began thus to stir, they of London, except such as were of their band, were greatly afraid. Then the Mayor of London and the rich men of the city took counsel together, and when they saw the people thus coming on every side, they caused the gates of the city to be closed and would suffer no man to enter into the city. But when they had well imagined, they advised not so to do, for they thought they should thereby put their suburbs in great peril to be burnt, and so they opened again the city; and there entered in at the gates in some place a hundred, two hundred, by twenty and by thirty. And so when they came to London they entered and lodged, and yet of truth the third part of these people could not tell what to ask or demand, but followed each other like beasts, as the shepherds did of old time, saying how they would go conquer the Holy Land, and at last all came to nothing. In likewise these villains and poor people came to London a hundred mile off, sixty mile, fifty mile, forty mile and twenty mile off, and from all countries about London, but the most part came from the countries before named. And as they came they demanded ever for the king. The gentlemen of the countries, knights and squires, began to doubt,[4] when they saw the people began to rebel, and though they were in doubt, it was good reason: for a less occasion they might have been afraid. So the gentlemen drew together as well as they might.

The same day that these unhappy people of Kent were coming to London, there returned from Canterbury the king's mother, Princess of Wales, coming from her pilgrimage. She was in great jeopardy to have been lost, for these people came to her carriage and dealt rudely with her, whereof the good lady was in great doubt lest they would have done some villainy to her or to her damosels. Howbeit, God kept her, and she came in one day from Canterbury to London, for she never durst tarry by the way. The same time King Richard her son was at the Tower of London. There his mother found him, and with him there was the Earl of Salisbury, the Archbishop of Canterbury, Sir Robert of Namur, the Lord of Gommegnies and divers other, who were in

---

3. Water: Walter
4. doubt: fear

doubt of these people that thus gathered together and wist not what they demanded. This rebellion was well-known in the king's court or [5] any of these people began to stir out of their houses, but the king nor his council did provide no remedy therefor, which was great marvel. And to the intent that all lords and good people, and such as would nothing but good, should take ensample to correct them that be evil and rebellious, I shall show you plainly all the matter as it was.

THE EVIL DEEDS THAT THESE COMMONS OF ENGLAND DID TO THE KING'S OFFICERS, AND HOW THEY SENT A KNIGHT TO SPEAK WITH THE KING

The Monday before the feast of Corpus Christi, the year of our Lord God a thousand three hundred and eighty-one, these people issued out of their houses to come to London to speak with the king to be made free, for they would have had no bondman in England. And so first they came to Saint Thomas of Canterbury, and there John Ball had thought to have found the Bishop of Canterbury, but he was at London with the king. When Wat Tyler and Jack Straw entered into Canterbury, all the common people made great feast for all the town was of their assent. And there they took counsel to go to London to the king, and to send some of their company over the river of Thames into Essex, into Sussex, and into the counties of Stafford and Bedford, to speak to the people that they should all come to the farther side of London, and thereby to close London round about so that the king should not stop their passages, and that they should all meet together on Corpus Christi day. They that were at Canterbury entered into Saint Thomas' church and did there much hurt, and robbed and brake up the bishop's chamber. And in robbing and bearing out their pillage they said, "Ah! this Chancellor of England hath had a good market to get together all this riches. He shall give us now account of the revenues of England and of the great profits that he hath gathered since the king's coronation."

When they had this Monday thus broken the abbey of Saint Vincent, they departed in the morning and all the people of Canterbury with them, and so took the way to Rochester and sent their people to the villages about. And in their going they beat down and robbed houses of advocates and of the procurors of the king's court and of the archbishop, and had mercy of none. And when they were come to Rochester, they had there good cheer, for the people of that town tarried for them, for they were of the same sect. And then they went to the castle there and took the knight that had the rule thereof: he was called Sir John Newton. And they said to him, "Sir, it behoveth you to go with us and you shall be our sovereign captain, and to do what we will have you." The knight excused himself honestly and showed them divers considerations and excuses, but all availed him nothing, for they said unto him, "Sir John, if ye do not as we will have you, ye are but dead." The knight seeing these people in that fury and ready to slay him, he then doubted death and

_____

5. Or: ere, before

agreed to them, and so they took him with them against his inward will. And in likewise did they of other countries in England, as Essex, Sussex, Stafford, Bedford, and Norfolk even to Lynn, for they brought the knights and gentlemen into such obeisance that they caused them to go with them whether they would or not, as the Lord Morley, a great baron, Sir Stephen of Hales and Sir Thomas of Cosington and other.

Now behold the great fortune. If they might have come to their intents, they would have destroyed all the noblemen of England, and thereafter all other nations would have followed the same and have taken foot and ensample by them and by them of Ghent and Flanders, who rebelled against their lord. The same year the Parisians rebelled in likewise and found out the mallets of iron, of whom there were more than twenty thousand, as ye shall hear after in this history, but first we will speak of them of England.

When these people thus lodged at Rochester departed and passed the river and came to Dartford, always keeping still their opinions, beating down before them and all about the places and houses of advocates and procurors, and striking off the heads of divers persons; and so long they went forward until they came within a four mile of London, and there lodged on a hill called Blackheath. And as they went, they said ever they were the king's men and the noble commons of England. And when they of London knew that they were come so near to them, the mayor, as ye have heard before, closed the gates and kept straitly all the passages: this order caused the mayor, who was called William Walworth, and divers other rich burgesses of the city who were not of their sect, but there were in London of their unhappy opinions more than thirty thousand. Then these people thus being lodged on Blackheath determined to send their knight to speak with the king, and to show him how all that they have done or will do is for him and his honour, and how the realm of England hath not been well governed a great space for the honour of the realm nor for the common profit by his uncles and by the clergy, and specially by the Archbishop of Canterbury his chancellor, whereof they would have account. This knight durst do none otherwise but so came by the river of Thames to the Tower. The king and they that were with him in the Tower, desiring to hear tidings, seeing this knight coming, made him way, and was brought before the king into a chamber. And with the knight was the princess his mother and his two brethren, the Earl of Kent and the Lord John Holland, the Earl of Salisbury, the Earl of Warwick, the Earl of Oxford, the Archbishop of Canterbury, the Lord of Saint John's, Sir Robert of Namur, the Lord of Vertaing, the Lord of Gommegnies, Sir Henry of Senzeille, the Mayor of London and divers other notable burgesses. This knight Sir John Newton, who was well known among them for he was one of the king's officers, he kneeled down before the king and said, "My right redoubted lord, let it not displease your Grace the message that I must needs show you, for, dear sir, it is by force and against my will." "Sir John," said the king, "say what ye will, I hold you excused." "Sir, the commons of this your realm hath sent me to you to desire you to come and speak with them on Blackheath, for they desire to have none but you. And, sir, ye need not to have any doubt of your person, for they will do you no hurt, for they hold and will hold you for their king; but, sir, they say they will show you divers things the which shall be right necessary for you to take heed of when they speak with you, of the which things, sir, I have no charge to show you. But, sir, an [6] it may please you to give me an answer such as may appease them, and that they may know for truth that I have spoken with you, for they have my children in hostage till I return again to them and without I return again they will slay my children incontinent." Then the king made him an answer and said, "Sir, ye shall have an answer shortly." Then the king took counsel what was best for him to do, and it was anon determined that the next morning the king should go down the river by water, and without fail to speak with them. And when Sir John Newton heard that answer he desired nothing else, and so took his leave of the king and of the lords and returned again into his vessel, and passed the Thames and went to Blackheath where he had left more than threescore thousand men. And there he answered them that the next morning they should send some of their council to the Thames, and there the king would come and speak with them. This answer greatly pleased them, and so passed that night as well as they might. . . .

How the Commons of England Entered into London, and of the Great Evil That They Did, and of the Death of the Bishop of Canterbury and Divers Other

In the morning on Corpus Christi day King Richard heard mass in the Tower of London, and all his lords, and then he took his barge with the Earl of Salisbury, the Earl of Warwick, the Earl of Oxford, and certain knights, and so rowed down along Thames to Rotherhithe, whereas was descended down the hill a ten thousand men to see the king and to speak with him. And when they saw the king's barge coming they began to shout and made such a cry as though all the devils in hell had been among them. And they had brought with them Sir John Newton, to the intent that if the king had not come they would have stricken him all to pieces, and so they had promised him. And when the king and his lords saw the demeanour of the people, the best assured of them were in dread, and so the king counselled by his barons not to take any landing there, but so rowed up and down the river. And the king demanded of them what they would, and said how he was come thither to speak with them. And they said all with one voice, "We would that ye should come a-land, and then we shall show you what we lack." Then the Earl of Salisbury answered for the king and said, "Sirs, ye be not in such order nor array that the king ought to speak with you"; and so with those words no more said. And then the king was counselled to return again to the Tower of London, and so he did. And when these people saw that, they were inflamed with ire and returned to the hill where the great band was, and there showed them what answer they had and how the king was returned to the Tower of London.

Then they cried all with one voice, "Let us go to London," and so they took their way thither. And in their going they beat down abbeys and houses

---

6. An: if

of advocates and of men of the court, and so came into the suburbs of London, which were great and fair, and there beat down divers fair houses, and specially they brake up the king's prisons, as the Marshalsea and other, and delivered out all the prisoners that were within and there they did much hurt. And at the bridge foot they threat them of London because the gates of the bridge were closed, saying how they would burn all the suburbs and so conquer London by force, and to slay and burn all the commons of the city. There were many within the city of their accord, and so they drew together and said, "Why do we not let these good people enter into the city? They are our fellows and that that they do is for us." So therewith the gates were opened, and then these people entered into the city and went into houses and sat down to eat and drink. They desired nothing but it was incontinent brought to them, for every man was ready to make them good cheer and to give them meat and drink to appease them.

Then the captains, as John Ball, Jack Straw and Wat Tyler, went throughout London, and a twenty thousand with them, and so came to the Savoy in the way to Westminster, which was a goodly house and it pertained to the Duke of Lancaster.[7] And when they entered they slew the keepers thereof and robbed and pilled the house, and when they had so done, then they set fire on it and clean destroyed and burnt it. And when they had done that outrage, they left not therewith but went straight to the fair hospital, minster and all. Then they went from street to street and slew all the Flemings [8] that they could find, in church or in any other place: there was none respited from death. And they brake up divers houses of the Lombards [9] and robbed them and took their goods at their pleasure, for there was none that durst say them nay.

. . . Ye may well know and believe that it was great pity for the danger that the king and such as were with him were in. For some time these unhappy people shouted and cried so loud, as though all the devils of hell had been among them.

In this evening the king was counselled by his brethren and lords, and by Sir William Walworth, Mayor of London, and divers other notable and rich burgesses, that in the night-time they should issue out of the Tower and enter into the city, and so to slay all these unhappy people while they were at their rest and asleep, for it was thought that many of them were drunken, whereby they should be slain like flies; also of twenty of them there was scant one in harness. And surely the good men of London might well have done this at their ease, for they had in their houses secretly their friends and servants ready in harness. And also Sir Robert Knowles was in his lodging, keeping his treasure, with a sixscore ready at his commandment. In likewise was Sir Perducas d'Albret, who was as then in London, insomuch that there might well [have] assembled together an eight thousand men ready in harness. Howbeit there was nothing done, for the residue of the commons of the city

7. Duke of Lancaster: John of Gaunt, one of the most powerful nobles in England and patron of the poet Geoffrey Chaucer. Gaunt was in Scotland at the time of the rebellion.

8. Flemings: wool-weavers from Flanders, many of whom settled in England to compete with native workers.

9. Lombards: Italian merchants and money-lenders.

were sore doubted, lest they should rise also, and the commons before were a threescore thousand or more. Then the Earl of Salisbury and the wise men about the king said, "Sir, if ye can appease them with fairness, it were best and most profitable, and to grant them everything that they desire: for if we should begin a thing the which we could not achieve, we should never recover it again, but we and our heirs ever to be disherited." So this counsel was taken and the mayor countermanded, and so commanded that he should not stir; and he did as he was commanded, as reason was. And in the city with the major there were twelve aldermen, whereof nine of them held with the king and the other three took part with these ungracious people, as it was after well-known, the which they full dearly bought.

And on the Friday in the morning, the people being at Saint Katherine's near to the Tower, began to apparel themselves and to cry and to shout and said, without the king would come out and speak with them, they would assail the Tower and take it by force and slay all them that were within. Then the king doubted these words, and so was counselled that he should issue out to speak with them. And then the king sent to them that they should all draw to a fair plain place, called Mile End, whereas the people in the city did sport them in the summer season, and there the king to grant them that they desired. And there it was cried in the king's name that whosoever would speak with the king, let him go to the said place, and there he should not fail to find the king.

Then the people began to depart, specially the commons of the villages, and went to the same place. But all went not thither, for they were not all of one condition; for there were some that desired nothing but riches and the utter destruction of the noblemen, and to have London robbed and pilled: that was the principal matter of their beginning, the which they well showed, for as soon as the Tower gate opened and that the king was issued out with his two brethren and the Earl of Salisbury, the Earl of Warwick, the Earl of Oxford, Sir Robert of Namur, the Lord of Vertaing, the Lord Gommegnies and divers other, then Wat Tyler, Jack Straw, and John Ball and more than four hundred, entered into the Tower and brake up chamber after chamber; and at last found the Archbishop of Canterbury, called Simon, a valiant man and a wise, and chief Chancellor of England, and a little before he had said mass before the king. These gluttons took him and struck off his head, and also they beheaded the Lord of Saint John's, and a friar minor, master in medicine pertaining to the Duke of Lancaster. They slew him in despite of his master and a sergeant-at-arms, called John Leg. And these four heads were set on four long spears and they made them to be borne before them through the streets of London and at last set them a-high on London Bridge, as though they had been traitors to the king and to the realm. Also these gluttons entered into the princess' chamber and brake her bed, whereby she was so sore afraid that she swooned, and there she was taken up and borne to the waterside and put into a barge and covered, and so conveyed to a place called the Queen's Wardrobe. And there she was all that day and night, like a woman half dead, till she was comforted with the king her son, as ye shall hear after.

How the Nobles of England Were in Great Peril to Have Been Destroyed, and How These Rebels Were Punished and Sent Home to Their Own Houses

When the king came to the said place of Mile End without London, he put out of his company his two brethren, the Earl of Kent and Sir John Holland, and the Lord of Gommegnies, for they durst not appear before the people. And when the king and his other lords were there, he found there a threescore thousand men of divers villages and of sundry countries in England. So the king entered in among them and said to them sweetly, "Ah! ye good people, I am your king. What lack ye? What will ye say?" Then such as understood him said, "We will that ye make us free for ever, ourselves, our heirs and our lands, and that we be called no more bond, nor so reputed." "Sirs," said the king "I am well agreed thereto. Withdraw ye home into your own houses and into such villages as ye came from, and leave behind you of every village two or three, and I shall cause writings to be made and seal them with my seal, the which they shall have with them, containing everything that ye demand. And to the intent that ye shall be the better assured, I shall cause my banners to be delivered into every bailiwick, shire, and counties."

These words appeased well the common people, such as were simple and good plain men, that were come thither and wist not why. They said, "It was well said, we desire no better." Thus these people began to be appeased and began to withdraw them into the city of London. And the king also said a word, the which greatly contented them. He said, "Sirs, among you good men of Kent, ye shall have one of my banners with you, and ye of Essex another, and ye of Sussex, of Bedford, of Cambridge, of Yarmouth, of Stafford, and of Lynn, each of you one; and also I pardon everything that ye have done hitherto, so that ye follow my banners and return home to your houses." They all answered how they would do so. Thus these people departed and went into London.

Then the king ordained more than thirty clerks the same Friday to write with all diligence letters patent, and sealed with the king's seal, and delivered them to these people. And when they had received the writing they departed and returned to their own countries. But the great venom remained still behind, for Wat Tyler, Jack Straw and John Ball said, for all that these people were thus appeased, yet they would not depart so, and they had of their accord more than thirty thousand. So they abode still and made no press to have the king's writing nor seal, for all their intents was to put the city to trouble in such wise as to slay all the rich and honest persons and to rob and pill their houses. They of London were in great fear of this, wherefore they kept their houses privily with their friends and such servants as they had, every man according to his puissance. And when these said people were this Friday thus somewhat appeased, and that they should depart as soon as they had their writings, every man home into his own country, then King Richard came into the Royal Palace where the queen his mother was, right sore afraid. So he comforted her as well as he could and tarried there with her all that night. . . .

The Saturday the king . . . went to Westminster and heard mass in the church there, and all his lords with him. And beside the church there was a little chapel with an image of our Lady, which did great miracles and in whom the Kings of England had ever great trust and confidence. The king made his orisons before this image and did there his offering, and then he leapt on his horse and all his lords, and so the king rode toward London. And when he had ridden a little way, on the left hand there was a way to pass without London.

The same proper morning Wat Tyler, Jack Straw and John Ball had assembled their company to commune together in a place called Smithfield, whereas every Friday there is a market of horses. And there were together all of affinity more than twenty thousand, and yet there were many still in the town, drinking and making merry in the taverns, and paid nothing, for they were happy that made them best cheer. And these people in Smithfield had with them the king's banners the which were delivered them the day before, and all these gluttons were in mind to overrun and to rob London the same day, for their captains said how they had done nothing as yet: "These liberties that the king hath given us is to us but a small profit: therefore let us be all of one accord, and let us overrun this rich and puissant city or they of Essex, of Sussex, of Cambridge, of Bedford, of Arundel, of Warwick, of Reading, of Oxford, of Guildford, of Lynn, of Stafford, of Yarmouth, of Lincoln, of York and of Durham do come hither, for all these will come hither; Baker and Lister will bring them hither. And if we be first lords of London and have the possession of the riches that is therein, we shall not repent us, for if we leave it, they that come after will have it from us."

To this counsel they all agreed. And therewith the king came the same way unaware of them, for he had thought to have passed that way without London, and with him a forty horse. And when he came before the abbey of Saint Bartholomew and beheld all these people, then the king rested and said how he would go no farther till he knew what these people ailed, saying if they were in any trouble how he would re-appease them again. The lords that were with him tarried also, as reason was when they saw the king tarry. And when Wat Tyler saw the king tarry he said to his people, "Sirs, yonder is the king, I will go and speak with him. Stir not from hence without I make you a sign, and when I make you that sign come on and slay all them except the king. But do the king no hurt, he is young, we shall do with him what we list and shall lead him with us all about England, and so shall we be lords of all the realm without doubt."

And there was a doublet-maker of London called John Tycle, and he had brought to these gluttons a sixty doublets, the which they wore. Then he demanded of these captains who should pay him for his doublets: he demanded thirty mark. Wat Tyler answered him and said, "Friend, appease yourself, thou shalt be well paid or this day be ended. Keep thee near me, I shall be your creditor." And therewith he spurred his horse and departed from his company, and came to the king, so near him that his horse's head touched the croup of the king's horse. And the first word that he said was this, "Sir king, seest thou all yonder people?" "Yea, truly," said the king, "wherefore sayest thou?" "Because," said he, "they be all at my commandment, and have sworn to me faith and troth to do all that I will have them." "In a good time," said the king, "I will well it be so." Then Wat Tyler said, as he that nothing demanded but riot, "What believest thou, king, that these people, and as many more as be in London at my commandment, that they will depart from thee thus without having thy letters?" "No," said the king, "ye shall have them; they be ordained for you, and shall be delivered every one each after other. Wherefore, good fellows, withdraw fair and easily to your people and cause them to depart out of London, for it is our intent that each of you by villages and townships shall have letters patent as I have promised you." With these words Wat Tyler cast his eyes on a squire that was there with the king bearing the king's sword, and Wat Tyler hated greatly the same squire, for the same squire had displeased him before for words between them. "What!" said Tyler, "art thou there? Give me thy dagger." "Nay," said the squire, "that will I not do. Wherefore should I give it thee?" The king beheld the squire and said, "Give it him, let him have it." And so the squire took it him sore against his will. And when this Wat Tyler had it he began to play therewith and turned it in his hand, and said again to the squire, "Give me also that sword." "Nay," said the squire, "it is the king's sword. Thou art not worthy to have it, for thou art but a knave, and if there were no more here but thou and I, thou durst not speak those words for as much gold in quantity as all yonder abbey!" "By my faith," said Wat Tyler, "I shall never eat meat till I have thy head!" And with those words the Mayor of London came to the king with a twelve horses well armed under their coats, and so he brake the press,[10] and saw and heard how Wat Tyler demeaned himself, and said to him, "Ha! thou knave, how art thou so hardy in the king's presence to speak such words? It is too much for thee so to do." Then the king began to chafe and said to the mayor, "Set hands on him." And while the king said so, Tyler said to the mayor, "A God's name, what have I said to displease thee?" "Yes, truly" quoth the mayor, "thou false stinking knave, shalt thou speak thus in the presence of the king my natural lord? I commit never to live, without thou shalt dearly abye it." And with those words the mayor drew out his sword and struck Tyler so great a stroke on the head that he fell down at the feet of his horse. And as soon as he was fallen, they environed him all about, whereby he was not seen of his company. Then a squire of the king's alighted, called John Standish, and he drew out his sword and put it into Wat Tyler's belly, and so he died. Then the ungracious people there assembled, perceiving their captain slain, began to murmur among themselves and said, "Ah! Our captain is slain, let us go and slay them all." And therewith they arranged themselves on the place in manner of battle, and their bows before them.

Thus the king began a great outrage; howbeit all turned to the best, for as soon as Tyler was on the earth, the king departed from all his company and all alone he rode to these people, and said to his own men, "Sirs, none of you follow me; let me alone." And so when he came before these ungracious people, who put themselves in ordinance to revenge their captain then the king said to them, "Sirs, what aileth you? Ye shall have no captain but me. I am

---

10. Brake the press: broke through the crowd.

your king. Be all in rest and peace." And so the most part of the people that heard the king speak and saw him among them, were shamefaced and began to wax peaceable and to depart. But some, such as were malicious and evil, would not depart, but made semblance as though they would do somewhat. . . .

There the king made three knights, the one the Mayor of London Sir William Walworth, Sir John Standish, and Sir Nicholas Bramber. Then the lords said among themselves, "What shall we do? We see here our enemies who would gladly slay us if they might have the better hand of us." Sir Robert Knowles counselled to go and fight with them and slay them all, yet the king would not consent thereto but said, "Nay, I will not so. I will send to them commanding them to send me again my banners, and thereby we shall see what they will do. Howbeit, either by fairness or otherwise, I will have them." "That is well said, sir," quoth the Earl of Salisbury. Then these new knights were sent to them, and these knights made token to them not to shoot at them, and when they came so near them that their speech might be heard, they said, "Sirs, the king commandeth you to send again his banners, and we think he will have mercy on you." And incontinent they delivered again the banners and sent them to the king. Also they were commanded on pain of their heads, that all such as had letters of the king to bring them forth and to send them again to the king; and so many of them delivered their letters, but not all. Then the king made them to be all torn in their presence. And as soon as the king's banners were delivered again these unhappy people kept none array, but the most part of them did cast down their bows, and so brake their array and returned into London. Sir Robert Knowles was sore displeased in that he might not go to slay them all, but the king would not consent thereto, but said he would be revenged of them well enough, and so he was after.

Thus these foolish people departed, some one way and some another; and the king and his lords and all his company right ordinately entered into London with great joy. And the first journey that the king made he went to the lady princess his mother, who was in a castle in the Royal called the Queen's Wardrobe, and there she had tarried two days and two nights right sore abashed, as she had good reason. And when she saw the king her son, she was greatly rejoiced and said, "Ah! fair son, what pain and great sorrow that I have suffered for you this day." Then the king answered and said, "Certainly, madam, I know it well; but now rejoice yourself and thank God for now it is time. I have this day recovered mine heritage and the realm of England, the which I had near lost." Thus the king tarried that day with his mother, and every lord went peaceably to their own lodgings.

Then there was a cry made in every street in the king's name that all manner of men, not being of the city of London and have not dwelt there the space of one year, to depart; and if any such be found there the Sunday by the sun-rising, that they should be taken as traitors to the king and to lose their heads. This cry thus made, there was none that durst break it, and so all manner of people departed and sparkled abroad every man to their own places.

John Ball and Jack Straw were found in an old house hidden, thinking to have stolen away, but they could not for they were accused by their own men.

Of the taking of them the king and his lords were glad, and then struck off their heads, and Wat Tyler's also, and they were set on London Bridge, and the valiant men's heads taken down that they had set on the Thursday before. These tidings anon spread abroad, so that the people of the strange countries, which were coming towards London, returned back again to their own houses and durst come no further.

ANONYMOUS, *Táborite Articles* (1420)

Among late-medieval revolutionary risings, only the Hussite movement in Bohemia achieved real power. The religious character of the movement is not simply a form of biblical fundamentalism; it reflects the Church's double role as the wealthiest of feudal institutions and ideological defender of the feudal social order. Both prelates and aristocrats owned land and castles, imposed rents and taxes, received free labor and goods from serfs, and maintained a luxurious way of life. Both prelates and aristocrats identified the existing social order as God's order: natural, eternal, and right.

John Hus (1370–1415), a scholar and cleric of peasant origins, believing that sinful authority ceases to be authority, began to preach against clerical and aristocratic corruption. Hus was excommunicated and burnt at the stake, but his followers continued to preach and to call the people to armed resistance. Masses of peasants, artisans, and bourgeois, convinced that a new world was at hand, began to assemble in the hills in regions throughout Bohemia. In 1420 they built the fortified new town of Tábor. Other towns were taken by the Hussites, and Prague itself was liberated when the Hussite army successfully defended it against a crusade. For several years the country was in their hands, but the issue of reform versus revolution split the movement from within. The poor were persecuted by their former allies of the middle class, who were defeated in turn by the Catholic nobility in 1434.

The Táborite articles represent the apocalyptic mode derived from the Revelation of St. John. Like Old Testament prophecy it is founded on direct revelation; like prophecy it permits no middle ground between those who observe God's law and those who oppose it. But for the prophet, punishment is in the future and can be averted by reformed conduct; in apocalyptic literature the time of reckoning is now and is historically inevitable. Prophecy allows man to create history, apocalypse creates it for him; prophecy puts off revolution with reform, apocalypse insists on revolution now. This uncompromising view of history perhaps accounts for the popularity of apocalyptic literature among the medieval and Renaissance poor; it reappears in Winstanley's Digger manifesto.

In our time there shall be an end of all things, that is, all evil shall be uprooted on this earth.

This age is no longer the time of grace or mercy or charity toward wicked men who resist the Law of God.

This is the time of vengeance and retaliation against wicked men by fire and sword so that all adversaries of God's Law shall be slain by fire and sword or otherwise done to death.

In this time whoever will hear the Word of Christ, then let those which are of the true faith flee to the mountains; and those that will not leave the towns, villages and hamlets for the mountains or for Tábor shall be guilty each one of mortal sin.

Everyone that will not go to the mountains shall perish amidst the towns, villages and hamlets by the blows of God.

In this time nobody can be saved nor shielded from God's blows but on the mountains.

In this time of vengeance all towns, villages and hamlets should be deserted by good people and forsaken.

When the people have thus gone away, no good man shall return there.

After this exodus, Prague, that great Babylon, together with all towns, villages and hamlets, shall be burnt and destroyed.

In this time of vengeance the Táborite brethren are God's angels sent to lead the righteous to the mountains out of towns, villages and hamlets as Lot was led out of Sodom.

The Táborite brethren are in this time of vengeance the messengers of God sent to purge away all offences and evil from Christ's kingdom, all wickedness from good people and from the Holy Church.

The Táborite brethren shall take revenge by fire and sword on God's enemies and on all towns, villages and hamlets.

The Táborite brethren are the body of which it has been said: for wheresoever the carcass is, there will the eagles be gathered together.

About these brethren it is written: every place whereon the soles of your feet shall tread shall be yours; because you have forsaken little to gain a lot.

Every lord, knight, citizen or peasant who has been admonished by the Táborite brethren to assist in these four things: first, to liberate every truth, second, to spread the praise of God, third, to work for the salvation of mankind, and fourth, to prevent sins; any man that does not do so shall be fought against like Satan or a dragon and slain, and all his property shall be taken from him or destroyed, and the same fate shall befall each town, village or hamlet.

Whosoever will grant money or help or show any good-will to such an enemy shall also suffer in body and in property.

Every church, chapel or altar built to the honour of the Lord God or of any saint, shall be destroyed and burnt as a place of idolatry.

Every house of a priest, canon, chaplain or any other cleric shall be destroyed and burnt.

In this time of vengeance only five towns shall remain in which those who flee to them shall be saved, but all other towns, villages, and hamlets, together with those who dwell in them, shall be destroyed and burnt like Sodom.

As in Tábor nothing is mine and nothing thine, but all is common, so everything shall be common to all forever and no one shall have anything of his own; because whoever owns anything himself commits a mortal sin.

Husband or wife shall leave for the mountains or for the five towns without seeking permission from each other, leaving behind children and everything else.

Debtors who flee to the mountains or the aforesaid five towns shall be acquitted of paying their debts.

Even now at this time of the end of things, which is called the day of vengeance, Christ is coming in secret like a thief that He may Himself or with the help of the angels, defeat all His enemies by fire and sword and, above all, by fire; because, as the deluge once renewed the world, so at this time it shall be renewed by fire; and therefore all towns, villages and hamlets shall be burnt.

Even now at the end of the ages, all shall see Christ bodily descend from Heaven to accept His kingdom here on earth. Here on these very mountains will He provide a great feast for His spouse the Holy Church and will enter among the feasters as King and throw into deep darkness all those who have not wedding garments, and likewise those who are not on the mountains.

When in this time Christ will arrive with His angels in clouds and majesty, those who have died in Christ, shall rise from the dead and they shall be the first to come with Him to judge the wicked, both the quick and the dead. And then those that are found alive at this time will be cast on high into the clouds to meet Christ, and this will come to pass soon in a few years. And many will live to see this and the saints who will rise from the dead; and among them they will see Master John Hus.

No king shall be elected on earth anymore, because Christ Himself shall rule.

In this time no king shall reign nor any lord rule on earth, there shall be no serfdom, all interests and taxes shall cease, nor shall any man force another to do anything, because all shall be equal, brothers and sisters.

Holy Mass shall not be sung or read in the Latin tongue, but only in the language of the people.

Missals sung in Latin, prayer books and other books, priestly vestments, surplices, silver or golden monstrances and the like chalices, silver or golden belts, ornamented or richly embroidered garments, finely made or costly robes: all these things shall not exist and must therefore be spoilt and destroyed.

Priests shall have no payments nor hamlets nor cattle nor estates nor houses in which to dwell nor anything of the like, even if they were given such things as alms, even if they held them by secular law and governance.

ANONYMOUS, *The Twelve Articles of the Swabian Peasants*

THOMAS MÜNTZER (1488–1525) *Most Highly Provoked Defense and Answer against the Spiritless, Soft-living Flesh at Wittenberg, which Has Befouled Pitiable Christianity in Perverted Fashion by Its Theft of Holy Scripture*

For more than a century before the Protestant Reformation, the peasants of central Europe had begun to rebel against their feudal lords and against the Catholic Church, which had become the most powerful of feudal institutions. When Martin Luther (1483–1546) renounced monasticism and papal authority to become a spokesman for the German Reformation, many German peasants seized his arguments as a theological justification for social reform. The "Twelve Articles" (1525)—like John Ball's sermon, the Táborite articles, Milton's tract, and Winstanley's vision—are based on independent scriptural exegesis, through which Luther had often criticized the Church. But Luther never intended his work to be used to justify insurrection; to attack "the kingdom of the world" was not his aim. He refuted the peasant articles with a long "Admonition to Peace," in which he counselled the rebels not to revolt against "the governing authorities that are instituted by God."

Thomas Müntzer, at first a disciple of Luther, had for several years sympathized with the cause of the German peasants and industrial workers and had become an influential preacher in several cities. When it became clear to Müntzer that the German aristocrats would do nothing to alleviate social conditions, he turned against both the aristocracy and the temporizing Luther. The tract below (1524) is the last and most vituperative of his several attacks on Luther, whom he blames for a luxurious way of life, alliance with the princes, and misinterpretation of scripture. The tract appeared in the midst of continued peasant revolts, which had now become sufficiently general and systematic to be called the Peasant War. But by May 1525 the peasant armies were defeated and the victorious princes, encouraged by another of Luther's tracts against the rebels, began a program of massacre and revenge in which Müntzer was tortured and beheaded.

Full of self-righteousness and sarcasm, Müntzer anticipates Kropotkin in his denunciation of the class basis of laws pertaining to property.

*

ANONYMOUS

The Twelve Articles of the Swabian Peasants

The basic and chief articles of all the peasants and subjects of spiritual and temporal lords, concerning the matters in which they feel they are being denied their rights.

To the Christian reader: Peace and the grace of God through Christ.

Many antichrists [I John 2:18] have recently taken advantage of the assembling of the peasants and used it as an excuse to speak scornfully about the gospel. They say, "Is this the fruit of the new gospel? Will no one be obedient anymore? Will the people rebel everywhere, revolt against their lords, gather and organize in crowds, and use their power to reform or even to overthrow their spiritual and temporal authorities? Indeed, they may even kill them." The following articles are our answer to these godless and blasphemous critics. Our intention is twofold: first, to remove this calumny from the word of God and, second, to excuse in a Christian way the disobedience and even the rebellion of the peasants.

First, the gospel does not cause rebellion and disturbance, because it is a message about Christ, the promised Messiah, whose words and life teach nothing but love, peace, patience, and unity. And all who believe in this Christ become loving, peaceful, patient, and agreeable. This is the basis of all the articles of the peasants (as will clearly appear), and they are basically concerned with hearing the word of God and living according to it. On what basis, then, can these antichrists call the gospel a cause of revolt and violence? That some antichrists and enemies of the gospel resist these demands and requests is not the fault of the gospel, but of the devil, the gospel's deadliest enemy, who by means of unbelief arouses opposition in his own. Through this opposition the word of God, which teaches love, peace, and unity, is suppressed and taken away.

Second, on this basis the conclusion is obvious that the peasants cannot properly be called disobedient and rebellious. For, as these articles indicate, they desire this gospel [to be the basis of] their teaching and life. Now if God wills to hear the peasants' earnest and fervent prayer that they may live according to his word, who will criticize the will of God? Who will meddle in his judgment? Who indeed will resist his majesty? Did he not hear the children of Israel when they cried to him and release them out of the hand of Pharaoh [Exod. 3:7-8]; and can he not today deliver his own? Yes, he will deliver them, and will do so quickly [Ps. 46:5]! Therefore, Christian reader, read the following articles carefully and then decide.

Here Follow the Articles

THE FIRST ARTICLE

First, we humbly ask and request—in accordance with our unanimous will and desire—that in the future the entire community have the power and authority to choose and appoint a pastor. We also desire the power to depose him, should he conduct himself improperly. The pastor whom we thus choose for ourselves shall preach the holy gospel to us clearly and purely. He is to add no teaching or commandment of men to the gospel, but rather is always to proclaim the true faith and encourage us to ask God for his grace. He is to instill and strengthen this true faith in us. For if the grace of God is not instilled in us, we remain mere flesh and blood. And mere flesh and blood is useless, as Scripture clearly says, for we can come to God only through true faith and can be saved only through his mercy. That is why we need such a leader and pastor; and thus our demand is grounded in Scripture.

Second, since the tithe is prescribed in the Old Testament, although it is fulfilled in the New, we are willing to pay the just tithe of grain, but it must be done in a proper way. Since men ought to give it to God and distribute it to those who are his, it belongs to the pastor who clearly proclaims the word of God, and we desire that in the future this tithe be gathered and received by our church provost, appointed by the community. With the consent of the whole community the pastor, who shall be chosen by an entire community, shall receive out of this tithe a modest sufficient maintenance for him and his; the remainder shall be distributed to the poor and needy in the same village, according to the circumstances and with the consent of the community. Anything that then remains shall be kept, so that if the needs of the land require the laying of a war tax, no general tax may be laid upon the poor, but it shall be paid out of this surplus.

If it should happen that there were one or more villages that had sold their tithes to meet certain needs, they are to be informed that he who has [bought] the tithes from a whole village is not to be deprived of them without compensation; for we will negotiate with him, in the proper way, form, and manner, to buy them back from him on suitable terms and at a suitable time. But in case anyone has not bought the tithes from any village, and his forbears have simply appropriated them to themselves, we will not, we ought not, nor do we intend to pay him anything further, but will keep them for the support of the aforesaid, our chosen pastor, and for distribution to the needy, as the Holy Scriptures [command]. It does not matter whether the holders of the tithes be spiritual or temporal lords. The small tithe we will not pay at all, for God the Lord created cattle for the free use of men, and we regard this tithe as an improper one which men have invented; therefore we will not give it any longer.

Third, it has been the custom for men to hold us as their own property. This situation is pitiable, for Christ has redeemed and bought us all with the precious shedding of his blood, the lowly as well as the great, excepting no one. Therefore, it agrees with Scripture that we be free and will to be so. It is not our intention to be entirely free. God does not teach us that we should desire no rulers. We are to live according to the commandments, not the free self-will of the flesh; but we are to love God, recognize him in our neighbor as our Lord, and do all (as we gladly would do) that God has commanded in the Lord's Supper; therefore, we ought to live according to his commandment. This commandment does not teach us to disobey our rulers; rather to humble ourselves, not before the rulers only, but before everyone. Thus we willingly obey our chosen and appointed rulers (whom God has appointed over us) in all Christian and appropriate matters. And we have no doubt that since they are true and genuine Christians, they will gladly release us from serfdom, or show us in the gospel that we are serfs.

Fourth, it has been the custom that no poor man has been allowed to catch game, wild fowl, or fresh-water fish, which seems to us altogether improper and unbrotherly, selfish, and not according to the word of God. In some places the rulers keep the game to our vexation and great loss, because the unreasoning animals wantonly devour our crops which God causes to grow for man's use; and we have to put up with this and keep quiet about it, though it is against God and neighbor. When God the Lord created man, he gave him authority over all animals, over the birds of the air, and over the fish in the water. Therefore it is our request that if anyone has waters, he offer satisfactory documentary evidence that the waters have been intentionally sold to him. In that case we do not wish to take them from him by force; on the contrary, for the sake of brotherly love, Christian consideration must be shown. But whoever cannot offer sufficient proof shall surrender these waters to the community in a proper manner.

Fifth, we also have a grievance about wood cutting, for our lords have appropriated all the forests solely to themselves, and when the poor man needs any wood, he must buy it at a double price. In our opinion the forests held by spiritual or temporal lords who have not bought them should revert to the entire community. This community should be free, in an orderly way, to allow anyone to take home what he needs for firewood without payment, and also to take for nothing any that he needs for wood-working; this is to be done with the approval of a supervisor appointed by the community. If there are any forests which have not been thus honestly purchased, a brotherly and Christian agreement should be reached about them; but if the property had first been expropriated and afterward sold, an agreement shall be made in accordance with the facts of the case, and according to brotherly love and the Holy Scriptures.

Sixth, we are grievously oppressed by the free labor which we are required to provide for our lords. The amount of labor required increases from day to day and [the variety of services required] increases from day to day. We ask that an appropriate investigation be made of this matter and that the burdens laid upon us not be too heavy. We ask that we be dealt with graciously, just as our ancestors were, who provided these services according to the word of God.

Seventh, in the future we will not allow ourselves to be further oppressed by the lords. Rather, a man shall possess his holding according to the terms on which it has been granted, that is, according to the agreement between the lord and the peasants. The lord shall not in any way put pressure on the peasant, or force him to render more services, or demand anything else from him without payment, so that the peasant may use and enjoy his property unburdened and in peace; but if the lord needs more services, the peasant shall be obedient, and willing to perform them. However, he is to do so at a time when the peasant's own affairs do not suffer, and he shall receive a fair wage for this labor.

THE EIGHTH ARTICLE

We are greatly aggrieved because many of us have holdings that do not produce enough to enable us to pay the rents due on them. As a result, the peasants bear the loss and are ruined. We ask that the lords have honorable men inspect the said holdings, and fix a fair rent, so that the peasant shall not labor for nothing; for every laborer is worthy of his hire.

THE NINTH ARTICLE

We are aggrieved by the great wrong of continually making new laws. Punishment is inflicted on us, not according to the facts in the case, but at times by great ill-will, at times by great partiality. In our opinion we should be punished by the ancient written law, and the cases dealt with according to the facts, and not according to partiality.

THE TENTH ARTICLE

We are aggrieved because some have expropriated meadows from the common fields which once belonged to a community. We would take these back again into the hands of our communities, unless they have been honestly purchased. If they have been improperly purchased, we should come to a kindly and brotherly agreement about them, according to the facts of the case.

THE ELEVENTH ARTICLE

We would have the custom called death tax[1] entirely abolished. We will not tolerate it or allow widows and orphans to be so shamefully robbed by those who ought to guard and protect them, as now happens in many places and under many forms, contrary to God and honor. They have disgraced and cheated us, and although they had little authority, they have taken what was left after that. God will no longer permit it; it shall be entirely done away with. Henceforth no man shall be required to pay any of this tax, whether large or small.

---

1. Death tax: a fee paid to the lord upon the death of a tenant.

CONCLUSION

Twelfth, it is our conclusion and final opinion that if one or more of the articles set forth here is not in agreement with the word of God (though we think this is not the case), and this disagreement is shown to us on the basis of Scripture, we shall withdraw such an article—after the matter is explained to us on the basis of Scripture. If some of our demands are granted and it is afterward found that they were unjust, they shall be null and void from that hour. Similarly, if additional articles are found to be properly based on Scripture and more offenses against God and our neighbor be revealed thereby [they will be added to these articles]. We, for our part, will and have determined to use forbearance, and will discipline ourselves in all Christian doctrine and practice. We will pray to God the Lord for this; for he, and no one else, can give it to us. The peace of Christ be with us all.

*

THOMAS MÜNTZER

Most Highly Provoked Defense and Answer against the Spiritless, Soft-living Flesh at Wittenberg, which Has Befouled Pitiable Christianity in Perverted Fashion by Its Theft of Holy Scripture

To the most high, firstborn Prince and omnipotent Lord Jesus Christ, gracious King of all kings, valiant Duke of all believers, my most gracious Lord and faithful Protector and to his own troubled bride, poor Christendom.[1]

All praise, honor, dignity, titles and glory belong to Thee alone, Thou eternal Son of God (Phil. 2). Thy Holy Spirit has always appeared, on account of the scribes, those graceless lions, as the worst of all devils (John 8).

Thus it is no great surprise that the most ambitious scribe of all, Doctor Liar,[2] becomes more and more a fool. Without mortifying his name and comfort, he covers himself with Thy Holy Scripture, using it in a deceiving manner, being in nothing less interested than to have dealings with Thee (Isa. 58). He pretends to have attained Thy knowledge (through Thee the gates of truth), acts impudently in Thy presence, and despises Thy true spirit immeasurably. For he shows irrevocably that, out of raging envy and the most bitter hatred, he ridicules me, Thy limb, which was purchased by Thee. This he does without sincere and true cause, in the presence of his sneering, mocking associates, and calls me a Satan or Devil before the simple, despising and mocking me with his perverted, blasphemous judgment.

In Thee, however, I rejoice and am altogether satisfied by Thy gentle com-

---

1. Müntzer's dedication is in deliberate ironic contrast to Luther's habit of dedicating his tracts to various princes.
2. Liar: in German, Lugner, a word play on Luther's name.

fort, for Thou has most lovingly told Thy true friends in Matthew 10 that the disciple is not above the master. Since they blasphemously called Thee, innocent Duke and blessed Savior, Beelzebub, how much more will they do this to me, Thy untiring soldier, since I left that flattering scoundrel at Wittenberg and followed Thy voice (John 10). Indeed, thus it must be, if one would not let these soft-living, self-styled believers carry on in their spurious faith and pharisaical tricks, but wishes to destroy their name and pomp. Thou wert not immune from this experience. They also thought themselves to be more learned than Thou and Thy disciples. (Indeed, with their literalistic stubbornness they probably were more learned than Doctor Ludibrii [3] can ever hope to be.) They also had sufficient reputation and name in all the world. Nonetheless it was not right that they set out against Thee with their reason and wanted to prove themselves against Thee with the clear evidence of Scripture. . . . Thus they did what is done to me today by that shrewd scribe. Where Scripture can be heard most pointedly, he mocks with fervent envy and calls the Spirit of God a devil. . . .

The Jews continually wanted to bring slander and downfall upon Christ, even as Luther now tries to do to me. He chides me emphatically and tells me of the mercy of the Son of God and of his dear friends [4] to whom I preached the sternness of the Law. I pointed out that it is not suspended because of the ungodly transgressors (even though they are rulers) and that it should be administered with all seriousness, as Paul instructed his disciple Timothy, and through him all ministers of souls (I Tim. 1), to preach to the people. He says clearly that all those shall be afflicted who fight and strive against sound doctrine. This no one can deny. Paul passes the same judgment against the lustful transgressor (I Cor. 5). I have printed this as I preached it before the Saxon Rulers, without deception, showing them the sword in the Scriptures that they should use it in order that no insurrection might develop. In short: transgression must be punished; neither the great nor the small may escape from it (Numbers 15).

But then Cousin Lightstep, that tame fellow, comes along and claims that I want to stir up insurrection. This he supposedly read in my letter to the miners. He mentions one, but omits the most incisive part. I stated clearly before the Rulers that the entire congregation is in possession of the sword and the key of loosing. Quoting from Daniel 7, Revelation 6, Romans 8, and I Kings 8, I said that the princes are not lords, but servants of the sword. They should not do as they pleased (Deut. 17), but should do right. According to ancient and honorable custom the people must be present if someone is to be tried and judged correctly according to the Law of God (Numbers 15). Why? If the magistrate misjudges, then the Christians present will repudiate and not tolerate it, for God demands an account of innocent blood (Psalm 78). It is the greatest monstrosity on earth that no one will take care of the needy. As is described in Job 41, the mighty do as they please.

The poor Flatterer wants to cover himself with a spurious mercy of Christ, greatly contrary to the word of Paul in I Tim. 1. In his booklet on commerce

---

3. Ludibrii: ludibrium (Latin) means idle play.
4. **Dear friends**: the princes, to whom Müntzer had preached a sermon on the necessity of reform.

he says that princes should punish thieves and robbers without hesitation. But he is silent about the origin of all thievery. He is a herald who wants to earn thanks through the shedding of the people's blood for the sake of worldly goods. This God assuredly had not told him. The origin of usury, theft, and robbery is our lords and princes, who claim all creatures as their own. All must be theirs—the fish in the water, the birds in the air, the harvest of the earth (Isa.5). They proclaim the so-called command of God among the poor, saying "God commanded that you shall not steal." But this does not help them, since they suppress all men, pinch and flay the poor farmer, the artisan, and all the living (Micah 3). If someone steals the smallest thing, he must hang. And Doctor Liar says "Amen!" Since the princes do not want to get rid of the cause of insurrection it is their own fault that the poor man becomes their enemy. How, under these conditions, could things ever be changed? If I say this, I am rebellious. So let it be. . . .

All who have become evildoers in Christendom on account of the first transgression must be justified by the Law, as Paul says, in order that the sternness of the Father can do away those godless Christians who oppose the saving doctrine of Christ. Thus the just have time and place to learn the will of God. Not a single Christian could ever follow his contemplation under such tyranny, if evil were free from being punished by the Law and the innocent were thus molested. Thus the godless tyrant says to the pious, I must torture you. Christ also suffered, therefore you are not to resist me (Matthew 5). This would be a great perversion. One must carefully discern why the persecutors want to be the best Christians. . . .

Christ was called a devil when He referred the Jews to the works of Abraham as giving them the best criterion for punishment and forgiveness, namely, to punish according to proper sternness. Thus He did not dissolve the Law. Accordingly He said in the seventh chapter of John, before going on to the eighth, "Judge not according to the appearance, but judge righteous judgment." They have no other judgments than those described in the Law, to judge according to the spirit of the Law. Thus one must forgive with the gospel and the spirit of Christ, to the furtherance and not hindrance of the gospel (II Cor. 3 and 13). On account of such distinction Doctor Liar wants to make me a devil and says with his scribes, "Did I not teach rightly in my writing and publication? But you can show no other fruit than insurrection. You are a Satan, an evil Satan indeed. Behold, you are a Samaritan possessed by the devil."

I consider myself unworthy, O Christ, to bear such precious suffering for the same cause, even though the enemy's pronouncement finds so many favorable, perverted supporters. I say, with Thee, to this proud, puffed-up dragon, "Do you hear? I am not possessed by the devil. Through my office I seek to proclaim the name of God, to bring comfort to the troubled, and destruction and sickness to the healthy (Isa. 6, Matt. 9, 13, Luke 8, 4). If I were to say that I would desist from this because of the bad name which is falsely given to me, I would be no better than you, Doctor Liar, with your perverted slander and outrage. You can do nothing but quarrel with the godless. After you succeeded in this, you occupied the place of the scoundrels whom you cast out. Now that you realize that things might go too far, you want to give your name, as bad as it is, to somebody else whom the world dislikes to begin with. You are trying to burn yourself clean, as the devil does, in order that no one may learn openly of your malice. Therefore the prophet calls you (Psalm 90) a basilisk, dragon, viper, and lion because you use your poison first to flatter and then to rave in madness as is your manner." . . .

But Doctor Liar is a simple man when he writes that I should not be prevented from preaching or that they should watch that the spirit at Alstedt keeps its fists quiet. Let us see, dear brethren in Christ, if he is a learned man. Of course, he is learned. In two or three years the world will have opportunity to see the terrible, insidious grief he has brought. But in writing in this manner he wants to wash his hands in innocence, so that no one might notice how he persecutes truth. He claims that his preaching is the Word of God because it evokes so much persecution. I am astounded how this shameless monk can claim to be terribly persecuted—sitting in front of his glass of wine and enjoying his whore's feast. He can do none other than be a scribe (John 10). We shall not do anything to you because of your good works, but because of your blasphemy we shall stone you to death. Thus they spoke to Christ, even as this fellow speaks to me: Not on account of your preaching, but your rebellion you must be expelled.

Beloved brethren. It is not a bad affair going on at the present, particularly since you have no judgment in the matter. You assume that if you stop supporting the parsons everything is in order. But you do not realize that you are now a hundred times one thousand worse off than before. From now on you will be bombarded with a new logic which is said to be the Word of God. But you have the command of Christ (Matthew 7). Study it by heart and no one will deceive you, whatever he writes or says. You must attend carefully to Paul's admonition to the Corinthians (II Cor. 11): See that your minds are not corrupted from the simplicity of Christ. The scribes have interpreted this simplicity with the full treasure of divine wisdom (Col. 2), greatly contrary to Genesis 3, where God warned Adam with a single commandment of future grief, that he be not led astray by the creaturely lust, but have his pleasure in God alone, as is written: Delight thyself in God. . . .

It would be more appropriate for me to instruct the poor folk with good doctrine than to get involved with this blasphemous monk who wants to be a new Christ, who with his blood brought much good for Christendom. Besides there was the gain of a fine thing: priests may get married! . . .

Be ashamed, you arch-scoundrel, that in servile fashion you want to be in favor of an erring world wishing to justify all mankind (Luke 9). You know well whom to rebuke. The poor monks and priests and merchants cannot defend themselves; therefore you can easily slander them. But no one is to judge the godless rulers, even if they trample on Christ with their feet.

To please the peasants, you write that the princes will perish through the Word of God.[5] You say in your commentary on the latest imperial mandate that the princes shall be pushed from their thrones. You prefer them, nonetheless, to merchants. You should pull your princes by their noses, for they have deserved it more than the others. Have they lowered their tribute and extortion? Although you have scolded the princes, you still cheer them up,

---

5. The Word of God: that is, the princes (according to Luther) will be judged in the afterlife.

you new pope, giving them monasteries and churches. They are well pleased with you. I warn you that the peasant may strike loose. You always speak of faith and you write that I fight against you under your shield and protection. Well, one can see my sincerity and your foolishness, for I have been under your shield and protection as a sheep among wolves (Matthew 10). Did you not have greater power over me there than elsewhere? Could you not anticipate what would yet come of this? I was in your territory in order that you would not have any excuse. You say: under our shield and protection. O, how do you reveal yourself! I take it that you consider yourself a ruler. Why do you boast of such shield and protection? In all my letters I never sought a ruler's protection.

. . . You say I desire a hasty and compelled faith, allowing no time to think. I reply with Christ that he is of God who hears His Word. Are you of God? Why do you not hear it? Why do you mock it, judging what you have not understood? Are you still pondering what to teach others? You should be called a criminal rather than judge. Poor Christendom will become aware how your carnal mind has acted against the undeceivable Spirit of God. Let Paul pronounce the judgment: II Cor. 11. Like a fox you have always treated everything with simplicity like an onion with nine skins. You have become a rabid fox who barks hoarsely before dawn. Now, when truth would rise up, you scold the lowly rather than the great. As we Germans say, you are going into the well: just as the fox jumped into a bucket and ate the fish, and then lured the stupid wolf into the bottom.[6] This will happen to the princes who follow you, and to the noble highwaymen whom you set upon the merchants. In his third chapter Ezekiel gives his judgment concerning the fox and in his thirty-fourth chapter concerning the beasts and wild animals whom Christ calls wolves (John 10). They all will share the fate of the trapped foxes (Psalm 72). Once the people begin to expect the light, the little dogs (Matthew 15) will rush into the den of the foxes, doing no more than tiredly biting their mouths. The rested dog, however, will shake the fox by his pelt until he has to leave his den. He has eaten enough chickens. Well, Martin, have you not smelled this roasted fox which, instead of hare, is given inexperienced hunters at the Lord's Court? You, Esau, deserved that Jacob pushed you away. Why did you sell your birthright for the sake of pottage?

Ezekiel 13 and Micah 3 give the answer. You have confounded Christendom with a false faith. Now that trouble has arisen you are unable to correct her. Therefore you flatter the princes and think that all is well so long as you have a great name, as at Leipzig, where you appeared before a most august assembly. Do you want to blind the people? You were quite comfortable at Leipzig, leaving the city with the wreath of carnations and drinking the good wine at Melchior Lother's. . . .

One could fall asleep through your boasting and your senseless foolishness. The merit for your appearance before the Empire at Worms goes to the German nobility, whose mouths you smeared full of honey. They were under the impression that your preaching would give them Bohemian gifts,[7] monas-

---

6. A reference to the popular medieval fable of the fox and the wolf.
7. Bohemian gifts: during the Hussite revolt in Bohemia, church properties had been expropriated. The German aristocracy hoped to profit similarly through the influence of Luther's anticlerical doctrine.

teries and convents. Such you promise now to the princes. Had you wavered at Worms the nobles would have pierced you with a sword instead of arranging your escape. Everybody knows this. You have no right to take the credit, unless you want to risk your noble blood again, as you boast. You and your supporters used wild treachery and cunning. You let yourself be taken prisoner at your own suggestion. You get very impatient with those who do not fall for your roguery. You swore to the saints that you were a pious Martin. Sleep softly, dear flesh. I would like to smell you roasted in your own stubbornness through the wrath of God in the pot on the fire (Jer. 1). Then, cooked in your own juice, the devil should eat you (Ezekiel 23). Your flesh is like that of the ass and would take a long while to cook thoroughly. It would be a tough dish for your soft-mouthed friends. . . .

You fox, with your lies you have saddened the heart of the just man, whom God has not afflicted. And you have strengthened the ungodly, so that they will not revert from their evil ways. For this you shall die; the just man will be liberated by God from your tyranny. You shall see that God is Lord.

JOHN MILTON (1608–1674), Selection from
The Doctrine and Discipline of Divorce

The Civil War of 1642 confirmed for the English middle classes the political influence commensurate with their economic role: parliamentary control of major policy, the limitation of royal and aristocratic power, the elimination of church hierarchies. But many of the rebels had more radical aims, and in 1649, under the tacit leadership of Oliver Cromwell and his New Model Army, Charles I was tried and executed, crown and church lands were confiscated and sold, and the House of Lords was abolished. The Commonwealth Government was established with Cromwell as Protector; it lasted until 1660 when, unable to solve grave financial and political problems, a new Parliament restored Charles II to the throne.

John Milton, the English poet, defended the revolution in a series of pamphlets, and under Cromwell he was appointed Secretary of State for Foreign Tongues. Milton's religious, political, and domestic views are rooted in the conviction that habit and ignorance "fill each state of life . . . with abject and servile principles, depressing the high and heaven-born spirit of man far beneath the condition wherein either God created him, or sin hath sunk him." The tract on divorce is addressed to Parliament as a subject for immediate action, for there was no divorce except on grounds of adultery. As Milton notes in his introduction, there can be no "true reformation in the state, while such an evil as [permanent domestic misery] lies undiscerned or unregarded in the house." Yet the work is motivated by experience as well as conviction, for in 1642 Milton married a young girl who left him after several unhappy months: a disappointment that may account for the special poignancy of the piece. But Milton's prose, like his poetry, moves us in order to instruct us. Its style is characterized by subtle argument, Latinate diction, the stately periodic sentence, and a wealth of scholarly reference.

THE PREFACE

That man is the occasion of his own miseries in most of those evils which he imputes to God's inflicting. The absurdity of our canonists in their decrees about divorce. The Christian imperial laws framed with more equity. The opinion of Hugo Grotius and Paulus Fagius: And the purpose in general of this discourse.

Many men, whether it be their fate or fond opinion, easily persuade themselves, if God would but be pleased a while to withdraw his just punishments from us and to restrain what power either the devil or any earthly enemy hath to work us woe, that then man's nature would find immediate rest and releasement from all evils. But verily they who think so, if they be such as have a mind large enough to take into their thoughts a general survey of human things, would soon prove themselves in that opinion far deceived. For though it were granted us by Divine indulgence to be exempt from all that can be harmful to us from without, yet the perverseness of our folly is so bent that we should never lin [1] hammering out of our own hearts, as it were out of a flint, the seeds and sparkles of new misery to ourselves, till all were in a blaze again.

And no marvel if out of our own hearts, for they are evil; but even out of those things which God meant us either for a principal good or a pure contentment, we are still hatching and contriving upon ourselves matter of continual sorrow and perplexity. What greater good to man than that revealed rule whereby God vouchsafes to show us how he would be worshipped? And yet that not rightly understood became the cause, that once a famous man in Israel [2] could not but oblige his conscience to be the sacrificer, or if not, the gaoler of his innocent and only daughter; and was the cause ofttimes that armies of valiant men have given up their throats to a heathenish enemy on the sabbath day, fondly thinking their defensive resistance to be as then a work unlawful. What thing more instituted to the solace and delight of man than marriage? And yet the mis-interpreting of some Scripture, directed mainly against the abusers of the law for divorce given by Moses, hath changed the blessing of matrimony not seldom into a familiar and co-inhabiting mischief; at least into a drooping and disconsolate household captivity without refuge or redemption. So ungoverned and so wild a race doth superstition run us from one extreme of abused liberty into the other of unmerciful restraint. For although God in the first ordaining of marriage taught us to what end he did it, in words expressly implying the apt and cheerful conversation of man with woman to comfort and refresh him against the evil of solitary life, not mentioning the purpose of generation till afterwards, as being but a secondary end in dignity, though not in necessity: yet now, if any two be but once handed in the church, and have tasted in any sort the nuptial bed, let them find themselves never so mistaken in their dispositions through any error, concealment, or misadventure, that through their different tempers, thoughts, and constitutions, they can neither be to one another a remedy against loneliness nor live in any union or contentment all their days; yet they shall, so they be but found suitably weaponed to the least possibility of sensual enjoyment, be made, spite of antipathy, to fadge together, and combine as they may to their unspeakable wearisomeness and despair of all social delight in the ordinance which God established to that very end.

What a calamity is this, and as the wise man,[3] if he were alive, would sigh out in his own phrase, what a "sore evil is this under the sun!" All which we

---

1. Lin: stop
2. Famous man: Jephthah, who, vowing to sacrifice the first thing he met after a military victory, met his daughter.
3. The wise man: the author of Ecclesiastes, from which the quotation is taken.

can refer justly to no other author than the canon law and her adherents, not consulting with charity, the interpreter and guide of our faith, but resting in the mere element of the text; doubtless by the policy of the devil to make that gracious ordinance become unsupportable, that what with men not daring to venture upon wedlock, and what with men wearied out of it, all inordinate licence might abound.

It was for many ages that marriage lay in disgrace with most of the ancient doctors as a work of the flesh, almost a defilement, wholly denied to priests and the second time dissuaded to all, as he that reads Tertullian or Jerome [4] may see at large. Afterwards it was thought so sacramental that no adultery or desertion could dissolve it; and this is the sense of our canon courts in England to this day, but in no other reformed church else. Yet there remains in them also a burden on it as heavy as the other two were disgraceful or superstitious, and of as much iniquity, crossing a law not only written by Moses but charactered in us by nature, of more antiquity and deeper ground than marriage itself; which law is to force nothing against the faultless proprieties of nature. Yet that this may be colourably done, our Saviour's words touching divorce are, as it were, congealed into a stony rigour inconsistent both with his doctrine and his office; and that which he preached only to the conscience is by canonical tyranny snatched into the compulsive censure of a judicial court, where laws are imposed even against the venerable and secret power of nature's impression, to love, whatever cause be found to loath: which is a heinous barbarism both against the honour of marriage, the dignity of man and his soul, the goodness of Christianity, and all the human respects of civility. Notwithstanding that some of the wisest and gravest among the Christian emperors, who had about them to consult with, those of the fathers then living; who for their learning and holiness of life are still with us in great renown, have made their statutes and edicts concerning this debate far more easy and relenting in many necessary cases, wherein the canon is inflexible. And Hugo Grotius,[5] a man of these times, one of the best learned, seems not obscurely to adhere in his persuasion to the equity of those imperial decrees, in his notes upon the Evangelists; much allaying the outward roughness of the text, which hath for the most part been too immoderately expounded; and excites the diligence of others to inquire further into this question, as containing many points that have not yet been explained. Which ever likely to remain intricate and hopeless upon the suppositions commonly stuck to, the authority of Paulus Fagius,[6] one so learned and so eminent in England once, if it might persuade, would straight acquaint us with a solution of these differences no less prudent than compendious. He, in his comment on the Pentateuch, doubted not to maintain that divorces might be as lawfully permitted by the magistrate to Christians, as they were to the Jews.

But because he is but brief, and these things of great consequence not to be kept obscure, I shall conceive it nothing above my duty, either for the difficulty or the censure that may pass thereon, to communicate such thoughts as I also have had, and do offer them now in this general labour of reformation

---

4. Tertullian or Jerome: early Christian theologians.
5. Hugo Grotius (1583–1645), Dutch jurist, humanist, and biblical scholar.
6. Paulus Fagius (1504–1549), German biblical scholar.

to the candid view both of church and magistrate; especially because I see it the hope of good men, that those irregular and unspiritual courts have spun their utmost date in this land, and some better course must now be constituted. This therefore shall be the task and period of this discourse to prove, FIRST, *that other reasons of divorce, besides adultery, were by the law of Moses, and are yet to be allowed by the Christian magistrate as a piece of justice, and that the words of Christ are not hereby contraried.* SECONDLY, *that to prohibit absolutely any divorce whatsoever, except those which Moses excepted, is against the reason of law;*—as in due place I shall show out of Fagius with many additions. He therefore who by adventuring, shall be so happy as with success to light the way of such an expedient liberty and truth as this, shall restore the much wronged and over-sorrowed state of matrimony, not only to those merciful and life-giving remedies of Moses, but as much as may be, to that serene and blissful condition it was in at the beginning, and shall deserve of all apprehensive men (considering the troubles and distempers which for want of this insight have been so oft in kingdoms, in states, and families), shall deserve to be reckoned among the public benefactors of civil and human life, above the inventors of wine and oil; for this is a far dearer, far nobler, and more desirable cherishing to man's life, unworthily exposed to sadness and mistake, which he shall vindicate. Not that licence and levity and unconsented breach of faith should herein be countenanced, but that some conscionable and tender pity might be had of those who have unwarily, in a thing they never practised before, made themselves the bondmen of a luckless and helpless matrimony. In which argument, he whose courage can serve him to give the first onset, must look for two several [7] oppositions; the one from those who having sworn themselves to long custom and the letter of the text, will not go out of the road; the other from those whose gross and vulgar apprehensions conceit but low of matrimonial purposes, and in the work of male and female think they have all. Nevertheless, it shall be here sought by due ways to be made appear that those words of God in the institution, promising a meet help against loneliness, and those words of Christ, "that his yoke is easy, and his burden light," [8] were not spoken in vain; for if the knot of marriage may in no case be dissolved but for adultery, all the burdens and services of the law are not so intolerable.

This only is desired of them who are minded to judge hardly of thus maintaining: that they would be still, and hear all out, nor think it equal to answer deliberate reason with sudden heat and noise; remembering this, that many truths now of reverend esteem and credit had their birth and beginning once from singular and private thoughts, while the most of men were otherwise possessed; and had the fate at first to be generally exploded and exclaimed on by many violent opposers. Yet I may err perhaps in soothing myself, that this present truth revived will deserve on all hands to be not sinisterly received, in that it undertakes the cure of an inveterate disease crept into the best part of human society; and to do this with no smarting corrosive but with a smooth and pleasing lesson, which received, hath the virtue to soften and dispel rooted and knotty sorrows, and without enchantment, if that be feared, or

---

7. Several: different
8. Matthew 11:30.

spell used, hath regard at once both to serious pity and upright honesty; that tends to the redeeming and restoring of none but such as are the object of compassion, having in an ill hour hampered themselves, to the utter dispatch of all their most beloved comforts and repose for this life's term. But if we shall obstinately dislike this new overture of unexpected ease and recovery, what remains but to deplore the frowardness of our hopeless condition, which neither can endure the estate we are in nor admit of remedy either sharp or sweet. Sharp we ourselves distaste; and sweet, under whose hands we are, is scrupled and suspected as too luscious. In such a posture Christ found the Jews, who were neither won with the austerity of John the Baptist, and thought it too much licence to follow freely the charming pipe of him who sounded and proclaimed liberty and relief to all distresses; yet truth in some age or other will find her witness and shall be justified at last by her own children.

Chapter VI

The fourth reason of this law, that God regards love and peace in the family more than a compulsive performance of marriage, which is more broke by a grievous continuance than by a needful divorce.

Fourthly; Marriage is a covenant, the very being whereof consists not in a forced cohabitation and counterfeit performance of duties, but in unfeigned love and peace. And of matrimonial love, no doubt but that was chiefly meant which by the ancient sages was thus parabled: that Love if he be not twin-born yet hath a brother wondrous like him, called Anteros, whom while he seeks all about, his chance is to meet with many false and feigning desires that wander singly up and down in his likeness. By then in their borrowed garb, Love (though not wholly blind as poets wrong him, yet having but one eye, as being born an archer aiming, and that eye not the quickest in this dark region here below which is not Love's proper sphere), partly out of the simplicity and credulity which is native to him, often deceived, embraces and consorts him with these obvious and suborned striplings, as if they were his mother's own sons; for so he thinks them while they subtly keep themselves most on his blind side. But after a while, as his manner is, when soaring up into the high tower of his Apogaeum [9] above the shadow of the earth, he darts out the direct rays of his then most piercing eye-sight upon the impostures and trim disguises that were used with him, and discerns that this is not his genuine brother as he imagined; he has no longer the power to hold fellowship with such a personated mate; for straight his arrows lose their golden heads and shed their purple feathers, his silken braids untwine and slip their knots, and that original and fiery virtue given him by fate all on a sudden goes out, and leaves him undeified and despoiled of all his force; till finding Anteros at last, he kindles and repairs the almost faded ammunition of his deity by the reflection of a co-equal and homogeneal fire. Thus mine author sung it to me: and by the leave of those who would be counted the only grave

---

9. Apogaeum: apogee, a planet's furthest point from the earth.

ones, this is no mere amatorious novel (though to be wise and skilful in these matters men heretofore of greatest name in virtue have esteemed it one of the highest arcs that human contemplation circling upwards can make from the globy sea whereon she stands); but this is a deep and serious verity, showing us that love in marriage cannot live nor subsist unless it be mutual; and where love cannot be, there can be left of wedlock nothing but the empty husk of an outside matrimony, as undelightful and unpleasing to God as any other kind of hypocrisy. So far is his command from tying men to the observance of duties which there is no help for, but they must be dissembled. If Solomon's advice be not over-frolic, "Live joyfully," saith he, "with the wife whom thou lovest, all thy days, for that is thy portion." [10] How then, where we find it impossible to rejoice or to love, can we obey this precept? How miserably do we defraud ourselves of that comfortable portion which God gives us, by striving vainly to glue an error together which God and nature will not join, adding but more vexation and violence to that blissful society by our importunate superstition, that will not hearken to St. Paul, 1 Cor. vii., who, speaking of marriage and divorce, determines plain enough in general, that God therein "hath called us to peace, and not to bondage." Yea, God himself commands in his law more than once, and by his Prophet Malachi, as Calvin and the best translations read, that "he who hates, let him divorce," that is, he who cannot love. Hence it is that the rabbins and Maimonides [11] . . . tell us that "divorce was permitted by Moses to preserve peace in marriage, and quiet in the family." Surely that Jews had their saving peace about them as well as we, yet care was taken that this wholesome provision for household peace should also be allowed them: and this must be denied to Christians? O perverseness! that the law [12] should be made more provident of peace-making than the gospel! that the gospel should be put to beg a most necessary help of mercy from the law, but must not have it; and that to grind in the mill of an undelighted and servile copulation, must be the only forced work of a Christian marriage, oft times with such a yokefellow from whom both love and peace, both nature and religion mourns to be separated. I cannot therefore be so diffident as not securely to conclude, that he who can receive nothing of the most important helps in marriage, being thereby disenabled to return that duty which is his with a clear and hearty countenance, and thus continues to grieve whom he would not and is no less grieved; that man ought even for love's sake and peace to move divorce upon good and liberal conditions to the divorced. And it is less a breach of wedlock to part with wise and quiet consent betimes, than still to foil and profane that mystery of joy and union with a polluting sadness and perpetual distemper: for it is not the outward continuing of marriage that keeps whole that covenant, but whosoever does most according to peace and love, whether in marriage or in divorce, he it is that breaks marriage least; it being so often written, that "Love only is the fulfilling of every commandment."

---

10. Ecclesiastes 9:9. Solomon was thought to be the author of the book.
11. Maimonides (1135–1204), Spanish-Jewish physician and philosopher.
12. The law: Jewish law, the Pentateuch.

CHAPTER XII

The eighth reason, It is probable or rather certain that every one who happens to marry hath not the calling; and therefore upon unfitness found and considered, force ought not to be used.

Eighthly; It is most sure that some even of those who are not plainly defective in body, yet are destitute of all other marriageable gifts, and consequently have not the calling to marry unless nothing be requisite thereto but a mere instrumental body; which to affirm is to that unanimous covenant a reproach. Yet it is sure that many such, not of their own desire but by the persuasion of friends or not knowing themselves, do often enter into wedlock; where finding the difference at length between the duties of a married life and the gifts of a single life, what unfitness of mind, what wearisomeness, scruples and doubts to an incredible offence and displeasure are like to follow between, may be soon imagined; whom thus to shut up and immure and shut up together, the one with a mischosen mate, the other in a mistaken calling, is not a course that Christian wisdom and tenderness ought to use. As for the custom that some parents and guardians have of forcing marriages, it will be better to say nothing of such a savage inhumanity, but only thus: that the law which gives not all freedom of divorce to any creature endued with reason so assassinated, is next in cruelty.

CHAPTER XLVII

The conclusion of this treatise.

These things, most renowned king, I have brought together, both to explain for what causes the unhappy but sometimes most necessary help of divorce ought to be granted according to God's word, by princes and rulers; as also to explain how the words of Christ do consent with such a grant. I have been large indeed both in handling those oracles of God, and in laying down those certain principles which he who will know what the mind of God is in this matter must ever think on and remember. But if we consider what mist and obscurïty hath been poured out by Antichrist upon this question, and how deep this pernicious contempt of wedlock and admiration of single life, even in those who are not called thereto, hath sunk into many men's persuasions: I fear lest all that hath been said be hardly enough to persuade such, that they would cease at length to make themselves wiser and holier than God himself, in being so severe to grant lawful marriage, and so easy to connive at all, not only whoredoms but deflowerings and adulteries: whenas among the people of God no whoredom was to be tolerated.

Our Lord Jesus Christ, who came to destroy the works of Satan, sent down his spirit upon all Christians and principally upon Christian governors both in church and commonwealth (for of the clear judgment of your royal majesty I nothing doubt, revolving the scripture so often as ye do) that they may acknowledge how much they provoke the anger of God against us, whenas all kind of unchastity is tolerated, fornications and adulteries winked at; but holy and honourable wedlock is oft withheld by the mere persuasion of Antichrist, from such as without this remedy cannot preserve themselves from damnation! For none who hath but a spark of honesty will deny that princes and states ought to use diligence toward the maintaining of pure and honest life among all men, without which all justice, all fear of God, and true religion decays.

And who knows not that chastity and pureness of life can never be restored or continued in the commonwealth, unless it be first established in private houses, from whence the whole breed of men is to come forth? To effect this, no wise man can doubt that it is necessary for princes and magistrates first with severity to punish whoredom and adultery; next to see that marriages be lawfully contracted and in the Lord; then that they be faithfully kept; and lastly, when that unhappiness urges, that they be lawfully dissolved and other marriage granted, according as the law of God and of nature and the constitutions of pious princes have decreed: as I have shown both by evident authorities of scripture, together with the writings of the ancient fathers, and other testimonies. Only the Lord grant that we may learn to prefer his ever just and saving word before the comments of Antichrist, too deeply rooted in many, and the false and blasphemous exposition of our Saviour's words. Amen.

GERRARD WINSTANLEY (born 1609), *The True Levellers' Standard Advanced*

Since the unorthodox religious ideas of the rebels played an important part in the English Civil War, it has often been called "the Puritan Revolution." The Episcopal state church dominated individual and political life: it owned extensive property and levied tithes; its bishops were administrators, legislators, and advisers to the government; education and the censorship of books were in its hands; parish clergy were appointed by wealthy patrons without consulting the congregation. As Charles I remarked to his son, "The dependency of the Church upon the crown is the chiefest support of regal authority."

The Puritans rejected all this, preferring a more secular state and a more democratic church. But there were many shades of Puritanism along the spectrum from reform to revolution: rich and poor Puritans, merchants and farmers, republicans and socialists. The Diggers, a tiny sect of artisans, farm workers, and small tradesmen, called for a fully revolutionary reorganization of society: not only universal suffrage and religious equality, but redistribution of land among the poor, communal cultivation, and ultimately the abolition of private property in land. On April 1, 1649, Winstanley and a band of his followers began to dig and plant the uncultivated common land at St. George's Hill (Surrey). After being harassed by the local population, the group was brought to court, and the communal experiment ended in failure.

Like most political theory of the time, the Digger manifesto (1649) is based on religious arguments; indeed a striking literary feature of the Revolution is the biblical language of its speeches and pamphlets. The piece is nearly contemporaneous with Milton's tract, and both were written by men who supported the Revolution. The works are as different stylistically as their authors were socially: the manifesto is an apocalyptic vision, the tract a scholarly exposition; Winstanley was ill-educated and often impoverished, Milton the comfortable cosmopolitan intellectual. In first principles, though, the essays are often closer than style alone might suggest.

In the beginning of Time, the great Creator Reason made the Earth to be a Common Treasury to preserve Beasts, Birds, Fishes, and Man, the lord that was to govern this Creation; for Man had Domination given to him over the Beasts, Birds, and Fishes; but not one word was spoken in the beginning that one branch of mankind should rule over another.

And the Reason is this: Every single man, Male and Female, is a perfect Creature of himself; and the same Spirit that made the Globe dwells in man to govern the Globe; so that the flesh of man being subject to Reason, his Maker, hath him to be his Teacher and Ruler within himself, therefore needs not run abroad after any Teacher and Ruler without him, for he needs not that any man should teach him, for the same Anointing that ruled in the Son of man, teacheth him all things.

But since human flesh (that king of Beasts) began to delight himself in the objects of the Creation more than in the Spirit Reason and Righteousness (who manifests himself to be the indweller in the Five Senses of Hearing, Seeing, Tasting, Smelling, Feeling), then he fell into blindness of mind and weakness of heart, and runs abroad for a Teacher and Ruler. And so selfish imagination, taking possession of the Five Senses and ruling as King in the room of Reason therein, and working with Covetousness, did set up one man to teach and rule over another; and thereby the Spirit was killed, and man was brought into bondage, and became a greater Slave to such of his own kind, than the Beasts of the field were to him.

And hereupon The Earth (which was made to be a Common Treasury of relief for all, both Beasts and Men) was hedged in to Inclosures by the teachers and rulers, and the others were made Servants and Slaves: And that Earth that is within this Creation, made a Common Store-house for all, is bought and sold and kept in the hands of a few, whereby the great Creator is mightily dishonored, as if he were a respecter of persons, delighting in the comfortable Livelihood of some, and rejoicing in the miserable poverty and straits of others. From the beginning it was not so.

But this coming in of Bondage, is called *A-dam,* because this ruling and teaching power without, doth *dam* up the Spirit of Peace and Liberty; First within the heart, by filling it with slavish fears of others. Secondly without, by giving the body of one to be imprisoned, punished and oppressed by the outward power of another. And this evil was brought upon us through his own Covetousness, whereby he is blinded and made weak and sees not the Law of Righteousness in his heart, which is the pure light of Reason, but looks abroad for it, and thereby the Creation is cast under bondage and curse, and the Creator is sleighted. . . .

But for the present state of the old World that is running up like parchment in the fire, and wearing away we see proud Imaginary flesh, which is the wise Serpent, rises up in flesh and gets dominion in some to rule over others, and so forces one part of the Creation (man) to be a slave to another; and thereby the Spirit is killed in both. The one looks upon himself as a teacher and ruler, and so is lifted up in pride over his fellow Creature. The other looks upon himself as imperfect, and so is dejected in his Spirit, and looks upon his fellow Creature of his own Image as a Lord above him.

And thus *Esau,* the man of flesh, which is Covetousness and Pride, hath killed *Jacob,* the Spirit of meeknesse and righteous government in the light of Reason, and rules over him. And so the Earth that was made a common Treasury for all to live comfortably upon, is become through men's unrighteous actions one over another, to be a place wherein one torments another.
. . .

But when once the Earth becomes a Common Treasury again (as it must, for all the Prophesies of Scriptures and Reason are Circled here in this Community, and mankind must have the Law of Righteousness once more writ in his heart, and all must be made of one heart and one mind).

Then this Enmity in all Lands will cease, for none shall dare to seek a Dominion over others, neither shall any dare to kill another, nor desire more of the Earth then another; for he that will rule over, imprison, oppress, and kill his fellow Creatures, under what pretence soever, is a destroyer of the Creation and an actor of the Curse, and walks contrary to the rule of righteousness: *Do as you would have others do to you; and love your Enemies, not in words, but in actions.*

Therefore you powers of the Earth, or Lord *Esau,* the Elder brother, because you have appeared to rule the Creation, first take notice, That the power that sets you to work is selfish Covetousness, and an aspiring Pride to live in glory and ease over *Iacob,* the meek Spirit; that is, the Seed that lies hid in & among the poor Common People, or younger Brother, out of whom the blessing of Deliverance is to rise and spring up to all Nations.

And Reason, the living king of righteousness, doth only look on and lets thee alone, That whereas thou counts thy self an Angel of Light, thou shalt appear in the light of the Sun to be a Devil, *A-dam,* and the Curse that the Creation groans under; and the time is now come for thy downfall, and *Jacob* must rise, who is the universal Spirit of love and righteousness that fills and will fill all the earth.

Thou teaching and ruling power of flesh, thou hast had three periods of time, to vaunt thy self over thy Brother; the first was from the time of thy coming in, called *A-dam,* or a stoppage, till *Moses* came . . .

And Secondly, From *Moses* till the *Son of Man* came, which was a time of the world that the man child could not speak like a man, but lisping, making signs to shew his meaning; as we see many Creatures that cannot speak do.

And then Thirdly from the time of the *Son of Man,* which was a time that the man-child began to speak like a child growing upward to manhood, till now, that the Spirit is rising up in strength. O thou teaching and ruling power of the earthy man, thou hast been an oppressor, by imprisonment, impoverishing, and martyrdom; and all thy power and wit hath been to make Laws, and execute them against such as stand for universal Liberty, which is the rising up of *Jacob;* as by those ancient enslaving Laws not yet blotted out, but held up as weapons against the man-child.

O thou Powers of *England,* though thou hast promised to make this People a Free People, yet thou hast so handled the matter, through thy self-seeking humour, that thou hast wrapped us up more in bondage, and oppression lies heavier upon us; not only bringing thy fellow Creatures, the Commoners, to a morsel of Bread, but by confounding all sorts of people by thy Government, of doing and undoing. . . .

And all this, because they stand to maintain an universal Liberty and Freedom, which not only is our Birthright, which our Maker gave us, but which thou hast promised to restore unto us, from under the former oppressing Powers that are gone before, and which likewise we have bought with our Money, in Taxes, Free-quarter, and Blood-shed; all which Sums thou hast received at our hands, and yet thou hast not given us our bargain.

O thou *A-dam,* thou *Esau,* thou *Cain,* thou Hypocritical man of flesh, when wilt thou cease to kill thy younger Brother? Surely thou must not do this great Work of advancing the Creation out of Bondage; for thou art lost extremely, and drowned in the Sea of Covetousness, Pride, and hardness of heart. *The blessing shall rise out of the dust which thou treadest under foot, Even the poor despised People, and they shall hold up Salvation to this Land, and to all Lands, and thou shalt be ashamed.*

Our Bodies as yet are in thy hand, our Spirit waits in quiet and peace upon our Father for Deliverance; and if he give our Blood into thy hand for thee to spill, know this, that he is our Almighty Captain: And if some of you will not dare to shed your blood, to maintain Tyranny and Oppression upon the Creation, know this, that our Blood and Life shall not be unwilling to be delivered up in meekness to maintain universal Liberty, that so the Curse on our part may be taken off the Creation.

And we shall not do this by force of Arms. We abhor it, for that is the work of the *Midianites* to kill one another. But by obeying the Lord of Hosts, who hath Revealed himself in us, and to us, by labouring the Earth in righteousness together, to eate our bread with the sweat of our brows, neither giving hire nor taking hire, but working together and eating together as one man or as one house of Israel restored from Bondage; and so by the power of Reason, the Law of righteousness in us, we endeavour to lift up the Creation from that bondage of Civil Propriety which it groans under.

We are made to hold forth this Declaration to you that are the Great Council, and to you the Great Army of the Land of *England,* that you may know what we would have and what you are bound to give us by your Covenants and Promises; and that you may join with us in this Work, and so find Peace. Or else, if you do oppose us, we have peace in our Work and in declaring this Report: And you shall be left without excuse.

The Work we are going about is this: To dig up *Georges-Hill* and the waste Ground thereabouts, and to Sow Corn, and to eat our bread together by the sweat of our brows.

And the First Reason is this: That we may work in righteousness, and lay the Foundation of making the Earth a Common Treasury for All, both Rich and Poor, that every one that is born in the Land may be fed by the Earth his Mother that brought him forth, according to the Reason that rules in the Creation. Not inclosing any part into any particular hand, but all as one man, working together, and feeding together as Sons of one Father, members of one Family; not one Lording over another, but all looking upon each other as equals in the Creation; so that our Maker may be glorified in the work of his own hands, and that every one may see he is no respecter of Persons, but equally loves his whole Creation and hates nothing but the Serpent, which is Covetousness, branching forth into selfish Imagination, Pride, Envy, Hypocrisy, Uncleanness; all seeking the ease and honor of flesh, and fighting against the Spirit Reason that made the Creation; for that is the Corruption, the Curse, the Devil, the Father of Lies; Death and Bondage that Serpent and Dragon that the Creation is to be delivered from.

And we are moved hereunto for that Reason, and others which hath been showed us both by Vision, Voice, and Revelation.

For it is showed us, that so long as we or any other doth own [1] the Earth

---

1. Own: admit.

to be the peculiar Interest of Lords and Landlords, and not common to others as well as them, we own the Curse, and hold the Creation under bondage; and so long as we or any other doth own Landlords and Tenants, for one to call the Land his or another to hire it of him, or for one to give hire and for another to work for hire; this is to dishonour the work of Creation; as if the righteous Creator should have respect to persons, and therefore made the Earth for some and not for all. And so long as we or any other maintain this Civil Propriety, we consent still to hold the Creation down under that bondage it groans under, and so we should hinder the work of Restoration, and sin against Light that is given into us, and so through the fear of the flesh man, lose our peace.

And that this Civil Propriety is the Curse, is manifest thus, Those that Buy and Sell Land and are landlords, have got it either by Oppression or Murder or Theft; and all landlords live in the breach of the Seventh and Eighth Commandments, *Thou shalt not steal, nor kill.*

First by their Oppression. They have by their subtle imaginary and covetous wit, got the plain-hearted poor, or younger Brethren, to work for them for small wages, and by their work have got a great increase; for the poor by their labour lift up Tyrants to rule over them; . . .

And such as these rise up to be rich in the objects of the Earth; then by their plausible words of flattery to the plain-hearted people, whom they deceive and that lies under confusion and blindness they are lifted up to be Teachers, Rulers, and Law makers over them that lifted them up; as if the Earth were made peculiarly for them, and not for others weal. If you cast your eye a little backward, you shall see that this outward Teaching and Ruling power is the Babylonish yoke laid upon Israel of old, under *Nebuchadnezzar;* and so Successively from that time, the Conquering Enemy have still laid these yokes upon Israel to keep *Jacob* down; and the last enslaving Conquest which the Enemy got over Israel, was the *Norman* [2] over *England;* . . .

O what mighty Delusion do you who are the powers of *England* live in! That while you pretend to throw down that *Norman* yoke and *Babylonish* power, and have promised to make the groaning people of *England* a Free People; yet you still lift up that *Norman* yoke and slavish Tyranny, and hold the People as much in bondage as the Bastard Conquerour himself, and his Council of War.

Take notice, that *England* is not a Free People, till the Poor that have no Land have a free allowance to dig and labour the Commons, and so live as Comfortably as the Landlords that live in their Inclosures. For the People have not laid out their Monies and shed their Blood, that their Landlords, the *Norman* power, should still have its liberty and freedom to rule in Tyranny in his Lords, landlords, Judges, Justices, Bailiffs, and State Servants; but that the Oppressed might be set Free, Prison doors opened, and the Poor peoples hearts comforted by a universal Consent of making the Earth a Common Treasury, that they may live together as one House of Israel, united in brotherly love into one Spirit and having a comfortable livelihood in the Community of one Earth their Mother.

---

2. Norman: in 1066, William, Duke of Normandy, invaded England and imposed on it French forms of government and culture.

If you look through the Earth you shall see, that the Landlords, Teachers and Rulers, are Oppressors, Murderers, and Thieves in this manner; but it was not thus from the Beginning. And this is one Reason of our digging and labouring the Earth one with another, that we might work in righteousness, and lift up the Creation from bondage: For so long as we own Landlords in this Corrupt Settlement, we cannot work in righteousness; for we should still lift up the Curse, and tread down the Creation, dishonour the Spirit of universal Liberty, and hinder the work of Restoration.

Secondly, In that we begin to dig upon *George-Hill,* to eat our Bread together by righteous labour and sweat of our browes; It was showed us by Vision in Dreams and out of Dreams, that that should be the Place we should begin upon; and though that Earth in view of Flesh be very barren, yet we should trust the Spirit for a blessing. And that not only this Common or Heath should be taken in and Manured by the People, but all the Commons and waste Ground in *England* and in the whole World shall be taken in by the People in righteousness, not owning any Propriety; but taking the Earth to be a Common Treasury, as it was first made for all.

Thirdly, it is shewed us, that all the Prophecies, Visions, and Revelations of Scriptures, of Prophets, and Apostles, concerning the calling of the Jews, the Restoration of Israel; and making of that People the Inheritors of the whole Earth; doth all seat Work of making the Earth a Common Treasury; . . .

Fourthly, This work to make the Earth a Common Treasury, was shewed us by Voice in Trance and out of Trance, which words were these,

Work together, Eat Bread together, Declare this all abroad.

Which Voice was heard Three times: And in Obedience to the Spirit, we have Declared this by Word of mouth, as occasion was offered. Secondly, we have declared it by writing, which others may read. Thirdly, we have now begun to declare it by Action, in Digging up the Common Land and casting in Seed, that we may eat our Bread together in righteousness. And every one that comes to work shall eat the Fruit of their own labours, one having as much Freedom in the Fruit of the Earth as another. Another Voice that was heard was this,

Israel shall neither take Hire nor give Hire.

And if so, then certainly none shall say, This is my Land, work for me and I'll give you Wages: For The Earth is the Lords, that is, Mans, who is Lord of the Creation, in every branch of mankind; for as divers members of our human bodies make but one body perfect; so every particular man is but a member or branch of mankind; and mankind living in the light and obedience to Reason, the King of righteousness, is thereby made a fit and complete Lord of the Creation. . . .

Fifthly, That which does encourage us to go on in this work, is this: We find the streaming out of Love in our hearts towards all; to enemies as well as friends; we would have none live in Beggary, Poverty, or Sorrow, but that every one might enjoy the benefit of his creation: we have peace in our hearts and quiet rejoicing in our work, and filled with sweet content, though we have but a dish of roots and bread for our food. . . .

Sixthly, We have another encouragement that this work shall prosper, because we see it to be the Fullness of Time: For whereas the Son of Man, the *Lamb,* came in the Fullness of Time, that is, when the Powers of the World made the Earth stink every where, by oppressing others, . . .

Even so now in this Age of the World, that the Spirit is upon his Resurrection, it is likewise the Fullness of Time in the higher measure. For whereas the People generally in former times did rest upon the very observation of the Sacrifices and Types, but persecuted the very name of the Spirit; Even so now, Professors do rest upon the bare observation of Forms and Customs, and pretend to the Spirit, and yet persecutes, grudges, and hates the power of the Spirit; and as it was then, so it is now: All places stink with the abomination of Self-seeking Teachers and Rulers: For do not I see that every one Preacheth for money, Counsels for money, and fights for money to maintain particular Interests? And none of these three that pretend to give liberty to the Creation, do give liberty to the Creation; neither can they, for they are enemies to universal liberty; so that the earth stinks with their Hypocrisy, Covetousness, Envy, sottish Ignorance, and Pride. . . .

And thus you Powers of England, and of the whole World, we have declared our Reasons, why we have begun to dig upon *George* hill in Surrey. One thing I must tell you more, in the close, which I received *in voce* likewise at another time; and when I received it, my eye was set towards you. The words were these:

Let Israel go free.

. . . Therefore, if thou wilt find Mercy, *Let Israel go Free;* break in pieces quickly the Band of particular Propriety, dis-own this oppressing Murder, Oppression and Thievery of Buying and Selling of Land, owning of landlords, and laying of Rents, and give thy Free Consent to make the Earth a Common Treasury, without grumbling; That the younger Brethren may live comfortably upon Earth, as well as the Elder: That all may enjoy the benefit of their Creation.

And hereby thou wilt *Honour thy Father and thy Mother:* Thy Father, which is the Spirit of Community that made all and that dwells in all. Thy Mother, which is the Earth that brought us all forth: That as a true Mother, loves all her Children. Therefore do not thou hinder the Mother Earth from giving all her Children suck, by thy Inclosing it into particular hands and holding up that cursed Bondage of Inclosure by thy Power.

And then thou wilt repent of thy *Theft,* in maintaining the breach of the eighth Commandment, by *Stealing* the Land as I say from thy fellow-creatures, or younger Brothers: which thou and all thy landlords have, and do live in the breach of that Commandment.

Then thou wilt *Own no other God,* or Ruling Power, *but One,* which is the King of Righteousness, ruling and dwelling in every one and in the whole; whereas now thou hast many gods: For Covetousness is thy God, Pride, and an Envious murdering Humor (to kill one by Prison or Gallows that crosses thee, though their cause be pure, sound, and good reason) is thy God, Self-love, and slavish Fear (lest others serve thee as thou hast served them) is thy god; Hypocrisy, Fleshly Imagination that keeps no Promise, Covenant, nor Protestation is thy God; love of Money, Honor, and Ease, is thy God. And all these, and the like Ruling Powers, make thee Blind and hard-hearted, that thou does not nor cannot lay to heart the affliction of others, though they die for want of bread, in that rich City, undone under your eyes.

Therefore once more, *Let Israel go Free,* that the poor may labour the Waste land and suck the Breasts of their mother *Earth,* that they starve not. And in so doing thou wilt keep the *Sabbath day,* which is a day of *Rest,* sweetly enjoying the Peace of the Spirit of Righteousness, and find Peace by living among a people that live in peace; this will be a day of *Rest* which thou never knew yet.

But I do not entreat thee, for thou art not to be intreated, but in the *Name of the Lord* that hath drawn me forth to speak to thee; I, yea I say, I Command thee, To *let Israel go Free,* and quietly *to gather together into the place where I shall appoint; and hold them no longer in bondage.*

And thou *A-dam* that holds the Earth in slavery under the Curse: If thou wilt not *let Israel go Free; . . .* Then know, that whereas I brought *Ten* Plagues upon him, I will *Multiply* my Plagues upon thee, till I make thee weary and miserably ashamed: And *I will bring out my People with a strong hand and stretched-out arm.*

Thus we have discharged our Souls in declaring the Cause of our Digging upon *George-Hill* in *Surrey,* that the Great Council and Army of the Land may take notice of it, That there is no intent of Tumult or Fighting, but only to get Bread to eat with the sweat of our brows; working together in righteousness and eating the blessings of the Earth in peace.

And if any of you that are the great Ones of the Earth, that have been bred tenderly and cannot work, do bring in your Stock into this Common Treasury as an Offering to the work of Righteousness; we will work for you, and you shall receive as we receive. But if you will not, but *Pharaoh*-like, cry, *Who is the Lord that we should obey him?* and endeavour to Oppose, then know, That he that delivered Israel from *Pharaoh* of old, is the same Power still in whom we trust and whom we serve; from this Conquest over thee shall be got, *not by Sword or Weapon, but by my Spirit saith the Lord of Hosts.*

JONATHAN SWIFT (1667–1745), *A Modest Proposal for Preventing the Children of Poor People in Ireland from being a burden to their parents or country, and for making them beneficial to the public*

"Here lies the body of Jonathan Swift . . . where savage indignation can no longer lacerate his heart. Go, traveller, and imitate if you can this tireless defender of manly liberty." Swift's epitaph in St. Patrick's Cathedral, Dublin, where he was Dean, commemorates his efforts in behalf of the people of his own country. Eighteenth-century Ireland was virtually an English colony. Important church and government positions were held by English appointees; huge estates were owned by absentee landlords; Catholics (the majority of the population) could not hold office, own land, or carry arms. The Irish Parliament was only a rubber stamp for the English Parliament —which, in order to protect its own commercial interests, had effectively crippled Ireland's agriculture, industry, and export trade.

Swift attacked these and other abuses in a series of popular pamphlets, proposals, and letters to the Irish people. In A Modest Proposal *(1729) he treats the consequences of English exploitation: poverty, starvation, moral degradation and the disintegration of family life. He speaks through the fictional persona of a naive, well-meaning patriot, carrying to its literal extreme the metaphorical perception that man is a beast to men. The sustained irony of the* Proposal *and the underlying ferocity of its plan reveal the "savage indignation" that moved Swift to write, as well as the frustration and despair he felt after observing the failure of his earlier attempts to mobilize the Irish against their own oppression.*

It is a melancholy object to those who walk through this great town or travel in the country, when they see the streets, the roads and cabin-doors crowded with beggars of the female sex, followed by three, four, or six children, all in rags, and importuning every passenger for an alms. These mothers, instead of being able to work for their honest livelihood, are forced to employ all their time in strolling, to beg sustenance for their helpless infants, who, as they grow up, either turn thieves for want of work, or leave their dear native country to fight for the Pretender in Spain, or sell themselves to the Barbadoes.

I think it is agreed by all parties that this prodigious number of children in the arms, or on the backs, or at the heels of their mothers, and frequently of their fathers, is in the present deplorable state of the kingdom a very great additional grievance; and therefore whoever could find out a fair, cheap, and easy method of making these children sound and useful members of the commonwealth would deserve so well of the public as to have his statue set up for a preserver of the nation.

But my intention is very far from being confined to provide only for the children of professed beggars; it is of a much greater intent, and shall take in the whole number of infants at a certain age who are born of parents in effect as little able to support them as those who demand our charity in the streets.

As to my own part, having turned my thoughts for many years upon this important subject, and maturely weighed the several schemes of other projectors, I have always found them grossly mistaken in their computation. It is true a child just dropped from its dam may be supported by her milk for a solar year with little other nourishment, at most not above the value of two shillings, which the mother may certainly get, or the value in scraps, by her lawful occupation of begging, and it is exactly at one year old that I propose to provide for them, in such a manner as, instead of being a charge upon their parents, or the parish, or wanting food and raiment for the rest of their lives, they shall, on the contrary, contribute to the feeding and partly to the clothing of many thousands.

There is likewise another great advantage of my scheme, that it will prevent those voluntary abortions, and that horrid practice of women murdering their bastard children, alas, too frequent among us, sacrificing the poor innocent babes, I doubt, more to avoid the expense than the shame, which would move tears and pity in the most savage and inhuman breast.

The number of souls in Ireland being usually reckoned one million and a half, of these I calculate there may be about two hundred thousand couples whose wives are breeders, from which number I subtract thirty thousand couples who are able to maintain their own children, although I apprehend there cannot be so many under the present distresses of the kingdom, but this being granted, there will remain an hundred and seventy thousand breeders. I again subtract fifty thousand for those women who miscarry, or whose children die by accident or disease within the year. There only remain an hundred and twenty thousand children of poor parents annually born: the question therefore is, how this number shall be reared, and provided for, which, as I have already said, under the present situation of affairs is utterly impossible by all the methods hitherto proposed, for we can neither employ them in handicraft nor agriculture; we neither build houses (I mean in the country), nor cultivate land: they can very seldom pick up a livelihood by stealing until they arrive at six years old, except where they are of towardly parts, although I confess they learn the rudiments much earlier, during which time they can however be properly looked upon only as probationers, as I have been informed by a principal gentleman in the County of Cavan, who protested to me that he never knew above one or two instances under the age of six, even in a part of the kingdom so renowned for the quickest proficiency in that art.

I am assured by our merchants that a boy or a girl before twelve years old, is no saleable commodity, and even when they come to this age, they will not yield above three pounds, or three pounds and a half-a-crown at most on the Exchange, which cannot turn to account either to the parents or the kingdom, the charge of nutriment and rags having been at least four times that value.

I shall now therefore humbly propose my own thoughts, which I hope will not be liable to the least objection.

I have been assured by a very knowing American of my acquaintance in London, that a young healthy child well nursed is at a year old a most delicious, nourishing and wholesome food, whether stewed, roasted, baked, or boiled, and I make no doubt that it will equally serve in a fricassee, or a ragout.

I do therefore humbly offer it to public consideration, that of the hundred and twenty thousand children already computed, twenty thousand may be reserved for breed, whereof only one fourth part to be males, which is more than we allow to sheep, black-cattle, or swine, and my reason is that these children are seldom the fruits of marriage, a circumstance not much regarded by our savages, therefore one male will be sufficient to serve four females. That the remaining hundred thousand may at a year old be offered in sale to the persons of quality, and fortune, through the kingdom, always advising the mother to let them suck plentifully in the last month, so as to render them plump, and fat for a good table. A child will make two dishes at an entertainment for friends, and when the family dines alone, the fore or hind quarter will make a reasonable dish, and seasoned with a little pepper or salt will be very good boiled on the fourth day, especially in winter.

I have reckoned upon a medium, that a child just born will weigh twelve pounds, and in a solar year if tolerably nursed increaseth to twenty-eight pounds.

I grant this food will be somewhat dear, and therefore very proper for landlords, who, as they have already devoured most of the parents, seem to have the best title to the children.

Infant's flesh will be in season throughout the year, but more plentiful in March, and a little before and after, for we are told by a grave author, an eminent French physician, that fish being a prolific diet, there are more children born in Roman Catholic countries about nine months after Lent than at any other season; therefore reckoning a year after Lent, the markets will be more glutted than usual, because the number of Papish infants is at least three to one in this kingdom, and therefore it will have one other collateral advantage by lessening the number of Papists among us.

I have already computed the charge of nursing a beggar's child (in which list I reckon all cottagers, labourers, and four-fifths of the farmers) to be about two shillings *per annum,* rags included, and I believe no gentleman would repine to give ten shillings for the carcass of a good fat child, which, as I have said, will make four dishes of excellent nutritive meat, when he hath only some particular friend or his own family to dine with him. Thus the Squire will learn to be a good landlord and grow popular among his tenants, the mother will have eight shillings net profit, and be fit for work until she produces another child.

Those who are more thrifty (as I must confess the times require) may flay the carcass; the skin of which artificially dressed, will make admirable gloves for ladies, and summer boots for fine gentlemen.

As to our city of Dublin, shambles may be appointed for this purpose, in the most convenient parts of it, and butchers we may be assured will not be wanting, although I rather recommend buying the children alive, and dressing them hot from the knife, as we do roasting pigs.

A very worthy person, a true lover of his country, and whose virtues I highly esteem, was lately pleased, in discoursing on this matter to offer a refinement upon my scheme. He said that many gentlemen of this kingdom, having of late destroyed their deer, he conceived that the want of venison might be well supplied by the bodies of young lads and maidens, not exceeding fourteen years of age, nor under twelve, so great a number of both sexes in every county being now ready to starve, for want of work and service: and these to be disposed of by their parents if alive, or otherwise by their nearest relations. But with due deference to so excellent a friend, and so deserving a patriot, I cannot be altogether in his sentiments. For as to the males, my American acquaintance assured me from frequent experience that their flesh was generally tough and lean, like that of our schoolboys, by continual exercise, and their taste disagreeable, and to fatten them would not answer the charge. Then as to the females, it would, I think with humble submission, be a loss to the public, because they soon would become breeders themselves: and besides, it is not improbable that some scrupulous people might be apt to censure such a practice (although indeed very unjustly) as a little bordering upon cruelty, which I confess, hath always been with me the strongest objection against any project, howsoever well intended.

But in order to justify my friend, he confessed that this expedient was put into his head by the famous Psalmanazar, a native of the island Formosa, who came from thence to London, above twenty years ago, and in conversation told my friend that in his country when any young person happened to be put to death, the executioner sold the carcass to persons of quality, as a prime dainty, and that, in his time, the body of a plump girl of fifteen, who was crucified for an attempt to poison the emperor, was sold to his Imperial Majesty's Prime Minister of State, and other great Mandarins of the Court, in joints from the gibbet, at four hundred crowns. Neither indeed can I deny that if the same use were made of several plump young girls in this town who, without one single groat to their fortunes, cannot stir abroad without a chair, and appear at the playhouse and assemblies in foreign fineries, which they never will pay for, the kingdom would not be the worse.

Some persons of a desponding spirit are in great concern about that vast number of poor people, who are aged, diseased, or maimed, and I have been desired to employ my thoughts what course may be taken to ease the nation of so grievous an encumbrance. But I am not in the least pain upon that matter, because it is very well known that they are every day dying, and rotting, by cold, and famine, and filth, and vermin, as fast as can be reasonably expected. And as to the younger labourers they are now in almost as hopeful a condition. They cannot get work, and consequently pine away from want of nourishment, to a degree that if at any time they are accidentally hired to common labour, they have not strength to perform it; and thus the country and themselves are in a fair way of being soon delivered from the evils to come.

I have too long digressed, and therefore shall return to my subject. I think the advantages by the proposal which I have made are obvious and many, as well as of the highest importance.

For first, as I have already observed, it would greatly lessen the number of Papists, with whom we are yearly over-run, being the principal breeders of the nation, as well as our most dangerous enemies, and who stay at home on purpose with a design to deliver the kingdom to the Pretender, hoping to take their advantage by the absence of so many good Protestants, who have chosen rather to leave their country than stay at home and pay tithes against their conscience to an idolatrous Episcopal curate.

Secondly, the poorer tenants will have something valuable of their own, which by law may be made liable to distress, and help to pay their landlord's rent, their corn and cattle being already seized, and money a thing unknown.

Thirdly, whereas the maintenance of an hundred thousand children, from two years old, and upwards, cannot be computed at less than ten shillings a piece *per annum,* the nation's stock will be thereby increased fifty thousand pounds *per annum,* besides the profit of a new dish, introduced to the tables of all gentlemen of fortune in the kingdom, who have any refinement in taste, and the money will circulate among ourselves, the goods being entirely of our own growth and manufacture.

Fourthly, the constant breeders, besides the gain of eight shillings sterling *per annum,* by the sale of their children, will be rid of the charge of maintaining them after the first year.

Fifthly, this food would likewise bring great custom to taverns, where the vintners will certainly be so prudent as to procure the best receipts for dressing it to perfection, and consequently have their houses frequented by all the fine gentlemen, who justly value themselves upon their knowledge in good eating; and a skilful cook, who understands how to oblige his guests, will contrive to make it as expensive as they please.

Sixthly, this would be a great inducement to marriage, which all wise nations have either encouraged by rewards, or enforced by laws and penalties. It would increase the care and tenderness of mothers towards their children, when they were sure of a settlement for life, to the poor babes, provided in some sort by the public to their annual profit instead of expense. We should soon see an honest emulation among the married women, which of them could bring the fattest child to the market. Men would become as fond of their wives, during the time of their pregnancy, as they are now of their mares in foal, their cows in calf, or sows when they are ready to farrow, nor offer to beat or kick them (as it is too frequent a practice) for fear of a miscarriage.

Many other advantages might be enumerated. For instance, the addition of some thousand carcasses in our exportation of barrelled beef; the propagation of swine's flesh, and improvement in the art of making good bacon, so much wanted among us by the great destruction of pigs, too frequent at our tables, are no way comparable in taste or magnificence to a well-grown, fat yearling child, which roasted whole will make a considerable figure at a Lord Mayor's feast, or any other public entertainment. But this and many others I omit, being studious of brevity.

Supposing that one thousand families in this city would be constant customers for infants flesh, besides others who might have it at merry meetings, particularly weddings and christenings; I compute that Dublin would take off annually about twenty thousand carcasses, and the rest of the kingdom (where probably they will be sold somewhat cheaper) the remaining eighty thousand.

I can think of no one objection that will possibly be raised against this proposal, unless it should be urged that the number of people will be thereby much lessened in the kingdom. This I freely own, and it was indeed one principal design in offering it to the world. I desire the reader will observe, that I calculate my remedy *for this one individual Kingdom of* Ireland, *and for no other that ever was, is, or, I think, ever can be upon earth.* Therefore let no man talk to me of other expedients: *Of taxing our absentees at five shillings a pound: Of using neither clothes, nor household furniture, except what is of our own growth and manufacture: Of utterly rejecting the materials and instruments that promote foreign luxury: Of curing the expensiveness of pride, vanity, idleness, and gaming in our women: Of introducing a vein of parsimony, prudence, and temperance: Of learning to love our country, wherein we differ even from* Laplanders, *and the inhabitants of* Topinamboo: *Of quitting our animosities and factions, nor act any longer like the* Jews, *who were murdering one another at the very moment their city was taken: Of being a little cautious not to sell our country and consciences for nothing: Of teaching landlords to have at least one degree of mercy towards their tenants.* Lastly, *of putting a spirit of honesty, industry, and skill into our shopkeepers, who, if a resolution could now be taken to buy only our native goods, would immediately unite to cheat and exact upon us in the price, the measure and the goodness, nor could ever yet be brought to make one fair proposal of just dealing, though often and earnestly invited to it.*

Therefore I repeat, let no man talk to me of these and the like expedients, till he hath at least a glimpse of hope that there will ever be some hearty and sincere attempt to put them in practice.

But as to myself, having been wearied out for many years with offering vain, idle, visionary thoughts, and at length utterly despairing of success, I fortunately fell upon this proposal, which as it is wholly new, so it hath something solid and real, of no expense and little trouble, full in our own power, and whereby we can incur no danger in disobliging England. For this kind of commodity will not bear exportation, the flesh being of too tender a consistence to admit a long continuance in salt, *although perhaps I could name a country which would be glad to eat up our whole nation without it.*

After all I am not so violently bent upon my own opinion as to reject any offer, proposed by wise men, which shall be found equally innocent, cheap, easy and effectual. But before some thing of that kind shall be advanced in contradiction to my scheme, and offering a better, I desire the author, or authors, will be pleased maturely to consider two points. First, as things now stand, how they will be able to find food and raiment for a hundred thousand useless mouths and backs? And secondly, there being a round million of creatures in human figure, throughout this kingdom, whose whole subsistence put into a common stock would leave them in debt two millions of pounds sterling; adding those who are beggars by profession, to the bulk of farmers, cottagers, and labourers with their wives and children, who are beggars in effect; I desire those politicians who dislike my overture, and may perhaps be so bold to attempt an answer, that they will first ask the parents of these mortals whether they would not at this day think it a great happiness to have been sold for food at a year old, in the manner I prescribe, and thereby have avoided such a perpetual scene of misfortunes as they have since gone through, by the oppression of landlords, the impossibility of paying rent without money or trade, the want of common sustenance, with neither house nor clothes to cover them from the inclemencies of weather, and the most inevitable prospect of entailing the like, or greater miseries upon their breed for ever.

I profess in the sincerity of my heart that I have not the least personal interest in endeavouring to promote this necessary work, having no other motive than the *public good of my country, by advancing our trade, providing for infants, relieving the poor, and giving some pleasure to the rich*. I have no children by which I can propose to get a single penny; the youngest being nine years old, and my wife past child-bearing.

PATRICK HENRY (1736–1799) *Speech to the Revolutionary Convention of Virginia; Speeches in the Virginia Convention to Consider the Adoption of the United States Constitution*

Virginia-born and bred, Patrick Henry practiced law in that state and was its first governor after the colonies declared their independence from England. Elected to the Virginia House of Burgesses in 1765, he became a well-known radical orator, defending the colony's legislative rights against the authority of the English king. During these early years Henry was often accused of treason; even Benjamin Franklin urged "a firm loyalty to the crown." But despite the opposition of landowners and wealthy merchants, Henry—representative of artisans, small farmers, and tradesmen—succeeded in mobilizing support for his most militant antiroyalist resolutions. His famous speech to the second revolutionary convention of Virginia (March 23, 1775) amounts to a declaration of war against England—an event for which the other colonies had also been preparing.

After independence was won, the Constitutional Convention of 1787 was called to resolve political questions that had remained uncertain: What was to be the relation between states and the Union? Which economic classes and geographical sections were to benefit most from the Union? Liberty having been won, was it now to be used or would it be subordinated to empire-building? The Convention met in secret sessions in Philadelphia, and it met without Patrick Henry, who—although he had been elected a delegate—refused to attend, and who became an influential opponent of the new form of government revealed in the document. His position reflects partly his class loyalty to the common man—whose interests, Henry thought, were plainly subordinated to those of the wealthy men who wrote the Constitution—and partly his sectional loyalty to the South, the basis of whose economic life—slavery—could, as Henry points out, be destroyed in accordance with the Constitution. This last argument against the Constitution reveals more clearly than any other of Henry's statements the ambivalent nature of bourgeois radicalism and the limitation of its rhetoric; those limits are further demonstrated in Caudwell's essay, "Liberty: A Study in Bourgeois Illusion." Within its limits, though, Henry's political vision was acute, and one recognizes in his warnings no more than what exists today.

*

Speech to the Revolutionary Convention, of Virginia

No man, Mr. President, thinks more highly than I do of the patriotism, as well as the abilities, of the very honorable gentlemen who have just addressed the House. But different men often see the same subject in different lights; and, therefore, I hope it will not be thought disrespectful to those gentlemen if, entertaining, as I do, opinions of a character very opposite to theirs, I should speak forth my sentiments freely, and without reserve. This is no time for ceremony. The question before the house is one of awful moment to this country. For my own part, I consider it as nothing less than a question of freedom or slavery. And in proportion to the magnitude of the subject ought to be the freedom of the debate. It is only in this way that we can hope to arrive at truth, and fulfil the great responsibility which we hold to God and our country. Should I keep back my opinions at such a time, through fear of giving offence, I should consider myself as guilty of treason towards my country, and of an act of disloyalty towards the majesty of Heaven, which I revere above all earthly kings.

Mr. President, it is natural to man to indulge in the illusions of Hope. We are apt to shut our eyes against a painful truth, and listen to the song of that siren till she transforms us into beasts. Is this the part of wise men, engaged in a great and arduous struggle for liberty? Are we disposed to be of the number of those who, having eyes, see not, and having ears, hear not, the things which so nearly concern their temporal salvation? For my part, whatever anguish of spirit it may cost, I am willing to know the whole truth; to know the worst, and to provide for it.

I have but one lamp by which my feet are guided, and that is the lamp of experience. I know of no way of judging of the future but by the past. And, judging by the past, I wish to know what there has been in the conduct of the British ministry, for the last ten years, to justify those hopes with which gentlemen have been pleased to solace themselves and the House. Is it that insidious smile with which our petition has been lately received? Trust it not, sir; it will prove a snare to your feet. Suffer not yourselves to be betrayed with a kiss. Ask yourselves how this gracious reception of our petition comports with those warlike preparations which cover our waters and darken our land. Are fleets and armies necessary to a work of love and reconciliation? Have we shown ourselves so unwilling to be reconciled, that force must be called in to win back our love? Let us not deceive ourselves, sir. These are the implements of war and subjugation—the last arguments to which kings resort.

I ask gentlemen, sir, what means this martial array, if its purpose be not to force us to submission? Can gentlemen assign any other possible motive for it? Has Great Britain any enemy in this quarter of the world, to call for all this accumulation of navies and armies? No sir, she has none. They are meant for us: they can be meant for no other. They are sent over to bind and rivet upon us those chains which the British ministry have been so long forging.

And what have we to oppose to them? Shall we try argument? Sir, we have been trying that for the last ten years. Have we anything new to offer upon the subject? Nothing. We have held the subject up in every light of which it is capable; but it has been all in vain. Shall we resort to entreaty, and humble supplication? What terms shall we find which have not been already exhausted?

Let us not, I beseech you, sir, deceive ourselves longer. Sir, we have done everything that could be done to avert the storm which is now coming on. We have petitioned; we have remonstrated; we have supplicated; we have prostrated ourselves before the throne, and have implored its interposition to arrest the tyrannical hands of the ministry and Parliament. Our petitions have been slighted; our remonstrances have produced additional violence and insult; our supplications have been disregarded; and we have been spurned with contempt from the foot of the throne.

In vain, after these things, may we indulge the fond hope of peace and reconciliation. There is no longer any room for hope. If we wish to be free; if we mean to preserve inviolate those inestimable privileges for which we have been so long contending; if we mean not basely to abandon the noble struggle in which we have been so long engaged, and which we have pledged ourselves never to abandon until the glorious object of our contest shall be obtained, —we must fight! I repeat it, sir—we must fight! An appeal to arms, and to the God of hosts, is all that is left us.

They tell us, sir, that we are weak, unable to cope with so formidable an adversary. But when shall we be stronger? Will it be the next week, or the next year? Will it be when we are totally disarmed, and when a British guard shall be stationed in every house? Shall we gather strength by irresolution and inaction? Shall we acquire the means of effectual resistance by lying supinely on our backs, and hugging the delusive phantom of Hope, until our enemies shall have bound us hand and foot?

Sir, we are not weak, if we make a proper use of those means which the God of nature hath placed in our power. Three millions of people armed in the holy cause of liberty, and in such a country as that which we possess, are invincible by any force which our enemy can send against us.

Besides, sir, we shall not fight our battles alone. There is a just God who presides over the destinies of nations, and who will raise up friends to fight our battles for us. The battle, sir, is not to the strong alone: it is to the vigilant, the active, the brave. Besides, sir, we have no election.[1] If we were base enough to desire it, it is now too late to retire from the contest. There is no retreat but in submission and slavery. Our chains are forged. Their clanking may be heard on the plains of Boston. The war is inevitable. And let it come! I repeat it, sir, let it come!

It is in vain, sir, to extenuate the matter. Gentlemen may cry peace, peace, but there is no peace. The war is actually begun. The next gale that sweeps from the north will bring to our ears the clash of resounding arms. Our brethren are already in the field. Why stand we here idle? What is it that gentle-

---

1. Election: choice.

men wish? what would they have? Is life so dear, or peace so sweet, as to be purchased at the price of chains and slavery? Forbid it, Almighty God! I know not what course others may take, but as for me, give me liberty, or give me death!

*

Speeches in the Virginia Convention to Consider the Adoption of the United States Constitution

JUNE 4

Mr. Chairman: The public mind, as well as my own is extremely uneasy at the proposed change of government. Give me leave to form one of the number of those who wish to be thoroughly acquainted with the reasons of this perilous and uneasy situation—and why we are brought hither to decide on this great national question. I consider myself as the servant of the people of this commonwealth, as a sentinel over their rights, liberty, and happiness. I represent their feelings when I say that they are exceedingly uneasy, being brought from that state of full security which they enjoyed, to the present delusive appearance of things. A year ago the minds of our citizens were at perfect repose. Before the meeting of the late federal convention at Philadelphia, a general peace, and an universal tranquillity prevailed in this country—but since that period they are exceedingly uneasy and disquieted. When I wished for an appointment to this convention, my mind was extremely agitated for the situation of public affairs. I conceive the republic to be in extreme danger. If our situation be thus uneasy, whence has arisen this fearful jeopardy? It arises from this fatal system—it arises from a proposal to change our government . . . And for what? I expected to have heard the reasons of an event so unexpected to my mind, and to many others. Was our civil polity, or public justice, endangered or sapped? Was the real existence of the country threatened—or was this preceded by a mournful progression of events? This proposal of altering our federal government is of a most alarming nature: make the best of this new government—say it is composed by anything but inspiration—you ought to be extremely cautious, watchful, jealous of your liberty; for instead of securing your rights, you may lose them forever. If a wrong step be now made, the republic may be lost forever. If this new government will not come up to the expectation of the people, and they should be disappointed—their liberty will be lost, and tyranny must and will arise. I repeat it again, and I beg gentlemen to consider, that a wrong step made now will plunge us into misery, and our republic will be lost. It will be necessary for this convention to have a faithful historical detail of the facts that preceded the session of the federal convention, and the reasons that actuated its members in proposing an entire alteration of government—and to demonstrate the dangers that awaited us: if they were of such awful magnitude as to warrant a proposal so extremely perilous as this, I must assert, that this convention has an absolute right to a thorough discovery of every circumstance relative to this great event. And here I would make this enquiry of those worthy characters who composed a part of the late federal convention. I am sure they were fully impressed with the necessity of forming a great consolidated government, instead of a confederation. That this is a consolidated government is demonstrably clear; and the danger of such a government is, to my mind, very striking. I have the highest veneration for those gentlemen; but, sir, give me leave to demand, what right had they to say, *We, the People?* My political curiosity, exclusive of my anxious solicitude for the public welfare, leads me to ask, who authorized them to speak the language of, *We, the People,* instead of *We, the States?* States are the characteristics and the soul of a confederation. If the states be not the agents of this compact, it must be one great consolidated national government of the people of all the states. I have the highest respect for those gentlemen who formed the convention, and were some of them not here, I would express some testimonial of esteem for them. America had on a former occasion put the utmost confidence in them; a confidence which was well placed: and I am sure, sir, I would give up anything to them; I would cheerfully confide in them as my representatives. But, sir, on this great occasion, I would demand the cause of their conduct. Even from that illustrious man, who saved us by his valor, I would have a reason for his conduct—that liberty which he has given us by his valor, tells me to ask this reason—and sure I am, were he here, he would give us that reason: but there are other gentlemen here, who can give us this information. The people gave them no power to use their name. That they exceeded their power is perfectly clear. It is not mere curiosity that actuates me—I wish to hear the real actual existing danger, which should lead us to take those steps so dangerous in my conception. Disorders have arisen in other parts of America, but here, sir, no dangers, no insurrection nor tumult, has happened—everything has been calm and tranquil. But notwithstanding this, we are wandering on the great ocean of human affairs. I see no landmark to guide us. We are running we know not whither. Difference in opinion has gone to a degree of inflammatory resentment in different parts of the country—which has been occasioned by this perilous innovation. The federal convention ought to have amended the old system—for this purpose they were solely delegated: the object of their mission extended to no other consideration. You must therefore forgive the solicitation of one unworthy member, to know what danger could have arisen under the present confederation, and what are the causes of this proposal to change our government.

JUNE 5

Mr. Chairman: I wish I was possessed of talents, or possessed of anything, that might enable me to elucidate this great subject. I am not free from suspicion: I am apt to entertain doubts: I rose yesterday to ask a question, which arose in my own mind. When I asked that question, I thought the meaning of my interrogation was obvious: the fate of this question and of America may depend on this. Have they said, we the states? Have they made a proposal of a compact between states? If they had, this would be a confederation: It is otherwise most clearly a consolidated government. The question turns, sir, on that poor little thing—the expression, *We the People,* instead of the states of America. I need not take much pains to show, that the principles of this system, are extremely pernicious, impolitic, and dangerous. Is this a monarchy, like England—a compact between prince and people: with checks on the former to secure the liberty of the latter? Is this a confederacy, like Holland —an association of a number of independent states, each of which retains its individual sovereignty? It is not a democracy, wherein the people retain all their rights securely. Had these principles been adhered to, we should not have been brought to this alarming transition, from a confederacy to a consolidated government. We have no detail of those great considerations which, in my opinion, ought to have abounded before we should recur to a government of this kind. Here is a revolution as radical as that which separated us from Great Britain. It is as radical, if in this transition, our rights and privileges are endangered, and the sovereignty of the states be relinquished: and cannot we plainly see that this is actually the case? The rights of conscience, trial by jury, liberty of the press, all your immunities and franchises, all pretensions to human rights and privileges, are rendered insecure, if not lost, by this change so loudly talked of by some, and inconsiderately by others. Is this tame relinquishment of rights worthy of freemen? Is it worthy of that manly fortitude that ought to characterize republicans? It is said eight states have adopted this plan. I declare that if twelve states and an half had adopted it, I would with manly firmness and in spite of an erring world, reject it. You are not to enquire how your trade may be increased nor how you are to become a great and powerful people, but how your liberties can be secured; for liberty ought to be the direct end of your government.

Having premised these things, I shall, with the aid of my judgment and information, which I confess are not extensive, go into the discussion of this system more minutely. Is it necessary for your liberty, that you should abandon those great rights by the adoption of this system? Is the relinquishment of the trial by jury, and the liberty of the press necessary for your liberty? Will the abandonment of your most sacred rights tend to the security of your liberty? Liberty the greatest of all earthly blessings—give us that precious jewel, and you may take everything else. But I am fearful I have lived long enough to become an old-fashioned fellow. Perhaps an invincible attachment to the dearest rights of man may, in these refined enlightened days, be deemed *old-fashioned*—if so, I am contented to be so: I say, the time has been, when every pulse of my heart beat for American liberty, and which, I believe, had a counterpart in the breast of every true American; but suspicions have gone forth—suspicions of my integrity—publicly reported that my professions are not real—twenty-three years ago I was supposed a traitor to my country: I was then said to be a bane of sedition, because I supported these rights of my country: I may be thought suspicious when I say our privileges and rights are in danger. But, sir, a number of the people of this country are weak enough to think these things are too true. I am happy to find that the gentleman on the other side declares they are groundless. But, sir, suspicion is a virtue, as long as its object is the preservation of the public good, and as long as it stays within proper bounds: should it fall on me, I am contented: conscious rectitude is a powerful consolation: I trust there are many who think my professions for the public good to be real. Let your suspicion look to both sides: there are many on the other side, who possibly may have been persuaded of the necessity of these measures, which I conceive to be dangerous to your liberty. Guard with jealous attention the public liberty. Suspect every one who approaches that jewel. Unfortunately, nothing will preserve it, but downright force. Whenever you give up that force, you are inevitably ruined. . . .

Some minds are agitated by foreign alarms: Happily for us, there is no real danger from Europe; that country is engaged in more arduous business; from that quarter there is no cause of fear: you may sleep in safety forever for them. Where is the danger? If, sir, there was any, I would recur to the American spirit to defend us—that spirit which has enabled us to surmount the greatest difficulties: to that illustrious spirit I address my most fervent prayer, to prevent our adopting a system destructive to liberty. Let not gentlemen be told, that it is not safe to reject this government. Wherefore is it not safe? We are told there are dangers; but those dangers are ideal; they cannot be demonstrated. To encourage us to adopt it, they tell us, that there is a plain easy way of getting amendments. When I come to contemplate this part, I suppose that I am mad, or, that my countrymen are so. The way to amendment, is, in my conception, shut. Let us consider this plain easy way. "The Congress, whenever two-thirds of both houses shall deem it necessary, shall propose amendments to this constitution, or, on the application of the legislatures of two-thirds of the several states, shall call a convention for proposing amendments, which, in either case, shall be valid to all intents and purposes, as part of this constitution, when ratified by the legislatures of three-fourths of the several states, or by conventions in three-fourths thereof, as the one or the other mode of ratification may be proposed by the Congress. Provided, that no amendment which may be made prior to the year 1808, shall in any manner affect the first and fourth clauses in the ninth section of the first article; and that no state, without its consent, shall be deprived of its equal suffrage in the Senate." Hence it appears that three-fourths of the states must ultimately agree to any amendments that may be necessary. Let us consider the consequences of this. However uncharitable it may appear, yet I must tell my opinion, that the most unworthy characters may get into power and prevent the introduction of amendments. Let us suppose (for the case is supposable, possible, and probable) that you happen to deal these powers to unworthy hands; will they relinquish powers already in their possession, or agree to amendments? Two-thirds of the congress, or, of the state legislatures, are necessary even to propose amendments. If one-third of these be unworthy men, they may prevent the application for amendments; but what is destructive and mischievous is, that three-fourths of the state legislatures, or of state conventions, must concur in the amendments when proposed: in such numerous bodies, there must necessarily be some designing bad men. To suppose that so large a number as three-fourths of the states will concur, is to suppose that they will possess genius, intelligence, and integrity, approaching to miraculous. It would indeed be miraculous that they should concur in the same amendments, or even in such as would bear some likeness to one another. For four of the smallest states, that do not collectively contain one-tenth part of the population of the United States, may obstruct the most salutary and necessary amendments. Nay, in these four states, six-tenths of the people may reject these amendments; and suppose, that amendments shall be opposed to amendments (which is highly probable) is it possible, that three-fourths can ever agree to the same amendments? A bare majority in these four small states may hinder the adoption of amendments; so that we may fairly and justly conclude, that one-twentieth part of the American people may prevent the removal of the most grievous inconveniences and oppression, by refusing to accede to amendments. A trifling minority may reject the most salutary amendments. Is this an easy mode of securing the public liberty? It is, sir, a most fearful situation, when the most contemptible minority can prevent the alteration of the most oppressive government; for it may in many respects prove to be such. Is this the spirit of republicanism?

What, sir, is the genius of democracy? Let me read that clause of the Bill of Rights of Virginia which relates to this: 3d cl. "That government is or ought to be instituted for the common benefit, protection, and security of the people, nation, or community; of all the various modes and forms of government, that is best which is capable of producing the greatest degree of happiness and safety, and is most effectually secured against the danger of mal-administration, and *that whenever any government shall be found inadequate, or contrary to these purposes, a majority of the community hath an indubitable, unalienable, and indefeasible right to reform, alter or abolish it in such manner as shall be judged most conducive to the public weal.*" This, sir, is the language of democracy; that a majority of the community have a right to alter their government when found to be oppressive; but how different is the genius of your new constitution from this? How different from the sentiments of freemen, that a contemptible minority can prevent the good of the majority? If then gentlemen standing on this ground are come to that point, that they are willing to bind themselves and their posterity to be oppressed, I am amazed and inexpressibly astonished. If this be the opinion of the majority, I must submit; but to me, sir, it appears perilous and destructive: I cannot help thinking so; perhaps it may be the result of my age; these may be feelings natural to a man of my years, when the American spirit has left him, and his mental powers, like the members of the body, are decayed. If, sir, amendments are left to the twentieth or to the tenth part of the people of America, your liberty is gone forever. We have heard that there is a great deal of bribery practised in the House of Commons in England; and that many of the members raised themselves to preferments by selling the rights of the people. But, sir, the tenth part of that body cannot continue oppressions on the rest of the people. English liberty is in this case, on a firmer foundation than American liberty. It will be easily contrived to procure the opposition of one-tenth of the people to any alteration, however judicious. The honorable gentleman who presides told us that to prevent abuses in our government, we will assemble in convention, recall our delegated powers, and punish our servants for abusing the trust reposed in them. Oh, sir, we should have fine times indeed, if to punish tyrants, it were only sufficient to assemble the people. Your arms wherewith you could defend yourselves are gone; and you have now an aristocratical, no longer a democratical spirit. Did you ever read of any revolution in any nation, brought about by the punishment of those in power, inflicted by those who had no power at all?

You read of a riot act in a country which is called one of the freest in the world, where a few neighbors cannot assemble without the risk of being shot by a hired soldiery, the engines of despotism. We may see such an act in America. A standing army we shall have also, to execute the execrable commands of tyranny: and how are you to punish them? Will you order them to be punished? Who shall obey these orders? Will your mace-bearer be a match for a disciplined regiment? In what situation are we to be? The clause before you gives a power of direct taxation, unbounded and unlimited: exclusive power of legislation in all cases whatsoever, for ten miles square; and over all places purchased for the erection of forts, magazines, arsenals, dock-yards, etc. What resistance could be made? The attempt would be madness. You will find all the strength of this country in the hands of your enemies: those garrisons will naturally be the strongest places in the country. Your militia is given up to congress also in another part of this plan: they will therefore act as they think proper: all power will be in their own possession: you cannot force them to receive their punishment: of what service would militia be to you, when most probably you will not have a single musket in the state? For as arms are to be provided by congress, they may or may not furnish them. Let me here call your attention to that part which gives the Congress power "To provide for organizing, arming, and disciplining the militia, and for governing such part of them as may be employed in the service of the United States, reserving to the states respectively, the appointment of the officers, and the authority of training the militia, according to the discipline prescribed by Congress." By this, sir, you see that their control over our last and best defence, is unlimited. If they neglect or refuse to discipline or arm our militia, they will be useless: the states can do neither—this power being exclusively given to Congress: the power of appointing officers over men not disciplined or armed is ridiculous: so that this pretended little remains of power left to the states may at the pleasure of Congress be rendered nugatory. Our situation will be deplorable indeed: nor can we ever expect to get this government amended, since I have already shown, that a very small minority may prevent it; and that small minority interested in the continuance of the oppression. Will the oppressor let go the oppressed? Was there ever an instance? Can the annals of mankind exhibit one single example, where rulers overcharged with power, willingly let go the oppressed, though solicited and requested most earnestly? The application for amendments will therefore be fruitless. Sometimes the oppressed have got loose by one of those bloody struggles that desolate a country. But a willing relinquishment of power is one of those things which human nature never was, nor ever will be capable of. . . .

The honorable gentleman then went on to the figure we make with foreign nations; the contemptible one we make in France and Holland; which, according to the substance of my notes, he attributes to the present feeble government. An opinion has gone forth, we find, that we are a contemptible people: the time has been when we were thought otherwise. Under this same despised government, we commanded the respect of all Europe: wherefore are we now reckoned otherwise? The American spirit has fled from hence: it has gone to regions, where it has never been expected: it has gone to the people of France in search of a splendid government—a strong energetic government. Shall we imitate the example of those nations who have gone from a simple to a splendid government? Are those nations more worthy of our imitation? What can make an adequate satisfaction to them for the loss they have suffered in attaining such a government—for the loss of their liberty? If we admit this consolidated government, it will be because we like a great splendid one. Some way or other we must be a great and mighty empire; we must have an army, and a navy, and a number of things. When the American spirit was in its youth, the language of America was different: liberty, sir, was then the primary object. We are descended from a people whose government was founded on liberty: our glorious forefathers of Great Britain made liberty the foundation of every thing. That country is become a great, mighty and splendid nation; not because their government is strong and energetic; but, sir, because liberty is its direct end and foundation. We drew the spirit of liberty from our British ancestors: by that spirit we have triumphed over every difficulty. But now, sir, the American spirit, assisted by the ropes and chains of consolidation, is about to convert this country into a powerful and mighty empire; if you make the citizens of this country agree to become the subjects of one great consolidated empire of America, your government will not have sufficient energy to keep them together: such a government is incompatible with the genius of republicanism. There will be no checks, no real balances, in this government. What can avail your specious, imaginary balances, your rope-dancing, chain-rattling, ridiculous idea checks and contrivances? But, sir, we are not feared by foreigners; we do not make nations tremble. Would this constitute happiness, or secure liberty? I trust, sir, our political hemisphere will ever direct their operations to the security of those objects.

Consider our situation, sir: go to the poor man, ask him what he does; he will inform you that he enjoys the fruits of his labor, under his own fig-tree, with his wife and children around him, in peace and security. Go to every other member of the society, you will find the same tranquil ease and content; you will find no alarms or disturbances! Why then tell us of dangers to terrify us into an adoption of this new form of government? And yet who knows the dangers that this new system may produce? They are out of the sight of the common people; they cannot foresee latent consequences. I dread the operation of it on the middling and lower classes of people: it is for them I fear the adoption of this system. I fear I tire the patience of the committee, but I beg to be indulged with a few more observations. When I thus profess myself an advocate for the liberty of the people, I shall be told, I am a designing man, that I am to be a great man, that I am to be a demagogue; and many similar illiberal insinuations will be thrown out; but, sir, conscious rectitude outweighs these things with me. I see great jeopardy in this new government. I see none from our present one. I hope some gentleman or other will bring forth, in full array, those dangers, if there be any, that we may see and touch them.

I have said that I thought this a consolidated government: I will now prove it. Will the great rights of the people be secured by this government? Suppose it should prove oppressive, how can it be altered? Our bill of rights declares, "That a majority of the community hath an *indubitable, unalienable, and indefeasible right* to reform, alter or abolish it, in such manner as shall be judged most conducive to the public weal." I have just proved that one-tenth, or less, of the people of America, a most despicable minority, may prevent this reform or alteration. Suppose the people of Virginia should wish to alter their government, can a majority of them do it? No, because they are connected with other men; or, in other words, consolidated with other states; when the people of Virginia at a future day shall wish to alter their government, though they should be unanimous in this desire, yet they may be prevented therefrom by a despicable minority at the extremity of the United States. The founders of your own constitution made your government changeable: but the power of changing it is gone from you! . . .

The next clause of the bill of rights tells you, "That all power of suspending law, or the execution of laws, by any authority without the consent of the representatives of the people, is injurious to their rights, and ought not to be exercised." This tells us that there can be no suspension of government, or laws without our own consent: yet this constitution can counteract and suspend any of our laws that contravene its oppressive operation; for they have the power of direct taxation, which suspends our bill of rights; and it is expressly provided that they can make all laws necessary for carrying their powers into execution; and it is declared paramount to the laws and constitutions of the states. Consider how the only remaining defence we have left is destroyed in this manner. Besides the expenses of maintaining the Senate and other house in as much splendor as they please, there is to be a great and mighty president, with very extensive powers—the powers of a king. He is to be supported in extravagant magnificence: so that the whole of our property may be taken by this American government, by laying what taxes they please, giving themselves what salaries they please, and suspending our laws at their pleasure. . . .

This constitution is said to have beautiful features; but when I come to examine these features, sir, they appear to me horribly frightful. Among other deformities it has an awful squinting; it squints toward monarchy; and does not this raise indignation in the breast of every true American? Your president may easily become king; your senate is so imperfectly constructed that your dearest rights may be sacrificed by what may be a small minority; and a very small minority may continue forever unchangeably this government although horridly defective: where are your checks in this government? Your strongholds will be in the hands of your enemies; it is on a supposition that your American governors shall be honest, that all the good qualities of this government are founded: but its defective and imperfect construction puts it in their power to perpetrate the worst of mischiefs, should they be bad men: and, sir, would not all the world, from the eastern to the western hemisphere, blame our distracted folly in resting our rights upon the contingency of our rulers being good or bad? Show me that age and country where the rights and liberties of the people were placed on the sole chance of their rulers being good men, without a consequent loss of liberty? I say that the loss of that dearest privilege has ever followed with absolute certainty every such mad attempt.

If your American chief be a man of ambition and abilities, how easy it is for him to render himself absolute! The army is in his hands, and, if he be a man of address, it will be attached to him; and it will be the subject of meditation with him to seize the first auspicious moment to accomplish his design; and, sir, will the American spirit solely relieve you when this happens? I would rather infinitely, and I am sure most of this convention are of the same opinion, have a king, lords, and commons, than a government so replete with such insupportable evils. If we make a king, we may prescribe the rules by which he shall rule his people, and interpose such checks as shall prevent him from infringing them: but the president in the field at the head of his army can prescribe the terms on which he shall reign master, so far that it will puzzle any American ever to get his neck from under the galling yoke. I cannot with patience think of this idea. If ever he violates the laws, one of two things will happen: he will come at the head of his army to carry everything before him; or, he will give bail, or do what Mr. Chief Justice will order him. If he be guilty, will not the recollection of his crimes teach him to make one bold push for the American throne? Will not the immense difference between being master of everything, and being ignominiously tried and punished, powerfully excite him to make this bold push? But, sir, where is the existing force to punish him? Can he not at the head of his army beat down every opposition? Away with your president, we shall have a king; the army will salute him monarch; your militia will leave you and assist in making him king, and fight against you, and what have you to oppose this force? What will then become of you and your rights? Will not absolute despotism ensue?

What can be more defective than the clause concerning the elections? The control given to Congress over the time, place and manner of holding elections, will totally destroy the end of suffrage. The elections may be held at one place, and the most inconvenient in the state; or they may be at remote distances from those who have a right of suffrage: hence nine out of ten must either not vote at all, or vote for strangers: for the most influential characters will be applied to, to know who are the most proper to be chosen. I repeat that the control of Congress over the *manner,* etc., of electing, well warrants the idea. The natural consequence will be that this democratic branch will possess none of the public confidence: the people will be prejudiced against representatives chosen in such an injudicious manner. The proceedings in the northern conclave will be hidden from the yeomanry of this country. We are told that the yeas and nays shall be taken and entered on the journals: this, sir, will avail nothing: it may be locked up in their chests, and concealed forever from the people; for they are not to publish what parts they think require secrecy: they *may* think, and *will think,* the whole requires it.

Another beautiful feature of this constitution is the publication from time to time of the receipts and expenditures of the public money. This expression, from time to time, is very indefinite and indeterminate: it may extend to a century. Grant that any of them are wicked, they may squander the public money so as to ruin you, and yet this expression will give you no redress. I say they may ruin you: for where, sir, is the responsibility? The yeas and nays will shew you nothing, unless they be fools as well as knaves: for after having wickedly trampled on the rights of the people, they would act like fools indeed, were they to publish and divulge their iniquity, when they have it equally in their power to suppress and conceal it. Where is the responsibility—that leading principle in the British government? In that government a punishment certain and inevitable is provided: but in this, there is no real actual punishment for the grossest mal-administration. They may go without punishment, though they commit the most outrageous violation on our immunities. That paper may tell me they will be punished. I ask, by what law? They must make the law—for there is no existing law to do it. What—will they make a law to punish themselves?

This, sir, is my great objection to the constitution, that there is no true responsibility—and that the preservation of our liberty depends on the single chance of men being virtuous enough to make laws to punish themselves. In the country from which we are descended, they have real and not imaginary responsibility—for there mal-administration has cost their heads to some of the most saucy geniuses that ever were. The Senate by making treaties may destroy your liberty and laws for want of responsibility. Two-thirds of those that shall happen to be present, can, with the president, make treaties that shall be the supreme law of the land; they may make the most ruinous treaties and yet there is no punishment for them. Whoever shows me a punishment provided for them will oblige me. So, sir, notwithstanding there are eight pillars, they want another. Where will they make another? I trust, sir, the exclusion of the evils wherewith this system is replete in its present form, will be made a condition precedent to its adoption, by this or any other state. . . . Public fame tells us, that the adopting states have already heart-burnings and animosity, and repent their precipitate hurry; this, sir, may occasion exceeding great mischief. When I reflect on these and many other circumstances, I must think those states will be found to be in confederacy with us. If we pay our quota of money annually, and furnish our ratable number of men, when necessary, I can see no danger from a rejection.

The history of Switzerland clearly proves that we might be in amicable alliance with those states without adopting this constitution. Switzerland is a confederacy, consisting of dissimilar governments. This is an example which proves that governments of dissimilar structures may be confederated. That confederate republic has stood upward of four hundred years; and although several of the individual republics are democratic, and the rest aristocratic, no evil has resulted from this dissimilarity, for they have braved all the power of France and Germany during that long period. The Swiss spirit, sir, has kept them together; they have encountered and overcome immense difficulties with patience and fortitude. In the vicinity of powerful and ambitious monarchs, they have retained their independence, republican simplicity and valor.

JUNE 9

. . . Congress by the power of taxation, by that of raising an army, and by their control over the militia, have the sword in one hand, and the purse in the other. Shall we be safe without either? Congress have an unlimited power over both: they are entirely given up by us. Let him candidly tell me, where and when did freedom exist, when the sword and purse were given up from the people? Unless a miracle in human affairs interposed, no nation ever retained its liberty after the loss of the sword and purse. Can you prove by any argumentative deduction that it is possible to be safe without retaining one of these? If you give them up you are gone.

Give us at least a plausible apology why Congress should keep their proceedings in secret. They have the power of keeping them secret as long as they please; for the provision for a periodical publication is too inexplicit and ambiguous to avail anything. The expression *from time to time,* as I have more than once observed, admits of any extension. They may carry on the most wicked and pernicious of schemes under the dark veil of secrecy. The liberties of a people never were nor ever will be secure, when the transactions of their rulers may be concealed from them. The most iniquitous plots may be carried on against their liberty and happiness. I am not an advocate for divulging indiscriminately all the operations of government, though the practice of our ancestors in some degree justifies it. Such transactions as relate to military operations, or affairs of great consequence, the immediate promulgation of which might defeat the interests of the community, I would not wish to be published, till the end which required their secrecy should have been effected. But to cover with the veil of secrecy the common routine of business, is an abomination in the eyes of every intelligent man, and every friend to his country. . . .

I shall make a few observations to prove that the power over elections, which is given to Congress, is contrived by the Federal Government, that the people may be deprived of their proper influence in the government, by destroying the force and effect of their suffrages. Congress is to have a discretionary control over the time, place and manner of elections. The representatives are to be elected, consequently, when and where they please. As to the time and place, gentlemen have attempted to obviate the objection by saying that the time is to happen once in two years, and that the place is to be within a particular district, or in the respective counties. But how will they obviate the danger of referring the *manner* of election to Congress? Those illumined genii may see that this may not endanger the rights of the people; but to my unenlightened understanding, it appears plain and clear that it will impair the popular weight in the government. Look at the Roman history. They had two ways of voting: the one by tribes, and the other by centuries. By the former, numbers prevailed: in the latter, riches preponderated. According to the mode prescribed, Congress may tell you that they have a right to make the vote of one gentleman go as far as the votes of one hundred poor men. The power over the manner admits of the most dangerous latitude. They may modify it as they please. They may regulate the number of votes by the quantity of property, without involving any repugnancy to the constitution. I should not have thought of this trick of contrivance had I not seen how the public liberty of Rome was trifled with by the mode of voting by centuries, whereby one rich man had as many votes as a multitude of poor men. The plebeians were trampled on till they resisted. The patricians trampled on the liberties of the plebeians till the latter had spirit to assert their right to freedom and equality. The result of the American mode of election may be similar. Perhaps I shall be told that I have gone through the regions of fancy—that I deal in noisy exclamations and mighty professions of patriotism. Gentlemen may retain their opinions; but I look on that paper as the most fatal plan that could possibly be conceived to enslave a free people. If such be your rage for novelty, take it and welcome, but you never shall have my consent. My sentiments may appear extravagant, but I can tell you that a number of my fellow-citizens have kindred sentiments, and I am anxious if my country should come into the hands of tyranny to exculpate myself from being in any degree the cause, and to exert my faculties to the utmost to extricate her. Whether I am gratified or not in my beloved form of government, I consider that the more she is plunged into distress the more it is my duty to relieve her. Whatever may be the result, I shall wait with patience till the day may come when an opportunity shall offer to exert myself in her cause.

But I should be led to take that man for a lunatic who should tell me to run into the adoption of a government, avowedly defective, in hopes of having it amended afterward. Were I about to give away the meanest particle of my own property, I should act with more prudence and discretion. My anxiety and fears are great, lest America, by the adoption of this system, should be cast into a fathomless bottom.

JUNE 24

. . . I exhort gentlemen to think seriously, before they ratify this Constitution, and persuade themselves that they will succeed in making a feeble effort to get amendments after adoption. With respect to that part of the proposal, which says, that every power not granted remains with the people; it must be previous to adoption, or it will involve this country in inevitable destruction. To talk of it, as a thing subsequent, not as one of your unalienable rights, is leaving it to the casual opinion of the Congress who shall take up the consideration of that matter. They will not reason with you about the effect of this Constitution. They will not take the opinion of this committee concerning its operation. They will construe it as they please. If you place it subsequently, let me ask the consequences? Among ten thousand implied powers which they may assume, they may, if we be engaged in war, liberate every one of your slaves if they please. And this must and will be done by men, a majority of whom have not a common interest with you. They will therefore have no feeling for your interests. It has been repeatedly said here, that the great object of a national government was national defence. That power which is said to be intended for security and safety may be rendered detestable and oppressive. If you give power to the general government to provide for the general defence, the means must be commensurate to the end. All the means in the possession of the people must be given to the government which is intrusted with the public defence. In this State there are 236,000 blacks, and there are many in several other States. But there are few or none in the Northern States, and yet if the Northern States shall be of opinion that our slaves are numberless, they may call forth every national resource. May Congress not say that every black man must fight? Did we not see a little of this in the last war? We were not so hard pushed as to make emancipation general. But acts of Assembly passed, that every slave who would go to the army should be free. Another thing will contribute to bring this event about—slavery is detested—we feel its fatal effects—we deplore it with all the pity of humanity. Let all these considerations, at some future period, press with full force on the minds of Congress. Let that urbanity, which I trust will distinguish America, and the necessity of national defence, let all these things operate on their minds. They will search that paper, and see if they have power of manumission. And have they not, sir? Have they not power to provide for the general defence and welfare? May they not think that these call for the abolition of slavery? May they not pronounce all slaves free, and will they not be warranted by that power? There is no ambiguous implication, or logical deduction—the paper speaks to the point. They have the power in clear unequivocal terms, and will clearly and certainly exercise it. As much as I deplore slavery, I see that prudence forbids its abolition. I deny that the general government ought to set them free, because a decided majority of the States have not the ties of sympathy and fellow-feeling for those whose interest would be affected by their emancipation. The majority of Congress is to the north, and the slaves are to the south. In this situation, I see a great deal of the property of the people of Virginia in jeopardy, and their peace and tranquillity gone away. I repeat it again, that it would rejoice my very soul that every one of my fellow-beings was emancipated. As we ought with gratitude to admire that decree of heaven which has numbered us among the free, we ought to lament and deplore the necessity of holding our fellow-men in bondage. But is it practicable, by any human means, to liberate them, without producing the most dreadful and ruinous consequences? We ought to possess them in the manner we have inherited them from our ancestors, as their manumission is incompatible with the felicity of the country. But we ought to soften, as much as possible, the rigor of their unhappy fate. I know that in a variety of particular instances, the legislature, listening to complaints, have admitted their emancipation. Let me not dwell on this subject. I will only add, that this, as well as every other property of the people of Virginia is in jeopardy, and put in the hands of those who have no similarity of situation with us. This is a local matter, and I can see no propriety in subjecting it to Congress.

THOMAS PAINE (1737–1809), *Crisis I;* Selection from *Rights of Man*

Although Thomas Paine was not by birth American, "It was," he wrote, "the cause of America that made me an author." In England he worked as a seaman, tax inspector, and teacher; he left for America in 1774 with a letter of recommendation from Benjamin Franklin. Paine's pamphlet Common Sense *(1776), a defense of the American Revolution, made his reputation on both sides of the Atlantic. During the war he wrote a series of morale-building tracts called* The Crisis; *the first (December 1776) appeared a few days before Washington crossed the Delaware to mount a victorious surprise attack on Trenton. His style exhibits many of the rhetorical devices common in eighteenth-century poetry—alliteration, assonance, cadenced rhythm, epigram, sentences balanced by parallel or antithetical construction. For the most part, though, it remains simple and direct, well-suited to describe action or to encourage it.*
*Paine welcomed the French Revolution of 1789, and when the English statesman and political writer Edmund Burke wrote a book against it (*Reflections on the Revolution in France*), Paine felt compelled to reply. The* Rights of Man *(1792) was his answer; as a result of it Paine was outlawed in England, where he was then living. Elected deputy in the newly created French National Assembly, Paine lost the trust of the Jacobins when he opposed the execution of Louis XVI. Too radical for England, not radical enough for France, he barely escaped the guillotine in Paris. On returning to America in 1802, he became convinced that "the principles of the Revolution were expiring on the soil that produced them"; he deplored American slavery, property-restricted suffrage and offices, antilabor and antifeminist legislation, and oligarchical leadership. Paine died* persona non grata *in the country whose independence he had helped to win.*

*

The Crisis

These are the times that try men's souls. The summer soldier and the sunshine patriot will, in this crisis, shrink from the service of their country; but he that stands it *now,* deserves the love and thanks of man and woman.

Tyranny, like hell, is not easily conquered; yet we have this consolation with us, that the harder the conflict, the more glorious the triumph. What we obtain too cheap, we esteem too lightly: it is dearness only that gives every thing its value. Heaven knows how to put a proper price upon its goods; and it would be strange indeed if so celestial an article as FREEDOM should not be highly rated. Britain, with an army to enforce her tyranny, has declared that she has a right (*not only to* TAX) but "to BIND *us in* ALL CASES WHATSOEVER," and if being *bound in that manner,* is not slavery, then is there not such a thing as slavery upon earth. Even the expression is impious; for so unlimited a power can belong only to God.

Whether the independence of the continent was declared too soon, or delayed too long, I will not now enter into as an argument; my own simple opinion is, that had it been eight months earlier, it would have been much better. We did not make a proper use of last winter, neither could we, while we were in a dependant state. However, the fault, if it were one, was all our own; we have none to blame but ourselves. But no great deal is lost yet. All that Howe [1] has been doing for this month past, is rather a ravage than a conquest, which the spirit of the Jerseys, a year ago, would have quickly repulsed, and which time and a little resolution will soon recover.

I have as little superstition in me as any man living, but my secret opinion has ever been, and still is, that God Almighty will not give up a people to military destruction, or leave them unsupportedly to perish, who have so earnestly and so repeatedly sought to avoid the calamities of war, by every decent method which wisdom could invent. Neither have I so much of the infidel in me, as to suppose that He has relinquished the government of the world, and given us up to the care of devils; and as I do not, I cannot see on what grounds the king of Britain can look up to heaven for help against us: a common murderer, highwayman, or a house-breaker, has as good a pretence as he.

'Tis surprising to see how rapidly a panic will sometimes run through a country. All nations and ages have been subject to them: Britain has trembled like an ague at the report of a French fleet of flat bottomed boats; and in the fifteenth century the whole English army, after ravaging the kingdom of France, was driven back like men petrified with fear; and this brave exploit was performed by a few broken forces collected and headed by a woman, Joan of Arc. Would that heaven might inspire some Jersey maid to spirit up her countrymen, and save her fair fellow sufferers from ravage and ravishment! Yet panics, in some cases, have their uses; they produce as much good as hurt. Their duration is always short; the mind soon grows through them, and acquires a firmer habit than before. But their peculiar advantage is, that they are the touchstones of sincerity and hypocrisy, and bring things and men to light, which might otherwise have lain forever undiscovered. In fact, they have the same effect on secret traitors, which an imaginary apparition would have upon a private murderer. They sift out the hidden thoughts of man, and hold them up in public to the world. Many a disguised tory [2] has lately shown

---

1. Howe: William, 5th Viscount Howe, general and commander-in-chief of English forces in the American colonies.

2. Tory: supporter of the power and privilege of king, aristocracy, and ecclesiastical hierarchy.

his head, that shall penitentially solemnize with curses the day on which Howe arrived upon the Delaware.

As I was with the troops at Fort Lee, and marched with them to the edge of Pennsylvania, I am well acquainted with many circumstances, which those who live at a distance know but little or nothing of. Our situation there was exceedingly cramped, the place being a narrow neck of land between the North River and the Hackensack. Our force was inconsiderable, being not one-fourth so great as Howe could bring against us. We had no army at hand to have relieved the garrison, had we shut ourselves up and stood on our defence. Our ammunition, light artillery, and the best part of our stores, had been removed, on the apprehension that Howe would endeavor to penetrate the Jerseys, in which case Fort Lee could be of no use to us; for it must occur to every thinking man, whether in the army or not, that these kind of field forts are only for temporary purposes, and last in use no longer than the enemy directs his force against the particular object, which such forts are raised to defend. . . . Howe, in my little opinion, committed a great error in generalship in not throwing a body of forces off from Staten Island through Amboy, by which means he might have seized all our stores at Brunswick, and intercepted our march into Pennsylvania; but if we believe the power of hell to be limited, we must likewise believe that their agents are under some providential control.

I shall not now attempt to give all the particulars of our retreat to the Delaware; suffice it for the present to say, that both officers and men, though greatly harassed and fatigued, frequently without rest, covering, or provision, the inevitable consequences of a long retreat, bore it with a manly and martial spirit. All their wishes centred in one, which was, that the country would turn out and help them to drive the enemy back. Voltaire has remarked that King William never appeared to full advantage but in difficulties and in action; the same remark may be made on General Washington, for the character fits him. There is a natural firmness in some minds which cannot be unlocked by trifles, but which, when unlocked, discovers a cabinet of fortitude; and I reckon it among those kind of public blessings, which we do not immediately see, that God hath blessed him with uninterrupted health, and given him a mind that can even flourish upon care.

I shall conclude this paper with some miscellaneous remarks on the state of our affairs; and shall begin with asking the following question, Why is it that the enemy have left the New-England provinces, and made these middle ones the seat of war? The answer is easy: New-England is not infested with tories, and we are. I have been tender in raising the cry against these men, and used numberless arguments to show them their danger, but it will not do to sacrifice a world either to their folly or their baseness. The period is now arrived, in which either they or we must change our sentiments, or one or both must fall. And what is a tory? Good God! what is he? I should not be afraid to go with a hundred whigs against a thousand tories, were they to attempt to get into arms. Every tory is a coward; for servile, slavish, self-interested fear is the foundation of toryism; and a man under such influence, though he may be cruel, never can be brave.

But, before the line of irrecoverable separation be drawn between us, let us reason the matter together: Your conduct is an invitation to the enemy, yet not one in a thousand of you has heart enough to join him. Howe is as much deceived by you as the American cause is injured by you. He expects you will all take up arms, and flock to his standard, with muskets on your shoulders. Your opinions are of no use to him, unless you support him personally, for 'tis soldiers, and not tories, that he wants.

I once felt all that kind of anger, which a man ought to feel, against the mean principles that are held by the tories: a noted one, who kept a tavern at Amboy, was standing at his door, with as pretty a child in his hand, about eight or nine years old, as I ever saw, and after speaking his mind as freely as he thought was prudent, finished with this unfatherly expression, *"Well! give me peace in my day."* Not a man lives on the continent but fully believes that a separation must some time or other finally take place, and a generous parent should have said, *"If there must be trouble, let it be in my day, that my child may have peace";* and this single reflection, well applied, is sufficient to awaken every man to duty. Not a place upon earth might be so happy as America. Her situation is remote from all the wrangling world, and she has nothing to do but to trade with them. A man can distinguish himself between temper and principle, and I am as confident, as I am that God governs the world, that America will never be happy till she gets clear of foreign dominion. Wars, without ceasing, will break out till that period arrives, and the continent must in the end be conqueror; for though the flame of liberty may sometimes cease to shine, the coal can never expire.

America did not, nor does not want force; but she wanted a proper application of that force. Wisdom is not the purchase of a day, and it is no wonder that we should err at the first setting off. From an excess of tenderness, we were unwilling to raise an army, and trusted our cause to the temporary defence of a well-meaning militia. A summer's experience has now taught us better; yet with those troops, while they were collected, we were able to set bounds to the progress of the enemy, and, thank God! they are again assembling. I always considered militia as the best troops in the world for a sudden exertion, but they will not do for a long campaign. Howe, it is probable, will make an attempt on this city;[3] should he fail on this side the Delaware, he is ruined: if he succeeds, our cause is not ruined. He stakes all on his side against a part on ours; admitting he succeeds, the consequence will be, that armies from both ends of the continent will march to assist their suffering friends in the middle states; for he cannot go everywhere, it is impossible. I consider Howe as the greatest enemy the tories have; he is bringing a war into their country, which, had it not been for him and partly for themselves, they had been clear of. Should he now be expelled, I wish with all the devotion of a Christian, that the names of whig and tory may never more be mentioned; but should the tories give him encouragement to come, or assistance if he come, I as sincerely wish that our next year's arms may expel them from the continent, and the congress appropriate their possessions to the relief of those who have suffered in well-doing. A single successful battle next year will settle the whole. America could carry on a two years war by the confiscation of the property of disaffected persons, and be made happy by their expulsion. Say not that this is revenge, call it rather the soft resentment of a

3. This city: Philadelphia.

suffering people, who, having no object in view but the *good* of *all,* have staked their *own all* upon a seemingly doubtful event. Yet it is folly to argue against determined hardness; eloquence may strike the ear, and the language of sorrow draw forth the tear of compassion, but nothing can reach the heart that is steeled with prejudice.

Quitting this class of men, I turn with the warm ardor of a friend to those who have nobly stood, and are yet determined to stand the matter out: I call not upon a few, but upon all: not on *this* state or *that* state, but on *every* state: up an help us; lay your shoulders to the wheel; better have too much force than too little, when so great an object is at stake. Let it be told to the future world, that in the depth of winter, when nothing but hope and virtue could survive, that the city and the country, alarmed at one common danger, came forth to meet and to repulse it. Say not that thousands are gone, turn out your tens of thousands; throw not the burden of the day upon Providence, but *"show your faith by your works,"* that God may bless you. It matters not where you live, or what rank of life you hold, the evil or the blessing will reach you all. The far and the near, the home counties and the back, the rich and the poor, will suffer or rejoice alike. The heart that feels not now, is dead: the blood of his children will curse his cowardice, who shrinks back at a time when a little might have saved the whole, and made *them* happy. I love the man that can smile in trouble, that can gather strength from distress, and grow brave by reflection. 'Tis the business of little minds to shrink; but he whose heart is firm, and whose conscience approves his conduct, will pursue his principles unto death. My own line of reasoning is to myself as straight and clear as a ray of light. Not all the treasures of the world, so far as I believe, could have induced me to support an offensive war, for I think it murder; but if a thief breaks into my house, burns and destroys my property, and kills or threatens to kill me, or those that are in it, and to *"bind me in all cases whatsoever"* to his absolute will, am I to suffer it? What signifies it to me, whether he who does it is a king or a common man; my countryman or not my countryman; whether it be done by an individual villain, or an army of them? If we reason to the root of things we shall find no difference; neither can any just cause be assigned why we should punish in the one case and pardon in the other. Let them call me rebel, and welcome, I feel no concern from it; but I should suffer the misery of devils, were I to make a whore of my soul by swearing allegiance to one whose character is that of a sottish, stupid, stubborn, worthless, brutish man. I conceive likewise a horrid idea in receiving mercy from a being, who at the last day shall be shrieking to the rocks and mountains to cover him, and fleeing with terror from the orphan, the widow, and the slain of America.

There are cases which cannot be overdone by language, and this is one. There are persons, too, who see not the full extent of the evil which threatens them; they solace themselves with hopes that the enemy, if he succeed, will be merciful. It is the madness of folly, to expect mercy from those who have refused to do justice; and even mercy, where conquest is the object, is only a trick of war; the cunning of the fox is as murderous as the violence of the wolf, and we ought to guard equally against both. Howe's first object is, partly by threats and partly by promises, to terrify or seduce the people to deliver up their arms and receive mercy. . . . Ye men of Pennsylvania, do reason upon these things! Were the back counties to give up their arms, they would fall an easy prey to the Indians, who are all armed: this perhaps is what some tories would not be sorry for. Were the home counties to deliver up their arms, they would be exposed to the resentment of the back counties, who would then have it in their power to chastise their defection at pleasure. And were any one state to give up its arms, *that* state must be garrisoned by all Howe's army of Britons and Hessians [4] to preserve it from the anger of the rest. Mutual fear is the principal link in the chain of mutual love, and woe be to that state that breaks the compact. Howe is mercifully inviting you to barbarous destruction, and men must be either rogues or fools that will not see it. I dwell not upon the vapours of imagination: I bring reason to your ears, and, in language as plain as A, B, C, hold up truth to your eyes.

I thank God, that I fear not. I see no real cause for fear. I know our situation well, and can see the way out of it. While our army was collected, Howe dared not risk a battle; and it is no credit to him that he decamped from the White Plains, and waited a mean opportunity to ravage the defenceless Jerseys; but it is great credit to us, that, with a handful of men, we sustained an orderly retreat for near an hundred miles, brought off our ammunition, all our field pieces, the greatest part of our stores, and had four rivers to pass. None can say that our retreat was precipitate, for we were near three weeks in performing it, that the country might have time to come in. Twice we marched back to meet the enemy, and remained out till dark. The sign of fear was not seen in our camp, and had not some of the cowardly and disaffected inhabitants spread false alarms through the country, the Jerseys had never been ravaged. Once more we are again collected and collecting; our new army at both ends of the continent is recruiting fast, and we shall be able to open the next campaign with sixty thousand men, well armed and clothed. This is our situation, and who will may know it. By perseverance and fortitude we have the prospect of a glorious issue; by cowardice and submission, the sad choice of a variety of evils—a ravaged country—a depopulated city —habitations without safety, and slavery without hope—our homes turned into barracks and bawdy-houses for Hessians, and a future race to provide for, whose fathers we shall doubt of. Look on this picture and weep over it! and if there yet remains one thoughtless wretch who believes it not, let him suffer it unlamented.

*

Selection from *Rights of Man*

Among the incivilities by which nations or individuals provoke and irritate each other, Mr. Burke's pamphlet on the French Revolution is an extraordinary instance. Neither the People of France, nor the National Assembly, were troubling themselves about the affairs of England, or the English Parliament; and that Mr. Burke should commence an unprovoked attack upon

---

4. Hessians: German mercenaries, many of whom settled in the United States after the war.

them, both in Parliament and in public, is a conduct that cannot be pardoned on the score of manners, nor justified on that of policy.

There is scarcely an epithet of abuse to be found in the English language, with which Mr. Burke has not loaded the French Nation and the National Assembly. Everything which rancour, prejudice, ignorance or knowledge could suggest, is poured forth in the copious fury of near four hundred pages. In the strain and on the plan Mr. Burke was writing, he might have written on to as many thousands. When the tongue or the pen is let loose in a frenzy of passion, it is the man, and not the subject, that becomes exhausted.

Hitherto Mr. Burke has been mistaken and disappointed in the opinions he had formed of the affairs of France; but such is the ingenuity of his hope, or the malignancy of his despair, that it furnishes him with new pretences to go on. There was a time when it was impossible to make Mr. Burke believe there would be any Revolution in France. His opinion then was, that the French had neither spirit to undertake it nor fortitude to support it; and now that there is one, he seeks an escape by condemning it. . . .

Not one glance of compassion, not one commiserating reflexion that I can find throughout his book, has he bestowed on those who lingered out the most wretched of lives, a life without hope in the most miserable of prisons.[1] It is painful to behold a man employing his talents to corrupt himself. Nature has been kinder to Mr. Burke than he is to her. He is not affected by the reality of distress touching his heart, but by the showy resemblance of it striking his imagination. He pities the plumage, but forgets the dying bird. Accustomed to kiss the aristocratical hand that hath purloined him from himself, he degenerates into a composition of art, and the genuine soul of nature forsakes him. His hero or his heroine must be a tragedy-victim expiring in show, and not the real prisoner of misery, sliding into death in the silence of a dungeon.

As Mr. Burke has passed over the whole transaction of the Bastille (and his silence is nothing in his favor), and has entertained his readers with reflections on supposed facts distorted into real falsehoods, I will give, since he has not, some account of the circumstances which preceded that transaction. They will serve to shew that less mischief could scarcely have accompanied such an event when considered with the treacherous and hostile aggravations of the enemies of the Revolution.

The mind can hardly picture to itself a more tremendous scene than what the city of Paris exhibited at the time of taking the Bastille, and for two days before and after, nor perceive the possibility of its quieting so soon. At a distance this transaction has appeared only as an act of heroism standing on itself, and the close political connection it had with the Revolution is lost in the brilliancy of the achievement. But we are to consider it as the strength of the parties brought man to man, and contending for the issue. The Bastille was to be either the prize or the prison of the assailants. The downfall of it included the idea of the downfall of despotism, and this compounded image was become as figuratively united as Bunyan's Doubting Castle and Giant Despair.

The National Assembly, before and at the time of taking the Bastille, was

---

1. The most miserable of prisons: the Bastille, a fortress and state prison erected in the fourteenth century and often used for political prisoners. Its guns commanded one of the gates of Paris.

sitting at Versailles, twelve miles distant from Paris. About a week before the rising of the Parisians, and their taking the Bastille, it was discovered that a plot was forming, at the head of which was the Count d'Artois, the king's youngest brother, for demolishing the National Assembly, seizing its members, and thereby crushing, by a *coup de main,* all hopes and prospects of forming a free government. For the sake of humanity, as well as freedom, it is well this plan did not succeed. Examples are not wanting to show how dreadfully vindictive and cruel are all old governments, when they are successful against what they call a revolt.

This plan must have been some time in contemplation; because, in order to carry it into execution, it was necessary to collect a large military force round Paris, and cut off the communication between that city and the National Assembly at Versailles. The troops destined for this service were chiefly the foreign troops in the pay of France, and who, for this particular purpose, were drawn from the distant provinces where they were then stationed. When they were collected to the amount of between twenty-five and thirty thousand, it was judged time to put the plan into execution. The ministry who were then in office, and who were friendly to the Revolution, were instantly dismissed and a new ministry formed of those who had concerted the project, among whom was Count de Broglio, and to his share was given the command of those troops. The character of this man as described to me in a letter which I communicated to Mr. Burke before he began to write his book, and from an authority which Mr. Burke well knows was good, was that of "a high-flying aristocrat, cool, and capable of every mischief."

While these matters were agitating, the National Assembly stood in the most perilous and critical situation that a body of men can be supposed to act in. They were the devoted victims, and they knew it. They had the hearts and wishes of their country on their side, but military authority they had none. The guards of Broglio surrounded the hall where the Assembly sat, ready, at the word of command, to seize their persons, as had been done the year before to the Parliament of Paris. Had the National Assembly deserted their trust, or had they exhibited signs of weakness or fear, their enemies had been encouraged and their country depressed. When the situation they stood in, the cause they were engaged in, and the crisis then ready to burst, which should determine their personal and political fate and that of their country, and probably of Europe, are taken into one view, none but a heart callous with prejudice or corrupted by dependence can avoid interesting itself in their success.

The Archbishop of Vienne was at this time President of the National Assembly—a person too old to undergo the scene that a few days or a few hours might bring forth. A man of more activity and bolder fortitude was necessary, and the National Assembly chose (under the form of a Vice-President, for the Presidency still resided in the Archbishop) M. de la Fayette; and this is the only instance of a Vice-President being chosen. It was at the moment that this storm was pending (July 11th) that a declaration of rights was brought forward by M. de la Fayette. . . . It was hastily drawn up, and makes only a part of the more extensive declaration of rights agreed upon and adopted afterwards by the National Assembly. The particular reason for bringing it forward at this moment (M. de la Fayette has since informed me) was that, if the National Assembly should fall in the threatened destruction that then surrounded it, some trace of its principles might have the chance of surviving the wreck.

Everything now was drawing to a crisis. The event was freedom or slavery. On one side, an army of nearly thirty thousand men; on the other, an unarmed body of citizens—for the citizens of Paris, on whom the National Assembly must then immediately depend, were as unarmed and as undisciplined as the citizens of London are now. The French guards had given strong symptoms of their being attached to the national cause; but their numbers were small, not a tenth part of the force that Broglio commanded, and their officers were in the interest of Broglio.

Matters being now ripe for execution, the new ministry made their appearance in office. The reader will carry in his mind that the Bastille was taken the 14th July; the point of time I am now speaking of is the 12th. Immediately on the news of the change of ministry reaching Paris, in the afternoon, all the playhouses and places of entertainment, shops and houses, were shut up. The change of ministry was considered as the prelude of hostilities, and the opinion was rightly founded.

The foreign troops began to advance towards the city. The Prince de Lambesc, who commanded a body of German cavalry, approached by the Place of Lewis XV., which connects itself with some of the streets. In his march, he insulted and struck an old man with a sword. The French are remarkable for their respect to old age; and the insolence with which it appeared to be done, uniting with the general fermentation they were in, produced a powerful effect, and a cry of "To arms! to arms!" spread itself in a moment over the city.

Arms they had none, nor scarcely anyone who knew the use of them; but desperate resolution, when every hope is at stake, supplies, for a while, the want of arms. Near where the Prince de Lambesc was drawn up, were large piles of stones collected for building the new bridge, and with these the people attacked the cavalry. A party of French guards upon hearing the firing, rushed from their quarters and joined the people; and night coming on, the cavalry retreated.

The streets of Paris, being narrow, are favorable for defence, and the loftiness of the houses, consisting of many stories, from which great annoyance might be given, secured them against nocturnal enterprises; and the night was spent in providing themselves with every sort of weapon they could make or procure: guns, swords, blacksmiths' hammers, carpenters' axes, iron crows, pikes, halberts, pitchforks, spits, clubs, etc., etc. The incredible numbers in which they assembled the next morning, and the still more incredible resolution they exhibited, embarrassed and astonished their enemies. Little did the new ministry expect such a salute. Accustomed to slavery themselves, they had no idea that liberty was capable of such inspiration, or that a body of unarmed citizens would dare to face the miliary force of thirty thousand men. Every moment of this day was employed in collecting arms, concerting plans, and arranging themselves into the best order which such an instantaneous movement could afford. Broglio continued lying round the city, but made no further advances this day, and the succeeding night passed with as much tranquility as such a scene could possibly produce.

But defence only was not the object of the citizens. They had a cause at stake, on which depended their freedom or their slavery. They every moment expected an attack, or to hear of one made on the National Assembly; and in such a situation, the most prompt measures are sometimes the best. The object that now presented itself was the Bastille; and the *éclat* of carrying such a fortress in the face of such an army, could not fail to strike terror into the new ministry, who had scarcely yet had time to meet. By some intercepted correspondence this morning, it was discovered that the Mayor of Paris, M. Deffleseslles, who appeared to be in the interest of the citizens, was betraying them; and from this discovery, there remained no doubt that Broglio would reinforce the Bastille the ensuing evening. It was therefore necessary to attack it that day; but before this could be done, it was first necessary to procure a better supply of arms than they were then possessed of.

There was, adjoining to the city a large magazine of arms deposited at the Hospital of the Invalids,[2] which the citizens summoned to surrender; and as the place was neither defensible, nor attempted much defence, they soon succeeded. Thus supplied, they marched to attack the Bastille; a vast mixed multitude of all ages, and of all degrees, armed with all sorts of weapons. Imagination would fail in describing to itself the appearance of such a procession, and of the anxiety of the events which a few hours or a few minutes might produce. What plans the ministry were forming, were as unknown to the people within the city, as what the citizens were doing was unknown to the ministry; and what movements Broglio might make for the support or relief of the place, were to the citizens equally as unknown. All was mystery and hazard.

That the Bastille was attacked with an enthusiasm of heroism, such only as the highest animation of liberty could inspire, and carried in the space of a few hours, is an event which the world is fully possessed of. I am not undertaking the detail of the attack, but bringing into view the conspiracy against the nation which provoked it, and which fell with the Bastille. The prison to which the new ministry were dooming the National Assembly, in addition to its being the high altar and castle of despotism, became the proper object to begin with. This enterprise broke up the new ministry, who began now to fly from the ruin they had prepared for others. The troops of Broglio dispersed, and himself fled also.

Mr. Burke has spoken a great deal about plots, but he has never once spoken of this plot against the National Assembly, and the liberties of the nation; and that he might not, he has passed over all the circumstances that might throw it in his way. The exiles who have fled from France, whose case he so much interests himself in, and from whom he has had his lesson, fled in consequence of the miscarriage of this plot. No plot was formed against them; they were plotting against others; and those who fell, met, not unjustly, the punishment they were preparing to execute. But will Mr. Burke say, that if this plot, contrived with the subtlety of an ambuscade, had succeeded, the successful party would have restrained their wrath so soon? Let the history of all governments answer the question.

---

2. Hospital of the Invalids: built during the seventeenth century as a home for disabled veterans; now a military museum and site of Napoleon's tomb.

Whom has the National Assembly brought to the scaffold? None.[3] They were themselves the devoted victims of this plot, and they have not retaliated; why, then, are they charged with revenge they have not acted? In the tremendous breaking forth of a whole people, in which all degrees, tempers and characters are confounded, delivering themselves, by a miracle of exertion, from the destruction meditated against them, is it to be expected that nothing will happen? When men are sore with the sense of oppressions, and menaced with the prospects of new ones, is the calmness of philosophy or the palsy of insensibility to be looked for? Mr. Burke exclaims against outrage; yet the greatest is that which himself has committed. His book is a volume of outrage, not apologised for by the impulse of a moment, but cherished through a space of ten months; yet Mr. Burke had no provocation—no life, no interest, at stake.

More of the citizens fell in this struggle than of their opponents: but four or five persons were seized by the populace, and instantly put to death; the Governor of the Bastille, and the Mayor of Paris, who was detected in the act of betraying them; and afterwards Foulon, one of the new ministry, and Berthier, his son-in-law, who had accepted the office of intendant of Paris. Their heads were struck upon spikes, and carried about the city; and it is upon this mode of punishment that Mr. Burke builds a great part of his tragic scene. Let us therefore examine how men came by the idea of punishing in this manner.

They learn it from the governments they live under; and retaliate the punishments they have been accustomed to behold. The heads stuck upon spikes, which remained for years upon Temple Bar, differed nothing in the horror of the scene from those carried about upon spikes at Paris; yet this was done by the English Government. It may perhaps be said that it signifies nothing to a man what is done to him after he is dead; but it signifies much to the living; it either tortures their feelings or hardens their hearts, and in either case it instructs them how to punish when power falls into their hands.

Lay then the axe to the root, and teach governments humanity. It is their sanguinary punishments which corrupt mankind. In England the punishment in certain cases is by *hanging, drawing* and *quartering;* the heart of the sufferer is cut out and held up to the view of the populace. In France, under the former Government, the punishments were not less barbarous. Who does not remember the execution of Damien, torn to pieces by horses? The effect of those cruel spectacles exhibited to the populace is to destroy tenderness or excite revenge; and by the base and false idea of governing men by terror, instead of reason, they become precedents. It is over the lowest class of mankind that government by terror is intended to operate, and it is on them that it operates to the worst effect. They have sense enough to feel they are the objects aimed at; and they inflict in their turn the examples of terror they have been instructed to practise.

There is in all European countries a large class of people of that description, which in England is called the *"mob."* Of this class were those who

---

3. None. True at the time of writing. Two years later (1793–1794), during the "Reign of Terror," several thousand were executed for counter-revolutionary activity or sympathies.

committed the burnings and devastations in London in 1780, and of this class were those who carried the heads on iron spikes in Paris. Foulon and Berthier were taken up in the country, and sent to Paris, to undergo their examination at the Hotel de Ville; for the National Assembly, immediately on the new ministry coming into office, passed a decree, which they communicated to the King and Cabinet, that they (the National Assembly) would hold the ministry, of which Foulon was one, responsible for the measures they were advising and pursuing; but the mob, incensed at the appearance of Foulon and Berthier, tore them from their conductors before they were carried to the Hotel de Ville, and executed them on the spot. Why then does Mr. Burke charge outrages of this kind on a whole people? As well may he charge the riots and outrages of 1780 on all the people of London, or those in Ireland on all his countrymen.

But everything we see or hear offensive to our feelings and derogatory to the human character should lead to other reflections than those of reproach. Even the beings who commit them have some claim to our consideration. How then is it that such vast classes of mankind as are distinguished by the appellation of the vulgar, or the ignorant mob, are so numerous in all old countries? The instant we ask ourselves this question, reflection feels an answer. They rise, as an unavoidable consequence, out of the ill construction of all old governments in Europe, England included with the rest. It is by distortedly exalting some men, that others are distortedly debased, till the whole is out of nature. A vast mass of mankind are degradedly thrown into the back-ground of the human picture, to bring forward, with greater glare, the puppet-show of state and aristocracy. In the commencement of a revolution, those men are rather the followers of the *camp* than of the *standard* of liberty, and have yet to be instructed how to reverence it.

I give to Mr. Burke all his theatrical exaggerations for facts, and I then ask him if they do not establish the certainty of what I here lay down? Admitting them to be true, they show the necessity of the French Revolution, as much as any one thing he could have asserted. These outrages were not the effect of the principles of the Revolution, but of the degraded mind that existed before the Revolution, and which the Revolution is calculated to reform. Place them then to their proper cause, and take the reproach of them to your own side.

It is the honour of the National Assembly and the city of Paris that, during such a tremendous scene of arms and confusion, beyond the control of all authority, they have been able, by the influence of example and exhortation, to restrain so much. Never were more pains taken to instruct and enlighten mankind, and to make them see that their interest consisted in their virtue, and not in their revenge, than have been displayed in the Revolution of France.

WILLIAM BLAKE (1757–1827), Selections from *The Marriage of Heaven and Hell*

To destroy the French Revolution abroad and to suppress popular sympathy for it at home: these were the two political aims of the British government from the execution of Louis XVI in 1793 until the monarchy was restored in 1814. Nevertheless, many English people supported the French Revolution, as twenty years earlier they had supported the cause of American independence. The painter, engraver, and poet William Blake was an English radical, and Blake's art, both graphic and literary, is full of the great events of his time.

But Blake's radicalism is not political only; to the mythic vision, politics itself is the manifestation in history of archetypal events and conditions. One such condition is the modern fragmentation of consciousness generated by the Industrial Revolution and reinforced by Christian dualism: men and women are divided from nature and from one another, mind is opposed to body, work to pleasure, sexual and creative energy to intellect. For this fragmentation Blake substitutes, in "The Marriage of Heaven and Hell" (1790–1792), a vision not of opposites but of complementary contraries. Blake's values therefore appear as an ironic inversion of traditional values: his Devil is the man of genius, energy, and perception, while his Angels represent conventional wisdom and morality. The gnomic, paradoxical, often symbolic Proverbs of Hell expose the tension between these two modes of consciousness. The "Marriage" parodies several biblical sources (Genesis, Proverbs, the Apocalypse) and is itself a book in "the Bible of Hell"—Blake's own work.

. . . Without Contraries is no progression. Attraction and Repulsion, Reason and Energy, Love and Hate, are necessary to Human existence.

From these contraries spring what the religious call Good & Evil. Good is the passive that obeys Reason. Evil is the active springing from Energy.

Good is Heaven. Evil is Hell.

THE VOICE OF THE DEVIL

ALL Bibles or sacred codes have been the causes of the following Errors:

1. That Man has two real existing principles, Viz. a Body & a Soul.

2. That Energy, call'd Evil, is alone from the Body; & that Reason, call'd Good, is alone from the Soul.

3. That God will torment Man in Eternity for following his Energies.

But the following Contraries to these are True:

1. Man has no Body distinct from his Soul; for that call'd Body is a portion of Soul discern'd by the five Senses, the chief inlets of Soul in this age.

2. Energy is the only life and is from the Body; and Reason is the bound or outward circumference of Energy.

3. Energy is Eternal Delight.

Those who restrain desire, do so because theirs is weak enough to be restrained; and the restrainer, or reason, usurps its place & governs the unwilling.

And being restrain'd, it by degrees becomes passive, till it is only the shadow of desire.

The history of this is written in Paradise Lost,[1] & the Governor, or Reason, is call'd Messiah.

And the original Archangel, or possessor of the command of the heavenly host, is call'd the Devil or Satan, and his children are call'd Sin & Death.

But in the Book of Job Milton's Messiah is call'd Satan.

For this history [2] has been adopted by both parties.

It indeed appear'd to Reason as if Desire was cast out, but the Devil's account is, that the Messiah fell, & formed a heaven of what he stole from the Abyss.

This is shewn in the Gospel, where he prays to the Father to send the comforter, or Desire, that Reason may have Ideas to build on; the Jehovah of the Bible being no other than he who dwells in flaming fire.

Know that after Christ's death, he became Jehovah.

But in Milton, the Father is Destiny, the Son a Ratio of the five senses, & the Holy-ghost Vacuum!

Note. The reason Milton wrote in fetters when he wrote of Angels & God, and at liberty when of Devils & Hell, is because he was a true Poet and of the Devil's party without knowing it.

A MEMORABLE FANCY

As I was walking among the fires of hell, delighted with the enjoyments of Genius, which to Angels look like torment and insanity, I collected some of their Proverbs, thinking that, as the sayings used in a nation mark its character, so the Proverbs of Hell shew the nature of Infernal wisdom better than any description of buildings or garments.

When I came home, on the abyss of the five senses, where a flat sided steep frowns over the present world, I saw a mighty Devil, folded in black

---

1. Paradise Lost: in Milton's epic poem on "man's first disobedience," the revolutionary has become an apologist for hierarchal order and the fallen world. The character of Satan is the most vivid in the poem, though, and Milton writes about Hell with far more poetic exuberance than he does about Heaven.

2. This history: the dualism of good and evil, in which reason is split off from faith (as in Job) or from energy (as in *Paradise Lost*).

clouds, hovering on the sides of the rock: with corroding fires he wrote the following sentence, now perceived by the minds of men, & read by them on earth:

> *"How do you know but ev'ry Bird that cuts the airy way,*
> *Is an immense world of delight, clos'd by your senses five?"*

PROVERBS OF HELL

In seed time learn; in harvest teach; in winter enjoy.
Drive your cart and your plow over the bones of the dead.
The road of excess leads to the palace of wisdom.
Prudence is a rich ugly old maid courted by Incapacity.
He who desires but acts not, breeds pestilence.
The cut worm forgives the plow.
Dip him in the river who loves water.
A fool sees not the same tree that a wise man sees.
He whose face gives no light shall never become a star.
Eternity is in love with the productions of time.
The busy bee has no time for sorrow.
The hours of folly are measur'd by the clock; but of wisdom no clock can measure.
All wholsom food is caught without a net or a trap.
Bring out number, weight & measure in a year of dearth.
No bird soars too high, if he soars with his own wings.
A dead body revenges not injuries.
The most sublime act is to set another before you.
If the fool would persist in his folly he would become wise.
Folly is the cloke of knavery.
Shame is Pride's cloke.
Prisons are built with stones of Law, Brothels with bricks of Religion.
The pride of the peacock is the glory of God.
The lust of the goat is the bounty of God.
The wrath of the lion is the wisdom of God.
The nakedness of woman is the work of God.
Excess of sorrow laughs. Excess of joy weeps.
The roaring of lions, the howling of wolves, the raging of the stormy sea, and the destructive sword are portions of eternity too great for the eye of man.
The fox condemns the trap, not himself.
Joys impregnate: Sorrows bring forth.
Let man wear the fell of the lion, woman the fleece of the sheep.
The bird a nest, the spider a web, man friendship.
The selfish smiling fool & the sullen frowning fool shall be both thought wise, that they may be a rod.
What is now proved was once only imagin'd.
The rat, the mouse, the fox, the rabbet watch the roots; the lion, the tyger, the horse, the elephant watch the fruits.
The cistern contains, the fountain overflows.
One thought fills immensity.
Always be ready to speak your mind, and a base man will avoid you.
Every thing possible to be believ'd is an image of truth.
The eagle never lost so much time as when he submitted to learn of the crow.
The fox provides for himself, but God provides for the lion.

Think in the morning. Act in the noon. Eat in the evening. Sleep in the Night.
He who has suffer'd you to impose on him knows you.
As the plow follows words, so God rewards prayers.
The tygers of wrath are wiser than the horses of instruction.
Expect poison from the standing water.
You never know what is enough, unless you know what is more than enough.
Listen to the fool's reproach: it is a kingly title.
The eyes of fire, the nostrils of air, the mouth of water, the beard of earth.
The weak in courage is strong in cunning.
The apple tree never asks the beech how he shall grow, nor the lion the horse how
*   he shall take his prey.*
The thankful reciever bears a plentiful harvest.
If others had not been foolish, we should be so.
The soul of sweet delight can never be defil'd.
When thou seest an Eagle, thou seest a portion of Genius: lift up thy head!
As the catterpiller chooses the fairest leaves to lay her eggs on, so the priest lays
his curse on the fairest joys.
To create a little flower is the labour of ages.
Damn braces. Bless relaxes.
The best wine is the oldest, the best water the newest.
Prayers plow not! Praises reap not!
Joys laugh not! Sorrows weep not!
The head Sublime, the heart Pathos, the genitals Beauty, the hands & feet Propor-
*   tion.*
As the air to a bird or the sea to a fish, so is contempt to the contemptible.
The crow wish'd every thing was black, the owl that every thing was white.
Exuberance is Beauty.
If the lion was advised by the fox, he would be cunning.
Improve [me]nt makes strait roads, but the crooked roads without Improvement
*   are roads of Genius.*
Sooner murder an infant in its cradle than nurse unacted desires.
Where man is not, nature is barren.
Truth can never be told so as to be understood, and not be believ'd.
                    Enough or Too much.

The ancient Poets animated all sensible objects with Gods or Geniuses, calling them by the names and adorning them with the properties of woods, rivers, mountains, lakes, cities, nations, and whatever their enlarged & numerous senses could percieve.

And particularly they studied the genius of each city & country, placing it under its mental deity:

Till a system was formed, which some took advantage of, & enslav'd the vulgar by attempting to realize or abstract the mental deities from their objects: thus began Priesthood,

Choosing forms of worship from poetic tales.

And at length they pronounc'd that the Gods had order'd such things.

Thus men forgot that All deities reside in the human breast.

A MEMORABLE FANCY

The Prophets Isaiah and Ezekiel dined with me, and I asked them how they dared so roundly to assert that God spoke to them; and whether they did not think at the time that they would be misunderstood, & so be the cause of imposition.

Isaiah answer'd: "I saw no God, nor heard any, in a finite organical perception; but my senses discover'd the infinite in every thing; and as I was then perswaded, & remain confirm'd, that the voice of honest indignation is the voice of God, I cared not for consequences, but wrote."

Then I asked: "Does a firm perswasion that a thing is so, make it so?"

He replied: "All poets believe that it does, & in ages of imagination this firm perswasion removed mountains; but many are not capable of a firm perswasion of any thing."

Then Ezekiel said: "The philosophy of the east taught the first principles of human perception. Some nations held one principle for the origin, & some another; we of Israel taught that the Poetic Genius (as you now call it) was the first principle, and all the others merely derivative, which was the cause of our despising the Priests & Philosophers of other countries, and prophecying that all Gods would at last be proved to originate in ours & to be the tributaries of the Poetic Genius. It was this that our great poet, King David desired so ferventy & invokes so patheticly, saying, by this he conquers enemies & governs kingdoms: and we so loved our God, that we cursed in his name all the deities of surrounding nations, and asserted that they had rebelled. From these opinions the vulgar came to think that all nations would at last be subject to the jews."

"This," said he, "like all firm perswasions, is come to pass; for all nations believe the jews' code and worship the jews' god, and what greater subjection can be?"

I heard this with some wonder, & must confess my own conviction. After dinner, I ask'd Isaiah to favour the world with his lost works; he said none of equal value was lost. Ezekiel said the same of his.

I also asked Isaiah what made him go naked and barefoot three years: he answer'd: "The same that made our friend Diogenes the Grecian."

I then asked Ezekiel why he eat dung, & lay so long on his right & left side. He answer'd: "The desire of raising other men into a perception of the infinite. This the North American tribes practise, & is he honest who resists his genius or conscience only for the sake of present ease or gratification?"

The ancient tradition that the world will be consumed in fire at the end of six thousand years is true, as I have heard from Hell.

For the cherub with his flaming sword is hereby commanded to leave his guard at the tree of life, and when he does, the whole creation will be consumed and appear infinite and holy, whereas it now appears finite & corrupt.

This will come to pass by an improvement of sensual enjoyment.

But first the notion that man has a body distinct from his soul is to be expunged; this I shall do by printing in the infernal method by corrosives, which in Hell are salutary and medicinal, melting apparent surfaces away, and displaying the infinite which was hid.

If the doors of perception were cleansed, every thing would appear to man as it is, infinite.

For man has closed himself up, till he sees all things thro' narrow chinks of his cavern.

A MEMORABLE FANCY

I was in a Printing house in Hell & saw the method in which knowledge is transmitted from generation to generation.

In the first chamber was a Dragon-Man, clearing away the rubbish from a cave's mouth; within, a number of Dragons were hollowing the cave.

In the second chamber was a Viper folding round the rock & the cave, and others adorning it with gold, silver and precious stones.

In the third chamber was an Eagle with wings and feathers of air; he caused the inside of the cave to be infinite: around were numbers of Eagle-like men who built palaces in the immense cliffs.

In the fourth chamber were Lions of flaming fire, raging around & melting the metals into living fluids.

In the fifth chamber were Unnam'd forms, which cast the metals into the expanse.

There they were reciev'd by Man who occupied the sixth chamber, and took the forms of books & were arranged in libraries.

The Giants who formed this world into its sensual existence and now seem to live in it in chains, are in truth the causes of its life & the sources of all activity; but the chains are the cunning of weak and tame minds which have power to resist energy: according to the proverb, the weak in courage is strong in cunning.

Thus one portion of being is the Prolific, the other the Devouring. To the devourer it seems as if the producer was in his chains; but it is not so; he only takes portions of existence and fancies that the whole.

But the Prolific would cease to be Prolific unless the Devourer as a sea received the excess of his delights.

Some will say: "Is not God alone the Prolific?" I answer: "God only Acts & Is, in existing beings or Men."

These two classes of men are always upon earth, & they should be enemies: whoever tries to reconcile them seeks to destroy existence.

Religion is an endeavour to reconcile the two.

Note. Jesus Christ did not wish to unite, but to separate them, as in the Parable of sheep and goats: & he says: "I came not to send Peace, but a Sword."

Messiah or Satan or Tempter was formerly thought to be one of the Antediluvians who are our Energies.

A MEMORABLE FANCY

Once I saw a Devil in a flame of fire, who arose before an Angel that sat on a cloud, and the Devil utter'd these words:

"The worship of God is: Honouring his gifts in other men, each according to his genius, and loving the greatest men best: those who envy or calumniate great men hate God; for there is no other God."

The Angel, hearing this, became almost blue; but mastering himself he grew yellow, & at last white, pink & smiling, and then replied:

"Thou Idolater, is not God One? & is not he visible in Jesus Christ? and has not Jesus Christ given his sanction to the law of ten commandments? and are not all other men fools, sinners & nothings? '

The Devil answer'd: "bray a fool in a morter with wheat, yet shall not his folly be beaten out of him. If Jesus Christ is the greatest man, you ought to love him in the greatest degree. Now hear how he has given his sanction to the law of ten commandments. Did he not mock at the sabbath, and so mock the sabbath's God, murder those who were murder'd because of him, turn away the law from the woman taken in adultery, steal the labor of others to support him, bear false witness when he omitted making a defence before Pilate, covet when he pray'd for his disciples and when he bid them shake off the dust of their feet against such as refused to lodge them? I tell you, no virtue can exist without breaking these ten commandments. Jesus was all virtue, and acted from impulse, not from rules."

When he had so spoken, I beheld the Angel, who stretched out his arms, embracing the flame of fire: & he was consumed, and arose as Elijah.

Note. This Angel, who is now become a Devil, is my particular friend: we often read the Bible together in its infernal or diabolical sense, which the world shall have if they behave well.

I have also The Bible of Hell, which the world shall have whether they will or no.

One Law for the Lion & Ox is Oppression.

MARY WOLLSTONECRAFT (1759–1797), *Of the Pernicious Effects Which Arise from the Unnatural Distinctions Established in Society,* from *A Vindication of the Rights of Women*

Like her friend Thomas Paine, Mary Wollstonecraft was moved to refute Edmund Burke's attack on the French Revolution and on the "swinish multitude" who produced it. Her answer, A Vindication of the Rights of Men *(1790) was followed by a companion book,* A Vindication of the Rights of Woman *(1792), in which she applied to womankind the principles of liberty and equality central to her defense of the revolution. In the chapter given below, Wollstonecraft notes a paradox that is still to be resolved by the women's liberation movement: the passive life that most women lead is unfulfilling, but so, ultimately, is the active life that most men lead, for both are controlled by property and class. Thus it is not simply freedom to work that she demands, but an end to the idea of "sexual character" (stereotyped sex roles) and to the hierarchal systems that both generate and reinforce that idea.*

Wollstonecraft's style—passionate, image-laden, and often hyperbolic—sometimes illustrates the abuse of rhetoric; but in general her metaphors advance her argument: the recurrent image of drapery is an example. The resentment raised by her political radicalism and by her open disregard for social propriety is movingly described in Blake's lyric "Mary" (1803), which is thought to be about Wollstonecraft:

> *Some said she was proud, some call'd her a whore,*
> *And some, when she passed by, shut to the door; . . .*
> *All faces have envy, sweet Mary, but thine.*

From the respect paid to property flow, as from a poisoned fountain, most of the evils and vices which render this world such a dreary scene to the contemplative mind. For it is in the most polished society that noissome reptiles and venomous serpents lurk under the rank herbage; and there is voluptuousness pampered by the still sultry air, which relaxes every good disposition before it ripens into virtue.

One class presses on another; for all are aiming to procure respect on account of their property: and property, once gained, will procure the respect due only to talents and virtue. Men neglect the duties incumbent on man, yet are treated like demi-gods; religion is also separated from morality by a cere-monial veil, yet men wonder that the world is almost, literally speaking, a den of sharpers or oppressors.

There is a homely proverb, which speaks a shrewd truth, that whoever the devil finds idle he will employ. And what but habitual idleness can hereditary wealth and titles produce? For man is so constituted that he can only attain a proper use of his faculties by exercising them, and will not exercise them un-less necessity of some kind first set the wheels in motion. Virtue likewise can only be acquired by the discharge of relative duties; but the importance of these sacred duties will scarcely be felt by the being who is cajoled out of his humanity by the flattery of sycophants. There must be more equality estab-lished in society, or morality will never gain ground, and this virtuous equal-ity will not rest firmly even when founded on a rock, if one half of mankind be chained to its bottom by fate, for they will be continually undermining it through ignorance or pride.

It is vain to expect virtue from women till they are in some degree inde-pendent of men; nay, it is vain to expect that strength of natural affection which would make them good wives and mothers. Whilst they are absolutely dependent on their husbands they will be cunning, mean, and selfish, and the men who can be gratified by the fawning fondness of spaniel-like affection have not much delicacy, for love is not to be bought, in any sense of the words; its silken wings are instantly shrivelled up when anything beside a re-turn in kind is sought. Yet whilst wealth enervates men, and women live, as it were, by their personal charms, how can we expect them to discharge those ennobling duties which equally require exertion and self-denial? Hereditary property sophisticates the mind, and the unfortunate victims to it, if I may so express myself, swathed from their birth, seldom exert the locomotive faculty of body or mind; and, thus viewing everything through one medium, and that a false one, they are unable to discern in what true merit and happiness con-sist. False, indeed, must be the light when the drapery of situation hides the man, and makes him stalk in masquerade, dragging from one scene of dissi-pation to another the nerveless limbs that hang with stupid listlessness, and rolling round the vacant eye which plainly tells us that there is no mind at home.

I mean, therefore, to infer that the society is not properly organized which does not compel men and women to discharge their respective duties, by making it the only way to acquire that countenance from their fellow-crea-tures which every human being wishes some way to attain. The respect, con-sequently, which is paid to wealth and mere personal charms, is a true north-east blast that blights the tender blossoms of affection and virtue. Na-ture has wisely attached affections to duties to sweeten toil, and to give that vigour to the exertions of reason which only the heart can give. But the affec-tion which is put on merely because it is the appropriated insignia of a cer-tain character, when its duties are not fulfilled, is one of the empty compli-ments which vice and folly are obliged to pay to virtue and the real nature of things.

To illustrate my opinion, I need only observe that when a woman is ad-mired for her beauty, and suffers herself to be so far intoxicated by the admi-ration she receives as to neglect to discharge the indispensable duty of a mother, she sins against herself by neglecting to cultivate an affection that would equally tend to make her useful and happy. True happiness, I mean all the contentment and virtuous satisfaction that can be snatched in this imperfect state, must arise from well regulated affections; and an affection includes a duty. Men are not aware of the misery they cause and the vicious weakness they cherish by only inciting women to render themselves pleasing; they do not consider that they thus make natural and artificial duties clash by sacrificing the comfort and respectability of a woman's life to voluptuous notions of beauty when in nature they all harmonize.

Cold would be the heart of a husband, were he not rendered unnatural by early debauchery, who did not feel more delight at seeing his child suckled by its mother, than the most artful wanton tricks could ever raise; yet this natural way of cementing the matrimonial tie and twisting esteem with fonder recollections, wealth leads women to spurn. To preserve their beauty and wear the flowery crown of the day, which gives them a kind of right to reign for a short time over the sex, they neglect to stamp impressions on their husbands' hearts that would be remembered with more tenderness when the snow on the head began to chill the bosom than even their virgin charms. The maternal solicitude of a reasonable affectionate woman is very interesting, and the chastened dignity with which a mother returns the caresses that she and her child receive from a father who has been fulfilling the serious duties of his station, is not only a respectable but a beautiful sight. So singular indeed are my feelings, and I have endeavoured not to catch factitious ones, that after having been fatigued with the sight of insipid grandeur and the slavish ceremonies that with cumbrous pomp supplied the place of domestic affections, I have turned to some other scene to relieve my eye by resting it on the refreshing green everywhere scattered by nature. I have then viewed with pleasure a woman nursing her children, and discharging the duties of her station with, perhaps, merely a servant maid to take off her hands the servile part of the household business. I have seen her prepare herself and children, with only the luxury of cleanliness, to receive her husband, who returning weary home in the evening found smiling babes and a clean hearth. My heart has loitered in the midst of the group, and has even throbbed with sympathetic emotion, when the scraping of the well known foot has raised a pleasing tumult.

Whilst my benevolence has been gratified by contemplating this artless picture, I have thought that a couple of this description, equally necessary and independent of each other, because each fulfilled the respective duties of their station, possessed all that life could give. Raised sufficiently above abject poverty not to be obliged to weigh the consequence of every farthing they spend, and having sufficient to prevent their attending to a frigid system of economy, which narrows both heart and mind. I declare, so vulgar are my conceptions, that I know not what is wanted to render this the happiest as well as the most respectable situation in the world, but a taste for literature, to throw a little variety and interest into social converse, and some superfluous money to give to the needy and to buy books. For it is not pleasant when the heart is opened by compassion and the head active in arranging plans of usefulness, to have a prim urchin continually twitching back the elbow to prevent the hand from drawing out an almost empty purse, whispering at the same time some prudential maxim about the priority of justice.

Destructive, however, as riches and inherited honours are to the human character, women are more debased and cramped, if possible, by them than men, because men may still, in some degree, unfold their faculties by becoming soldiers and statesmen.

As soldiers, I grant, they can now only gather, for the most part, vainglorious laurels, whilst they adjust to a hair the European balance, taking especial care that no bleak northern nook or sound incline the beam. But the days of true heroism are over, when a citizen fought for his country like a Fabricius or a Washington, and then returned to his farm to let his virtuous fervour run in a more placid, but not a less salutary, stream. No, our British heroes are oftener sent from the gaming table than from the plough; and their passions have been rather inflamed by hanging with dumb suspense on the turn of a die, than sublimated by panting after the adventurous march of virtue in the historic page.

The statesman, it is true, might with more propriety quit the faro bank, or card table, to guide the helm, for he has still but to shuffle and trick. The whole system of British politics, if system it may courteously be called, consisting in multiplying dependents and contriving taxes which grind the poor to pamper the rich; thus a war, or any wild goose chase, is, as the vulgar use the phrase, a lucky turn-up of patronage for the minister, whose chief merit is the art of keeping himself in place. It is not necessary then that he should have bowels for the poor, so he can secure for his family the odd trick. Or should some show of respect, for what is termed with ignorant ostentation an Englishman's birthright, be expedient to bubble the gruff mastiff that he has to lead by the nose, he can make an empty show very safely by giving his single voice and suffering his light squadron to file off to the other side. And when a question of humanity is agitated he may dip a sop in the milk of human kindness to silence Cerberus, and talk of the interest which his heart takes in an attempt to make the earth no longer cry for vengeance as it sucks in its children's blood, though his cold hand may at the very moment rivet their chains by sanctioning the abominable traffic. A minister is no longer a minister than while he can carry a point which he is determined to carry. Yet it is not necessary that a minister should feel like a man, when a bold push might shake his seat.

But, to have done with these episodical observations, let me return to the more specious slavery which chains the very soul of woman, keeping her for ever under the bondage of ignorance.

The preposterous distinctions of rank, which render civilization a curse by dividing the world between voluptuous tyrants and cunning envious dependents, corrupt, almost equally, every class of people, because respectability is not attached to the discharge of the relative duties of life, but to the station, and when the duties are not fulfilled the affections cannot gain sufficient strength to fortify the virtue of which they are the natural reward. Still there are some loopholes out of which a man may creep, and dare to think and act for himself; but for a woman it is a herculean task, because she has difficulties peculiar to her sex to overcome which require almost superhuman powers.

A truly benevolent legislator always endeavours to make it the interest of each individual to be virtuous; and thus private virtue becoming the cement of public happiness, an orderly whole is consolidated by the tendency of all the parts towards a common centre. But, the private or public virtue of woman is very problematical; for Rousseau, and a numerous list of male writers, insist that she should all her life be subjected to a severe restraint, that of propriety. Why subject her to propriety—blind propriety, if she be capable of acting from a nobler spring, if she be an heir of immortality? Is sugar always to be produced by vital blood? Is one half of the human species, like the poor African slaves, to be subject to prejudices that brutalize them, when principles would be a surer guard, only to sweeten the cup of man? Is not this indirectly to deny woman reason? for a gift is a mockery, if it be unfit for use.

Women are, in common with men, rendered weak and luxurious by the relaxing pleasures which wealth procures; but added to this they are made slaves to their persons, and must render them alluring that man may lend them his reason to guide their tottering steps aright. Or should they be ambitious, they must govern their tyrants by sinister tricks, for without rights there cannot be any incumbent duties. The laws respecting woman, which I mean to discuss in a future part, make an absurd unit of a man and his wife; and then, by the easy transition of only considering him as responsible, she is reduced to a mere cypher.

The being who discharges the duties of its station is independent; and, speaking of women at large, their first duty is to themselves as rational creatures, and the next in point of importance, as citizens, is that which includes so many, of a mother. The rank in life which dispenses with their fulfilling this duty necessarily degrades them by making them mere dolls. Or, should they turn to something more important than merely fitting drapery upon a smooth block, their minds are only occupied by some soft platonic attachment; or, the actual management of an intrigue may keep their thoughts in motion; for when they neglect domestic duties, they have it not in their own power to take the field and march and counter-march like soldiers, or wrangle in the senate to keep their faculties from rusting.

I know that, as a proof of the inferiority of the sex, Rousseau has exultingly exclaimed, How can they leave the nursery for the camp! And the camp has by some moralists been termed the school of the most heroic virtues; though, I think, it would puzzle a keen casuist to prove the reasonableness of the greater number of wars that have dubbed heroes. I do not mean to consider this question critically; because, having frequently viewed these freaks of ambition as the first natural mode of civilization, when the ground must be torn up, and the woods cleared by fire and sword, I do not choose to call them pests; but surely the present system of war has little connection with virtue of any denomination, being rather the school of *finesse* and effeminacy than of fortitude.

Yet if defensive war, the only justifiable war, in the present advanced state of society, where virtue can show its face and ripen amidst the rigours which purify the air on the mountain's top, were alone to be adopted as just and glorious, the true heroism of antiquity might again animate female bosoms. But fair and softly, gentle reader, male or female, do not alarm thyself, for though I have compared the character of a modern soldier with that of a civilized woman, I am not going to advise them to turn their distaff into a musket, though I sincerely wish to see the bayonet converted into a pruning-hook. I only recreated an imagination, fatigued by contemplating the vices and follies which all proceed from a feculent stream of wealth that has muddied the pure rills of natural affection, by supposing that society will some time or other be so constituted, that man must necessarily fulfil the duties of a citizen or be despised, and that while he was employed in any of the departments of civil life, his wife, also an active citizen, should be equally intent to manage her family, educate her children, and assist her neighbours.

But, to render her really virtuous and useful, she must not, if she discharge her civil duties, want, individually, the protection of civil laws; she must not be dependent on her husband's bounty for her subsistence during his life or support after his death—for how can a being be generous who has nothing of its own? or virtuous, who is not free? The wife, in the present state of things, who is faithful to her husband, and neither suckles nor educates her children, scarcely deserves the name of a wife, and has no right to that of a citizen. But take away natural rights, and duties become null.

Women then must be considered as only the wanton solace of men when they become so weak in mind and body that they cannot exert themselves, unless to pursue some frothy pleasure or to invent some frivolous fashion. What can be a more melancholy sight to a thinking mind than to look into the numerous carriages that drive helter-skelter about this metropolis in a morning full of pale-faced creatures who are flying from themselves. I have often wished, with Dr. Johnson, to place some of them in a little shop with half a dozen children looking up to their languid countenances for support. I am much mistaken if some latent vigour would not soon give health and spirit to their eyes, and some lines drawn by the exercise of reason on the blank cheeks, which before were only undulated by dimples, might restore lost dignity to the character, or rather enable it to attain the true dignity of its nature. Virtue is not to be acquired even by speculation, much less by the negative supineness that wealth naturally generates.

Besides, when poverty is more disgraceful than even vice, is not morality cut to the quick? Still to avoid misconstruction, though I consider that women in the common walks of life are called to fulfill the duties of wives and mothers, by religion and reason, I cannot help lamenting that women of a superior cast have not a road open by which they can pursue more extensive plans of usefulness and independence. I may excite laughter by dropping a hint which I mean to pursue some future time, for I really think that women ought to have representatives, instead of being arbitrarily governed without having any direct share allowed them in the deliberations of government.

But, as the whole system of representation is now in this country only a convenient handle for despotism, they need not complain, for they are as well represented as a numerous class of hard-working mechanics, who pay for the support of royalty when they can scarcely stop their children's mouths with bread. How are they represented whose very sweat supports the splendid stud of an heir apparent, or varnishes the chariot of some female favourite who looks down on shame? Taxes on the very necessaries of life enable an endless tribe of idle princes and princesses to pass with stupid pomp before a gaping crowd, who almost worship the very parade which costs them so dear. This is mere gothic grandeur, something like the barbarous useless parade of having sentinels on horseback at Whitehall, which I could never view without a mixture of contempt and indignation.

How strangely must the mind be sophisticated when this sort of state impresses it! But, till these monuments of folly are levelled by virtue, similar follies will leaven the whole mass. For the same character, in some degree, will prevail in the aggregate of society; and the refinements of luxury, or the vicious repinings of envious poverty, will equally banish virtue from society, considered as the characteristic of that society, or only allow it to appear as one of the stripes of the harlequin coat worn by the civilized man.

In the superior ranks of life every duty is done by deputies, as if duties could ever be waived, and the vain pleasures which consequent idleness forces the rich to pursue appear so enticing to the next rank that the numerous scramblers for wealth sacrifice everything to tread on their heels. The most sacred trusts are then considered as sinecures, because they were procured by interest, and only sought to enable a man to keep *good company.* Women, in particular, all want to be ladies. Which is simply to have nothing to do, but listlessly to go they scarcely care where, for they cannot tell what.

But what have women to do in society? I may be asked, but to loiter with easy grace; surely you would not condemn them all to suckle fools and chronicle small beer! No. Women might certainly study the art of healing, and be physicians as well as nurses. And midwifery, decency seems to allot to them, though I am afraid the word midwife in our dictionaries will soon give place to *accoucheur,* and one proof of the former delicacy of the sex be effaced from the language.

They might also study politics, and settle their benevolence on the broadest basis; for the reading of history will scarcely be more useful than the perusal of romances, if read as mere biography; if the character of the times, the political improvements, arts, &c., be not observed. In short, if it be not considered as the history of man; and not of particular men, who filled a niche in the temple of fame, and dropped into the black rolling stream of time, that silently sweeps all before it, into the shapeless void called— eternity. For shape, can it be called, "that shape hath none"?

Business of various kinds they might likewise pursue, if they were educated in a more orderly manner, which might save many from common and legal prostitution. Women would not then marry for a support, as men accept of places under government, and neglect the implied duties; nor would an attempt to earn their own subsistence—a most laudable one!—sink them almost to the level of those poor abandoned creatures who live by prostitution. For are not milliners and mantua-makers reckoned the next class? The few employments open to women, so far from being liberal, are menial; and when a superior education enables them to take charge of the education of children as governesses, they are not treated like the tutors of sons, though even clerical tutors are not always treated in a manner calculated to render them respectable in the eyes of their pupils, to say nothing of the private comfort of the individual. But as women educated like gentlewomen are never designed for the humiliating situation which necessity sometimes forces them to fill, these situations are considered in the light of a degradation; and they know little of the human heart, who need to be told that nothing so painfully sharpens sensibility as such a fall in life.

Some of these women might be restrained from marrying by a proper spirit or delicacy, and others may not have had it in their power to escape in this pitiful way from servitude; is not that government then very defective, and very unmindful of the happiness of one half of its members, that does not provide for honest, independent women, by encouraging them to fill respectable stations? But in order to render their private virtue a public benefit, they must have a civil existence in the state, married or single; else we shall continually see some worthy woman, whose sensibility has been rendered painfully acute by undeserved contempt, droop like "the lily broken down by a plow-share."

It is a melancholy truth—yet such is the blessed effect of civilization!—the most respectable women are the most oppressed; and, unless they have understandings far superior to the common run of understandings, taking in both sexes, they must, from being treated like contemptible beings, become contemptible. How many women thus waste life away the prey of discontent, who might have practised as physicians, regulated a farm, managed a shop, and stood erect, supported by their own industry, instead of hanging their heads surcharged with the dew of sensibility, that consumes the beauty to which it at first gave lustre; nay, I doubt whether pity and love are so near akin as poets feign, for I have seldom seen much compassion excited by the helplessness of females, unless they were fair; then, perhaps pity was the soft handmaid of love, or the harbinger of lust.

How much more respectable is the woman who earns her own bread by fulfilling any duty, than the most accomplished beauty!—beauty did I say?—so sensible am I of the beauty of moral loveliness, or the harmonious propriety that attunes the passions of a well-regulated mind, that I blush at making the comparison; yet I sigh to think how few women aim at attaining this respectability by withdrawing from the giddy whirl of pleasure, or the indolent calm that stupefies the good sort of women it sucks in.

Proud of their weakness, however, they must always be protected, guarded from care, and all the rough toils that dignify the mind. If this be the fiat of fate, if they will make themselves insignificant and contemptible, sweetly to waste "life away," let them not expect to be valued when their beauty fades, for it is the fate of the fairest flowers to be admired and pulled to pieces by the careless hand that plucked them. In how many ways do I wish, from the purest benevolence, to impress this truth on my sex; yet I fear that they will not listen to a truth that dear-bought experience has brought home to many an agitated bosom, nor willingly resign the privileges of rank and sex for the privileges of humanity, to which those have no claim who do not discharge its duties.

Those writers are particularly useful, in my opinion, who make man feel for man, independent of the station he fills, or the drapery of factitious sentiments. I then would fain convince reasonable men of the importance of some of my remarks; and prevail on them to weigh dispassionately the whole tenor of my observations. I appeal to their understandings; and, as a fellow-creature, claim, in the name of my sex, some interest in their hearts. I entreat them to assist to emancipate their companion, to make her a *help meet* for them!

Would men but generously snap our chains, and be content with rational fellowship instead of slavish obedience, they would find us more observant daughters, more affectionate sisters, more faithful wives, more reasonable mothers—in a word, better citizens. We should then love them with true affection, because we should learn to respect ourselves; and, the peace of mind of a worthy man would not be interrupted by the idle vanity of his wife, nor the babes sent to nestle in a strange bosom, having never found a home in their mother's.

PERCY BYSSHE SHELLEY (1792–1822),
The Necessity of Atheism

Although he was described by Matthew Arnold as "a beautiful and ineffectual angel, beating in the void his luminous wings in vain," the poet Shelley was in fact a prolific social critic, both in his poetry and in his prose. While at Oxford he published "The Necessity of Atheism" (1811). It was one of the first essays in England to argue openly for atheism, and for refusing to answer questions about his authorship, Shelley was expelled from the university. Many of Shelley's political ideas are expressed in his longer poems: denunciation of war, tyranny, and repressive religion; support of various popular revolutions. He also wrote and personally distributed essays and broadsheet ballads on political subjects. Shelley admired the work of Thomas Paine and thought of editing a selection of Paine's writings; another important influence was the work of William Godwin (the political philosopher and husband of Mary Wollstonecraft), who became Shelley's friend and father-in-law.

The pamphlet on atheism is tersely, almost impatiently, argued. Its bare, pedantic style and deliberate avoidance of formal rhetoric emphasize the scientific impartiality with which the author claims to examine his subject. Given the intensely controversial nature of that subject, he could not hope to persuade by fulsome rhetoric, but only by the driest rationality. But the tone of objective detachment so scrupulously maintained in the body of the piece breaks down in the last paragraphs, suggesting that detachment is not always objective.

A close examination of the validity of the proofs adduced to support any proposition has ever been allowed to be the only sure way of attaining truth, upon the advantages of which it is unnecessary to descant. Our knowledge of the existence of a Deity is a subject of such importance that it cannot be too minutely investigated; in consequence of this conviction, we proceed briefly and impartially to examine the proofs which have been adduced. It is necessary first to consider the nature of Belief.

When a proposition is offered to the mind, it perceives the agreement or disagreement of the ideas of which it is composed. A perception of their agreement is termed belief. Many obstacles frequently prevent this perception from being immediate; these the mind attempts to remove in order that the perception may be distinct. The mind is active in the investigation, in order to perfect the state of perception which is passive; the investigation being confused with the perception has induced many falsely to imagine that the mind is active in belief, that belief is an act of volition, in consequence of which it may be regulated by the mind; pursuing, continuing this mistake they have attached a degree of criminality to disbelief of which in its nature it is incapable; it is equally so of merit.

The strength of belief like that of every other passion is in proportion to the degrees of excitement.

The degrees of excitement are three.

The senses are the sources of all knowledge to the mind, consequently their evidence claims the strongest assent.

The decision of the mind founded upon our own experience derived from these sources, claims the next degree.

The experience of others which addresses itself to the former one, occupies the lowest degree.—

Consequently no testimony can be admitted which is contrary to reason, reason is founded on the evidence of our senses.

Every proof may be referred to one of these three divisions. We are naturally led to consider what arguments we receive from each of them to convince us of the existence of a Deity.

1st. The evidence of the senses.—If the Deity should appear to us, if he should convince our senses of his existence; this revelation would necessarily command belief;—Those to whom the Deity has thus appeared, have the strongest possible conviction of his existence.

Reason claims the 2nd place. It is urged that man knows that whatever is, must either have had a beginning or existed from all eternity; he also knows that whatever is not eternal must have had a cause.—Where this is applied to the existence of the universe, it is necessary to prove that it was created; until that is clearly demonstrated, we may reasonably suppose that it has endured from all eternity.—In a case where two propositions are diametrically opposite, the mind believes that which is less incomprehensible. It is easier to suppose that the Universe has existed from all eternity, than to conceive a being capable of creating it; if the mind sinks beneath the weight of one, is it an alleviation to increase the intolerability of the burden?—The other argument which is founded upon a man's knowledge of his own existence, stands thus: A man knows not only he now is, but that there was a time when he did not exist, consequently there must have been a cause. But what does this prove? we can only infer from effects causes exactly adequate to those effects. There certainly is a generative power which is effected by particular instruments; we cannot prove that it is inherent in these instruments, nor is the contrary hypothesis capable of demonstration; we admit that the generative power is incomprehensible, but to suppose that the same effect is produced by an eternal, omniscient, Almighty Being, leaves the cause in the obscurity, but renders it more incomprehensible.

The 3rd and last degree of assent is claimed by Testimony. It is required that it should not be contrary to reason. The testimony that the Deity convinces the senses of men of his existence can only be admitted by us, if our mind considers it less probable that these men should have been deceived, than that the Deity should have appeared to them. Our reason can never admit the testimony of men, who not only declare that they were eye-witnesses of miracles but that the Deity was irrational, for he commanded that he should be believed, he proposed the highest rewards for faith, eternal punishments for disbelief. We can only command voluntary actions. Belief is not an act of volition, the mind is even passive; from this it is evident that we have not sufficient testimony, or rather that testimony is insufficient to prove the being of a God, we have before shewn that it cannot be deduced from reason. They who have been convinced by the evidence of the senses, they only can believe it.

From this it is evident that having no proofs from any of the three sources of conviction, the mind *cannot* believe the existence of a God. It is also evident that as belief is a passion of the mind, no degree of criminality can be attached to disbelief; they only are reprehensible who willingly neglect to remove the false medium thro' which their mind views the subject.

It is almost unnecessary to observe, that the general knowledge of the deficiency of such proof, cannot be prejudicial to society: Truth has always been found to promote the best interests of mankind. Every reflecting mind must allow that there is no proof of the existence of a Deity.—Q.E.D.

THOMAS CARLYLE (1795–1881), *Midas* and *Gospel of Mammonism*, from *Past and Present*

When Thomas Carlyle was writing Past and Present *(1843), and was asked to lecture for a political club, he responded, "I am already engaged for a far bigger League (that of the oppressed poor against the idle rich; that of God against the Devil)." The book is a comparative study of England in the twelfth and nineteenth centuries; it is also a fierce indictment of the modern bourgeoisie—their greed, their destruction of communal values, their replacement of moral principle with the "cash nexus." But if Carlyle presents as passionate a denunciation of industrial capitalism as do Engels and Marx in their Manifesto, it is from a wholly different premise. The ordered community in which Carlyle sees salvation is the feudal society of the medieval past, not the socialist society of the future. Such Tory radicalism Engels and Marx describe as "half lamentation, half lampoon; half echo of the past, half menace of the future; at times, by its bitter, witty, and incisive criticism, striking the bourgeoisie to the very heart's core; but always ludicrous in its effect, through total incapacity to comprehend the march of modern history."*

In Past and Present *Carlyle consciously assumes the prophetic stance. His style, formally structured and intensely energetic, displays a tonal range that is unusually extensive even in Victorian imaginative prose.*

*

Midas

The condition of England, on which many pamphlets are now in the course of publication, and many thoughts unpublished are going on in every reflective head, is justly regarded as one of the most ominous, and withal one of the strangest, ever seen in this world. England is full of wealth, of multifarious produce, supply for human want in every kind; yet England is dying of inanition. With unabated bounty the land of England blooms and grows; waving with yellow harvests; thick-studded with workshops, industrial implements, with fifteen millions of workers, understood to be the strongest, the cunningest and the willingest our Earth ever had; these men are here; the work they have done, the fruit they have realised is here, abundant, exuberant on every hand of us: and behold, some baleful fiat as of Enchantment has gone forth, saying, "Touch it not, ye workers, ye master-workers, ye master-idlers; none of you can touch it, no man of you shall be the better for it; this is enchanted fruit!" On the poor workers such fiat falls first, in its rudest shape; but on the rich master-workers too it falls; neither can the rich master-idlers, nor any richest or highest man escape, but all are like to be brought low with it, and made "poor" enough, in the money-sense or a far fataller one.

Of these successful skillful workers some two millions, it is now counted, sit in Workhouses, Poor-law Prisons; or have "out-door relief" flung over the wall to them,—the workhouse Bastille being filled to bursting, and the strong Poor-law [1] broken asunder by a stronger. They sit there, these many months now; their hope of deliverance as yet small. In workhouses, pleasantly so named, because work cannot be done in them. Twelve hundred thousand workers in England alone; their cunning right-hand lamed, lying idle in their sorrowful bosom; their hopes, outlooks, share of this fair world, shut in by narrow walls. They sit there, pent up, as in a kind of horrid enchantment; glad to be imprisoned and enchanted, that they may not perish starved. The picturesque Tourist, in a sunny autumn day, through this bounteous realm of England, descries the Union Workhouse on his path. "Passing by the Workhouse of St. Ives in Huntingdonshire, on a bright day last autumn," says the picturesque Tourist, "I saw sitting on wooden benches, in front of their Bastille and within their ring-wall and its railings, some half-hundred or more of these men. Tall robust figures, young mostly or of middle age; of honest countenance, many of them thoughtful and even intelligent-looking men. They sat there, near by one another; but in a kind of torpor, especially in a silence, which was very striking. In silence: for, alas, what word was to be said? An Earth all lying round, crying, Come and till me, come and reap me; —yet we here sit enchanted! In the eyes and brows of these men hung the gloomiest expression, not of anger, but of grief and shame and manifold inarticulate distress and weariness; they returned my glance with a glance that seemed to say, 'Do not look at us. We sit enchanted here, we know not why. The Sun shines and the Earth calls; and, by the governing Powers and Impotences of this England, we are forbidden to obey. It is impossible, they tell us!' There was something that reminded me of Dante's Hell in the look of all this; and I rode swiftly away."

So many hundred thousands sit in workhouses: and other hundred thousands have not yet got even workhouses; and in thrifty Scotland itself, in Glasgow or Edinburgh City, in their dark lanes, hidden from all but the eye of God, and of rare Benevolence the minister of God, there are scenes of woe and destitution and desolation, such as, one may hope, the Sun never saw before in the most barbarous regions where men dwelt. Competent witnesses, the brave and humane Dr. Alison, who speaks what he knows, whose noble Healing Art in his charitable hands becomes once more a truly sacred one,

---

1. Poor law: legislation governing state assistance to the poor. Nineteenth-century poor laws, assuming unemployment to be the result of laziness, established work houses "as like prisons as possible," with "a discipline so severe and repulsive as to make them a terror to the poor and prevent them from entering" (the words of a contemporary assistant commissioner).

report these things for us: these things are not of this year, or of last year, have no reference to our present state of commercial stagnation, but only to the common state. Not in sharp fever-fits, but in chronic gangrene of this kind is Scotland suffering. A Poor-law, any and every Poor-law, it may be observed, is but a temporary measure; an anodyne, not a remedy: Rich and Poor, when once the naked facts of their condition have come into collision, cannot long subsist together on a mere Poor-law. True enough:—and yet, human beings cannot be left to die! Scotland too, till something better come, must have a Poor-law, if Scotland is not to be a byword among the nations. O, what a waste is there; of noble and thrice-noble national virtues; peasant Stoicisms, Heroisms; valiant manful habits, soul of a Nation's worth,—which all the metal of Potosi [2] cannot purchase back; to which the metal of Potosi, and all you can buy with *it,* is dross and dust!

Why dwell on this aspect of the matter? It is too indisputable, not doubtful now to any one. Descend where you will into the lower class, in Town or Country, by what avenue you will, by Factory Inquiries, Agricultural Inquiries, by Revenue Returns, by Mining-Labourer Committees, by opening your own eyes and looking, the same sorrowful result discloses itself: you have to admit that the working body of this rich English Nation has sunk or is fast sinking into a state, to which, all sides of it considered, there was literally never any parallel. At Stockport Assizes,—and this too has no reference to the present state of trade, being of date prior to that,—a Mother and a Father are arraigned and found guilty of poisoning three of their children, to defraud a "burial-society" of some *3l.8s.* due on the death of each child: they are arraigned, found guilty; and the official authorities, it is whispered, hint that perhaps the case is not solitary, that perhaps you had better not probe farther into that department of things. This is in the autumn of 1841; the crime itself is of the previous year or season. "Brutal savages, degraded Irish," mutters the idle reader of Newspapers; hardly lingering on this incident. Yet it is an incident worth lingering on; the depravity, savagery and degraded Irishism being never so well admitted. In the British land, a human Mother and Father, of white skin and professing the Christian religion, had done this thing; they, with their Irishism and necessity and savagery, had been driven to do it. Such instances are like the highest mountain apex emerged into view; under which lies a whole mountain region and land, not yet emerged. A human Mother and Father had said to themselves, What shall we do to escape starvation? We are deep sunk here, in our dark cellar; and help is far.—Yes, in the Ugolino [3] Hunger-tower stern things happen; best-loved little Gaddo fallen dead on his Father's knees!—The Stockport Mother and Father think and hint: Our poor little starveling Tom, who cries all day for victuals, who will see only evil and not good in this world: if he were out of misery at once; he well dead, and the rest of us perhaps kept alive? It is thought, and hinted; at last it is done. And now Tom being killed, and all

---

2. Potosi: Bolivian city located on one of the world's richest deposits of silver.

3. Ugolino: in Dante's *Divine Comedy* (Inferno), Ugolino is shown gnawing the head of his political enemy, the Archbishop Ruggieri, who had imprisoned Ugolino in a tower with his small sons. After his sons had died of starvation, Ugolino's "hunger overcame [his] grief."

spent and eaten, Is it poor little starveling Jack that must go, or poor little starveling Will?—What an inquiry of ways and means!

In starved sieged cities, in the uttermost doomed ruin of old Jerusalem fallen under the wrath of God, it was prophesied and said, "The hands of the pitiful women have sodden their own children." The stern Hebrew imagination could conceive no blacker gulf of wretchedness; that was the ultimatum of degraded god-punished man. And we here, in modern England, exuberant with supply of all kinds, besieged by nothing if it be not by invisible Enchantments, are we reaching that?——How come these things? Wherefore are they, wherefore should they be?

Nor are they of the St. Ives workhouses, of the Glasgow lanes, and Stockport cellars, the only unblessed among us. This successful industry of England, with its plethoric wealth, has as yet made nobody rich; it is an enchanted wealth, and belongs yet to nobody. We might ask, Which of us has it enriched? We can spend thousands where we once spent hundreds; but can purchase nothing good with them. In Poor and Rich, instead of noble thrift and plenty, there is idle luxury alternating with mean scarcity and inability. We have sumptuous garnitures for our Life, but have forgotten to *live* in the middle of them. It is an enchanted wealth; no man of us can yet touch it. The class of men who feel that they are truly better off by means of it, let them give us their name!

Many men eat finer cookery, drink dearer liquors,—with what advantage they can report, and their Doctors can: but in the heart of them, if we go out of the dyspeptic stomach, what increase of blessedness is there? Are they better, beautifuller, stronger, braver? Are they even what they call "happier?" Do they look with satisfaction on more things and human faces in this God's-Earth; do more things and human faces look with satisfaction on them? Not so. Human faces gloom discordantly, disloyally on one another. Things, if it be not mere cotton and iron things, are growing disobedient to man. The Master Worker is enchanted, for the present, like his Workhouse Workman; clamours, in vain hitherto, for a very simple sort of "Liberty": the liberty "to buy where he finds it cheapest, to sell where he finds it dearest." With guineas jingling in every pocket, he was no whit richer; but now, the very guineas threatening to vanish, he feels that he is poor indeed. Poor Master Worker! And the Master Unworker, is not he in a still fataller situation? Pausing amid his game-preserves, with awful eye,—as he well may! Coercing fifty-pound tenants; coercing, bribing, cajoling; doing what he likes with his own. His mouth full of loud futilities, and arguments to prove the excellence of his Corn-law; and in his heart the blackest misgiving, a desperate half-consciousness that his excellent Corn-law is *in*defensible, that his loud arguments for it are of a kind to strike men too literally *dumb*.

To whom, then, is this wealth of England wealth? Who is it that it blesses; makes happier, wiser, beautifuller, in any way better? Who has got hold of it, to make it fetch and carry for him, like a true servant, not like a false mock-servant; to do him any real service whatsoever? As yet no one. We have more riches than any Nation ever had before; we have less good of them than any Nation ever had before. Our successful industry is hitherto unsuccessful; a strange success, if we stop here! In the midst of plethoric plenty, the people perish; with gold walls, and full barns, no man feels himself safe or satisfied.

Workers, Master Workers, Unworkers, all men, come to a pause; stand fixed, and cannot farther. Fatal paralysis spreading inwards, from the extremities, in St. Ives workhouses, in Stockport cellars, through all limbs, as if towards the heart itself. Have we actually got enchanted, then; accursed by some god?—

Midas longed for gold, and insulted the Olympians. He got gold, so that whatsoever he touched became gold,—and he, with his long ears, was little the better for it. Midas had misjudged the celestial music-tones; Midas had insulted Apollo and the gods: the gods gave him his wish, and a pair of long ears, which also were a good appendage to it. What a truth in these old Fables!

*

Gospel of Mammonism

Reader, even Christian Reader as thy title goes, hast thou any notion of Heaven and Hell? I rather apprehend, not. Often as the words are on our tongue, they have got a fabulous or semi-fabulous character for most of us, and pass on like a kind of transient similitude, like a sound signifying little.

Yet it is well worth while for us to know, once and always, that they are not a similitude, nor a fable nor semi-fable; that they are an everlasting highest fact! "No Lake of Sicilian or other sulphur burns now anywhere in these ages," sayest thou? Well, and if there did not! Believe that there does not; believe it if thou wilt, nay hold by it as a real increase, a rise to higher stages, to wider horizons and empires. All this has vanished, or has not vanished; believe as thou wilt as to all this. But that an Infinite of Practical Importance, speaking with strict arithmetical exactness, an *Infinite,* has vanished or can vanish from the Life of any Man: this thou shalt not believe! O brother, the Infinite of Terror, of Hope, of Pity, did it not at any moment disclose itself to thee, indubitable, unnameable? Came it never, like the gleam of *preter*-natural eternal Oceans, like the voice of old Eternities, far-sounding through thy heart of hearts? Never? Alas, it was not thy Liberalism then; it was thy Animalism! The Infinite is more sure than any other fact. But only men can discern it; mere building beavers, spinning arachnes, much more the predatory vulturous and vulpine species, do not discern it well!—

"The word Hell," says Sauerteig,[1] "is still frequently in use among the English People: but I could not without difficulty ascertain what they meant by it. Hell generally signifies the Infinite Terror, the thing a man *is* infinitely afraid of, and shudders and shrinks from, struggling with his whole soul to escape from it. There is a Hell therefore, if you will consider, which accompanies man, in all stages of his history, and religious or other development: but the Hells of men and Peoples differ notably. With Christians it is the infinite terror of being found guilty before the Just Judge. With old Romans, I conjecture, it was the terror not of Pluto, for whom probably they cared little,

---

1. Sauerteig: Carlyle's fictional persona; literally, sourdough, used to leaven or ferment a mass of dough.

but of doing unworthily, doing unvirtuously, which was their word for un-*man*fully. And now what is it, if you pierce through his Cants, his oft-repeated Hearsays, what he calls his Worships and so forth,—what is it that the modern English soul does, in very truth, dread infinitely, and contemplate with entire despair? What *is* his Hell; after all these reputable, oft-repeated Hearsays, what is it? With hesitation, with astonishment, I pronounce it to be: The terror of 'Not succeeding'; of not making money, fame, or some other figure in the world,—chiefly of not making money! Is not that a somewhat singular Hell?"

Yes, O Sauerteig, it is very singular. If we do not "succeed," where is the use of us? We had better never have been born. "Tremble intensely," as our friend the Emperor of China says: *there* is the black Bottomless of Terror; what Sauerteig calls the "Hell of the English!"—But indeed this Hell belongs naturally to the Gospel of Mammonism, which also has its corresponding Heaven. For there *is* one Reality among so many Phantasms; about one thing we are entirely in earnest: The making of money. Working Mammonism does divide the world with idle game-preserving Dilettantism:—thank Heaven that there is even a Mammonism, *any*thing we are in earnest about! Idleness is worst, Idleness alone is without hope: work earnestly at anything, you will by degrees learn to work at almost all things. There is endless hope in work, were it even work at making money.

True, it must be owned, we for the present, with our Mammon-Gospel, have come to strange conclusions. We call it a Society; and go about professing openly the totalest separation, isolation. Our life is not a mutual helpfulness; but rather, cloaked under due laws-of-war, named "fair competition" and so forth, it is a mutual hostility. We have profoundly forgotten everywhere that *Cash-payment* is not the sole relation of human beings; we think, nothing doubting, that *it* absolves and liquidates all engagements of man. "My starving workers?" answers the rich Mill-owner: "Did not I hire them fairly in the market? Did I not pay them, to the last sixpence, the sum covenanted for? What have I to do with them more?"—Verily Mammon-worship is a melancholy creed. When Cain, for his own behoof, had killed Abel, and was questioned, "Where is thy brother?" he too made answer, "Am I my brother's keeper?" Did I not pay my brother *his* wages, the thing he had merited from me?

O sumptuous Merchant-Prince, illustrious game-preserving Duke, is there no way of "killing" thy brother but Cain's rude way! "A good man by the very look of him, by his very presence with us as a fellow wayfarer in this Life-pilgrimage, *promises* so much": wo to him if he forget all such promises, if he never know that they were given! To a deadened soul, seared with the brute Idolatry of Sense, to whom going to Hell is equivalent to not making money, all "promises," and moral duties, that cannot be pleaded for in Courts of Requests, address themselves in vain. Money he can be ordered to pay, but nothing more. I have not heard in all Past History, and expect not to hear in all Future History, of any Society anywhere under God's Heaven supporting itself on such Philosophy. The Universe is not made so; it is made otherwise than so. The man or nation of men that thinks it is made so, marches forward nothing doubting, step after step; but marches—whither we know! In these last two centuries of Atheistic Government (near two centuries now, since the blessed restoration of his Sacred Majesty, and Defender of the Faith, Charles Second), I reckon that we have pretty well exhausted what of "firm earth" there was for us to march on;—and are now, very ominously, shuddering, reeling, and let us hope trying to recoil, on the cliff's edge!—

For out of this that we call Atheism come so many other *isms* and falsities, each falsity with its misery at its heels!—A SOUL is not like wind (*spiritus,* or breath) contained within a capsule; the ALMIGHTY MAKER is not like a Clockmaker that once, in old immemorial ages, having *made* his Horologe of a Universe, sits ever since and sees it go! Not at all. Hence comes Atheism; come, as we say, many other *isms;* and as the sum of all, comes Valetism, the *reverse* of Heroism; sad root of all woes whatsoever. For indeed, as no man ever saw the above-said wind-element enclosed within its capsule, and finds it at bottom more deniable than conceivable; so too he finds, in spite of Bridgewater Bequests, your Clockmaker Almighty an entirely questionable affair, a deniable affair;—and accordingly denies it, and along with it so much else. Alas, one knows not what and how much else! For the faith in an Invisible, Unnameable, Godlike, present everywhere in all that we see and work and suffer, is the essence of all faith whatsoever; and that once denied, or still worse, asserted with lips only, and out of bound prayerbooks only, what other thing remains believable? That Cant well-ordered is marketable Cant; that Heroism means gas-lighted Histrionism; that seen with "clear eyes" (as they call Valet-eyes), no man is a Hero, or ever was a Hero, but all men are Valets and Varlets. The accursed practical quintessence of all sorts of Unbelief! For if there be now no Hero, and the Histrio himself begin to be seen into, what hope is there for the seed of Adam here below? We are the doomed everlasting prey of the Quack; who, now in this guise, now in that, is to filch us, to pluck and eat us, by such modes as are convenient for him. For the modes and guises I care little. The Quack once inevitable, let him come swiftly, let him pluck and eat me;—swiftly, that I may at least have done with him; for in his Quack-world I can have no wish to linger. Though he slay me, yet will I despise him. Though he conquer nations, and have all the Flunkeys of the Universe shouting at his heels, yet will I know well that *he* is an Inanity; that for him and his there is no continuance appointed, save only in Gehenna and the Pool. Alas, the Atheist world, from its utmost summits of Heaven and Westminster Hall, downwards through poor seven-feet Hats and "Unveracities fallen hungry," down to the lowest cellars and neglected hunger-dens of it, is very wretched.

One of Dr. Alison's Scotch facts struck us much.* A poor Irish Widow, her husband having died in one of the Lanes of Edinburgh, went forth with her three children, bare of all resource, to solicit help from the Charitable Establishments of that City. At this Charitable Establishment and then at that she was refused; referred from one to the other, helped by none;—till she had exhausted them all; till her strength and heart failed her: she sank down in typhus-fever; died, and infected her Lane with fever, so that "seventeen other persons" died of fever there in consequence. The humane Physician asks thereupon, as with a heart too full for speaking, Would it not have been

---

* Observations on the Management of the Poor in Scotland: By William Pulteney Alison, M.D. (Edinburgh, 1840). [Carlyle's note.]

economy to help this poor Widow? She took typhus-fever, and killed seventeen of you!—Very curious. The forlorn Irish Widow applies to her fellow-creatures, as if saying, "Behold I am sinking, bare of help: ye must help me! I am your sister, bone of your bone; one God made us: ye must help me!" They answer, "No; impossible: thou art no sister of ours." But she proves her sisterhood; her typhus-fever kills *them:* they actually were her brothers, though denying it! Had man ever to go lower for a proof?

For, as indeed was very natural in such case, all government of the Poor by the Rich has long ago been given over to Supply-and-demand, Laissez-faire and such like, and universally declared to be "impossible." "You are no sister of ours; what shadow of proof is there? Here are our parchments, our padlocks, proving indisputably our money-safes to be *ours,* and you to have no business with them. Depart! It is impossible!"—Nay, what wouldst thou thyself have us do? cry indignant readers. Nothing, my friends,—till you have got a soul for yourselves again. Till then all things are "impossible." Till then I cannot even bid you buy, as the old Spartans would have done, two-pence worth of powder and lead, and compendiously shoot to death this poor Irish Widow: even that is "impossible" for you. Nothing is left but that she prove her sisterhood by dying, and infecting you with typhus. Seventeen of you lying dead will not deny such proof that she *was* flesh of your flesh; and perhaps some of the living may lay it to heart.

"Impossible": of a certain two-legged animal with feathers, it is said if you draw a distinct chalk-circle round him, he sits imprisoned, as if girt with the iron ring of Fate; and will die there, though within sight of victuals,—or sit in sick misery there, and be fatted to death. The name of this poor two-legged animal is—Goose; and they make of him, when well fattened, *Pâté de foie gras,* much prized by some!

KARL MARX (1818–1883) AND
FREDERICK ENGELS (1820–1895),
Manifesto of the Communist Party

The Communist Manifesto of 1848 appeared during the kind of struggle whose origin it was the purpose of the document to explain. Since 1789 the revolutionary experience of France had dominated European politics, so that when the French king, Louis Philippe—representative of the wealthiest industrial and financial interests—was deposed in 1848, it seemed to Marx and Engels that "once again the signal had gone forth for general revolutionary change." "Moreover," wrote Engels, "when the Paris upheaval found its echo in the victorious insurrections in Vienna, Milan, and Berlin; when the whole of Europe right up to the Russian frontier was swept into the movement; . . . for us, under the circumstances of the time, there could be no doubt that the great decisive struggle had broken out . . . [and] that it could only end in the final victory of the proletariat." Although such optimism was premature, and the continental movements of 1848 were soon crushed, revolutionary socialism became from this time a significant force in international political life.

Marx and Engels formed their lifelong friendship in Paris in 1844. After the failure of the 1848 revolution they settled in London, where they devoted themselves to research, writing, and organizing the international working class. Despite some financial support from Engels (whose father was a wealthy manufacturer), Marx lived in poverty, finding occasional work as a newspaper correspondent.

Commissioned by the newly founded Communist League as a statement of its theoretical and practical aims, the Manifesto is polemic at its best. The argument is unusually tight and dense; the tone often indignant or ironic; yet there is no sacrifice of clarity or precision in the exposition of the nature of class struggle.

A spectre is haunting Europe—the spectre of Communism. All the Powers of old Europe have entered into a holy alliance to exorcise this spectre: Pope and Czar, Metternich and Guizot, French Radicals and German police-spies.

Where is the party in opposition that has not been decried as Communistic by its opponents in power? Where the Opposition that has not hurled back the branding reproach of Communism, against the more advanced opposition parties, as well as against its reactionary adversaries?

Two things result from this fact.

I. Communism is already acknowledged by all European Powers to be itself a Power.

II. It is high time that Communists should openly, in the face of the whole world, publish their views, their aims, their tendencies, and meet this nursery tale of the Spectre of Communism with a Manifesto of the party itself.

To this end, Communists of various nationalities have assembled in London, and sketched the following Manifesto, to be published in the English, French, German, Italian, Flemish and Danish languages.

I

BOURGEOIS AND PROLETARIANS [1]

The history of all hitherto existing society is the history of class struggles.

Freeman and slave, patrician and plebeian, lord and serf, guildmaster and journeyman, in a word, oppressor and oppressed, stood in constant opposition to one another, carried on an uninterrupted, now hidden, now open fight, a fight that each time ended, either in a revolutionary re-constitution of society at large, or in the common ruin of the contending classes.

In the earlier epochs of history, we find almost everywhere a complicated arrangement of society into various orders, a manifold gradation of social rank. In ancient Rome we have patricians, knights, plebeians, slaves; in the Middle Ages, feudal lords, vassals, guild-masters, journeymen, apprentices, serfs; in almost all of these classes, again, subordinate gradations.

The modern bourgeois society that has sprouted from the ruins of feudal society has not done away with class antagonisms. It has but established new classes, new conditions of oppression, new forms of struggle in place of the old ones.

Our epoch, the epoch of the bourgeoisie, possesses, however, this distinctive feature: it has simplified the class antagonisms. Society as a whole is more and more splitting up into two great hostile camps, into two great classes directly facing each other: Bourgeoisie and Proletariat.

From the serfs of the Middle Ages sprang the chartered burghers of the earliest towns. From these burgesses the first elements of the bourgeoisie were developed.

The discovery of America, the rounding of the Cape, opened up fresh ground for the rising bourgeoisie. The East-Indian and Chinese markets, the colonisation of America, trade with the colonies, the increase in the means of exchange and in commodities generally, gave to commerce, to navigation, to industry, an impulse never before known, and thereby, to the revolutionary element in the tottering feudal society, a rapid development.

The feudal system of industry, under which industrial production was monopolised by closed guilds, now no longer sufficed for the growing wants of the new markets. The manufacturing system took its place. The guild-masters

---

1. By bourgeoisie is meant the class of modern capitalists, owners of the means of social production and employers of wage-labour. By proletariat, the class of modern wage-labourers who, having no means of production of their own, are reduced to selling their labour-power in order to live. [*Note by Engels to the English edition of 1888.*]

were pushed on one side by the manufacturing middle class; division of labour between the different corporate guilds vanished in the face of division of labour in each single workshop.

Meantime the markets kept ever growing, the demand ever rising. Even manufacture no longer sufficed. Thereupon, steam and machinery revolutionised industrial production. The place of manufacture was taken by the giant, Modern Industry, the place of the industrial middle class, by industrial millionaires, the leaders of whole industrial armies, the modern bourgeois.

Modern industry has established the world-market, for which the discovery of America paved the way. This market has given an immense development to commerce, to navigation, to communication by land. This development has, in its turn, reacted on the extension of industry; and in proportion as industry, commerce, navigation, railways extended, in the same proportion the bourgeoisie developed, increased its capital,[2] and pushed into the background every class handed down from the Middle Ages.

We see, therefore, how the modern bourgeoisie is itself the product of a long course of development, of a series of revolutions in the modes of production and of exchange.

Each step in the development of the bourgeoisie was accompanied by a corresponding political advance of that class. An oppressed class under the sway of the feudal nobility, an armed and self-governing association in the mediaeval commune;[3] here independent urban republic (as in Italy and Germany), there taxable "third estate" of the monarchy (as in France), afterwards, in the period of manufacture proper, serving either the semi-feudal or the absolute monarchy as a counterpoise against the nobility, and, in fact, corner-stone of the great monarchies in general, the bourgeoisie has at last, since the establishment of Modern Industry and of the world-market, conquered for itself, in the modern representative State, exclusive political sway. The executive of the modern State is but a committee for managing the common affairs of the whole bourgeoisie.

The bourgeoisie, historically, has played a most revolutionary part.

The bourgeoisie, wherever it has got the upper hand, has put an end to all feudal, patriarchal, idyllic relations. It has pitilessly torn asunder the motley feudal ties that bound man to his "natural superiors," and has left remaining no other nexus between man and man than naked self-interest, than callous "cash payment." It has drowned the most heavenly ecstasies of religious fervour, of chivalrous enthusiasm, of philistine sentimentalism, in the icy water of egotistical calculation. It has resolved personal worth into exchange value, and in place of the numberless indefeasible chartered freedoms, has set up that single, unconscionable freedom—Free Trade. In one word, for exploitation veiled by religious and political illusions, it has substituted naked, shameless, direct, brutal exploitation.

The bourgeoisie has stripped of its halo every occupation hitherto honoured and looked up to with reverent awe. It has converted the physician, the

---

2. Capital: materials, machines, or money that generates profit for the owner through another's labor.

3. This was the name given their urban communities by the townsmen of Italy and France, after they had purchased or wrested their initial rights of self-government from their feudal lords. [*Note by Engels to the German edition of 1890.*]

lawyer, the priest, the poet, the man of science, into its paid wage-labourers.

The bourgeoisie has torn away from the family its sentimental veil, and has reduced the family relation to a mere money relation.

The bourgeoisie has disclosed how it came to pass that the brutal display of vigour in the Middle Ages, which Reactionists so much admire, found its fitting complement in the most slothful indolence. It has been the first to show what man's activity can bring about. It has accomplished wonders far surpassing Egyptian pyramids, Roman aqueducts, and Gothic cathedrals; it has conducted expeditions that put in the shade all former Exoduses of nations and crusades.

The bourgeoisie cannot exist without constantly revolutionising the instruments of production, and thereby the relations of production, and with them the whole relations of society. Conservation of the old modes of production in unaltered form, was, on the contrary, the first condition of existence for all earlier industrial classes. Constant revolutionising of production, uninterrupted disturbance of all social conditions, everlasting uncertainty and agitation distinguish the bourgeois epoch from all earlier ones. All fixed, fast-frozen relations, with their train of ancient and venerable prejudices and opinions, are swept away, all newformed ones become antiquated before they can ossify. All that is solid melts into air, all that is holy is profaned, and man is at last compelled to face with sober senses, his real conditions of life, and his relations with his kind.

The need of a constantly expanding market for its products chases the bourgeoisie over the whole surface of the globe. It must nestle everywhere, settle everywhere, establish connexions everywhere.

The bourgeoisie has through its exploitation of the world-market given a cosmopolitan character to production and consumption in every country. To the great chagrin of Reactionists, it has drawn from under the feet of industry the national ground on which it stood. All old-established national industries have been destroyed or are daily being destroyed. They are dislodged by new industries, whose introduction becomes a life and death question for all civilised nations, by industries that no longer work up indigenous raw material, but raw material drawn from the remotest zones; industries whose products are consumed, not only at home, but in every quarter of the globe. In place of the old wants, satisfied by the productions of the country, we find new wants, requiring for their satisfaction the products of distant lands and climes. In place of the old local and national seclusion and self-sufficiency, we have intercourse in every direction, universal inter-dependence of nations. And as in material, so also in intellectual production. The intellectual creations of individual nations become common property. National one-sidedness and narrow-mindedness become more and more impossible, and from the numerous national and local literatures, there arises a world literature.

The bourgeoisie, by the rapid improvement of all instruments of production, by the immensely facilitated means of communication, draws all, even the most barbarian, nations into civilisation. The cheap prices of its commodities are the heavy artillery with which it batters down all Chinese walls, with which it forces the barbarians' intensely obstinate hatred of foreigners to capitulate. It compels all nations, on pain of extinction, to adopt the bourgeois mode of production; it compels them to introduce what it calls civilisation into their midst, *i.e.,* to become bourgeois themselves. In one word, it creates a world after its own image.

The bourgeoisie has subjected the country to the rule of the towns. It has created enormous cities, has greatly increased the urban population as compared with the rural, and has thus rescued a considerable part of the population from the idiocy of rural life. Just as it has made the country dependent on the towns, so it has made barbarian and semi-barbarian countries dependent on the civilised ones, nations of peasants on nations of bourgeois, the East on the West.

The bourgeoisie keeps more and more doing away with the scattered state of the population, of the means of production, and of property. It has agglomerated population, centralised means of production, and has concentrated property in a few hands. The necessary consequence of this was political centralisation. Independent, or but loosely connected provinces, with separate interests, laws, governments and systems of taxation, become lumped together into one nation, with one government, one code of laws, one national classinterest, one frontier and one customs-tariff.

The bourgeoisie, during its rule of scarce one hundred years, has created more massive and more colossal productive forces than have all preceding generations together. Subjection of Nature's forces to man, machinery, application of chemistry to industry and agriculture, steam-navigation, railways, electric telegraphs, clearing of whole continents for cultivation, canalisation of rivers, whole populations conjured out of the ground—what earlier century had even a presentiment that such productive forces slumbered in the lap of social labour?

We see then: the means of production and of exchange, on whose foundation the bourgeoisie built itself up, were generated in feudal society. At a certain stage in the development of these means of production and of exchange, the conditions under which feudal society produced and exchanged, the feudal organisation of agriculture and manufacturing industry, in one word, the feudal relations of property became no longer compatible with the already developed productive forces; they became so many fetters. They had to be burst asunder; they were burst asunder.

Into their place stepped free competition, accompanied by a social and political constitution adapted to it, and by the economical and political sway of the bourgeois class.

A similar movement is going on before our own eyes. Modern bourgeois society with its relations of production, of exchange and of property, a society that has conjured up such gigantic means of production and of exchange, is like the sorcerer, who is no longer able to control the powers of the nether world whom he has called up by his spells. For many a decade past the history of industry and commerce is but the history of the revolt of modern productive forces against modern conditions of production, against the property relations that are the conditions for the existence of the bourgeoisie and of its rule. It is enough to mention the commercial crises that by their periodical return put on its trial, each time more threateningly, the existence of the entire bourgeois society. In these crises a great part not only of the existing products, but also of the previously created productive forces, are periodically destroyed. In these crises there breaks out an epidemic that, in all earlier epochs, would have seemed an absurdity—the epidemic of over-production. Society suddenly finds itself put back into a state of momentary barbarism; it appears as if a famine, a universal war of devastation had cut off the supply of every means of subsistence; industry and commerce seem to be destroyed; and why? Because there is too much civilisation, too much means of subsistence, too much industry, too much commerce. The productive forces at the disposal of society no longer tend to further the development of the conditions of bourgeois property; on the contrary, they have become too powerful for these conditions, by which they are fettered, and so soon as they overcome these fetters, they bring disorder into the whole of bourgeois society, endanger the existence of bourgeois property. The conditions of bourgeois society are too narrow to comprise the wealth created by them. And how does the bourgeoisie get over these crises? On the one hand by enforced destruction of a mass of productive forces; on the other, by the conquest of new markets, and by the more thorough exploitation of the old ones. That is to say, by paving the way for more extensive and more destructive crises, and by diminishing the means whereby crises are prevented.

The weapons with which the bourgeoisie felled feudalism to the ground are now turned against the bourgeoisie itself.

But not only has the bourgeoisie forged the weapons that bring death to itself; it has also called into existence the men who are to wield those weapons—the modern working class—the proletarians.

In proportion as the bourgeoisie, *i.e.,* capital, is developed, in the same proportion is the proletariat, the modern working class, developed—a class of labourers, who live only so long as they find work, and who find work only so long as their labour increases capital. These labourers, who must sell themselves piecemeal, are a commodity, like every other article of commerce, and are consequently exposed to all the vicissitudes of competition, to all the fluctuations of the market. . . .

Modern industry has converted the little workshop of the patriarchal master into the great factory of the industrial capitalist. Masses of labourers, crowded into the factory, are organised like soldiers. As privates of the industrial army they are placed under the command of a perfect hierarchy of officers and sergeants. Not only are they slaves of the bourgeois class, and of the bourgeois State; they are daily and hourly enslaved by the machine, by the overlooker, and, above all, by the individual bourgeois manufacturer himself. The more openly this despotism proclaims gain to be its end and aim, the more petty, the more hateful and the more embittering it is.

The less the skill and exertion of strength implied in manual labour, in other words, the more modern industry becomes developed, the more is the labour of men superseded by that of women. Differences of age and sex have no longer any distinctive social validity for the working class. All are instruments of labour, more or less expensive to use, according to their age and sex.

No sooner is the exploitation of the labourer by the manufacturer, so far, at an end, and he receives his wages in cash, than he is set upon by the other portions of the bourgeoisie, the landlord, the shopkeeper, the pawnbroker, etc.

The lower strata of the middle class—the small tradespeople, shopkeepers, and retired tradesmen generally, the handicraftsmen and peasants—all these sink gradually into the proletariat, partly because their diminutive capital does not suffice for the scale on which Modern Industry is carried on, and is swamped in the competition with the large capitalists, partly because their specialised skill is rendered worthless by new methods of production. Thus the proletariat is recruited from all classes of the population.

The proletariat goes through various stages of development. With its birth begins its struggle with the bourgeoisie. At first the contest is carried on by individual labourers, then by the workpeople of a factory, then by the operatives of one trade, in one locality, against the individual bourgeois who directly exploits them. They direct their attacks not against the bourgeois conditions of production, but against the instruments of production themselves; they destroy imported wares that compete with their labour, they smash to pieces machinery, they set factories ablaze, they seek to restore by force [4] the vanished status of the workman of the Middle Ages.

At this stage the labourers still form an incoherent mass scattered over the whole country, and broken up by their mutual competition. If anywhere they unite to form more compact bodies, this is not yet the consequence of their own active union, but of the union of the bourgeoisie, which class, in order to attain its own political ends, is compelled to set the whole proletariat in motion, and is moreover yet, for a time, able to do so. At this stage, therefore, the proletarians do not fight their enemies, but the enemies of their enemies, the remnants of absolute monarchy, the landowners, the non-industrial bourgeois, the petty bourgeoisie. Thus the whole historical movement is concentrated in the hands of the bourgeoisie; every victory so obtained is a victory for the bourgeoisie.

But with the development of industry the proletariat not only increases in number; it becomes concentrated in greater masses, its strength grows, and it feels that strength more. The various interests and conditions of life within the ranks of the proletariat are more and more equalised, in proportion as machinery obliterates all distinctions of labour, and nearly everywhere reduces wages to the same low level. The growing competition among the bourgeois, and the resulting commercial crises, make the wages of the workers ever more fluctuating. The unceasing improvement of machinery, ever more rapidly developing, makes their livelihood more and more precarious; the collisions between individual workmen and individual bourgeois take more and more the character of collisions between two classes. Thereupon the workers begin to form combinations (Trades' Unions) against the bourgeois; they club together in order to keep up the rate of wages; they found permanent associations in order to make provision beforehand for these occasional revolts. Here and there the contest breaks out into riots.

Now and then the workers are victorious, but only for a time. The real fruit of their battles lies, not in the immediate result, but in the ever-expanding union of the workers. This union is helped on by the improved means of communication that are created by modern industry and that place the workers of different localities in contact with one another. It was just this contact

---

4. Restore by force: all this had in fact been done, especially in England, by industrial and agricultural workers, in both spontaneous and organized movements.

that was needed to centralise the numerous local struggles, all of the same character, into one national struggle between classes. But every class struggle is a political struggle. And that union, to attain which the burghers of the Middle Ages, with their miserable highways, required centuries, the modern proletarians, thanks to railways, achieve in a few years.

This organisation of the proletarians into a class, and consequently into a political party, is continually being upset again by the competition between the workers themselves. But it ever rises up again, stronger, firmer, mightier. It compels legislative recognition of particular interests of the workers, by taking advantage of the divisions among the bourgeoisie itself. Thus the ten-hours' bill [5] in England was carried.

Altogether collisions between the classes of the old society further, in many ways, the course of development of the proletariat. The bourgeoisie finds itself involved in a constant battle. At first with the aristocracy; later on, with those portions of the bourgeoisie itself, whose interests have become antagonistic to the progress of industry; at all times, with the bourgeoisie of foreign countries. In all these battles it sees itself compelled to appeal to the proletariat, to ask for its help, and thus, to drag it into the political arena. The bourgeoisie itself, therefore, supplies the proletariat with its own elements of political and general education, in other words, it furnishes the proletariat with weapons for fighting the bourgeoisie.

Further, as we have already seen, entire sections of the ruling classes are, by the advance of industry, precipitated into the proletariat, or are at least threatened in their conditions of existence. These also supply the proletariat with fresh elements of enlightenment and progress.

Finally, in times when the class struggle nears the decisive hour, the process of dissolution going on within the ruling class, in fact within the whole range of old society, assumes such a violent, glaring character, that a small section of the ruling class cuts itself adrift, and joins the revolutionary class, the class that holds the future in its hands. Just as, therefore, at an earlier period, a section of the nobility went over to the bourgeoisie, so now a portion of the bourgeoisie goes over to the proletariat, and in particular, a portion of the bourgeois ideologists, who have raised themselves to the level of comprehending theoretically the historical movement as a whole.

Of all the classes that stand face to face with the bourgeoisie today, the proletariat alone is a really revolutionary class. The other classes decay and finally disappear in the face of Modern Industry; the proletariat is its special and essential product.

The lower middle class, the small manufacturer, the shopkeeper, the artisan, the peasant, all these fight against the bourgeoisie, to save from extinction their existence as fractions of the middle class. They are therefore not revolutionary, but conservative. Nay more, they are reactionary, for they try to roll back the wheel of history. If by chance they are revolutionary, they are so only in view of their impending transfer into the proletariat, they thus defend not their present, but their future interests, they desert their own standpoint to place themselves at that of the proletariat.

---

5. Ten-hours' bill: passed in 1847, after thirty years of intensive agitation, the bill limited the working day to ten hours for women and children. Sixteen hours in the mills and mines had not been uncommon until then.

The "dangerous class," the social scum, that passively rotting mass thrown off by the lowest layers of old society, may, here and there, be swept into the movement by a proletarian revolution; its conditions of life, however, prepare it far more for the part of a bribed tool of reactionary intrigue.

In the conditions of the proletariat, those of old society at large are already virtually swamped. The proletarian is without property; his relation to his wife and children has no longer anything in common with the bourgeois family-relations; modern industrial labour, modern subjection to capital, the same in England as in France, in America as in Germany, has stripped him of every trace of national character. Law, morality, religion, are to him so many bourgeois prejudices, behind which lurk in ambush just as many bourgeois interests.

All the preceding classes that got the upper hand, sought to fortify their already acquired status by subjecting society at large to their conditions of appropriation. The proletarians cannot become masters of the productive forces of society, except by abolishing their own previous mode of appropriation, and thereby also every other previous mode of appropriation. They have nothing of their own to secure and to fortify; their mission is to destroy all previous securities for, and insurances of, individual property.

All previous historical movements were movements of minorities, or in the interests of minorities. The proletarian movement is the self-conscious, independent movement of the immense majority, in the interests of the immense majority. The proletariat, the lowest stratum of our present society, cannot stir, cannot raise itself up, without the whole superincumbent strata of official society being sprung into the air.

Though not in substance, yet in form, the struggle of the proletariat with the bourgeoisie is at first a national struggle. The proletariat of each country must, of course, first of all settle matters with its own bourgeoisie.

In depicting the most general phases of the development of the proletariat, we traced the more or less veiled civil war, raging within existing society, up to the point where that war breaks out into open revolution, and where the violent overthrow of the bourgeoisie lays the foundation for the sway of the proletariat.

Hitherto, every form of society has been based, as we have already seen, on the antagonism of oppressing and oppressed classes. But in order to oppress a class, certain conditions must be assured to it under which it can, at least, continue its slavish existence. The serf, in the period of serfdom, raised himself to membership in the commune, just as the petty bourgeois, under the yoke of feudal absolutism, managed to develop into a bourgeois. The modern labourer, on the contrary, instead of rising with the progress of industry, sinks deeper and deeper below the conditions of existence of his own class. He becomes a pauper, and pauperism develops more rapidly than population and wealth. And here it becomes evident, that the bourgeoisie is unfit any longer to be the ruling class in society, and to impose its conditions of existence upon society as an over-riding law. It is unfit to rule because it is incompetent to assure an existence to its slave within his slavery, because it cannot help letting him sink into such a state, that it has to feed him, instead of being fed by him. Society can no longer live under this bourgeoisie, in other words, its existence is no longer compatible with society.

The essential condition for the existence, and for the sway of the bourgeois class, is the formation and augmentation of capital; the condition for capital is wage-labour. Wage-labour rests exclusively on competition between the labourers. The advance of industry, whose involuntary promoter is the bourgeoisie, replaces the isolation of the labourers, due to competition, by their revolutionary combination, due to association. The development of Modern Industry, therefore, cuts from under its feet the very foundation on which the bourgeoisie produces and appropriates products. What the bourgeoisie, therefore, produces, above all, is its own grave-diggers. Its fall and the victory of the proletariat are equally inevitable.

II

PROLETARIANS AND COMMUNISTS

In what relation do the Communists stand to the proletarians as a whole?

The Communists do not form a separate party opposed to other working-class parties.

They have no interests separate and apart from those of the proletariat as a whole.

They do not set up any sectarian principles of their own, by which to shape and mould the proletarian movement.

The Communists are distinguished from the other working-class parties by this only: (1) In the national struggles of the proletarians of the different countries, they point out and bring to the front the common interests of the entire proletariat, independently of all nationality. (2) In the various stages of development which the struggle of the working class against the bourgeoisie has to pass through, they always and everywhere represent the interests of the movement as a whole.

The Communists, therefore, are on the one hand, practically, the most advanced and resolute section of the working-class parties of every country, that section which pushes forward all others; on the other hand, theoretically, they have over the great mass of the proletariat the advantage of clearly understanding the line of march, the conditions, and the ultimate general results of the proletarian movement.

The immediate aim of the Communists is the same as that of all the other proletarian parties: formation of the proletariat into a class, overthrow of the bourgeois supremacy, conquest of political power by the proletariat.

The theoretical conclusions of the Communists are in no way based on ideas or principles that have been invented, or discovered, by this or that would-be universal reformer.

They merely express, in general terms, actual relations springing from an existing class struggle, from a historical movement going on under our very eyes. The abolition of existing property relations is not at all a distinctive feature of Communism.

All property relations in the past have continually been subject to historical change consequent upon the change in historical conditions.

The French Revolution, for example, abolished feudal property in favour of bourgeois property.

The distinguishing feature of Communism is not the abolition of property generally, but the abolition of bourgeois property. But modern bourgeois private property is the final and most complete expression of the system of producing and appropriating products, that is based on class antagonisms, on the exploitation of the many by the few.

In this sense, the theory of the Communists may be summed up in the single sentence: Abolition of private property.

We Communists have been reproached with the desire of abolishing the right of personally acquiring property as the fruit of a man's own labour, which property is alleged to be the groundwork of all personal freedom, activity and independence.

Hard-won, self-acquired, self-earned property! Do you mean the property of the petty artisan and of the small peasant, a form of property that preceded the bourgeois form? There is no need to abolish that; the development of industry has to a great extent already destroyed it, and is still destroying it daily.

Or do you mean modern bourgeois private property?

But does wage-labour create any property for the labourer? Not a bit. It creates capital, *i.e.,* that kind of property which exploits wage-labour, and which cannot increase except upon condition of begetting a new supply of wage-labour for fresh exploitation. Property, in its present form, is based on the antagonism of capital and wage-labour. Let us examine both sides of this antagonism.

To be a capitalist, is to have not only a purely personal, but a social *status* in production. Capital is a collective product, and only by the united action of many members, nay, in the last resort, only by the united action of all members of society, can it be set in motion.

Capital is, therefore, not a personal, it is a social power.

When, therefore, capital is converted into common property, into the property of all members of society, personal property is not thereby transformed into social property. It is only the social character of the property that is changed. It loses its class-character.

Let us now take wage-labour.

The average price of wage-labour is the minimum wage, *i.e.,* that quantum of the means of subsistence, which is absolutely requisite to keep the labourer in bare existence as a labourer. What, therefore, the wage-labourer appropriates by means of his labour, merely suffices to prolong and reproduce a bare existence. We by no means intend to abolish this personal appropriation of the products of labour, an appropriation that is made for the maintenance and reproduction of human life, and that leaves no surplus wherewith to command the labour of others. All that we want to do away with, is the miserable character of this appropriation, under which the labourer lives merely to increase capital, and is allowed to live only in so far as the interest of the ruling class requires it.

In bourgeois society, living labour is but a means to increase accumulated labour. In Communist society, accumulated labour is but a means to widen, to enrich, to promote the existence of the labourer.

In bourgeois society, therefore, the past dominates the present; in Communist society, the present dominates the past. In bourgeois society capital is independent and has individuality, while the living person is dependent and has no individuality.

And the abolition of this state of things is called by the bourgeois, abolition of individuality and freedom! And rightly so. The abolition of bourgeois individuality, bourgeois independence, and bourgeois freedom is undoubtedly aimed at.

By freedom is meant, under the present bourgeois conditions of production, free trade, free selling and buying.

But if selling and buying disappears, free selling and buying disappears also. This talk about free selling and buying, and all the other "brave words" of our bourgeoisie about freedom in general, have a meaning, if any, only in contrast with restricted selling and buying, with the fettered traders of the Middle Ages, but have no meaning when opposed to the Communistic abolition of buying and selling, of the bourgeois conditions of production, and of the bourgeoisie itself.

You are horrified at our intending to do away with private property. But in your existing society, private property is already done away with for nine-tenths of the population; its existence for the few is solely due to its non-existence in the hands of those nine-tenths. You reproach us, therefore, with intending to do away with a form of property, the necessary condition for whose existence is the non-existence of any property for the immense majority of society.

In one word, you reproach us with intending to do away with your property. Precisely so; that is just what we intend.

From the moment when labour can no longer be converted into capital, money, or rent, into a social power capable of being monopolised, *i.e.,* from the moment when individual property can no longer be transformed into bourgeois property, into capital, from that moment, you say, individuality vanishes.

You must, therefore, confess that by "individual" you mean no other person than the bourgeois, than the middle-class owner of property. This person must, indeed, be swept out of the way, and made impossible.

Communism deprives no man of the power to appropriate the products of society; all that it does is to deprive him of the power to subjugate the labour of others by means of such appropriation.

It has been objected that upon the abolition of private property all work will cease, and universal laziness will overtake us.

According to this, bourgeois society ought long ago to have gone to the dogs through sheer idleness; for those of its members who work, acquire nothing, and those who acquire anything, do not work. The whole of this objection is but another expression of the tautology: that there can no longer be any wage-labour when there is no longer any capital.

All objections urged against the Communistic mode of producing and appropriating material products, have, in the same way, been urged against the Communistic modes of producing and appropriating intellectual products. Just as, to the bourgeois, the disappearance of class property is the disappearance of production itself, so the disappearance of class culture is to him identical with the disappearance of all culture.

That culture, the loss of which he laments, is, for the enormous majority, a mere training to act as a machine.

But don't wrangle with us so long as you apply, to our intended abolition of bourgeois property, the standard of your bourgeois notions of freedom, culture, law, etc. Your very ideas are but the outgrowth of the conditions of your bourgeois production and bourgeois property, just as your jurisprudence is but the will of your class made into a law for all, a will, whose essential character and direction are determined by the economical conditions of existence of your class.

The selfish misconception that induces you to transform into eternal laws of nature and of reason, the social forms springing from your present mode of production and form of property—historical relations that rise and disappear in the progress of production—this misconception you share with every ruling class that has preceded you. What you see clearly in the case of ancient property, what you admit in the case of feudal property, you are of course forbidden to admit in the case of your own bourgeois form of property.

Abolition of the family! Even the most radical flare up at this infamous proposal of the Communists.

On what foundation is the present family, the bourgeois family, based? On capital, on private gain. In its completely developed form this family exists only among the bourgeoisie. But this state of things finds its complement in the practical absence of the family among the proletarians, and in public prostitution.

The bourgeois family will vanish as a matter of course when its complement vanishes, and both will vanish with the vanishing of capital.

Do you charge us with wanting to stop the exploitation of children by their parents? To this crime we plead guilty.

But, you will say, we destroy the most hallowed of relations, when we replace home education by social.

And your education! Is not that also social, and determined by the social conditions under which you educate, by the intervention, direct or indirect, of society, by means of schools, &c.? The Communists have not invented the intervention of society in education; they do but seek to alter the character of that intervention, and to rescue education from the influence of the ruling class.

The bourgeois clap-trap about the family and education, about the hallowed co-relation of parent and child, becomes all the more disgusting, the more, by the action of Modern Industry, all family ties among the proletarians are torn asunder, and their children transformed into simple articles of commerce and instruments of labour.

But you Communists would introduce community of women, screams the whole bourgeoisie in chorus.

The bourgeois sees in his wife a mere instrument of production. He hears that the instruments of production are to be exploited in common, and, naturally, can come to no other conclusion than that the lot of being common to all will likewise fall to the women.

He has not even a suspicion that the real point aimed at is to do away with the status of women as mere instruments of production.

For the rest, nothing is more ridiculous than the virtuous indignation of our bourgeois at the community of women which, they pretend, is to be openly and officially established by the Communists. The Communists have no need to introduce community of women; it has existed almost from time immemorial.

Our bourgeois, not content with having the wives and daughters of their proletarians at their disposal, not to speak of common prostitutes, take the greatest pleasure in seducing each other's wives.

Bourgeois marriage is in reality a system of wives in common and thus, at the most, what the Communists might possibly be reproached with, is that they desire to introduce, in substitution for a hypocritically concealed, an openly legalised community of women. For the rest, it is self-evident that the abolition of the present system of production must bring with it the abolition of the community of women [6] springing from that system, *i.e.,* of prostitution both public and private.

The Communists are further reproached with desiring to abolish countries and nationality.

The working men have no country. We cannot take from them what they have not got. Since the proletariat must first of all acquire political supremacy, must rise to be the leading class of the nation, must constitute itself *the* nation, it is, so far, itself national, though not in the bourgeois sense of the word.

National differences and antagonisms between peoples are daily more and more vanishing, owing to the development of the bourgeoisie, to freedom of commerce, to the world-market, to uniformity in the mode of production and in the conditions of life corresponding thereto.

The supremacy of the proletariat will cause them to vanish still faster. United action, of the leading civilised countries at least, is one of the first conditions for the emancipation of the proletariat.

In proportion as the exploitation of one individual by another is put an end to, the exploitation of one nation by another will also be put an end to. In proportion as the antagonism between classes within the nation vanishes, the hostility of one nation to another will come to an end.

The charges against Communism made from a religious, a philosophical, and, generally, from an ideological standpoint, are not deserving of serious examination.

Does it require deep intuition to comprehend that man's ideas, views and conceptions, in one word, man's consciousness, changes with every change in the conditions of his material existence, in his social relations and in his social life?

What else does the history of ideas prove, than that intellectual production changes its character in proportion as material production is changed? The ruling ideas of each age have ever been the ideas of its ruling class.

When people speak of ideas that revolutionise society, they do but express the fact, that within the old society, the elements of a new one have been created, and that the dissolution of the old ideas keeps even pace with the dissolution of the old conditions of existence.

When the ancient world was in its last throes, the ancient religions were overcome by Christianity. When Christian ideas succumbed in the 18th cen-

---

6. Community of women: in fact both Marx and Engels believed in monogamy and were opposed to community of women or universal free love, which they considered exploitive and dehumanizing. See Marx, *Economic and Philosophic Manuscripts* ("Crude Communism") and Engels, *The Origin of the Family, Private Property, and the State* ("The Monogamous Family").

tury to rationalist ideas, feudal society fought its death battle with the then revolutionary bourgeoisie. The ideas of religious liberty and freedom of conscience merely gave expression to the sway of free competition within the domain of knowledge. . . .

The Communist revolution is the most radical rupture with traditional property relations; no wonder that its development involves the most radical rupture with traditional ideas.

But let us have done with the bourgeois objections to Communism.

We have seen above, that the first step in the revolution by the working class, is to raise the proletariat to the position of ruling class, to win the battle of democracy.

The proletariat will use its political supremacy to wrest, by degrees, all capital from the bourgeoisie, to centralise all instruments of production in the hands of the State, *i.e.,* of the proletariat organised as the ruling class; and to increase the total of productive forces as rapidly as possible.

Of course, in the beginning, this cannot be effected except by means of despotic inroads on the rights of property, and on the conditions of bourgeois production; by means of measures, therefore, which appear economically insufficient and untenable, but which, in the course of the movement, outstrip themselves, necessitate further inroads upon the old social order, and are unavoidable as a means of entirely revolutionising the mode of production.

These measures will of course be different in different countries.

Nevertheless in the most advanced countries, the following will be pretty generally applicable.

1. Abolition of property in land and application of all rents of land to public purposes.

2. A heavy progressive or graduated income tax.

3. Abolition of all right of inheritance.

4. Confiscation of the property of all emigrants and rebels.

5. Centralisation of credit in the hands of the State, by means of a national bank with State capital and an exclusive monopoly.

6. Centralisation of the means of communication and transport in the hands of the State.

7. Extension of factories and instruments of production owned by the State; the bringing into cultivation of waste-lands, and the improvement of the soil generally in accordance with a common plan.

8. Equal liability of all to labour. Establishment of industrial armies, especially for agriculture.

9. Combination of agriculture with manufacturing industries; gradual abolition of the distinction between town and country, by a more equable distribution of the population over the country.

10. Free education fo all children in public schools. Abolition of children's factory labour in its present form. Combination of education with industrial production, &c., &c.

When, in the course of development, class distinctions have disappeared, and all production has been concentrated in the hands of a vast association of the whole nation, the public power will lose its political character. Political power, properly so called, is merely the organized power of one class for oppressing another. If the proletariat during its contest with the bourgeoisie is compelled, by the force of circumstances, to organise itself as a class, if, by means of a revolution, it makes itself the ruling class, and, as such, sweeps away by force the old conditions of production, then it will, along with these conditions, have swept away the conditions for the existence of class antagonisms and of classes generally, and will thereby have abolished its own supremacy as a class.

In place of the old bourgeois society, with its classes and class antagonisms, we shall have an association, in which the free development of each is the condition for the free development of all. . . .

IV

Position of the Communists in Relation to the Various Existing Opposition Parties

Section II has made clear the relations of the Communists to the existing working-class parties, such as the Chartists in England and the Agrarian Reformers in America.

The Communists fight for the attainment of the immediate aims, for the enforcement of the momentary interests of the working class; but in the movement of the present, they also represent and take care of the future of that movement. In France the Communists ally themselves with the Social-Democrats, against the conservative and radical bourgeoisie, reserving, however, the right to take up a critical position in regard to phrases and illusions traditionally handed down from the great Revolution.

In Switzerland they support the Radicals, without losing sight of the fact that this party consists of antagonistic elements, partly of Democratic Socialists, in the French sense, partly of radical bourgeois.

In Poland they support the party that insists on an agrarian revolution as the prime condition for national emancipation, that party which fomented the insurrection of Cracow in 1846.

In Germany they fight with the bourgeoisie whenever it acts in a revolutionary way, against the absolute monarchy, the feudal squirearchy, and the petty bourgeoisie.

But they never cease, for a single instant, to instil into the working class the clearest possible recognition of the hostile antagonism between bourgeoisie and proletariat, in order that the German workers may straightway use, as so many weapons against the bourgeoisie, the social and political conditions that the bourgeoisie must necessarily introduce along with its supremacy, and in order that, after the fall of the reactionary classes in Germany, the fight against the bourgeoisie itself may immediately begin.

The Communists turn their attention chiefly to Germany, because that country is on the eve of a bourgeois revolution that is bound to be carried out under more advanced conditions of European civilisation, and with a much more developed proletariat, than that of England was in the seventeenth, and of France in the eighteenth century, because the bourgeois revolution in Germany will be but the prelude to an immediately following proletarian revolution.

In short, the Communists everywhere support every revolutionary movement against the existing social and political order of things.

In all these movements they bring to the front, as the leading question in each, the property question, no matter what its degree of development at the time.

Finally, they labour everywhere for the union and agreement of the democratic parties of all countries.

The Communists disdain to conceal their views and aims. They openly declare that their ends can be attained only by the forcible overthrow of all existing social conditions. Let the ruling classes tremble at a Communistic revolution. The proletarians have nothing to lose but their chains. They have a world to win.

WORKING MEN OF ALL COUNTRIES UNITE!

HENRY DAVID THOREAU (1817–1862), *A Plea for Captain John Brown*

Thoreau, the Concord naturalist and author, is usually thought of as the apostle of passive resistance. He was jailed for refusing to pay taxes in protest against slavery and the expansionist war with Mexico; his famous essay "On the Duty of Civil Disobedience" (1848) influenced the strategy of such leaders as Mohandas Gandhi and Martin Luther King. Yet even in "Civil Disobedience" Thoreau reaffirms the right to revolution, noting that "when oppression and robbery are organized . . . it is not too soon for honest men to rebel and revolutionize."

The abolitionist John Brown was, in Thoreau's view, an honest man who thought it time to "rebel and revolutionize." He did so in Pennsylvania, where he kept a station on the Underground Railroad that helped slaves to escape north; he did so in Kansas, where with his men he killed a group of southern terrorists who wanted Kansas to enter the Union as a slave state; he did so at Harpers' Ferry, where his band attempted to capture a U.S. arsenal in order to provide arms for slaves. The attempt failed. Thoreau's "Plea" (1859), delivered as a lecture before the citizens of Concord while Brown was still in jail, defends the man as well as the action; it argues ad hominem *because Brown's personal life, moral character, and politics were inseparable. The plea is a funeral oration for a man about to die. In method, intention, and effect it may be compared with Che Guevara's brief eulogy of Camilo.*

I trust that you will pardon me for being here. I do not wish to force my thoughts upon you, but I feel forced myself. Little as I know of Captain Brown, I would fain do my part to correct the tone and the statements of the newspapers, and of my countrymen generally, respecting his character and actions. It costs us nothing to be just. We can at least express our sympathy with, and admiration of, him and his companions, and that is what I now propose to do.

First, as to his history. I will endeavor to omit, as much as possible, what you have already read. I need not describe his person to you, for probably most of you have seen and will not soon forget him. I am told that his grandfather, John Brown, was an officer in the Revolution; that he himself was

born in Connecticut about the beginning of this century, but early went with
his father to Ohio. I heard him say that his father was a contractor who furnished beef to the army there, in the war of 1812; that he accompanied him
to the camp, and assisted him in that employment, seeing a good deal of military life,—more, perhaps, than if he had been a soldier; for he was often present at the councils of the officers. Especially, he learned by experience how
armies are supplied and maintained in the field,—a work which, he observed,
requires at least as much experience and skill as to lead them in battle. He
said that few persons had any conception of the cost, even the pecuniary cost,
of firing a single bullet in war. He saw enough, at any rate, to disgust him
with a military life; indeed, to excite in him a great abhorrence of it; so much
so, that though he was tempted by the offer of some petty office in the army,
when he was about eighteen, he not only declined that, but he also refused to
train when warned, and was fined for it. He then resolved that he would
never have anything to do with any war, unless it were a war for liberty.

When the troubles in Kansas began, he sent several of his sons thither to
strengthen the party of the Free State men, fitting them out with such weapons as he had; telling them that if the troubles should increase, and there
should be need of him, he would follow, to assist them with his hand and
counsel. This, as you all know, he soon after did; and it was through his
agency, far more than any other's, that Kansas was made free.

For a part of his life he was a surveyor, and at one time he was engaged
in wool-growing, and he went to Europe as an agent about that business.
There, as everywhere, he had his eyes about him, and made many original
observations. He said, for instance, that he saw why the soil of England was
so rich, and that of Germany (I think it was) so poor, and he thought of writing to some of the crowned heads about it. It was because in England the
peasantry live on the soil which they cultivate, but in Germany they are gathered into villages at night. It is a pity that he did not make a book of his observations.

I should say that he was an old-fashioned man in his respect for the Constitution, and his faith in the permanence of this Union. Slavery he deemed to
be wholly opposed to these, and he was its determined foe.

He was by descent and birth a New England farmer, a man of great
common sense, deliberate and practical as that class is, and tenfold more so.
He was like the best of those who stood at Concord Bridge once, on Lexing-
ton Common, and on Bunker Hill, only he was firmer and higher principled
than any that I have chanced to hear of as there. It was no abolition lecturer
that converted him. Ethan Allen [1] and Stark, with whom he may in some respects be compared, were rangers in a lower and less important field. They
could bravely face their country's foes, but he had the courage to face his
country herself when she was in the wrong. A Western writer says, to account
for his escape from so many perils, that he was concealed under a "rural ex-
terior"; as if, in that prairie land, a hero should, by good rights, wear a citizen's dress only.

He did not go to the college called Harvard, good old Alma Mater as she

---

1. Ethan Allen, independent military leader in the American revolution. John Stark
was another New England soldier known for his daring and courage.

is. He was not fed on the pap that is there furnished. As he phrased it, "I know no more of grammar than one of your calves." But he went to the great university of the West, where he sedulously pursued the study of Liberty, for which he had early betrayed a fondness, and having taken many degrees, he finally commenced the public practice of Humanity in Kansas, as you all know. Such were *his humanities,* and not any study of grammar. He would have left a Greek accent slanting the wrong way, and righted up a falling man.

He was one of that class of whom we hear a great deal, but, for the most part, see nothing at all,—the Puritans. It would be in vain to kill him. He died lately in the time of Cromwell, but he reappeared here. Why should he not? Some of the Puritan stock are said to have come over and settled in New England. They were a class that did something else than celebrate their forefathers' day, and eat parched corn in remembrance of that time. They were neither Democrats nor Republicans, but men of simple habits, straightforward, prayerful; not thinking much of rulers who did not fear God, not making many compromises, nor seeking after available candidates.

"In his camp," as one has recently written, and as I have myself heard him state, "he permitted no profanity; no man of loose morals was suffered to remain there, unless, indeed, as a prisoner of war. 'I would rather,' said he, 'have the small-pox, yellow fever, and cholera, all together in my camp, than a man without principle. . . . It is a mistake, sir, that our people make, when they think that bullies are the best fighters, or that they are the fit men to oppose these Southerners. Give me men of good principles,—God-fearing men,—men who respect themselves, and with a dozen of them I will oppose any hundred such men as these Buford ruffians.' " He said that if one offered himself to be a soldier under him, who was forward to tell what he could or would do if he could only get sight of the enemy, he had but little confidence in him.

He was never able to find more than a score or so of recruits whom he would accept, and only about a dozen, among them his sons, in whom he had perfect faith. When he was here some years ago, he showed to a few a little manuscript book,—his "orderly book" I think he called it,—containing the names of his company in Kansas, and the rules by which they bound themselves; and he stated that several of them had already sealed the contract with their blood. When some one remarked that, with the addition of a chaplain, it would have been a perfect Cromwellian troop, he observed that he would have been glad to add a chaplain to the list, if he could have found one who could fill that office worthily. It is easy enough to find one for the United States army. I believe that he had prayers in his camp morning and evening, nevertheless.

He was a man of Spartan habits, and at sixty was scrupulous about his diet at your table excusing himself by saying that he must eat sparingly and fare hard, as became a soldier, or one who was fitting himself for difficult enterprises, a life of exposure.

A man of rare common sense and directness of speech, as of action; a transcendentalist above all, a man of ideas and principles,—that was what distinguished him. Not yielding to a whim or transient impulse, but carrying out the purpose of a life. I noticed that he did not overstate anything, but spoke within bounds. I remember, particularly, how, in his speech here, he referred to what his family had suffered in Kansas, without ever giving the least vent to his pent-up fire. It was a volcano with an ordinary chimney-flue. Also referring to the deeds of certain Border Ruffians, he said, rapidly paring away his speech, like an experienced soldier, keeping a reserve of force and meaning, "They had a perfect right to be hung." He was not in the least a rhetorician, was not talking to Buncombe [2] or his constituents anywhere, had no need to invent anything but to tell the simple truth, and communicate his own resolution; therefore he appeared incomparably strong, and eloquence in Congress and elsewhere seemed to me at a discount. It was like the speeches of Cromwell compared with those of an ordinary king.

As for his tact and prudence, I will merely say, that at a time when scarcely a man from the Free States was able to reach Kansas by any direct route, at least without having his arms taken from him, he, carrying what imperfect guns and other weapons he could collect, openly and slowly drove an ox-cart through Missouri, apparently in the capacity of a surveyor, with his surveying compass exposed in it, and so passed unsuspected, and had ample opportunity to learn the designs of the enemy. For some time after his arrival he still followed the same profession. When, for instance, he saw a knot of the ruffians on the prairie, discussing, of course, the single topic which then occupied their minds, he would, perhaps, take his compass and one of his sons, and proceed to run an imaginary line right through the very spot on which that conclave had assembled, and when he came up to them, he would naturally pause and have some talk with them, learning their news, and, at last, all their plans perfectly; and having thus completed his real survey he would resume his imaginary one, and run on his line till he was out of sight.

When I expressed surprise that he could live in Kansas at all, with a price set upon his head, and so large a number, including the authorities, exasperated against him, he accounted for it by saying, "It is perfectly well understood that I will not be taken." Much of the time for some years he has had to skulk in swamps, suffering from poverty and from sickness, which was the consequence of exposure, befriended only by Indians and a few whites. But though it might be known that he was lurking in a particular swamp, his foes commonly did not care to go in after him. He could even come out into a town where there were more Border Ruffians than Free State men, and transact some business, without delaying long, and yet not be molested; for, said he, "no little handful of men were willing to undertake it, and a large body could not be got together in season."

As for his recent failure, we do not know the facts about it. It was evidently far from being a wild and desperate attempt. His enemy, Mr. Vallandigham,[3] is compelled to say that "it was among the best planned and executed conspiracies that ever failed."

Not to mention his other successes, was it a failure, or did it show a want of good management, to deliver from bondage a dozen human beings, and

2. Buncombe: a county in North Carolina, whose representative in Congress spoke long and often, "not to the house, but to Buncombe." Hence, any speech made simply to please a constituency.

3. Vallandigham, Clement L., congressman from Ohio and sympathizer with the southern cause.

walk off with them by broad daylight, for weeks if not months, at a leisurely pace, through one State after another, for half the length of the North, conspicuous to all parties, with a price set upon his head, going into a court-room on his way and telling what he had done, thus convincing Missouri that it was not profitable to try to hold slaves in his neighborhood?—and this, not because the government menials were lenient, but because they were afraid of him.

Yet he did not attribute his success, foolishly, to "his star," or to any magic. He said, truly, that the reason why such greatly superior numbers quailed before him was, as one of his prisoners confessed, because they *lacked a cause,*—a kind of armor which he and his party never lacked. When the time came, few men were found willing to lay down their lives in defense of what they knew to be wrong; they did not like that this should be their last act in this world.

But to make haste to *his* last act, and its effects.

The newspapers seem to ignore, or perhaps are really ignorant, of the fact that there are at least as many as two or three individuals to a town throughout the North who think much as the present speaker does about him and his enterprise. I do not hesitate to say that they are an important and growing party. We aspire to be something more than stupid and timid chattels, pretending to read history and our Bibles, but desecrating every house and every day we breathe in. Perhaps anxious politicians may prove that only seventeen white men and five negroes were concerned in the late enterprise; but their very anxiety to prove this might suggest to themselves that all is not told. Why do they still dodge the truth? They are so anxious because of a dim consciousness of the fact, which they do not distinctly face, that at least a million of the free inhabitants of the United States would have rejoiced if it had succeeded. They at most only criticise the tactics. Though we wear no crape, the thought of that man's position and probable fate is spoiling many a man's day here at the North for other thinking. If any one who has seen him here can pursue successfully any other train of thought, I do not know what he is made of. If there is any such who gets his usual allowance of sleep, I will warrant him to fatten easily under any circumstances which do not touch his body or purse. I put a piece of paper and a pencil under my pillow, and when I could not sleep I wrote in the dark.

On the whole, my respect for my fellow-men, except as one may outweigh a million, is not being increased these days. I have noticed the cold-blooded way in which newspaper writers and men generally speak of this event, as if an ordinary malefactor, though one of unusual "pluck,"—as the Governor of Virginia is reported to have said, using the language of the cock-pit, "the gamest man he ever saw,"—had been caught, and were about to be hung. He was not dreaming of his foes when the governor thought he looked so brave. It turns what sweetness I have to gall, to hear, or hear of, the remarks of some of my neighbors. When we heard at first that he was dead, one of my townsmen observed that "he died as the fool dieth;" which, pardon me, for an instant suggested a likeness in him dying to my neighbor living. Others, craven-hearted, said disparagingly, that "he threw his life away," because he resisted the government. Which way have they thrown *their* lives, pray?— such as would praise a man for attacking singly an ordinary band of thieves or murderers. I hear another ask, Yankee-like, "What will he gain by it?" as if he expected to fill his pockets by this enterprise. Such a one has no idea of gain but in this worldly sense. If it does not lead to a "surprise" party, if he does not get a new pair of boots, or a vote of thanks, it must be a failure. "But he won't gain anything by it."

Well, no, I don't suppose he could get four-and-sixpence a day for being hung, take the year round; but then he stands a chance to save a considerable part of his soul,—and *such* a soul!—when *you* do not. No doubt you can get more in your market for a quart of milk than for a quart of blood, but that is not the market that heroes carry their blood to.

Such do not know that like the seed is the fruit, and that, in the moral world, when good seed is planted, good fruit is inevitable, and does not depend on our watering and cultivating; that when you plant, or bury, a hero in his field, a crop of heroes is sure to spring up. This is a seed of such force and vitality, that it does not ask our leave to germinate.

The momentary charge at Balaklava, in obedience to a blundering command, proving what a perfect machine the soldier is, has, properly enough, been celebrated by a poet laureate;[4] but the steady, and for the most part successful, charge of this man, for some years, against the legions of Slavery, in obedience to an infinitely higher command, is as much more memorable than that as an intelligent and conscientious man is superior to a machine. Do you think that that will go unsung?

"Served him right,"—"A dangerous man,"—"He is undoubtedly insane." So they proceed to live their sane, and wise, and altogether admirable lives, reading their Plutarch a little, but chiefly pausing at that feat of Putnam,[5] who was let down into a wolf's den; and in this wise they nourish themselves for brave and patriotic deeds some time or other. The Tract Society could afford to print that story of Putnam. You might open the district schools with the reading of it, for there is nothing about Slavery or the Church in it; unless it occurs to the reader that some pastors are *wolves* in sheep's clothing. "The American Board of Commissioners for Foreign Missions," even, might dare to protest against *that* wolf. I have heard of boards, and of American boards, but it chances that I never heard of this particular lumber till lately. And yet I hear of Northern men, and women, and children, by families, buying a "life-membership" in societies as these. A life-membership in the grave! You can get buried cheaper than that.

Our foes are in our midst and all about us. There is hardly a house but is divided against itself, for our foe is the all but universal woodenness of both head and heart, the want of vitality in man, which is the effect of our vice; and hence are begotten fear, superstition, bigotry, persecution, and slavery of all kinds. We are mere figure-heads upon a hulk, with livers in the place of hearts. The curse is the worship of idols, which at length changes the worshiper into a stone image himself; and the New Englander is just as much an idolater as the Hindoo. This man was an exception, for he did not set up even a political graven image between him and his God.

---

4. Poet laureate: Alfred Lord Tennyson, who commemorated this episode of the Crimean War in "The Charge of the Light Brigade." The poem contains the famous lines, "Theirs not to reason why, / Theirs but to do and die."

5. Putnam: Israel Putnam, American revolutionary fighter. The story of the wolf was often told to illustrate his courage.

A church that can never have done with excommunicating Christ while it exists! Away with your broad and flat churches, and your narrow and tall churches! Take a step forward, and invent a new style of out-houses. Invent a salt that will save you, and defend our nostrils.

The modern Christian is a man who has consented to say all the prayers in the liturgy, provided you will let him go straight to bed and sleep quietly afterward. All his prayers begin with "Now I lay me down to sleep," and he is forever looking forward to the time when he shall go to his *"long* rest." He has consented to perform certain old-established charities, too, after a fashion, but he does not wish to hear of any new-fangled ones; he doesn't wish to have any supplementary articles added to the contract, to fit it to the present time. He shows the whites of his eyes on the Sabbath, and the blacks all the rest of the week. The evil is not merely a stagnation of blood, but a stagnation of spirit. Many, no doubt, are well disposed, but sluggish by constitution and by habit, and they cannot conceive of a man who is actuated by higher motives than they are. Accordingly they pronounce this man insane, for they know that *they* could never act as he does, as long as they are themselves.

We dream of foreign countries, of other times and races of men, placing them at a distance in history or space; but let some significant event like the present occur in our midst, and we discover, often, this distance and this strangeness between us and our nearest neighbors. *They* are our Austrias, and Chinas, and South Sea Islands. Our crowded society becomes well spaced all at once, clean and handsome to the eye,—a city of magnificent distances. We discover why it was that we never got beyond compliments and surfaces with them before; we become aware of as many versts between us and them as there are between a wandering Tartar and a Chinese town. The thoughtful man becomes a hermit in the thoroughfares of the market-place. Impassable seas suddenly find their level between us, or dumb steppes stretch themselves out there. It is the difference of constitution, of intelligence, and faith, and not streams and mountains, that make the true and impassable boundaries between individuals and between states. None but the like-minded can come plenipotentiary to our court.

I read all the newspapers I could get within a week after this event, and I do not remember in them a single expression of sympathy for these men. I have since seen one noble statement, in a Boston paper, not editorial. Some voluminous sheets decided not to print the full report of Brown's words to the exclusion of other matter. It was as if a publisher should reject the manuscript of the New Testament, and print Wilson's last speech. The same journal which contained this pregnant news was chiefly filled, in parallel columns, with the reports of the political conventions that were being held. But the descent to them was too steep. They should have been spared this contrast,—been printed in an extra, at least. To turn from the voices and deeds of earnest men to the *cackling* of political conventions! Office-seekers and speech-makers, who do not so much as lay an honest egg, but wear their breasts bare upon an egg of chalk! Their great game is the game of straws, or rather that universal aboriginal game of the platter, at which the Indians cried *hub, bub!* Exclude the reports of religious and political conventions, and publish the words of a living man.

But I object not so much to what they have omitted as to what they have inserted. Even the *Liberator* [6] called it "a misguided, wild, and apparently insane effort." As for the herd of newspapers and magazines, I do not chance to know an editor in the country who will deliberately print anything which he knows will ultimately and permanently reduce the number of his subscribers. They do not believe that it would be expedient. How then can they print truth? If we do not say pleasant things, they argue, nobody will attend to us. And so they do like some traveling aucioneers, who sing an obscene song, in order to draw a crowd around them. Republican editors, obliged to get their sentences ready for the morning edition, and accustomed to look at everything by the twilight of politics, express no admiration, nor true sorrow even, but call these men "deluded fanatics,"—"mistaken men," —"insane," or "crazed." It suggests what a *sane* set of editors we are blessed with, *not* "mistaken men"; who know very well on which side their bread is buttered, at least.

A man does a brave and humane deed, and at once, on all sides, we hear people and parties declaring, "I didn't do it, nor countenance *him* to do it, in any conceivable way. It can't be fairly inferred from my past career." I, for one, am not interested to hear you define your position. I don't know that I ever was or ever shall be. I think it is mere egotism, or impertinent at this time. Ye needn't take so much pains to wash your skirts of him. No intelligent man will ever be convinced that he was any creature of yours. He went and came, as he himself informs us, "under the auspices of John Brown and nobody else." The Republican party does not perceive how many his *failure* will make to vote more correctly than they would have them. They have counted the votes of Pennsylvania & Co., but they have not correctly counted Captain Brown's vote. He has taken the wind out of their sails,—the little wind they had,—and they may as well lie to and repair.

What though he did not belong to your clique! Though you may not approve of his method or his principles, recognize his magnanimity. Would you not like to claim kindredship with him in that, though in no other thing he is like, or likely, to you? Do you think that you would lose your reputation so? What you lost at the spile, you would gain at the bung.

If they do not mean all this, then they do not speak the truth, and say what they mean. They are simply at their old tricks still.

"It was always conceded to him," *says one who calls him crazy,* "that he was a conscientious man, very modest in his demeanor, apparently inoffensive, until the subject of Slavery was introduced, when he would exhibit a feeling of indignation unparalleled."

The slave-ship is on her way, crowded with its dying victims; new cargoes are being added in mid-ocean; a small crew of slaveholders, countenanced by a large body of passengers, is smothering four millions under the hatches, and yet the politician asserts that the only proper way by which deliverance is to be obtained is by "the quiet diffusion of the sentiments of humanity," without any "outbreak." As if the sentiments of humanity were ever found unaccompanied by its deeds, and you could disperse them, all finished to order, the pure article, as easily as water with a watering-pot, and so lay the dust. What is

---

6. *Liberator:* William Lloyd Garrison's abolitionist newspaper. Garrison believed in persuasion, not force, as a way of ending slavery.

that that I hear cast overboard? The bodies of the dead that have found deliverance. That is the way we are "diffusing" humanity, and its sentiments with it.

Prominent and influential editors, accustomed to deal with politicians, men of an infinitely lower grade, say, in their ignorance, that he acted "on the principle of revenge." They do not know the man. They must enlarge themselves to conceive of him. I have no doubt that the time will come when they will begin to see him as he was. They have got to conceive of a man of faith and of religious principle, and not a politician or an Indian; of a man who did not wait till he was personally interfered with or thwarted in some harmless business before he gave his life to the cause of the oppressed.

If Walker may be considered the representative of the South, I wish I could say that Brown was the representative of the North. He was a superior man. He did not value his bodily life in comparison with ideal things. He did not recognize unjust human laws, but resisted them as he was bid. For once we are lifted out of the trivialness and dust of politics into the region of truth and manhood. No man in America has ever stood up so persistently and effectively for the dignity of human nature, knowing himself for a man, and the equal of any and all governments. In that sense he was the most American of us all. He needed no babbling lawyer, making false issues, to defend him. He was more than a match for all the judges that American voters, or office-holders of whatever grade, can create. He could not have been tried by a jury of his peers, because his peers did not exist. When a man stands up serenely against the condemnation and vengeance of mankind, rising above them literally *by a whole body*,—even though he were of late the vilest murderer, who has settled that matter with himself,—the spectacle is a sublime one,—didn't ye know it, ye *Liberators,* ye *Tribunes,* ye *Republicans?*—and we become criminal in comparison. Do yourselves the honor to recognize him. He needs none of your respect.

As for the Democratic journals, they are not human enough to affect me at all. I do not feel indignation at anything they may say.

I am aware that I anticipate a little,—that he was still, at the last accounts, alive in the hands of his foes; but that being the case, I have all along found myself thinking and speaking of him as physically dead.

I do not believe in erecting statues to those who still live in our hearts, whose bones have not yet crumbled in the earth around us, but I would rather see the statue of Captain Brown in the Massachusetts State-House yard than that of any other man whom I know. I rejoice that I live in this age, that I am his contemporary.

What a contrast, when we turn to that political party which is so anxiously shuffling him and his plot out of its way, and looking around for some available slaveholder, perhaps, to be its candidate, at least for one who will execute the Fugitive Slave Law, and all those other unjust laws which he took up arms to annul!

Insane! A father and six sons, and one son-in-law, and several more men besides,—as many at least as twelve disciples,—all struck with insanity at once; while the sane tyrant holds with a firmer grip than ever his four millions of slaves, and a thousand sane editors, his abettors, are saving their country and their bacon! Just as insane were his efforts in Kansas. Ask the tyrant who is his most dangerous foe, the sane man or the insane? Do the thousands who know him best, who have rejoiced at his deeds in Kansas, and have afforded him material aid there, think him insane? Such a use of this word is a mere trope with most who persist in using it, and I have no doubt that many of the rest have already in silence retracted their words.

Read his admirable answers to Mason and others. How they are dwarfed and defeated by the contrast! On the one side, half-brutish, half-timid questioning; on the other, truth, clear as lightning, crashing into their obscene temples. They are made to stand with Pilate, and Gessler, and the Inquisition. How ineffectual their speech and action! and what a void their silence! They are but helpless tools in this great work. It was no human power that gathered them about this preacher.

What have Massachusetts and the North sent a few *sane* representatives to Congress for, of late years?—to declare with effect what kind of sentiments? All their speeches put together and boiled down—and probably they themselves will confess it—do not match for manly directness and force, and for simple truth, the few casual remarks of crazy John Brown on the floor of the Harper's Ferry engine-house,—that man whom you are about to hang, to send to the other world, though not to represent *you* there. No, he was not our representative in any sense. He was too fair a specimen of a man to represent the like of us. Who, then, *were* his constituents? If you read his words understandingly you will find out. In his case there is no idle eloquence, no made, nor maiden speech, no compliments to the oppressor. Truth is his inspirer, and earnestness the polisher of his sentences. He could afford to lose his Sharps rifles, while he retained his faculty of speech,—a Sharps rifle of infinitely surer and longer range.

And the New York *Herald* reports the conversation *verbatim!* It does not know of what undying words it is made the vehicle.

I have no respect for the penetration of any man who can read the report of that conversation and still call the principal in it insane. It has the ring of a saner sanity than an ordinary discipline and habits of life, than an ordinary organization, secure. Take any sentence of it,—"Any questions that I can honorably answer, I will; not otherwise. So far as I am myself concerned, I have told everything truthfully. I value my word, sir." The few who talk about his vindictive spirit, while they really admire his heroism, have no test by which to detect a noble man, no amalgam to combine with his pure gold. They mix their own dross with it.

It is a relief to turn from these slanders to the testimony of his more truthful, but frightened jailers and hangmen. Governor Wise speaks far more justly and appreciatingly of him than any Northern editor, or politician, or public personage, that I chance to have heard from. I know that you can afford to hear him again on this subject. He says: "They are themselves mistaken who take him to be a madman. . . . He is cool, collected, and indomitable, and it is but just to him to say that he was humane to his prisoners. . . . And he inspired me with great trust in his integrity as a man of truth. He is a fanatic, vain and garrulous" (I leave that part to Mr. Wise), "but firm, truthful, and intelligent. His men, too, who survive, are like him. . . . Colonel Washington says that he was the coolest and firmest man he ever saw in defying danger and death. With one son dead by his side, and another shot through, he felt the pulse of his dying son with one hand, and held his rifle with the other, and commanded his men with the utmost composure, encouraging them to be firm, and to sell their lives as dear as they could. Of the three white prisoners, Brown, Stevens, and Coppoc, it was hard to say which was most firm."

Almost the first Northern men whom the slaveholder has learned to respect!

The testimony of Mr. Vallandigham, though less valuable, is of the same purport, that "it is vain to underrate either the man or his conspiracy. . . . He is the farthest possible removed from the ordinary ruffian, fanatic, or madman."

"All is quiet at Harper's Ferry," say the journals. What is the character of that calm which follows when the law and the slaveholder prevail? I regard this event as a touchstone designed to bring out, with glaring distinctness, the character of this government. We needed to be thus assisted to see it by the light of history. It needed to see itself. When a government puts forth its strength on the side of injustice, as ours to maintain slavery and kill the liberators of the slave, it reveals itself a merely brute force, or worse, a demoniacal force. It is the head of the Plug-Uglies. It is more manifest than ever that tyranny rules. I see this government to be effectually allied with France and Austria in oppressing mankind. There sits a tyrant holding fettered four millions of slaves; here comes their heroic liberator. This most hypocritical and diabolical government looks up from its seat on the gasping four millions, and inquires with an assumption of innocence: "What do you assault me for? Am I not an honest man? Cease agitation on this subject, or I will make a slave of you, too, or else hang you."

We talk about a *representative* government; but what a monster of a government is that where the noblest faculties of the mind, and the *whole* heart, are not *represented*. A semi-human tiger or ox, stalking over the earth, with its heart taken out and the top of its brain shot away. Heroes have fought well on their stumps when their legs were shot off, but I never heard of any good done by such a government as that.

The only government that I recognize—and it matters not how few are at the head of it, or how small its army—is that power that establishes justice in the land, never that which establishes injustice. What shall we think of a government to which all the truly brave and just men in the land are enemies, standing between it and those whom it oppresses? A government that pretends to be Christian and crucifies a million Christs every day!

Treason! Where does such treason take its rise? I cannot help thinking of you as you deserve, ye governments. Can you dry up the fountains of thought? High treason, when it is resistance to tyranny here below, has its origin in, and is first committed by, the power that makes and forever recreates man. When you have caught and hung all these human rebels, you have accomplished nothing but your own guilt, for you have not struck at the fountainhead. You presume to contend with a foe against whom West Point cadets and rifled cannon *point* not. Can all the art of the cannon founder tempt matter to turn against its maker? Is the form in which the founder thinks he casts it more essential than the constitution of it and of himself?

The United States have a coffle of four millions of slaves. They are determined to keep them in this condition; and Massachusetts is one of the confederated overseers to prevent their escape. Such are not all the inhabitants of Massachusetts, but such are they who rule and are obeyed here. It was Massachusetts, as well as Virginia, that put down this insurrection at Harper's Ferry. She sent the marines there, and she will have *to pay the penalty of her sin.*

Suppose that there is a society in this State that out of its own purse and magnanimity saves all the fugitive slaves that run to us, and protects our colored fellow-citizens, and leaves the other work to the government, so called. Is not that government fast losing its occupation, and becoming contemptible to mankind? If private men are obliged to perform the offices of government, to protect the weak and dispense justice, then the government becomes only a hired man, or clerk, to perform menial or indifferent services. Of course, that is but the shadow of a government whose existence necessitates a Vigilant Committee. What should we think of the Oriental Cadi even, behind whom worked in secret a Vigilant Committee? But such is the character of our Northern States generally; each has its Vigilant Committee. And, to a certain extent, these crazy governments recognize and accept this relation. They say, virtually, "We'll be glad to work for you on these terms, only don't make a noise about it." And thus the government, its salary being insured, withdraws into the back shop, taking the constitution with it, and bestows most of its labor on repairing that. When I hear it at work sometimes, as I go by, it reminds me, at best, of those farmers who in winter contrive to turn a penny by following the coopering business. And what kind of spirit is their barrel made to hold? They speculate in stocks, and bore holes in mountains, but they are not competent to lay out even a decent highway. The only *free* road, the Underground Railroad, is owned and managed by the Vigilant Committee. *They* have tunneled under the whole breadth of the land. Such a government is losing its power and respectability as surely as water runs out of a leaky vessel, and is held by one that can contain it.

I hear many condemn these men because they were so few. When were the good and the brave ever in a majority? Would you have had him wait till that time came?—till you and I came over to him? The very fact that he had no rabble or troop of hirelings about him would alone distinguish him from ordinary heroes. His company was small indeed, because few could be found worthy to pass muster. Each one who there laid down his life for the poor and oppressed was a picked man, culled out of many thousands, if not millions; apparently a man of principle, of rare courage, and devoted humanity; ready to sacrifice his life at any moment for the benefit of his fellow-man. It may be doubted if there were as many more their equals in these respects in all the country,—I speak of his followers only,—for their leader, no doubt, scoured the land far and wide, seeking to swell his troop. These alone were ready to step between the oppressor and the oppressed. Surely they were the very best men you could select to be hung. That was the greatest compliment which this country could pay them. They were ripe for her gallows. She has tried a long time, she has hung a good many, but never found the right one before.

When I think of him, and his six sons, and his son-in-law, not to enumerate the others, enlisted for this fight, proceeding coolly, reverently, humanely to work, for months if not years, sleeping and waking upon it, summering

and wintering the thought, without expecting any reward but a good conscience, while almost all America stood ranked on the other side,—I say
again that it affects me as a sublime spectacle. If he had had any journal advocating *"his cause,"* any organ, as the phrase is, monotonously and weari-
somely playing the same old tune, and then passing round the hat, it would
have been fatal to his efficiency. If he had acted in any way so as to be let
alone by the government, he might have been suspected. It was the fact that
the tyrant must give place to him, or he to the tyrant, that distinguished him
from all the reformers of the day that I know.

It was his peculiar doctrine that a man has a perfect right to interfere by
force with the slaveholder, in order to rescue the slave. I agree with him.
They who are continually shocked by slavery have some right to be shocked
by the violent death of the slaveholder, but no others. Such will be more
shocked by his life than by his death. I shall not be forward to think him mistaken in his method who quickest succeeds to liberate the slave. I speak for
the slave when I say that I prefer the philanthropy of Captain Brown to that
philanthropy which neither shoots me nor liberates me. At any rate, I do not
think it is quite sane for one to spend his whole life in talking or writing
about this matter, unless he is continuously inspired, and I have not done so.
A man may have other affairs to attend to. I do not wish to kill nor to be
killed, but I can foresee circumstances in which both these things would be
by me unavoidable. We preserve the so-called peace of our community by
deeds of petty violence every day. Look at the policeman's billy and hand-
cuffs! Look at the jail! Look at the gallows! Look at the chaplain of the regiment! We are hoping only to live safely on the outskirts of *this* provisional
army. So we defend ourselves and our hen-roosts, and maintain slavery. I
know that the mass of my countrymen think that the only righteous use that
can be made of Sharps rifles and revolvers is to fight duels with them, when
we are insulted by other nations, or to hunt Indians, or shoot fugitive slaves
with them, or the like. I think that for once the Sharps rifles and the revolvers
were employed in a righteous cause. The tools were in the hands of one who
could use them.

The same indignation that is said to have cleared the temple once will
clear it again. The question is not about the weapon, but the spirit in which
you use it. No man has appeared in America, as yet, who loved his fellow-
man so well, and treated him so tenderly. He lived for him. He took up his
life and he laid it down for him. What sort of violence is that which is encouraged, not by soldiers, but by peaceable citizens, not so much by laymen
as by ministers of the Gospel, not so much by the fighting sects as by the
Quakers, and not so much by Quaker men as by Quaker women?

This event advertises me that there is such a fact as death,—the possibility of a man's dying. It seems as if no man had ever died in America before;
for in order to die you must first have lived. I don't believe in the hearses,
and palls, and funerals that they have had. There was no death in the case,
because there had been no life; they merely rotted or sloughed off, pretty
much as they had rotted or sloughed along. No temple's veil was rent, only a
hole dug somewhere. Let the dead bury their dead. The best of them fairly
ran down like a clock. Franklin,—Washington,—they were let off without
dying; they were merely missing one day. I hear a good many pretend that

they are going to die; or that they have died, for aught that I know. Nonsense! I'll defy them to do it. They haven't got life enough in them. They'll deliquesce like fungi, and keep a hundred eulogists mopping the spot where they left off. Only half a dozen or so have died since the world began. Do you think that you are going to die, sir? No! there's no hope of you. You haven't got your lesson yet. You've got to stay after school. We make a needless ado about capital punishment,—taking lives, when there is no life to take. *Memento mori!* We don't understand that sublime sentence which some worthy got sculptured on his gravestone once. We've interpreted it in a groveling and sniveling sense; we've wholly forgotten how to die.

But be sure you do die nevertheless. Do your work, and finish it. If you know how to begin, you will know when to end.

These men, in teaching us how to die, have at the same time taught us how to live. If this man's acts and words do not create a revival, it will be the severest possible satire on the acts and words that do. It is the best news that America has ever heard. It has already quickened the feeble pulse of the North, and infused more and more generous blood into her veins and heart than any number of years of what is called commercial and political prosperity could. How many a man who was lately contemplating suicide has now something to live for!

One writer says that Brown's peculiar monomania made him to be "dreaded by the Missourians as a supernatural being." Sure enough, a hero in the midst of us cowards is always so dreaded. He is just that thing. He shows himself superior to nature. He has a spark of divinity in him.

> *Unless above himself he can*
> *Erect himself, how poor a thing is man!*

Newspaper editors argue also that it is a proof of his *insanity* that he thought he was appointed to do this work which he did,—that he did not suspect himself for a moment! They talk as if it were impossible that a man could be "divinely appointed" in these days to do any work whatever; as if vows and religion were out of date as connected with any man's daily work; as if the agent to abolish slavery could only be somebody appointed by the President, or by some political party. They talk as if a man's death were a failure, and his continued life, be it of whatever character, were a success.

When I reflect to what a cause this man devoted himself, and how religiously, and then reflect to what cause his judges and all who condemn him so angrily and fluently devote themselves, I see that they are as far apart as the heavens and earth are asunder.

The amount of it is, our *"leading men"* are a harmless kind of folk, and they know *well enough* that *they* were not divinely appointed, but elected by the votes of their party.

Who is it whose safety requires that Captain Brown be hung? Is it indispensable to any Northern man? Is there no resource but to cast this man also to the Minotaur? If you do not wish it, say so distinctly. While these things are being done, beauty stands veiled and music is a screeching lie. Think of him,—of his rare qualities!—such a man as it takes ages to make, and ages to understand; no mock hero, nor the representative of any party. A man such as the sun may not rise upon again in this benighted land. To whose making went the costliest material, the finest adamant; sent to be the redeemer of those in captivity; and the only use to which you can put him is to hang him at the end of a rope! You who pretend to care for Christ crucified, consider what you are about to do to him who offered himself to be the saviour of four millions of men.

Any man knows when he is justified, and all the wits in the world cannot enlighten him on that point. The murderer always knows that he is justly punished; but when a government takes the life of a man without the consent of his conscience, it is an audacious government, and is taking a step towards its own dissolution. Is it not possible that an individual may be right and a government wrong? Are laws to be enforced simply because they were made? or declared by any number of men to be good, if they are *not* good? Is there any necessity for a man's being a tool to perform a deed of which his better nature disapproves? Is it the intention of law-makers that *good* men shall be hung ever? Are judges to interpret the law according to the letter, and not the spirit? What right have *you* to enter into a compact with yourself that you *will* do thus or so, against the light within you? Is it for *you* to *make up* your mind,—to form any resolution whatever,—and not accept the convictions that are forced upon you, and which ever pass your understanding? I do not believe in lawyers, in that mode of attacking or defending a man, because you descend to meet the judge on his own ground, and, in cases of the highest importance, it is of no consequence whether a man breaks a human law or not. Let lawyers decide trivial cases. Business men may arrange that among themselves. If they were the interpreters of the everlasting laws which rightfully bind man, that would be another thing. A counterfeiting law-factory, standing half in a slave land and half in a free! What kind of laws for free men can you expect from that?

I am here to plead his cause with you. I plead not for his life, but for his character,—his immortal life; and so it becomes your cause wholly, and is not his in the least. Some eighteen hundred years ago Christ was crucified; this morning, perchance, Captain Brown was hung. These are the two ends of a chain which is not without its links. He is not Old Brown any longer; he is an angel of light.

I see now that it was necessary that the bravest and humanest man in all the country should be hung. Perhaps he saw it himself. I *almost fear* that I may yet hear of his deliverance, doubting if a prolonged life, if *any* life, can do as much good as his death.

"Misguided!" "Garrulous!" "Insane!" "Vindictive!" So ye write in your easy-chairs, and thus he wounded responds from the floor of the Armory, clear as a cloudless sky, true as the voice of nature is: "No man sent me here; it was my own prompting and that of my Maker. I acknowledge no master in human form."

And in what a sweet and noble strain he proceeds, addressing his captors, who stand over him: "I think, my friends, you are guilty of a great wrong against God and humanity, and it would be perfectly right for any one to interfere with you so far as to free those you willfully and wickedly hold in bondage."

And, referring to his movement: "It is, in my opinion, the greatest service a man can render to God."

"I pity the poor in bondage that have none to help them; that is why I am here; not to gratify any personal animosity, revenge, or vindictive spirit. It is my sympathy with the oppressed and the wronged, that are as good as you, and as precious in the sight of God."

You don't know your testament when you see it.

"I want you to understand that I respect the rights of the poorest and weakest of colored people, oppressed by the slave power, just as much as I do those of the most wealthy and powerful."

"I wish to say, furthermore, that you had better, all you people at the South, prepare yourselves for a settlement of that question, that must come up for settlement sooner than you are prepared for it. The sooner you are prepared the better. You may dispose of me very easily. I am nearly disposed of now; but this question is still to be settled,—this negro question, I mean; the end of that is not yet."

I foresee the time when the painter will paint that scene, no longer going to Rome for a subject; the poet will sing it; the historian record it; and, with the Landing of the Pilgrims and the Declaration of Independence, it will be the ornament of some future national gallery, when at least the present form of slavery shall be no more here. We shall then be at liberty to weep for Captain Brown. Then, and not till then, we will take our revenge.

FREDERICK DOUGLASS (1817–1895), *The Slaveholders' Rebellion*

Born into slavery, Frederick Douglass escaped to become a famous orator, editor of the abolitionist journal North Star, *ambassador to Haiti, and an incisive critic of American domestic politics—especially the Civil War. To abolish slavery was not at first the government's intention in entering the war; as Abraham Lincoln noted in his Second Inaugural Address, "the government claimed no right to do more than to restrict the territorial enlargement of it [slavery]." That is, it intended, by requiring new states to enter the Union as free states, to secure the dominance in Congress of northern industrial interests. Slavery was nonetheless basic to the war: not primarily as a moral problem, but as an economic institution whose perpetuation and extension were essential to the southern plantation oligarchy. From the beginning of the war in 1861, it was clear to Douglass that emancipation must become an explicit issue and a war tactic if the Confederacy were to be defeated. Gradually this became evident to the administration as well, and emancipation was proclaimed, effective January 1, 1863.*

Lincoln was shot on April 14, 1865, a few days after the Union victory. When his funeral procession passed through New York City, blacks were denied permission to participate. Douglass had viewed the Civil War as an opportunity to make good what the war of independence had neglected. After the Civil War, when slavery was replaced by organized terrorism and oppressive "black codes," when blacks were given neither physical protection nor civil rights, the remainder of Douglass' life was devoted to the effort of transforming emancipation into freedom.

The oratorical style for which Douglass was known is amply displayed in the speech below: it is a theatrical, leisurely, elaborate style, full of adjectives and images, and slipping at times into bombast.

Fellow Citizens:

Eighty-six years ago the fourth of July was consecrated and distinguished among all the days of the year as the birthday of American liberty and Independence. The fathers of the Republic recommended that this day be celebrated with joy and gladness by the whole American people, to their latest posterity. Probably not one of those fathers ever dreamed that this hallowed day could possibly be made to witness the strange and portentous Events now transpiring before our eyes, and which even now cast a cloud of more than midnight blackness over the face of the whole country. We are the observers of strange and fearful transactions.

Never was this national anniversary celebrated in circumstances more trying, more momentous, more solemn and perilous, than those by which this nation is now so strongly environed. We present to the world at this moment, the painful spectacle of a great nation, undergoing all the bitter pangs of a gigantic and bloody revolution. We are torn and rent asunder, we are desolated by large and powerful armies of our own kith and kin, converted into desperate and infuriated rebels and traitors, more savage, more fierce and brutal in their modes of warfare, than any recognized barbarians making no pretentions to civilization.

In the presence of this troubled and terrible state of the country, in the appalling jar and rumbling of this social Earthquake, when sorrow and sighing are heard throughout our widely extended borders, when the wise and brave men of the land are everywhere deeply and sadly contemplating this solemn crisis as one which may permanently decide the fate of the nation, I should greatly transgress the law of fitness, and violate my own feelings and yours, if I should on this occasion attempt to entertain you by delivering anything of the usual type of our 4th of July orations.

The hour is one for sobriety, thoughtfulness and stern truthfulness. When the house is on fire, when destruction is spreading its baleful wings everywhere, when helpless women and children are to be rescued from devouring flames, a true man can neither have ear nor heart for anything but the thrilling and heart-rending cry for help. Our country is now on fire. No man can now tell what the future will bring forth. The question now is whether this great Republic before it has reached a century from its birth, is to fall in the wake of unhappy Mexico, and become the constant theatre of civil war, or whether it shall become like old Spain, the mother of Mexico, and by folly and cruelty part with its renown among the nations of the earth, and spend the next seventy years in vainly attempting to regain what it has lost in the space of this one slaveholding rebellion.

Looking thus at the state of the country, I know of no better use to which I can put this sacred day, I know of no higher duty resting upon me, than to enforce my views and convictions, and especially to hold out to reprobation, the short sighted and ill judged, and inefficient modes adopted to suppress the rebels. The past may be dismissed with a single word. The claims of our fathers upon our memory, admiration and gratitude, are founded in the fact that they wisely, and bravely, and successfully met the crisis of their day. And if the men of this generation would deserve well of posterity they must like their fathers, discharge the duties and responsibilities of their age.

Men have strange notions nowadays as to the manner of showing their respect for the heroes of the past. They every where prefer the form to the substance, the seeming to the real.—One of our Generals, and some of our editors, seem to think that the fathers are honored by guarding a well, from which those fathers may have taken water, or the house in which they may have passed a single night, while our sick soldiers need pure water, and are dying in the open fields for water and shelter. This is not honoring, but dishonoring your noble dead. Nevertheless, I would not even in words do violence to the grand events, and thrilling associations, that gloriously cluster around the birth of our national independence. There is no need of any such violence. The thought of to-day and the work of to-day, are alike linked, and interlinked with the thought and work of the past. The conflict between liberty and slavery, between civilization and barbarism, between enlightened progress, and stolid indifference and inactivity is the same in all countries, in all ages, and among all peoples. Your fathers drew the sword for free and independent Government, Republican in its form, Democratic in its spirit; to be administered by officers duly elected by the free and unbought suffrages of the people, and the war of to-day on the part of the loyal north, the east and west, is waged for the same grand and all commanding objects. We are only continuing the tremendous struggle, which your fathers and my fathers began eighty-six years ago. Thus identifying the present with the past, I propose to consider the great present question, uppermost and all absorbing in all minds and hearts throughout the land.

I shall speak to you of the origin, the nature, the objects of this war, the manner of conducting, and its possible and probable results.

ORIGIN OF THE WAR

It is hardly necessary at this very late day of this war, and in view of all the discussion through the press and on the platform which has transpired concerning it, to enter now upon any elaborate enquiry or explanation as to whence came this foul and guilty attempt to break up and destroy the national Government. All but the willfully blind or the malignantly traitorous, know and confess that this whole movement which now so largely distracts the country, and threatens ruin to the nation, has its root and its sap, its trunk and its branches, and the bloody fruit it bears only from the one source of all abounding abomination, and that is slavery. It has sprung out of a malign selfishness and a haughty and imperious pride which only the practice of the most hateful oppression and cruelty could generate and develop. No ordinary love of gain, no ordinary love of power, could have stirred up this terrible revolt.—The legitimate objects of property, such as houses, land, fruits of the earth, the products of art, science and invention, powerful as they are, could never have stirred and kindled this malignant flame, and set on fire this rebellious fury. The monster was brought to its birth by pride, lust and cruelty which could not brook the sober restraints of law, order and justice. The monster publishes its own parentage. Grim and hideous as this rebellion is, its shocking practices, digging up the bones of our dead soldiers slain in battle, making drinking vessels out of their skulls, drumsticks out of their arm bones, slaying our wounded soldiers on the field of carnage, when their gaping wounds appealed piteously for mercy, poisoning wells, firing upon unarmed men, stamp it with all the horrid characteristics of the bloody and barbarous system and society from which it derived its life.

Of course you know, and I know that there have been and still are, in certain out of the way places here at the north, where rebels, in the smooth disguise of loyal men, do meet and promulgate a very opposite explanation of the origin of this war, and that grave attempts have been made to refute their absurd theories. I once heard Hon. Edward Everett entertain a large audience by a lengthy and altogether unnecessary argument to prove that the south did not revolt on account of the fishing bounty paid to northern fishermen, nor because of any inequalities or discrimination in the revenue laws. It was the Irishman's gun aimed at nothing and hitting it every time. Yet the audience seemed pleased with the learning and skill of the orator, and I among the number, though I hope to avoid his bad example in the use of time.

There is however one false theory of the origin of the war to which a moment's reply may be properly given here. It is this. The abolitionists by their insane and unconstitutional attempt to abolish slavery have brought on the war. All that class of men who opposed what they were pleased to call coercion at the first, and a vigorous prosecution of the war at the present, charge the war directly to the abolitionists. In answer to this charge, I lay down this rule as a basis to which all candid men will assent. Whatever is said or done by any class of citizens, strictly in accordance with rights guaranteed by the Constitution, cannot be fairly charged as against the Union, or as inciting to a dissolution of the Union.

Now the slaveholders came into the Union with their eyes wide open, subject to a Constitution wherein the right to be abolitionists was sacredly guaranteed to all the people. They knew that slavery was to take its chance with all other evils against the power of free speech and national enlightenment. They came on board the national ship subject to these conditions, they signed the articles after having duly read them, and the fact that those rights, plainly written, have been exercised is no apology whatever for the slaveholder's mutiny and their attempt to lay piratical hands on the ship and its officers. When therefore I hear a man denouncing abolitionists on account of the war, I know that I am listening to a man who either does not know what he is talking about, or to one who is a traitor in disguise.

THE NATURE OF THE REBELLION

There is something quite distinct and quite individual in the nature and character of this rebellion. In its motives and objects it stands entirely alone, in the annals of great social disturbances. Rebellion is no new thing under the sun. The best governments in the world are liable to these terrible social disorders. All countries have experienced them. Generally however, rebellions are quite respectable in the eyes of the world, and very properly so. They naturally command the sympathy of mankind, for generally they are on the side of progress. They would overthrow and remove some old and festering abuse not to be otherwise disposed of, and introduce a higher civilization, and a larger measure of liberty among men. But this rebellion is in no wise analogous to such.—The pronounced and damning peculiarity of the present rebellion, is found in the fact, that it was conceived, undertaken, planned, and persevered in, for the guilty purpose of handing down to the latest generations that accursed system of human bondage. Its leaders have plainly told us by words as well as by deeds, that they are fighting for slavery. They have been stirred to this perfidious revolt, by a certain deep and deadly hate, which they warmly cherish toward every possible contradiction of slavery whether found in theory or in practice. For this cause they hate free society, free schools, free states, free speech, the freedom asserted in the Declaration of Independence, and guaranteed in the Constitution.—Herein is the whole secret of the rebellion.—The plan is and was to withdraw the slave system from the hated light of liberty, and from the natural operations of free principles. While the slaveholders could hold the reins of government they could and did pervert the free principles of the Constitution to slavery, and could afford to continue in the union, but when they saw that they could no longer control the union as they had done for sixty years before, they appealed to the sword and struck for a government which should forever shut out all light from the southern conscience, and all hope of Emancipation from the southern slave. This rebellion therefore, has no point of comparison with that which has brought liberty to America, or with those of Europe, which have been undertaken from time to time, to throw off the galling yoke of despotism. It stands alone in its infamy.

Our slaveholding rebels with an impudence only belonging to themselves, have sometimes compared themselves to Washington, Jefferson, and the long list of worthies who led in the revolution of 1776, when in fact they would hang either of these men if they were now living, as traitors to slavery, because they each and all considered the system an evil.

THE CONFLICT UNAVOIDABLE

I hold that this conflict is the logical and inevitable result of a long and persistent course of national transgression. Once in a while you will meet with men who will tell you that this war ought to have been avoided. In telling you this, they only make the truth serve the place and perform the office of a lie. I too say that this war ought never to have taken place. The combustible material which has produced this terrible explosion ought long ago to have been destroyed.—For thirty years the abolitionists have earnestly sought to remove this guilty cause of our troubles. There was a time when this might have been done, and the nation set in permanent safety. Opportunities have not been wanting. They have passed by unimproved. They have sometimes been of a character to suggest the very work which might have saved us from all the dreadful calamities, the horrors and bloodshed, of this war. Events, powerful operators, have eloquently pleaded with the American people to put away the hateful slave system. For doing this great work we have had opportunities innumerable. One of these was presented upon the close of the war for Independence, when the moral sentiment of the country was purified by that great struggle for national life. At that time slavery was young and small, the nation might have easily abolished it, and thus relieved itself forever of this alien element, the only disturbing and destructive force in our republican system of Government. Again there was another opportunity for putting away this evil in 1789, when we assembled to form the Constitution of the United States. At that time the anti-slavery sentiment was strong both in church and state, and many believed that by giving slavery no positive recognition in the Constitution and providing for the abolition of the slave trade, they had given slavery its death blow already. They made the great mistake of supposing that the existence of the slave trade was necessary to the existence of slavery, and having provided that the slave trade should cease, they flattered themselves that slavery itself must also speedily cease. They did not comprehend the radical character of the evil. Then again in 1819 the Missouri question gave us another opportunity to seal the doom of the slave system, by simply adhering to the early policy of the fathers and sternly refusing the admission of another State into the Union with a Constitution tolerating slavery. Had this been done in the case of Missouri, we should not now be cursed with this terrible rebellion. Slavery would have fallen into gradual decay. The moral sentiment of the country, instead of being vitiated as it is, would have been healthy and strong against the slave system. Political parties and politicians would not, as they have done since, courted the slave power for votes and thus increased the importance of slavery.

THE FIRST PALPABLE DEPARTURE FROM RIGHT POLICY

The date of the Missouri Compromise forms the beginning of that political current which has swept us on to this rebellion, and made the conflict unavoidable. From this dark date in our nation's history, there started forth a new political and social power. Until now slavery had been on its knees, only asking time to die in peace. But the Missouri Compromise gave it a new lease of life. It became at once a tremendous power. The line of thirty-six degrees, thirty minutes, at once stamped itself upon our national politics, our morals, manners, character and religion.—From this time there was a south side to everything American, and the country was at once subjected to the slave power, a power as restless and vigilant as the eye of an escaping murderer. We became under its sway an illogical nation. Pure and simple truth lost its attraction for us. We became a nation of Compromisers.

It is curious to remark the similarity of national to individual demoralization. A man sets out in life with honest principles and with high purposes inspired at the family hearthstone, and for a time steadily and scrupulously keeps them in view. But at last under the influence of some powerful temptation he is induced to violate his principles and push aside his sense of right. The water for the first moment is smooth about him, but soon he finds himself in the rapids. He has lost his footing. The broad flood, resistless as the power of fate, sweeps him onward, from bad to worse, he becomes more hardened, blind and shameless in his crimes till he is overtaken by dire calamity, and at last sinks to ruin. Precisely this has been the case with the American people. No people ever entered upon the pathway of nations, with higher and grander ideas of justice, liberty and humanity than ourselves. There are principles in the Declaration of Independence which would release every slave in the world and prepare the earth for a millenium of righteousness and peace.—But alas! we have seen that declaration intended to be viewed like some colossal statue at the loftiest altitude, by the broad eye of the whole world, meanly subjected to a microscopic examination and its glorious universal truths craftily perverted into seeming falsehoods. Instead of treating it, as it was intended to be treated, as a full and comprehensive declaration of the equal and sacred rights of mankind, our contemptible Negro-hating and slaveholding critics have endeavored to turn it into absurdity by treating it as a declaration of the equality of man in his physical proportions and mental endowments. This gross and scandalous perversion of the true intents and meaning of the declaration did not long stand alone. It was soon followed by the heartless dogma, that the rights declared in that instrument did not apply to any but white men. The slave power at last succeeded, in getting this doctrine proclaimed from the bench of the Supreme Court of the United States. It was there decided that "all men" only means some men, and those white men. And all this in face of the fact, that white people only form one fifth of the whole human family—and that some who pass for white are nearly as black as your humble speaker. While all this was going on, lawyers, priests and politicians were at work upon national prejudice against the colored man.—They raised the cry and put it into the mouth of the ignorant, and vulgar and narrow minded, that "this is the white man's country," and other cries which readily catch the ear of the crowd. This popular method of dealing with an oppressed people has, while crushing the blacks, corrupted and demoralized the whites. It has cheered on the slave power, increased its pride and pretension, till ripe for the foulest treason against the life of the nation. Slavery, that was before the Missouri Compromise couchant, on its knees, asking meekly to be let alone within its own limits to die, became in a few years after rampant, throttling free speech, fighting friendly Indians, annexing Texas, warring with Mexico, kindling with malicious hand the fires of war and bloodshed on the virgin soil of Kansas, and finally threatening to pull down the pillars of the Republic, if you Northern men should dare vote in accordance with your constitutional and political convictions. You know the history; I will not dwell upon it. What I have said, will suffice to indicate the point at which began the downward career of the Republic. It will be seen that it began by bartering away an eternal principle of right for present peace. We undertook to make slavery the full equal of Liberty, and to place it on the same footing of political right with Liberty. It was by permitting the dishonor of the Declaration of Independence, denying the rights of human nature to the man of color, and by yielding to the extravagant pretensions set up by the slaveholder under the plausible color of State rights. In a word it was by reversing the wise and early policy of the nation, which was to confine slavery to its original limits, and thus leave the system to die out under the gradual operation of the principles of the Constitution and the spirit of the age. Ten years had not elapsed, after this compromise, when the demon disunion lifted its ugly front, in the shape of nullification. . . .

THE CONDUCT OF THE WAR

To-day we have to deal not with dead traitors . . . but with a class of men incomparably more dangerous to the country. They are our weak, paltering and incompetent rulers in the Cabinet at Washington and our rebel worshipping Generals in the field, the men who sacrifice the brave loyal soldiers of the North by thousands, while refusing to employ the black man's arm in suppressing the rebels, for fear of exasperating these rebels: men who never interfere with the orders of Generals, unless those orders strike at slavery, the heart of the Rebellion. These are the men to whom we have a duty to discharge to-day, when the country is bleeding at every pore, and when disasters thick and terrible convert this national festal day, into a day of alarm and mourning. I do not underrate the power of the rebels, nor the vastness of the work required for suppressing them. Jefferson Davis [1] is a powerful man, but Jefferson Davis has no such power to blast the hope and break down the strong heart of this nation, as that possessed and exercised by Abraham Lincoln. With twenty millions of men behind him, with wealth and resources at his command such as might pride the heart of the mightiest monarch of Europe, and with a cause which kindles in every true heart the fires of valor and patriotism, we have a right to hold Abraham Lincoln sternly responsible for any disaster or failure attending the suppression of this rebellion. I hold that the rebels can do us no serious harm, unless it is done through the culpable weakness, imbecility or unfaithfulness of those who are charged with the high duty of seeing that the Supreme Law of the land is everywhere enforced and obeyed. Common sense will confess that five millions ought not to be a match for twenty millions. I know of nothing in the mettle of the slaveholder which should make him superior in any of the elements of a warrior to an honest Northern man. One slaveholder ought not longer to be allowed to maintain the boast that he is equal to three Northern men; and yet that boast will not be entirely empty, if we allow those five millions much longer to thwart all our efforts to put them down. It will be most mortifyingly shown that after all our appliances, our inventive genius, our superior mechanical skill, our great industry, our muscular energy, our fertility in strategy, our vast powers of endurance, our overwhelming numbers, and admitted bravery, that the eight or ten rebel slave States, sparsely populated, and shut out from the world by our possession of the sea, are invincible to the arms of the densely populated and every way powerful twenty free States. I repeat, these rebels can do nothing against us, cannot harm a single hair of the national head, if the men at Washington, the President and Cabinet, and the commanding Generals in the field will but earnestly do their most obvious duty.—I repeat Jeff. Davis and his malignant slaveholding Republic, can do this union no harm except by the permission of the reigning powers at Washington.

I am quite aware that some who hear me will question the wisdom of any criticisms upon the conduct of this war at this time and will censure me for making them. I do not dread those censures. I have on many occasions, since the war began, held my breath when even the stones of the street would seem to cry out. I can do so no longer. I believe in the absence of martial law, a citizen may properly express an opinion as to the manner in which our Government has conducted, and is still conducting this war. I hold that it becomes this country, the men who have to shed their blood and pour out their wealth to sustain the Government at this crisis, to look very sharply into the movements of the men who have our destiny in their hands.

Theoretically this is a responsible Government. Practically it can be made the very reverse. Experience demonstrates that our safety as a nation depends

---

1. Jefferson Davis, Mississippi planter, politician, and president of the Southern Confederacy.

upon holding every officer of the nation strictly responsible to the people for the faithful performance of duty. This war has developed among other bad tendencies, a tendency to shut our eyes to the mistakes and blunders of those in power. When the President has avowed a policy, sanctioned a measure, or commended a general, we have been told that his action must be treated as final. I scout this assumption. A doctrine more slavish and abject than this does not obtain under the walls of St. Peter. Even in the Rebel States, the Confederate Government is sharply critical, and Jefferson Davis is held to a rigid responsibility.—There is no reason of right or of sound policy for a different course towards the Federal Government. Our rulers are the agents of the people. They are fallible men. They need instruction from the people, and it is no evidence of a factious disposition that any man presumes to condemn a public measure if in his judgment that measure is opposed to the public good.

This is already an old war. The statesmanship at Washington with all its admitted wisdom and sagacity, utterly failed for a long time to comprehend the nature and extent of this rebellion. Mr. Lincoln and his Cabinet will have by and by to confess with many bitter regrets, that they have been equally blind and mistaken as to the true method of dealing with the rebels.—They have fought the rebels with the olive branch. The people must teach them to fight them with the sword. They have sought to conciliate obedience. The people must teach them to compel obedience.

There are many men connected with the stupendous work of suppressing this slaveholding rebellion, and it is the right of the American people to keep a friendly and vigilant eye upon them all, but there are three men in the nation, from whose conduct the attention of the people should never be withdrawn: The first is President Lincoln, the Commander-in-chief of the army and navy. The single word of this man can set a million of armed men in motion: He can make and unmake generals, can lift up or cast down at will. The other two men are McClellan and Halleck.[2] Between these two men nearly a half a million of your brave and loyal sons are divided, the one on the Potomac and the other on the Mississippi. They are the two extended arms of the nation, stretched out to save the Union.

Are those two men loyal? are they in earnest? are they competent? We have a right, and it is our duty to make these inquiries, and report and act in reference to them according to the truth.

Whatever may be said of the loyalty or competency of McClellan, I am fully persuaded by his whole course that he is not in earnest against the rebels, that he is to-day, as heretofore, in war as in peace a real pro-slavery Democrat. His whole course proves that his sympathies are with the rebels, and that his ideas of the crisis make him unfit for the place he holds. He kept the army of the Potomac standing still on that river, marching and countermarching, giving show parades during six months. He checked and prevented every movement which was during that time proposed against the rebels East and West.

Bear in mind the fact that this is a slaveholding rebellion, bear in mind that slavery is the very soul and life of all the vigor which the rebels have

---

2. George B. McClellan and Henry W. Halleck: Union generals in the Civil War.

thus far been able to throw into their daring attempt to overthrow and ruin this country. Bear in mind that in time of war, it is the right and duty of each belligerent to adopt that course which will strengthen himself and weaken his enemy.

Bear in mind also that nothing could more directly and powerfully tend to break down the rebels, and put an end to the struggle than the Insurrection or the running away of a large body of their slaves, and then, read General McClellan's proclamation, declaring that any attempt at a rising of the slaves against their rebel masters would be put down, and put down with an iron hand. Let it be observed too, that it has required the intervention of Congress, by repeated resolutions to prevent this General from converting the army of the Potomac from acting as the slave dogs of the rebels, and that even now while our army are compelled to drink water from the muddy swamps, and from the Pamunky river, forbidden by George B. McClellan to take pure water from the Rebel General Lee's well. Let it be understood that Northern loyal soldiers have been compelled by the orders of this same General, to keep guard over the property of a leading rebel, because of a previous understanding between the loyal, and the traitor General. Bear in mind the fact that this General has in deference to the slaveholding rebels forbidden the singing of anti-slavery songs in his camp, and you will learn that this General's ideas of the demands of the hour are most miserably below the mark, and unfit him for the place he fills. . . . This is only one class of facts. They are not the only facts, nor the chief ones that shake my faith in the General of the Army of the Potomac.

Unquestionably time is the mightiest ally that the rebels can rely on. Every month they can hold out against the Government gives them power at home, and prestige abroad, and increases the probabilities of final success. Time favors foreign intervention, time favors heavy taxation upon the loyal people, time favors reaction, and a clamor for peace. Time favors fevers, and pestilence, wasting and destroying our army. Therefore *time, time* is the great ally of the rebels.

Now I undertake to say that General McClellan has from the beginning so handled the army of the Potomac as to give the rebels the grand advantage of time. From the time he took command of the Potomac army in August 1861 until now, he has been the constant cause of delay, and probably would not have moved when he did, but that he was compelled to move or be removed. Then behold his movement. He moved upon Manassas when the enemy had been gone from there seven long days. When he gets there he is within sixty miles of Richmond. Does he go on? Oh! no, but he just says hush, to the press and the people, I am going to do something transcendentally brilliant in strategy. Three weeks pass away, and knowing ones wink and smile as much as to say you will see something wonderful soon. And so indeed we do, at the end of three weeks we find that General McClellan has actually marched back from Manassas to the Potomac, gotten together an endless number of vessels at a cost of untold millions, to transport his troops to Yorktown, where he is just as near to Richmond and not a bit nearer than he was just three weeks before, and where he is opposed by an army every way as strongly posted as any he could have met with by marching straight to Richmond from Manassas. Here we have two hundred and thirty thousand men moved to attack empty fortifications, and moved back again.

Now what is the state of facts concerning the nearly four months of campaign between the James and the York Rivers? The first is that Richmond is not taken, and in all the battles yet fought, the rebels have claimed them as victories, we have lost between thirty and forty thousand men, and the general impression is that there is an equal chance that our army will be again repulsed before Richmond and driven away.

You may not go the length that I do, in regard to Gen. McClellan, at this time, but I feel quite sure that this country will yet come to the conclusion that Geo. B. McClellan is either a cold blooded Traitor, or that he is an unmitigated military Impostor. He has shown no heart in his conduct, except when doing something directly in favor of the rebels, such as guarding their persons and property and offering his services to suppress with an iron hand any attempt on the part of the slaves against their rebel masters.

THE POLICY OF THE ADMINISTRATION

I come now to the policy of President Lincoln in reference to slavery. An administration without a policy is confessedly an administration without brains, since while a thing is to be done, it implies a known way to do it and he who professes his ability to do it, but cannot show how it is to be done, confesses his own imbecility. I do not undertake to say that the present administration has no policy, but if it has, the people have a right to know what it is, and to approve or disapprove of it as they shall deem it wise or unwise.

Now the policy of an administration can be learned in two ways. The first by what it says, and the second by what it does, and the last is far more certain and reliable than the first. It is by what President Lincoln has done in reference to slavery, since he assumed the reins of government, that we are to know what he is likely to do, and deems best to do in the premises. We all know how he came into power. He was elected and inaugurated as the representative of the anti-slavery policy of the Republican party. He had laid down and maintained the doctrine that Liberty and Slavery were the great antagonistic political elements in this country. That Union of these States could not long continue half free and half slave, that they must in the end be all free or all slave.

In the conflict between these two elements he arrayed himself on the side of freedom, and was elected with a view to the ascendancy of free principles. Now what has been the tendency of his acts since he became Commander in chief of the army and navy? I do not hestitate to say, that whatever may have been his intentions, the action of President Lincoln has been calculated in a marked and decided way to shield and protect slavery from the very blows which its horrible crimes have loudly and persistently invited. He has scornfully rejected the policy of arming the slaves, a policy naturally suggested and enforced by the nature and necessities of the war. He has steadily refused to proclaim, as he had the constitutional and moral right to proclaim, complete emancipation to all the slaves of rebels who should make their way into the lines of our army. He has repeatedly interfered with and arrested the anti-slavery policy of some of his most earnest and reliable generals. He has assigned to the most important positions, generals who are notoriously pro-slavery, and hostile to the party and principles which raised him to power.—He has permitted rebels to recapture their runaway slaves in sight of the capital. He has allowed General Halleck to openly violate the spirit of a solemn resolution by Congress forbidding the army of the United States to return the fugitive slaves to their cruel masters, and has evidently from the first submitted himself to the guidance of the half loyal slave States, rather than to the wise and loyal suggestions of those States upon which must fall, and have fallen, the chief expense and danger involved in the prosecution of the war. It is from such action as this, that we must infer the policy of the Administration. To my mind that policy is simply and solely to reconstruct the union on the old and corrupting basis of compromise, by which slavery shall retain all the power that it ever had, with the full assurance of gaining more, according to its future necessities.

The question now arises, "Is such a reconstruction possible or desirable?" To this I answer from the depth of my soul, no. Mr. Lincoln is powerful, Mr. Lincoln can do many things, but Mr. Lincoln will never see the day when he can bring back or charm back, the scattered fragments of the Union into the shape and form they stood when they were shattered by this slaveholding rebellion.

. . . Having thus condemned as impossible and undesirable the policy which seems to be that of the administration you will naturally want to know what I consider to be the true policy to be pursued by the Government and people in relation to slavery and the war. I will tell you: Recognise the fact, for it is the great fact, and never more palpable than at the present moment, that the only choice left to this nation, is abolition or destruction. You must abolish slavery or abandon the union. It is plain that there can never be any union between the north and the south, while the south values slavery more than nationality. A union of interest is essential to a union of ideas, and without this union of ideas, the outward form of the union will be but as a rope of sand. Now it is quite clear that while slavery lasts at the south, it will remain hereafter as heretofore, the great dominating interest, overtopping all others, and shaping the sentiments and opinions of the people in accordance with itself. We are not to flatter ourselves that because slavery has brought great troubles upon the South by this war, that therefore the people of the South will be stirred up against it. If we can bear with slavery after the calamities it has brought upon us, we may expect that the South will be no less patient. Indeed we may rationally expect that the South will be more devoted to slavery than ever. The blood and treasure poured out in its defense will tend to increase its sacredness in the eyes of southern people, and if slavery comes out of this struggle, and is retaken under the forms of old compromises, the country will witness a greater amount of insolence and bluster in favor of the slave system, than was ever shown before in or out of Congress. —But it is asked how will you abolish slavery. You have no power over the system before the rebellion is suppressed, and you will have no right or power when it is suppressed. I will answer this argument when I have stated how the thing may be done. The fact is there would be no trouble about the way, if the government only possessed the will. But several ways have been suggested. One is a stringent Confiscation Bill by Congress. Another is by a proclamation by the President at the head of the nation. Another is by the commanders of each division of the army. Slavery can be abolished in any or all these ways. There is plausibility in the argument that we cannot reach slavery until we have suppressed the rebellion. Yet it is far more true to say that we cannot reach the rebellion until we have suppressed slavery. For slavery is the life of the rebellion. Let the loyal army but inscribe upon its banner, Emancipation and protection to all who will rally under it, and no power could prevent a stampede from slavery, such as the world has not witnessed since the Hebrews crossed the Red Sea. I am convinced that this rebellion and slavery are twin monsters, and that they must fall or flourish together, and that all attempts at upholding one while putting down the other, will be followed by continued trains of darkening calamities, such as make this anniversary of our national Independence, a day of mourning instead of a day of transcendant joy and gladness.

But a proclamation of Emancipation, says one, would only be a paper order. I answer, so is any order emanating from our Government. The President's proclamation calling his countrymen to arms, was a paper order. The proposition to retake the property of the Federal Government in the southern States, was a paper order. Laws fixing the punishment of traitors are paper orders. All laws, all written rules for the Government of the army and navy and people, are "paper orders," and would remain only such were they not backed up by force, still we do not object to them as useless, but admit their wisdom and necessity. Then these paper orders carry with them a certain moral force which makes them in a large measure self-executing. I know of none which would possess this self-executing power in larger measure than a proclamation of Emancipation. It would act on the rebel masters, and even more powerfully upon their slaves. It would lead the slaves to run away, and the masters to emancipate, and thus put an end to slavery. The conclusion of the whole matter is this: The end of slavery and only the end of slavery, is the end of the war, the end of secession, the end of disunion, and the return of peace, prosperity and unity to the nation. Whether Emancipation comes from the North or from the South, from Jeff Davis or from Abraham Lincoln, it will come alike for the healing of the nation, for slavery is the only mountain interposed to make enemies of the North and South.

Fellow Citizens: let me say in conclusion. This slavery-begotten and slavery-sustained, and slavery-animated war, has now cost this nation more than a hundred thousand lives, and more than five hundred millions of treasure. It has weighed down the national heart with sorrow and heaviness, such as no speech can portray. It has cast a doubt upon the possibility of liberty and self government which it will require a century to remove.—The question is, shall this stupendous and most outrageous war be finally and forever ended? Or shall it be merely suspended for a time, and again revived with increased and aggravated fury in the future? Can you afford a repetition of this costly luxury? Do you wish to transmit to your children the calamities and sorrows of to-day? The way to either class of these results is open to you. By urging upon the nation the necessity and duty of putting an end to slavery, you put an end to the war, and put an end to the cause of the war, and make any repetition of it impossible. But just take back the pet monster again into the bosom of the nation, proclaim an amnesty to the slaveholders, let them have their slaves, and command your services in helping to catch and hold them, and so sure as like causes will ever produce like effects, you will hand down to your children here, and hereafter, born and to be born all the horrors through which you are now passing. I have told you of great national opportunities in the past, a greater than any in the past is the opportunity of the present. If now we omit the duty it imposes, steel our hearts against its teachings, or shrink in cowardice from the work of to-day, your fathers will have fought and bled in vain to establish free Institutions, and American Republicanism will become a hissing and a byword to a mocking earth.

PETER KROPOTKIN (1842–1921),
Law and Authority

"We [Russian revolutionaries] have had to endure every form of persecution, every thinkable misery; but we have been spared one disgrace, one humiliation; we at least have no anarchists." This statement of George Plekhanov in 1893 reveals the hostility between socialists and anarchists. The latter—individualists opposed to any form of coercive authority—favored the abolition of private property and of the wage system, but rejected the idea of a socialist state, or of any state at all. Some groups practised "propaganda by deed"—acts of individual terrorism such as bombing or assassination. Anarchism developed a significant following throughout Europe, in America, and in England where its chief theoretician was the Russian refugee, Prince Kropotkin.

A distinguished scientist and member of the old nobility, Kropotkin worked with a secret revolutionary circle in St. Petersburg. He was arrested but escaped from prison and made his way to England, where he spent most of the next forty years speaking, writing, and organizing for the anarchist cause. Kropotkin returned to Russia during the 1917 revolution, though he took no active part in either the revolution or the new state. He spent his last years peacefully, doing scientific research and advising anarchists abroad.

The essay below, written as a propaganda pamphlet in 1886, displays tight organization and the graceful, literate style for which Kropotkin was known. Its logic, however, reveals the aristocrat: Kropotkin implies that the choice is bourgeois law or no law. Christopher Caudwell's essay on liberty, also assuming that law serves class interests, comes to a very different conclusion: one that leaves rather more room for hope than Kropotkin's.

I

"When ignorance reigns in society and disorder in the minds of men, laws are multiplied, legislation is expected to do everything, and each fresh law being a fresh miscalculation, men are continually led to demand from it what can proceed only from themselves, from their own education and their own morality." It is no revolutionist who says this, not even a reformer. It is the jurist, Dalloy, author of the collection of French law known as *Répertoire de la Législation*. And yet, though these lines were written by a man who was himself a maker and admirer of law, they perfectly represent the abnormal condition of our society.

In existing States a fresh law is looked upon as a remedy for evil. Instead of themselves altering what is bad, people begin by demanding a *law* to alter it. If the road between two villages is impassable, the peasant says:—"There should be a law about parish roads." If a park-keeper takes advantage of the want of spirit in those who follow him with servile observance and insults one of them, the insulted man says, "There should be a law to enjoin more politeness upon park-keepers." If there is stagnation in agriculture or commerce, the husbandman, cattle-breeder, or corn speculator argues, "It is protective legislation that we require." Down to the old clothesman there is not one who does not demand a law to protect his own little trade. If the employer lowers wages or increases the hours of labor, the politician in embryo exclaims, "We must have a law to put all that to rights." In short, a law everywhere and for everything! A law about fashions, a law about mad dogs, a law about virtue, a law to put a stop to all the vices and all the evils which result from human indolence and cowardice.

We are so perverted by an education which from infancy seeks to kill in us the spirit of revolt, and to develop that of submission to authority; we are so perverted by this existence under the ferrule of a law, which regulates every event in life—our birth, our education, our development, our love, our friendship—that, if this state of things continues, we shall lose all initiative, all habit of thinking for ourselves. Our society seems no longer able to understand that it is possible to exist otherwise than under the reign of law, elaborated by a representative government and administered by a handful of rulers. And even when it has gone so far as to emancipate itself from the thralldom, its first care has been to reconstitute it immediately. "The Year I of Liberty" has never lasted more than a day, for after proclaiming it men put themselves the very next morning under the yoke of law and authority.

Indeed, for some thousands of years, those who govern us have done nothing but ring the changes upon "Respect for law, obedience to authority." This is the moral atmosphere in which parents bring up their children, and school only serves to confirm the impression. Cleverly assorted scraps of spurious science are inculcated upon the children to prove necessity of law; obedience to the law is made a religion; moral goodness and the law of the masters are fused into one and the same divinity. The historical hero of the schoolroom is the man who obeys the law, and defends it against rebels.

Later when we enter upon public life, society and literature, impressing us day by day and hour by hour as the water-drop hollows the stone, continue to inculcate the same prejudice. Books of history, of political science, of social economy, are stuffed with this respect for law. Even the physical sciences have been pressed into the service by introducing artificial modes of expression, borrowed from theology and arbitrary power, into knowledge which is purely the result of observation. Thus our intelligence is successfully befogged, and always to maintain our respect for law. The same work is done by newspapers. They have not an article which does not preach respect for law, even where the third page proves every day the imbecility of that law, and shows how it is dragged through every variety of mud and filth by those charged with its administration. Servility before the law has become a virtue, and I doubt if there was ever even a revolutionist who did not begin in his youth as the defender of law against what are generally called "abuses," although these last are inevitable consequences of the law itself.

Art pipes in unison with would-be science. The hero of the sculptor, the painter, the musician, shields Law beneath his buckler, and with flashing eyes and distended nostrils stands ever ready to strike down the man who would lay hands upon her. Temples are raised to her; revolutionists themselves hesitate to touch the high priests consecrated to her service, and when revolution is about to sweep away some ancient institution, it is still by law that it endeavors to sanctify the deed.

The confused mass of rules of conduct called law, which has been bequeathed to us by slavery, serfdom, feudalism, and royalty, has taken the place of those stone monsters, before whom human victims used to be immolated, and whom slavish savages dared not even touch lest they should be slain by the thunderbolts of heaven.

This new worship has been established with especial success since the rise to supreme power of the middle class—since the great French Revolution. Under the ancient régime, men spoke little of laws; unless, indeed, it were, with Montesquieu, Rousseau and Voltaire, to oppose them to royal caprice. Obedience to the good pleasure of the king and his lackeys was compulsory on pain of hanging or imprisonment. But during and after the revolutions, when the lawyers rose to power, they did their best to strengthen the principle upon which their ascendancy depended. The middle class at once accepted it as a dyke to dam up the popular torrent. The priestly crew hastened to sanctify it, to save their bark from foundering amid the breakers. Finally the people received it as an improvement upon the arbitrary authority and violence of the past.

To understand this, we must transport ourselves in imagination into the eighteenth century. Our hearts must have ached at the story of the atrocities committed by the all-powerful nobles of that time upon the men and women of the people before we can understand what must have been the magic influence upon the peasant's mind of the words, "Equality before the law, obedience to the law without distinction of birth or fortune." He who until then had been treated more cruelly than a beast, he who had never had any rights, he who had never obtained justice against the most revolting actions on the part of a noble, unless in revenge he killed him and was hanged—he saw himself recognized by this maxim, at least in theory, at least with regard to his personal rights, as the equal of his lord. Whatever this law might be, it promised to affect lord and peasant alike; it proclaimed the equality of rich and poor before the judge. The promise was a lie, and to-day we know it; but at that period it was an advance, a homage to justice, as hypocrisy is a homage rendered to truth. This is the reason that when the saviors of the menaced middle class (the Robespierres and the Dantons) took their stand upon the writings of the Rousseaus and the Voltaires, and proclaimed "respect for law, the same for every man," the people accepted the compromise; for their revolutionary impetus had already spent its force in the contest with a foe whose ranks drew closer day by day; they bowed their neck beneath the yoke of law to save themselves from the arbitrary power of their lords.

The middle class has ever since continued to make the most of this maxim, which with another principle, that of representative government, sums up the whole philosophy of the bourgeois age, the nineteenth century. It has preached this doctrine in its schools, it has propagated it in its writings, it has moulded its art and science to the same purpose, it has thrust its beliefs into every hole and corner—like a pious Englishwoman, who slips tracts under the door—and it has done all this so successfully that today we behold the issue in the detestable fact that men who long for freedom begin the attempt to obtain it by entreating their masters to be kind enough to protect them by modifying the laws which these masters themselves have created!

But times and tempers are changed. Rebels are everywhere to be found who no longer wish to obey the law without knowing whence it comes, what are its uses, and whither arises the obligation to submit to it, and the reverence with which it is encompassed. The rebels of our day are criticizing the very foundations of society which have hitherto been held sacred, and first and foremost amongst them that fetish, law.

The critics analyze the sources of law, and find there either a god, product of the terrors of the savage, and stupid, paltry and malicious as the priests who vouch for its supernatural origin, or else, bloodshed, conquest by fire and sword. They study the characteristics of law, and instead of perpetual growth corresponding to that of the human race, they find its distinctive trait to be immobility, a tendency to crystallize what should be modified and developed day by day. They ask how law has been maintained, and in its service they see the atrocities of Byzantinism, the cruelties of the Inquisition, the tortures of the middle ages, living flesh torn by the lash of the executioner, chains, clubs, axes, the gloomy dungeons of prisons, agony, curses and tears. In our own days they see, as before, the axe, the cord, the rifle, the prison; on the one hand, the brutalized prisoner, reduced to the condition of a caged beast by the debasement of his whole moral being, and on the other, the judge, stripped of every feeling which does honor to human nature, living like a visionary in a world of legal fictions, revelling in the infliction of imprisonment and death, without even suspecting, in the cold malignity of his madness, the abyss of degradation into which he has himself fallen before the eyes of those whom he condemns.

They see a race of law-makers legislating without knowing what their laws are about; today voting a law on the sanitation of towns, without the faintest notion of hygiene, tomorrow making regulations for the armament of troops, without so much as understanding a gun; making laws about teaching and education without ever having given a lesson of any sort, or even an honest education to their own children; legislating at random in all directions, but never forgetting the penalties to be meted out to ragamuffins, the prison and the galleys, which are to be the portion of men a thousand times less immoral than these legislators themselves.

Finally, they see the jailer on the way to lose all human feeling, the detective trained as a blood-hound, the police spy despising himself; "informing," metamorphosed into a virtue; corruption, erected into a system; all the vices, all the evil qualities of mankind countenanced and cultivated to insure the triumph of law.

All this we see, and, therefore, instead of inanely repeating the old formula, "Respect the law," we say, "Despise law and all its attributes!" In place of the cowardly phrase, "Obey the law," our cry is "Revolt against all laws!"

Only compare the misdeeds accomplished in the name of each law with the good it has been able to effect, and weigh carefully both good and evil, and you will see if we are right.

II

Relatively speaking, law is a product of modern times. For ages and ages mankind lived without any written law, even that graved in symbols upon the entrance stones of a temple. During that period, human relations were simply regulated by customs, habits and usages, made sacred by constant repetition, and acquired by each person in childhood, exactly as he learned how to obtain his food by hunting, cattle-rearing, or agriculture.

All human societies have passed through this primitive phase, and to this day a large proportion of mankind have no written law. Every tribe has its own manners and customs; customary law, as the jurists say. It has social habits, and that suffices to maintain cordial relations between the inhabitants of the village, the members of the tribe or community. Even amongst ourselves—the "civilized" nations—when we leave large towns, and go into the country, we see that there the mutual relations of the inhabitants are still regulated according to ancient and generally accepted customs, and not according to the written law of the legislators. The peasants of Russia, Italy and Spain, and even of a large part of France and England, have no conception of written law. It only meddles with their lives to regulate their relations with the State. As to relations between themselves, though these are sometimes very complex, they are simply regulated according to ancient custom. Formerly, this was the case with mankind in general.

Two distinctly marked currents of custom are revealed by analysis of the usages of primitive people.

As man does not live in a solitary state, habits and feelings develop within him which are useful for the preservation of society and the propagation of the race. Without social feelings and usages, life in common would have been absolutely impossible. It is not law which has established them; they are anterior to all law. Neither is it religion which has ordained them; they are anterior to all religions. They are found amongst all animals living in society. They are spontaneously developed by the very nature of things, like those habits in animals which men call instinct. They spring from a process of evolution, which is useful, and, indeed, necessary, to keep society together in the struggle it is forced to maintain for existence. Savages end by no longer eating one another because they find it in the long run more advantageous to devote themselves to some sort of cultivation than to enjoy the pleasure of feasting upon the flesh of an aged relative once a year. Many travelers have depicted the manners of absolutely independent tribes, where laws and chiefs are unknown, but where the members of the tribe have given up stabbing one another in every dispute, because the habit of living in society has ended by developing certain feelings of fraternity and oneness of interest, and they prefer appealing to a third person to settle their differences. The hospitality of primitive peoples, respect for human life, the sense of reciprocal obligation, compassion for the weak, courage, extending even to the sacrifice of self for others which is first learnt for the sake of children and friends, and later for that of members of the same community—all these qualities are developed in man anterior to all law, independently of all religion, as in the case of the social animals. Such feelings and practices are the inevitable results of social life. Without being, as say priests and metaphysicians, inherent in man, such qualities are the consequence of life in common.

But side by side with these customs, necessary to the life of societies and the preservation of the race, other desires, other passions, and therefore other habits and customs, are evolved in human association. The desire to dominate others and impose one's own will upon them; the desire to seize upon the products of the labor of a neighboring tribe; the desire to surround oneself with comforts without producing anything, while slaves provide their master with the means of procuring every sort of pleasure and luxury—these selfish, personal desires give rise to another current of habits and customs. The priest and the warrior, the charlatan who makes a profit out of superstition, and after freeing himself from the fear of the devil cultivates it in others; and the bully, who procures the invasion and pillage of his neighbors that he may return laden with booty and followed by slaves. These two, hand in hand, have succeeded in imposing upon primitive society customs advantageous to both of them, but tending to perpetuate their domination of the masses. Profiting by the indolence, the fears, the inertia of the crowd, and thanks to the continual repetition of the same acts, they have permanently established customs which have become a solid basis for their own domination.

For this purpose, they would have made use, in the first place, of that tendency to run in a groove, so highly developed in mankind. In children and all savages it attains striking proportions, and it may also be observed in animals. Man, when he is at all superstitious, is always afraid to introduce any sort of change into existing conditions; he generally venerates what is ancient. "Our fathers did so and so; they got on pretty well; they brought you up; they were not unhappy; do the same!" the old say to the young every time the latter wish to alter things. The unknown frightens them, they prefer to cling to the past even when that past represents poverty, oppression and slavery.

It may even be said that the more miserable a man is, the more he dreads every sort of change, lest it may make him more wretched still. Some ray of hope, a few scraps of comfort, must penetrate his gloomy abode before he can begin to desire better things, to criticize the old ways of living, and prepare to imperil them for the sake of bringing about a change. So long as he is not imbued with hope, so long as he is not freed from the tutelage of those who utilize his superstition and his fears, he prefers remaining in his former position. If the young desire any change, the old raise a cry of alarm against the innovators. Some savages would rather die than transgress the customs of their country because they have been told from childhood that the least infraction of established routine would bring ill-luck and ruin the whole tribe. Even in the present day, what numbers of politicians, economists, and would-be revolutionists act under the same impression, and cling to a vanishing past. How many care only to seek for precedents. How many fiery innovators are mere copyists of bygone revolutions.

The spirit of routine, originating in superstition, indolence, and cowardice, has in all times been the mainstay of oppression. In primitive human societies it was cleverly turned to account by priests and military chiefs. They perpetuated customs useful only to themselves, and succeeded in imposing them on the whole tribe. So long as this conservative spirit could be exploited so as to assure the chief in his encroachments upon individual liberty, so long as the only inequalities between men were the work of nature, and these were not increased a hundred-fold by the concentration of power and wealth, there was no need for law and the formidable paraphernalia of tribunals and ever-augmenting penalties to enforce it.

But as society became more and more divided into two hostile classes, one seeking to establish its domination, the other struggling to escape, the strife began. Now the conqueror was in a hurry to secure the results of his actions in a permanent form, he tried to place them beyond question, to make them holy and venerable by every means in his power. Law made its appearance under the sanction of the priest, and the warrior's club was placed at its service. Its office was to render immutable such customs as were to the advantage of the dominant minority. Military authority undertook to ensure obedience. This new function was a fresh guarantee to the power of the warrior; now he had not only mere brute force at his service; he was the defender of law.

If law, however, presented nothing but a collection of prescriptions serviceable to rulers, it would find some difficulty in insuring acceptance and obedience. Well, the legislators confounded in one code the two currents of custom of which we have just been speaking, the maxims which represent principles of morality and social union wrought out as a result of life in common, and the mandates which are meant to ensure external existence to inequality. Customs, absolutely essential to the very being of society, are, in the code, cleverly intermingled with usages imposed by the ruling caste, and both claim equal respect from the crowd. "Do not kill," says the code, and hastens to add, "And pay tithes to the priest." "Do not steal," says the code, and immediately after, "He who refuses to pay taxes, shall have his hand struck off."

Such was law; and it has maintained its two-fold character to this day. Its origin is the desire of the ruling class to give permanence to customs imposed by themselves for their own advantage. Its character is the skilful commingling of customs useful to society, customs which have no need of law to insure respect, with other customs useful only to rulers, injurious to the mass of the people, and maintained only by the fear of punishment.

Like individual capital, which was born of fraud and violence, and developed under the auspices of authority, law has no title to the respect of men. Born of violence and superstition, and established in the interests of consumer, priest and rich exploiter, it must be utterly destroyed on the day when the people desire to break their chains. . . .

IV

The millions of laws which exist for the regulation of humanity appear upon investigation to be divided into three principal categories: protection of property, protection of persons, protection of government. And by analyzing each of these three categories, we arrive at the same logical and necessary conclusion: *the uselessness and hurtfulness of law.*

Socialists know what is meant by protection of property. Laws on property are not made to guarantee either to the individual or to society the enjoyment of the produce of their own labor. On the contrary, they are made to rob the producer of a part of what he has created, and to secure to certain other people that portion of the produce which they have stolen either from the producer or from society as a whole. When, for example, the law establishes Mr. So-and-So's right to a house, it is not establishing his right to a cottage he has built for himself, or to a house he has erected with the help of some of his friends. In that case no one would have disputed his right. On the contrary, the law is establishing his right to a house which is *not* the product of his labor; first of all because he has had it built for him by others to whom he has not paid the full value of their work, and next because the house represents a social value which he could not have produced for himself. The law is establishing his right to what belongs to everybody in general and to nobody in particular. The same house built in the midst of Siberia would not have the value it possesses in a large town, and, as we know, that value arises from the labor of something like fifty generations of men who have built the town, beautified it, supplied it with water and gas, fine promenades, colleges, theatres, shops, railways and roads leading in all directions. Thus, by recognizing the right of Mr. So-and-So to a particular house in Paris, London or Rouen, the law is unjustly appropriating to him a certain portion of the produce of the labor of mankind in general. And it is precisely because this appropriation and all other forms of property bearing the same character are a crying injustice, that a whole arsenal of laws and a whole army of soldiers, policemen and judges are needed to maintain it against the good sense and just feeling inherent in humanity.

Half our laws—the civil code in each country—serves no other purpose than to maintain this appropriation, this monopoly for the benefit of certain individuals against the whole of mankind. Three-fourths of the causes decided by the tribunals are nothing but quarrels between monopolists—two robbers disputing over their booty. And a great many of our criminal laws have the same object in view, their end being to keep the workman in a subordinate position towards his employer, and thus afford security for exploitation.

As for guaranteeing the product of his labor to the producer, there are no laws which even attempt such a thing. It is so simple and natural, so much a part of the manners and customs of mankind, that law has not given it so much as a thought. Open brigandage, sword in hand, is no feature of our age. Neither does one workman ever come and dispute the produce of his labor with another. If they have a misunderstanding they settle it by calling in a third person, without having recourse to law. The only person who exacts from another what that other has produced, is the proprietor, who comes in and deducts the lion's share. As for humanity in general, it everywhere respects the right of each to what he has created, without the interposition of any special laws.

As all the laws about property which make up thick volumes of codes and are the delight of our lawyers have no other object than to protect the unjust appropriation of human labor by certain monopolists, there is no reason for their existence, and, on the day of the revolution, social revolutionists are thoroughly determined to put an end to them. Indeed, a bonfire might be made with perfect justice of all laws bearing upon the so-called rights of property, all title-deeds, all registers, in a word, of all that is in any way connected with an institution which will soon be looked upon as a blot in the history of humanity, as humiliating as the slavery and serfdom of past ages.

The remarks just made upon laws concerning property are quite as applicable to the second category of laws; those for the maintenance of government, i. e., constitutional law.

It again is a complete arsenal of laws, decrees, ordinances, orders in council, and what not, all serving to protect the diverse forms of representative government, delegated or usurped, beneath which humanity is writhing. We know very well—anarchists have often enough pointed out in their perpetual criticism of the various forms of government—that the mission of all governments, monarchical, constitutional, or republican, is to protect and maintain by force the privileges of the classes in possession, the aristocracy, clergy and traders. A good third of our laws—and each country possesses some tens of thousands of them—the fundamental laws on taxes, excise duties, the organization of ministerial departments and their offices, of the army, the police, the church, etc., have no other end than to maintain, patch up, and develop the administrative machine. And this machine in its turn serves almost entirely to protect the privileges of the possessing classes. Analyze all these laws, observe them in action day by day, and you will discover that not one is worth preserving.

About such laws there can be no two opinions. Not only anarchists, but more or less revolutionary radicals also, are agreed that the only use to be made of laws concerning the organization of government is to fling them into the fire.

The third category of law still remains to be considered; that relating to the protection of the person and the detection and prevention of "crime." This is the most important because most prejudices attach to it; because, if law enjoys a certain amount of consideration, it is in consequence of the belief that this species of law is absolutely indispensable to the maintenance of security in our societies. These are laws developed from the nucleus of customs useful to human communities, which have been turned to account by rulers to sanctify their own domination. The authority of the chiefs of tribes, of rich families in towns, and of the king, depended upon their judicial functions, and even down to the present day, whenever the necessity of government is spoken of, its function as supreme judge is the thing implied. "Without a government men would tear one another to pieces," argues the village orator. "The ultimate end of all government is to secure twelve honest jurymen to every accused person," said Burke.

Well, in spite of all the prejudices existing on this subject, it is quite time that anarchists should boldly declare this category of laws as useless and injurious as the preceding ones.

First of all, as to so-called crimes—assaults upon persons—it is well known that two-thirds, and often as many as three-fourths, of such "crimes" are instigated by the desire to obtain possession of someone's wealth. This immense class of so-called crimes and misdemeanors will disappear on the day on which private property ceases to exist. "But," it will be said, "there will always be brutes who will attempt the lives of their fellow citizens, who will lay their hands to a knife in every quarrel, and revenge the slightest offense by murder, if there are no laws to restrain and punishments to withhold them." This refrain is repeated every time the right of society *to punish* is called in question.

Yet there is one fact concerning this head which at the present time is thoroughly established; the severity of punishment does not diminish the amount of crime. Hang, and, if you like, quarter murderers, and the number of murders will not decrease by one. On the other hand, abolish the penalty of death, and there will not be one murder more; there will be fewer. Statistics prove it. But if the harvest is good, and bread cheap, and the weather fine, the number of murders immediately decreases. This again is proved by statistics. The amount of crime always augments and diminishes in proportion to the price of provisions and the state of the weather. Not that all murderers are actuated by hunger. That is not the case. But when the harvest is good, and provisions are at an obtainable price, and when the sun shines, men, lighter-hearted and less miserable than usual, do not give way to gloomy passions, do not from trivial motives plunge a knife into the bosom of a fellow creature.

Moreover, it is also a well known fact that the fear of punishment has never stopped a single murderer. He who kills his neighbor from revenge or misery does not reason much about consequences; and there have been few murderers who were not firmly convinced that they should escape prosecution.

Without speaking of a society in which a man will receive a better education, in which the development of all his faculties, and the possibility of exercising them, will procure him so many enjoyments that he will not seek to poison them by remorse—even in our society, even with those sad products of misery whom we see today in the public houses of great cities—on the day when no punishment is inflicted upon murderers, the number of murders will not be augmented by a single case. And it is extremely probable that it will be, on the contrary, diminished by all those cases which are due at present to habitual criminals, who have been brutalized in prisons.

We are continually being told of the benefits conferred by law, and the beneficial effect of penalties, but have the speakers ever attempted to strike a balance between the benefits attributed to laws and penalties, and the degrading effect of these penalties upon humanity? Only calculate all the evil passions awakened in mankind by the atrocious punishments formerly inflicted in our streets! Man is the cruelest animal upon earth. And who has pampered and developed the cruel instincts unknown, even among monkeys, if it is not the king, the judge, and the priests, armed with law, who caused flesh to be torn off in strips, boiling pitch to be poured into wounds, limbs to be dislocated, bones to be crushed, men to be sawn asunder to maintain their authority? Only estimate the torrent of depravity let loose in human society by the "informing" which is countenanced by judges, and paid in hard cash by governments, under pretext of assisting in the discovery of "crime." Only go into the jails and study what man becomes when he is deprived of freedom and shut up with other depraved beings, steeped in the vice and corruption which oozes from the very walls of our existing prisons. Only remember that the more these prisons are reformed, the more detestable they become. Our model modern penitentiaries are a hundred-fold more abominable than the dungeons of the middle ages. Finally, consider what corruption, what depravity of mind is kept up among men by the idea of obedience, the very essence of law; of chastisement; of authority having the right to punish, to judge irrespective of our conscience and the esteem of our friends; of the necessity for executioners, jailers, and informers—in a word, by all the attributes of law and authority. Consider all this, and you will assuredly agree with us in saying that a law inflicting penalties is an abomination which should cease to exist.

Peoples without political organization, and therefore less depraved than ourselves, have perfectly understood that the man who is called "criminal" is simply unfortunate; that the remedy is not to flog him, to chain him up, or to kill him on the scaffold or in prison, but to help him by the most brotherly care, by treatment based on equality, by the usages of life among honest men. In the next revolution we hope that this cry will go forth:

"Burn the guillotines; demolish the prisons; drive away the judges, policemen and informers—the impurest race upon the face of the earth; treat as a brother the man who has been led by passion to do ill to his fellow; above all, take from the ignoble products of middle-class idleness the possibility of displaying their vices in attractive colors; and be sure that but few crimes will mar our society."

The main supports of crime are idleness, law and authority; laws about property, laws about government, laws about penalties and misdemeanors; and authority, which takes upon itself to manufacture these laws and to apply them.

No more laws! No more judges! Liberty, equality, and practical human sympathy are the only effectual barriers we can oppose to the anti-social instincts of certain among us.

ELIZABETH CADY STANTON (1815–1902), *How the Woman Suffrage Movement Began*

Leader and historian of the woman suffrage movement, Elizabeth Cady Stanton devoted much of her life to combating the prevalent idea that "in marriage man and wife become one, and that one is the husband." In the address below, delivered at a convention of the International Council of Women (March 1888), she relates how the experience of women in the abolition movement gave them the insight and courage to confront their own oppression; for women too were "second-class citizens," forbidden by law to vote or hold office, own property, bring suit for divorce, or gain custody of children after divorce. Women were also excluded from colleges and professional schools and, as a matter of course, were paid far less than men in the few jobs to which they were admitted. Not until 1920 was Mrs. Stanton's battle won, when the nineteenth amendment to the Constitution gave women the vote. But just as blacks had learned that emancipation did not mean freedom, so women learned that suffrage did not mean equality. Taking up where their nineteenth-century antecedents left off, black militants and the women's liberation movement have begun to identify the source of their exploitation not as laws or individuals, but as an exploitive economic system.

As an example of first-person narrative, the address is engagingly simple, frank, and humorous, devoid of such theatrical amplitude as that of Frederick Douglass—an ardent supporter of women's rights—to whose well-known style Mrs. Stanton good-naturedly refers.

In 1840 the World's Anti-Slavery Convention was called in London. In harmony with the invitation, the Anti-Slavery Societies in this country sent over several women as delegates. I was not a delegate, although I am often so recorded. My husband was, and that was the occasion of our wedding trip to the Old World.

When we reached the convention we found there was a good deal of objection to women being received as delegates. It was something that had never been heard of in England, women as delegates to a convention; to sit as councilors; to have a vote in its proceedings. So the whole of the first day was taken up in discussing the merits of that question. The objections were chiefly drawn from the Bible.

At last it was decided that they could not enter the convention, but they were very carefully concealed in some side seats hidden by a curtain, just as you find the choirs in some of our churches. Joseph Sturge occupied the chair. Sitting near to Lucretia, I said to her: "Suppose now the spirit should move you to speak, what could Joseph Sturge do, as a Quaker, in the chair?" And said she: "Where the Spirit of the Lord is, there is liberty. There is no danger of the Spirit moving me to speak here."

After listening to all the arguments, which were very insulting to women, as I walked home, arm in arm, with Mrs. Mott, I said, "It seems to me high time to call a Woman's Convention. Here are these men from all parts of the globe to discuss the rights of the negroes to freedom, and yet they have no idea of any rights of freedom for women." Eight years after, when I was living in the western part of the State of New York, Lucretia Mott came out there to visit a sister, Mrs. Martha C. Wright. I then proposed to her to call a convention. I had no more idea of what was involved in calling a convention —no more idea how to do it, than to make a steam engine. Nevertheless, I was determined to do it somehow, so half a dozen of us assembled and decided that we would advertise, and we did advertise in the county paper, occupying a space about as long as your finger, no more. We wrote a few letters to friends, and that was all the announcement we gave.

The next point was a declaration. So we rummaged over all the reports of all the different societies—peace, anti-slavery, and temperance—but none of them were sufficiently pronounced for us; they didn't touch the case. A happy thought struck us—that our fathers' Declaration of Independence was exactly suited to our needs. We read it carefully over, and found that precisely the grievances that our fathers had to complain of against old King George, we had to complain of against our own Saxon fathers. So we adopted the Declaration of Independence, and we were delighted with our success, that we had a grand document, and were not obliged to write it ourselves. So, gentlemen, your ancestors did that good thing for us. It was equally satisfactory to find that we had the same number of grievances with the fathers—exactly eighteen.

Then came the resolutions, and with them we had a great deal of difficulty; however, the help of one or two gentlemen enabled us to succeed in getting up a pretty good series; but when they were finished they were not exactly what I wanted. I wanted to demand the right of suffrage then and there, because I saw that was the fundamental right out of which all others should necessarily flow, so I drew up a very short resolution, and my husband said to me, "Now you make the whole thing ridiculous. So long as you advocated simply rights of education, rights of property, rights of children, and all that sort of thing, it was very well, but the idea of demanding the right of suffrage!" And Lucretia Mott said the same thing, and all the committee who were interested in getting up the meeting were opposed to this resolution. So I seemingly gave it up, but when I got into the convention I determined to push forward my resolution. Unfortunately, I had never said a word in public, and how to put two sentences together I did not know. So I surveyed the Convention, and there I saw Frederick Douglass, and I knew that Frederick, from personal experience, was just the man for the work, so I presented my resolution, then hurried to his side, and whispered in his ear what I wanted said, and he went along awhile very well, but he didn't speak quite fast enough for me, nor say all I wanted said, and the first thing I knew I was on my feet defending the resolution, and in due time Douglass and I carried the whole convention, and the resolution was passed unanimously.

Well, I assure you, my friends, I was delighted with the success of the whole thing. I had read the Constitution and the Declaration of Independence, and understood the genius of our Government, and I had read the opinions of great men, and I found they were all in favor of woman suffrage. Now, said I, the world will accept the argument at once. It is just, it is right, and everybody must see it as plainly as I do. Imagine my surprise after the joy I felt in the perfect success of the convention, for we had a crowded house, and Lucretia Mott and her sister, Martha C. Wright, and other women from the Society of Friends, had made admirable speeches, and we had a magnificent man in the chair, James Mott, the husband of Lucretia Mott, tall and stately, and very distinguished in appearance.

In a few days the papers began to come in. I believe every paper from Maine to Louisiana published that declaration and made comments and ridiculed the whole thing. I was astounded. I had no idea there would be one word of ridicule about the matter. My good father, who was then attending supreme court in New York, hearing of this, took the night train and rushed up to Seneca Falls to see if I was insane. If I hadn't had a remarkably good constitution and a very cheerful temperament, I think I should have been put into the insane asylum. I heard nothing but ridicule. Many of the women who had put their names down in the enthusiasm of the convention, as subscribers to the declaration, in a few days hurried to take them off. Men were in consternation about the conduct of their sisters, mothers, and wives in that convention. I never can tell you, I never can describe to any one the humiliation I felt, and especially as I knew perfectly well that I was right. When I met my father, my sister, who had also given her adhesion to the principles, was in great consternation as to what we should say in defense of ourselves. I said I thought we had everything to say, and I really couldn't see what my father had to say on the other side. We talked the matter over until midnight, and I was more than ever convinced that I was right, for my father was a logical and sensible man, and he could not answer my arguments.

Perhaps I might have subsided altogether if it hadn't been that shortly after that I met Susan B. Anthony, whom we have always called the Napoleon of our movement. Then we put our heads together and we commenced our work in earnest with a general attack all along the line. We besieged the legislature every year; we looked all around the country and wherever we saw a convention of men having a nice time, we at once sent a resolution demanding recognition. And I will tell you how we managed. I would write the speeches and resolutions, and Susan would go to the conventions and fire them off. I had a family of young children and it was not convenient for me to go, but I accepted every invitation to do everything, because I knew Susan could do it.

Martha C. Wright, Mrs. Seward, Susan B. Anthony, and myself were often in consultation to see what more we could do to keep up the agitation. We tormented our legislators for the woman's property bill in New York, the first State that ever passed that bill, and the first State in the world that ever gave to married women the rights of property. Until that time we had been under the old common law of England, under which women were practically slaves, having no rights whatever that white men were bound to respect. Year after year some new civil rights were accorded us. Then we made an attack on the schools and the colleges, although at one time in all the educational conventions not a woman's voice was heard, though perhaps six or seven hundred of them would be sitting around like so many wall-flowers.

And so in the temperance meetings—but I leave Antoinette Brown Blackwell to tell you about that. But when we think of all that has been done, we can hardly believe what we see possible. From that time on, our conventions began to be held all over the country; the key-note was struck in New York, then, Ohio, Massachusetts and Indiana soon followed, holding their conventions from time to time, year by year growing larger and larger. The advanced legislation in New York was copied by many of the new States as they came into the Union and by some of the older States. It is hardly possible to give you in detail all that we did from year to year and all that we encountered in the way of ridicule and persecution.

Ridicule was the chief weapon of the press. We were caricatured in all the papers until really the majority of people supposed that the women on the suffrage platform had horns and hoofs. And now, as we sit here, how changed is the scene! Although at our first convention we were in a small Methodist church, and held many afterwards in the open air, in barns, in depots, in the dining-rooms of hotels, here to-day, at the end of forty years, we have the most beautiful building in the Capital, with magnificent audiences, and most complimentary notices by the press from one end of the country to the other. This is a great encouragement to the women who are present, and I want to give you a word to take to your homes. As soon as you see a grand truth, utter it, and though you may be ridiculed in starting, as the years go by, it will be received. In this long struggle I have never felt that we stood alone, for as representatives of a living truth we are ever linked with the great and grand of all ages, in every latitude and clime, with those able and willing to live or die for a principle.

WILLIAM MORRIS (1834–1896), *Art and Industry in the Fourteenth Century*

Like many of his contemporaries, the artist, craftsman, and poet William Morris looked to the Middle Ages as an example of the social coherence so conspicuously wanting in his own time. But Morris' medievalism, unlike Carlyle's, did not spring from reactionary politics: as a Marxist, Morris came to see in the Middle Ages primitive forms of communal life which —though they did not survive the growth of industrial capital—could be fully realized through revolutionary communism. In 1884 Morris helped to found the Socialist League and edited its journal; he worked closely with Marx's youngest daughter, Eleanor, and also with Engels, who lived in London. On the death of Tennyson in 1892, Morris was offered the Poet Laureateship; he declined, as he saw in Queen Victoria little more than "a respectable officer, who has always been careful to give the minimum of work for the maximum of pay."

For Morris, art and politics are closely connected: art expresses the consciousness that economic and political institutions help to create. "Surely anyone," he wrote, "who professes to think that the question of art and cultivation must go before that of the knife and fork . . . does not understand what art means, or how that its roots must have a soil of a thriving and unanxious life." Morris' literary and artistic gifts are evident in the following essay written in 1890: his sensitivity to form, color, and pattern, his narrative skill, and the ready sympathy that enabled him to recreate in his works the lives of heroes and ordinary men.

In England, at least, if not on the Continent of Europe, there are some towns and cities which have indeed a name that recalls associations with the past, but have no other trace left them of the course of that history which has made them what they are. Besides these, there are many more which have but a trace or two left; sometimes, indeed, this link with the past is so beautiful and majestic in itself that it compels us when we come across it to forget for a few moments the life of today with which we are so familiar that we do not mark its wonders or its meannesses, its follies or its tragedies. It compels us to turn away from our life of habit which is all about us on our right hand

and our left, and which therefore we cannot see, and forces on us the consideration of past times which we can picture to ourselves as a whole, rightly or wrongly, because they are so far off.

Sometimes, as we have been passing through the shabby streets of ill-burnt bricks, we have come on one of these links with the past and wondered. Before the eyes of my mind is such a place now. You travel by railway, get to your dull hotel by night, get up in the morning and breakfast in company with one or two men of the usual middle-class types, who even as they drink their tea and eat their eggs and glance at the sheet of lies, inanity, and ignorance, called a newspaper, by their sides, are obviously doing their business to come, in a vision. You go out into the street and wander up it; all about the station, and stretching away to the left, is a wilderness of small, dull houses built of a sickly-coloured yellow brick pretending to look like stone, and not even able to blush a faint brown blush at the imposture, and roofed with thin, cold, purple-coloured slates. They cry out at you at the first glance, workmen's houses; and a kind of instinct of information whispers to you: railway workmen and engineers. Bright as the spring morning is, a kind of sick feeling of hopeless disgust comes over you, and you go on further, sure at any rate that you cannot fare worse. The street betters a little as you go on; shabbyish shops indeed, and mean houses of the bourgeoisie of a dull market town, exhibiting in their shop fronts a show of goods a trifle below the London standard, and looking "flash" at the best; and above them dull houses, greyish and reddish, recalling some associations of the stage-coach days and Mr. Pickwick and Sam Weller, which would cheer you a little if you didn't see so many gaps in their lines filled up with the sickly yellow-white brick and blue slate, and with a sigh remember that even the romance surrounding Mr. Winkle is fast vanishing from the world. You let your eyes fall to the pavement and stop and stare a little, revolving many things, at a greengrocer's shop whose country produce probably comes mostly from Covent Garden,[1] but looks fresh and green as a relief from the jerry building. Then you take a step or two onward and raise your eyes, and stand transfixed with wonder, and a wave of pleasure and exultation sweeps away the memory of the squalidness of today and the shabby primness of yesterday; such a feeling as takes hold of the city-dweller when, after a night journey, he wakes and sees through his windows some range of great and noble mountains. And indeed this at the street's end is a mountain also; but wrought by the hand and the brain of man, and bearing the impress of his will and his aspirations; for there heaves itself up above the meanness of the street and its petty commercialism a mass of grey stone traceried and carved and moulded into a great triple portico beset with pinnacles and spires, so orderly in its intricacy, so elegant amidst its hugeness, that even without any thought of its history or meaning it fills your whole soul with satisfaction.

You walk on a little and see before you at last an ancient gate that leads into the close of the great church, but as if dreading that when you come nearer you may find some piece of modern pettiness or incongruity which will mar it, you turn away down a cross street from which the huge front is no longer visible, though its image is still in your mind's eye. The street leads

---

1. Covent Garden: London square, in which the central produce market is located.

you in no long while to a slow-flowing river crossed by an ugly modern iron bridge, and you are presently out in the fields, and going down a long causeway with a hint of Roman work in it. It runs along the river through a dead flat of black, peaty-looking country where long rows of men and women are working with an overlooker near them, giving us uncomfortable suggestions of the land on the other side of the Atlantic as it was; and you half expect as you get near some of these groups to find them black and woolly haired; but they are white as we call it, burned and grimed to dirty brown though; fair-sized and strong-looking enough, both men and women; but the women roughened and spoilt, with no remains of gracefulness, or softness of face or figure; the men heavy and depressed-looking; all that are not young, bent and beaten, and twisted and starved and weathered out of shape; in short, English field-labourers. You turn your face away with a sigh toward the town again, and see towering over its mean houses and the sluggish river and the endless reclaimed fen the flank of that huge building, whose front you saw just now, plainer and severer than the front, but harmonious and majestic still. A long roof tops it and a low, square tower rises from its midst. The day is getting on now, and the wind setting from the north-west is driving the smoke from the railway-works round the long roof and besmirching it somewhat; but still it looks out over the huddle of houses and the black fen with its bent rows of potato-hoers, like some relic of another world. What does it mean? Over there the railway-works with their monotonous hideousness of dwelling-houses for the artisans; here the gangs of the field-labourers; twelve shillings a week for ever and ever, and the workhouse for all day of judgment, of rewards and punishments; on each side and all around the nineteenth century, and rising solemnly in the midst of it, that token of the "dark ages," their hope in the past, grown now a warning for our future.

A thousand years ago our forefathers called the place Medehamstead, the abode of the meadows. They used the Roman works and doubtless knew little who wrought them, as by the side of the river Nene they drew together some stockaded collection of wooden and wattled houses. Then came the monks and built a church, which they dedicated to St. Peter; a much smaller and ruder building than that whose beauty has outlasted so many hundred years of waste and neglect and folly, but which seemed grand to them; so grand, that what for its building, what for the richness of its shrines, Medehamstead got to be called the Golden Burg. Doubtless that long stretching water there knew more than the monks' barges and the coracles of the fenmen, and the oars of the Norsemen have often beaten it white; but records of the sacking of the Golden Burg I have not got till the time when a valiant man of the country, in desperate contest with Duke William,[2] the man of Blood and Iron of the day, led on the host of the Danes to those rich shrines, and between them they stripped the Golden Burg down to its stone and timber. Hereward, that valiant man, was conquered and died, and what was left of the old tribal freedom of East England sank lower and lower into the Romanized feudality that crossed the Channel with the Frenchmen. But the country grew richer,

2. Duke William: William I (1027–1087), Duke of Normandy, also called William the Conqueror, invaded England in 1066. His followers were given important offices and large estates. Hereward, leader of resistance against the Norman conquest, became a folk hero.

and the craftsmen defter, and some three generations after that sacking of the Golden Burg, St. Peter's Church rose again, a great and noble pile, the most part of which we have seen to-day.

Time passed again; the feudal system had grown to its full height, and the cloud as big as a man's hand was rising up to overshadow it in the end. Doubtless this town played its part in this change: had a great gild changing to a commune, federating the craft-gilds under it; and was no longer called Medehamstead or the Golden Burg, but after its patron saint, Peterborough. And as a visible token of those times, the gilds built for the monks in the thirteenth century that wonderful piece of ordered beauty which you saw just now rising from out the grubby little streets of the early nineteenth century. They added to the great Church here and there in the fourteenth century, traceried windows to the aisles, two spirelets to the front, that low tower in the midst. The fifteenth century added certain fringes and trimmings, so to say, to the building; and so it was left to bear as best it could the successive waves of degradation, the blindness of middle-class puritanism, the brutality of the eighteenth-century squirearchy, and the stark idealless stupidity of the early nineteenth century; and there it stands now, with the foul sea of modern civilization washing against it; a token, as I said, of the hopes that were, and which civilization has destroyed. Might it but give a lesson to the hopes that are, and which shall some day destroy civilization!

For what was the world so utterly different from ours of this day, the world that completed the glories of the Golden Burg, which to-day is called Peterborough, and is chiefly known, I fear, as the depôt of the Great Northern Railway? This glorious building is a remnant of the feudal system, which even yet is not so well understood amongst us as it should be; and especially, people scarcely understand how great a gulf lies between the life of that day and the life of ours. The hypocrisy of so-called constitutional development has blinded us to the greatness of the change which has taken place; we use the words King, Parliament, Commerce, and so on, as if their connotation was the same as in that past time. Let us very briefly see, for the sake of a better understanding of the art and industry embodied in such works as Peterborough Cathedral, what was the relation of the complete feudal system with its two tribes, the one the unproductive masters, the other the productive servants, to the older incomplete feudality which it superseded; or in other words, what the Middle Ages came to before the development of the seeds of decay in them became obvious.

. . . Commerce, in our sense of the word, did not exist: people produced for their own consumption, and only exchanged the overplus of what they did not consume. A man would then sell the results of his labour in order to buy wherewithal to live upon or to live better; whereas at present he buys other people's labour in order to sell its results, that he may buy yet more labour, and so on to the end of the chapter; the mediæval man began with production, the modern begins with money. That is, there was no capital in our sense of the word; nay, it was a main care of the crafts, as we shall see later on, that there should be none. The money lent at usury was not lent for the purposes of production, but as spending-money for the proprietors of land: and their land was not capitalizable as it now is; they had to eat its produce from day to day, and used to travel about the country doing this like bands of an invading army, which was indeed what they were; but they could not, while the system lasted, drive their now tenants, erewhile serfs, off their lands, or fleece them beyond what the custom of the manor allowed, unless by sheer violence or illegal swindling; and also every free man had at least the use of some portion of the soil on which he was born. All this means that there was no profit to be made out of anything but the land; and profit out of that was confined to the lords of the soil, the superior tribe, the invading army, as represented in earlier times by Duke William and his hirelings. But even they could not accumulate their profit: the very serfdom that enabled them to live as an unproductive class forbade them to act as land capitalists: the serfs had to perform the customary services and nothing more, and thereby got a share of the produce over and above the economic rent, which surplus would to-day certainly not go to the cultivators of the soil. Now since all the class-robbery that there was was carried on by means of the land, and that not by any means closely or carefully, in spite of distinct arbitrary laws directed against the workers, which again were never fully carried out, it follows that it was easy for the productive class to live. Poor men's money was good, says one historian; necessaries were very cheap, that is, ordinary food (not the cagmag of to-day), ordinary clothing and housing; but luxuries were dear. Spices from the East, foreign fruits, cloth of gold, gold and silver plate, silk, velvet, Arras tapestries, Iceland gerfalcons, Turkish dogs, lions, and the like, doubtless cost far more than they do to-day. For the rest, men's desires keep pace with their power over nature, and in those days their desires were comparatively few; the upper class did not live so much more comfortably then than the lower; so there were not the same grounds or room for discontent as there are nowadays. A workman then might have liked to possess a canopy of cloth of gold or a big cupboard of plate; whereas now the contrast is no longer between splendour and simplicity, but between ease and anxiety, refinement and sordidness.

The ordinary life of the workman then was easy; what he suffered from was either the accidents of nature, which the society of the day had not yet learned to conquer, or the violence of his masters, the business of whose life was then open war, as it is now veiled war. Storm, plague, famine and battle, were his foes then; scarcity and the difficulty of bringing goods from one place to another were what pinched him, not as now, superabundance and the swiftness of carriage. Yet, in some respects even here, the contrast was not so violent as it is nowadays between rich and poor; for, if the artisan was apt to find himself in a besieged city, and had to battle at all adventure for his decent life and easy work, there were vicissitudes enough in the life of the lord also, and the great prince who sat in his hall like a god one day, surrounded by his gentlemen and men-at-arms, might find himself presently as the result of some luckless battle riding barefoot and bareheaded to the gallows-tree: distinguished politicians risked more then than they do now. A change of government was apt to take heads off shoulders.

What was briefly the process that led to this condition of things, a condition certainly not intended by the iron feudalism which aimed at embracing all life in its rigid grasp, and would not, if it had not been forced to it, have suffered the serf to escape from serfdom, the artisan to have any status except that of a serf, the gild to organize labour, or the town to become free? The necessities of the feudal lord were the opportunities of the towns: the former not being able to squeeze his serf-tenants beyond a certain point, and having no means of making his money grow, had to keep paying for his main position by yielding up what he thought he could spare of it to the producing classes. Of course, that is clear enough to see in reading mediaeval history; but what gave the men of the towns the desire to sacrifice their hard earnings for the sake of position, for the sake of obtaining a status alongside that of the baron and the bishop? The answer to my mind is clear: the spirit of association which had never died out of the peoples of Europe, and which in Northern Europe at least had been kept alive by the gilds which in turn it developed; the strong organization that feudalism could not crush.

The tale of the origin and development of the gilds is as long as it is interesting, and it can only be touched on here; for the history of the gilds is practically the history of the people in the Middle Ages, and what follows must be familiar to most of my readers. And I must begin by saying that it was not, as some would think (speaking always of Northern Europe), the towns that made the gilds, but the gilds that made the towns. These latter, you must remember once more, important as they grew to be before the Middle Ages ended, did not start with being organized centres of life political and intellectual, with tracts of country whose business it was just to feed and nourish them; in other words, they did not start with being mere second-rate imitations of the Greek and Roman cities. They were simply places on the face of the country where the population drawn together by convenience was thicker than in the ordinary country, a collection of neighbours associating themselves together for the ordinary business of life, finding it convenient in those disturbed times to palisade the houses and closes which they inhabited and lived by. But even before this took place, and while the unit of habitation was not even a village, but a homestead (or tun), our Teutonic and Scandinavian forefathers, while yet heathens, were used to band themselves together for feasts and sacrifices and for mutural defence and relief against accident and violence into what would now be called benefit societies, but which they called gilds. The change of religion from heathenism to Christianity did not make any difference to these associations; but as society grew firmer and more peaceful, as the commerce of our forefathers became something more than the selling to one town what the traders had plundered from another, these gilds developed in one direction into associations for the defence of the carriers and sellers of goods (who you must remember in passing had little in common with our merchants and commercial people); and on the other side began to grow into associations for the regulation of the special crafts, amongst which the building and clothing crafts were naturally pre-eminent. The development of these two sides of the gilds went on together, but at first the progress of the trading gilds, being administrative or political, was more marked than that of the craft-gilds, and their status was recognized much more readily by the princes of the feudal hierarchy; though I should say once for all that the direct development of the gilds did not flourish except in those countries where the undercurrent of the customs of the free tribes was too strong to be quite merged in the main stream of Romanized feudality. Popes, bishops, emperors, and kings in their early days fulminated against them; for instance, an association in Northern France for resistance to the Norse sea-robbers was condemned under ferocious penalties. In England, at any rate, where the king was always carrying on a struggle with his baronage, he was generally glad to acknowledge the claims of the towns or communes to a free administration as a makeweight to the power of the great feudatories; and here as well as in Flanders, Denmark, and North Germany, the merchant-gild was ready to form that administrative power, and so slid insensibly into the government of the growing towns under the name of the Great Gild, the Porte, the Lineage, and so on. These Great Gilds, the corporations of the towns, were from the first aristocratic and exclusive, even to the extent of excluding manual workmen; in the true spirit of Romanized feudalism, so diametrically opposed to that of the earlier tribal communities, in the tales of which the great chiefs are shown smithying armour, building houses and ships, and sowing their fields, just as the heroes of the Iliad and the Odyssey do. They were also exclusive in another way, membership in them being in the main an hereditary privilege, and they became at last very harsh and oppressive. But these bodies, divorced from labour and being nothing but governors, or at most administrators, on the one hand, and on the other not being an integral portion of the true feudal hierarchy, could not long hold their own against the gilds of craft, who all this while were producing and organizing production. There was a continuous and fierce struggle between the aristocratic and democratic elements in the towns, and plenty of downright fighting, bitter and cruel enough after the fashion of the times; besides a gradual progress of the crafts in getting hold of the power in the communes or municipalities. This went on all through the thirteenth century, and in the early part of the fourteenth the artisans had everywhere succeeded, and the affairs of the towns were administered by the federated craft-gilds. This brings us to the culminating period of the Middle Ages, the period to which my remarks on the condition of labourers apply most completely; though you must remember that the spirit which finally won the victory for the craft-gilds had been at work from the first, contending not only against the mere tyranny and violence incidental to those rough times, but also against the hierarchical system, the essential spirit of feudality. The progress of the gilds, which from the first were social, was the form which the class-struggle took in the Middle Ages.

I will now try to go a little more in detail into the conditions of art and industry in those days, conditions which it is clear, even from the scattered hints given above, are very different from those of to-day; so different indeed, that many people cannot conceive of them. The rules of the crafts in the great towns of Flanders will give us as typical examples as can be got at; since the mechanical arts, especially of weaving, were there farther advanced than anywhere else in Northern Europe. Let us take then the cloth-weavers of Flanders, and see under what rules they worked. No master to employ more than three journeymen in his workshop: no one under any pretence to have more than one workshop: the wages fixed per day, and the number of hours also: no work to be done on holidays. If piecework (which was allowed), the price per yard fixed: but only so much and no more to be done in a day. No one allowed to buy wool privately, but at open sales duly announced. No mixing of wools allowed; the man who uses English wool (the best) not to have any other on his premises. English and other foreign cloth not allowed to be sold. Workmen not belonging to the commune not admitted unless hands fell short. Most of these rules and many others may be considered to have been made in the direct interest of the workmen. Now for safeguards for the public: the workman must prove that he knows his craft duly: he serves as apprentice first, then as journeyman, after which he is a master if he can manage capital enough to set up three looms besides his own, which, of course, he generally could do. Width of web is settled; colour of list according to quality; no work to be done in a frost, or in a bad light. All cloth must be "walked" or fulled a certain time, and to a certain width; and so on, and so on. And finally every piece of cloth must stand the test of examination, and if it fall short, goes back to the maker, who is fined; if it come up to the due standard it is marked as satisfactory.

Now you will see that the accumulation of capital is impossible under such regulations as this, and it was meant to be impossible. The theory of industry among these communes was something like this. There is a certain demand for the goods which we can make, and a certain settled population to make them: if the goods are not thoroughly satisfactory we shall lose our market for them and be ruined: we must therefore keep up their quality to the utmost. Furthermore, the work to be done must be shared amongst the whole of those who can do it, who must be sure of work always as long as they are well behaved and industrious, and also must have a fair livelihood and plenty of leisure; as why should they not?

We shall find plenty of people to-day to cry out on this as slavery; but to begin with, history tells us that these workmen did not fight like slaves at any rate; and certainly a condition of slavery in which the slaves were well fed, and clothed, and housed, and had abundance of holidays, has not often been realized in the world's history. Yes, some will say, but their minds were enslaved. Were they? Their thoughts moved in the narrow circle maybe; and yet I can't say that a man is of slavish mind who is free to express his thoughts, such as they are; still less if he habitually expresses them; least of all if he expresses them in a definite form which gives pleasure to other people, what we call producing works of art; and these workmen of the communes did habitually produce works of art.

I have told you that the chief contrast between the upper and lower classes of those days was that the latter lacked the showy pomp and circumstance of life, and that the contrast rather lay there than in refinement and non-refinement. It is possible that some readers might judge from our own conditions that this lack involved the lack of art; but here, indeed, there was little cause for discontent on the part of the lower classes in those days; it was splendour rather than art in which they could feel any lack. It is, I know, so difficult to conceive of this nowadays that many people don't try to do so, but simply deny this fact; which is, however, undeniable by any one who had studied closely the art of the Middle Ages and its relation to the workers. I must say what I have often said before, that in those times there was no such thing as a piece of handicraft being ugly; that everything made had a due and befitting form; that most commonly, however ordinary its use might be, it was elaborately ornamented; such ornament was always both beautiful and inventive, and the mind of the workman was allowed full play and freedom in producing it; and also that for such art there was no extra charge made; it was a matter of course that such and such things should be ornamented, and the ornament was given and not sold. And this condition of the ordinary handicrafts with reference to the arts was the foundation of all that nobility of beauty which we were considering in a building like Peterborough Cathedral, and without that its beauty would never have existed. As it was, it was no great task to rear a building that should fill men's minds with awe and admiration when people fell to doing so of set purpose, in days when every cup and plate and knife-handle was beautiful.

When I had the Golden Burg in my eye just now, it was by no means only on account of its external beauty that I was so impressed by it, and wanted my readers to share my admiration, but it was also on account of the history embodied in it. To me it & its like are tokens of the aspirations of the workers five centuries ago; aspirations of which time alone seemed to promise fulfilment, & which were definitely social in character. If the leading element of association in the life of the mediæval workman could have cleared itself of certain drawbacks, and have developed logically along the road that seemed to be leading it onward, it seems to me it could scarcely have stopped short of forming a true society founded on the equality of labour: the Middle Ages, so to say, saw the promised land of Socialism from afar, like the Israelites, and like them had to turn back again into the desert. For the workers of that time, like us, suffered heavily from their masters: the upper classes who lived on their labour, finding themselves barred from progress by their lack of relation to the productive part of society, and at the same time holding all political power, turned towards aggrandizing themselves by perpetual war and shuffling of the political positions, and so opened the door to the advance of bureaucracy, and the growth of that thrice-accursed spirit of nationality which so hampers us even now in all attempts towards the realization of a true society. Furthermore, the association of the time, instinct as it was with hopes of something better, was exclusive. The commune of the Middle Ages, like the classical city, was unhappily only too often at strife with its sisters, and so became a fitting instrument for the greedy noble or bureaucratic king to play on. The gildsman's duties were bounded on the one hand by the limits of his craft, and on the other by the boundaries of the liberties of his city or town. The instinct of union was there, otherwise the course of the progress of association would not have had the unity which it did have: but the means of intercourse were lacking, and men were forced to defend the interests of small bodies against all comers, even those whom they should have received as brothers.

But, after all, these were but tokens of the real causes that checked the development of the Middle Ages towards Communism; that development can be traced from the survival of the primitive Communism which yet lived in the early days of the Middle Ages. The birth of tradition, strong in instinct, was weak in knowledge, and depended for its existence on its checking the desire of mankind for knowledge and the conquest of material nature: its own success in developing the resources of labour ruined it; it opened chances to men of growing rich and powerful if they could succeed in breaking down the artificial restrictions imposed by the gilds for the sake of the welfare of their members. The temptation was too much for the craving ignorance of the times, that were yet not so ignorant as not to have an instinct of what boundless stores of knowledge lay before the bold adventurer. As the need for the social and political organization of Europe blotted out the religious feeling of the early Middle Ages which produced the Crusades, so the need for knowledge and the power over material nature swept away the communistic aspirations of the fourteenth century, and it was not long before people had forgotten that they had ever existed.

The world had to learn another lesson; it had to gain power, and not be able to use it; to gain riches, and starve upon them like Midas on his gold; to gain knowledge, and then have newspapers for its teachers; in a word, to be so eager to gather the results of the deeds of the life of man that it must forget the life of man itself. Whether the price of the lesson was worth the lesson we can scarcely tell yet; but one comfort is that we are fast getting perfect in it; we shall, at any rate, not have to begin at the beginning of it again. The hope of the renaissance of the time when Europe first opened its mouth wide to fill its belly with the east wind of commercialism, that hope is passing away, and the ancient hope of the workmen of Europe is coming to life again. Times troublous and rough enough we shall have, doubtless, but not that dull time over again during which labour lay hopeless and voiceless under the muddle of self-satisfied competition.

It is not so hard now to picture to oneself those grey masses of stone, which our forefathers raised in their hope, standing no longer lost and melancholy over the ghastly misery of the fields and the squalor of the towns, but smiling rather on their new-born sisters the houses and halls of the free citizens of the new Communes, and the garden-like fields about them where there will be labour still, but the labour of the happy people who have shaken off the curse of labour and kept its blessing only. Between the time when the hope of the workman disappeared in the fifteenth century and our own times, there is a great gap indeed, but we know now that it will be filled up before long, and that our own lives from day to day may help to fill it. That is no little thing and is well worth living for, whatever else may fail us.

W. E. B. DUBOIS (1868–1963), *Of the Quest of the Golden Fleece*

The Massachusetts-born sociologist W. E. B. DuBois was educated at Fisk, Harvard, and Berlin Universities, during the period when lynchings, segregation, and Booker T. Washington helped to keep the black man "in his place." Washington—supported by many influential whites—urged blacks to become morally superior, to train themselves as artisans, to adjust to their lot. "In all things purely social," Washington announced, "we can be as separate as the five fingers, and yet one as the hand in all things essential to mutual progress." However, Washington's definition of "things purely social" included political power, civil rights, and higher education. In opposition to this approach, DuBois insisted that blacks must continue to demand full equality in all areas of life, and that they must defend themselves against lynchings and other forms of violence. On these principles he founded, in 1905, the short-lived Niagara Movement. This was a forerunner of the National Association for the Advancement of Colored People (NAACP), of whose journal, Crisis, *DuBois became editor. DuBois supported the Pan-African movement and the Bolshevik revolution, though his relations with American socialists were never cordial. In 1961 DuBois emigrated to Ghana, where he directed the planned* Encyclopedia Africana *and where he lived until his death.*

In The Souls of Black Folk—*a study of the economic and psychological oppression of American blacks—DuBois describes the experience of being in, but not of, one's world: "One ever feels his two-ness—an American, a Negro; two souls, two thoughts, two unreconciled strivings; two warring ideals in one dark body." The chapter below focuses on the effects of the cotton economy on the lives of rural southern blacks, and on the conditions that motivated their flight to the cities. As DuBois notes, "the sin of the country districts is visited on the town"—a statement we have only recently come to understand in full. Both aspects of DuBois' remarkable education are evident in the chapter—classical rhetoric and sociological analysis—but vignettes, dialogue, and vivid description make the study as moving as it is incisive.*

Have you ever seen a cotton-field white with the harvest,—its golden fleece hovering above the black earth like a silvery cloud edged with dark green, its bold white signals waving like the foam of billows from Carolina to Texas across that Black and human Sea? I have sometimes half suspected that here the winged ram Chrysomallus left that Fleece after which Jason and his Argonauts went vaguely wandering into the shadowy East three thousand years ago; and certainly one might frame a pretty and not far-fetched analogy of witchery and dragon's teeth, and blood and armed men, between the ancient and the modern quest of the Golden Fleece in the Black Sea.

And now the golden fleece is found; not only found, but, in its birthplace, woven. For the hum of the cotton-mills is the newest and most significant thing in the New South to-day. All through the Carolinas and Georgia, away down to Mexico, rise these gaunt red buildings, bare and homely, and yet so busy and noisy withal that they scarce seem to belong to the slow and sleepy land. Perhaps they sprang from dragons' teeth. So the Cotton Kingdom still lives; the world still bows beneath her sceptre. Even the markets that once defied the *parvenu* have crept one by one across the seas, and then slowly and reluctantly, but surely, have started toward the Black Belt.

To be sure, there are those who wag their heads knowingly and tell us that the capital of the Cotton Kingdom has moved from the Black to the White Belt,—that the Negro of to-day raises not more than half of the cotton crop. Such men forget that the cotton crop has doubled, and more than doubled, since the era of slavery, and that, even granting their contention, the Negro is still supreme in a Cotton Kingdom larger than that on which the Confederacy builded its hopes. So the Negro forms to-day one of the chief figures in a great world-industry; and this, for its own sake, and in the light of historic interest, makes the field-hands of the cotton country worth studying.

We seldom study the condition of the Negro to-day honestly and carefully. It is so much easier to assume that we know it all. Or perhaps, having already reached conclusions in our own minds, we are loth to have them disturbed by facts. And yet how little we really know of these millions,—of their daily lives and longings, of their homely joys and sorrows, of their real shortcomings and the meaning of their crimes! All this we can only learn by intimate contact with the masses, and not by wholesale arguments covering millions separate in time and space, and differing widely in training and culture. To-day, then, my reader, let us turn our faces to the Black Belt of Georgia and seek simply to know the condition of the black farm-laborers of one county there.

Here in 1890 lived ten thousand Negroes and two thousand whites. The country is rich, yet the people are poor. The keynote of the Black Belt is debt; not commercial credit, but debt in the sense of continued inability on the part of the mass of the population to make income cover expense. This is the direct heritage of the South from the wasteful economies of the slave *régime;* but it was emphasized and brought to a crisis by the Emancipation of the slaves. In 1860, Dougherty County had six thousand slaves, worth at least two and a half millions of dollars; its farms were estimated at three millions, —making five and a half millions of property, the value of which depended largely on the slave system, and on the speculative demand for land once marvellously rich but already partially devitalized by careless and exhaustive culture. The war then meant a financial crash; in place of the five and a half millions of 1860, there remained in 1870 only farms valued at less than two millions. With this came increased competition in cotton culture from the rich lands of Texas; a steady fall in the normal price of cotton followed, from about fourteen cents a pound in 1860 until it reached four cents in 1898. Such a financial revolution was it that involved the owners of the cotton-belt in debt. And if things went ill with the master, how fared it with the man?

The plantations of Dougherty County in slavery days were not as imposing and aristocratic as those of Virginia. The Big House was smaller and usually one-storied, and sat very near the slave cabins. Sometimes these cabins stretched off on either side like wings; sometimes only on one side, forming a double row, or edging the road that turned into the plantation from the main thoroughfare. The form and disposition of the laborers' cabins throughout the Black Belt is to-day the same as in slavery days. Some live in the self-same cabins, others in cabins rebuilt on the sites of the old. All are sprinkled in little groups over the face of the land, centering about some dilapidated Big House where the head-tenant or agent lives. The general character and arrangement of these dwellings remains on the whole unaltered. There were in the county, outside the corporate town of Albany, about fifteen hundred Negro families in 1898. Out of all these, only a single family occupied a house with seven rooms; only fourteen have five rooms or more. The mass live in one- and two-room homes.

The size and arrangements of a people's homes are no unfair index of their condition. If, then, we inquire more carefully into these Negro homes, we find much that is unsatisfactory. All over the face of the land is the one-room cabin,—now standing in the shadow of the Big House, now staring at the dusty road, now rising dark and sombre amid the green of the cotton-fields. It is nearly always old and bare, built of rough boards, and neither plastered nor ceiled. Light and ventilation are supplied by the single door and by the square hole in the wall with its wooden shutter. There is no glass, porch, or ornamentation without. Within is a fireplace, black and smoky, and usually unsteady with age. A bed or two, a table, a wooden chest, and a few chairs compose the furniture; while a stray show-bill or a newspaper makes up the decorations for the walls. Now and then one may find such a cabin kept scrupulously neat, with merry steaming fireplace and hospitable door; but the majority are dirty and dilapidated, smelling of eating and sleeping, poorly ventilated, and anything but homes.

Above all, the cabins are crowded. We have come to associate crowding with homes in cities almost exclusively. This is primarily because we have so little accurate knowledge of country life. Here in Dougherty County one may find families of eight and ten occupying one or two rooms, and for every ten rooms of house accommodation for the Negroes there are twenty-five persons. The worst tenement abominations of New York do not have above twenty-two persons for every ten rooms. Of course, one small, close room in a city, without a yard, is in many respects worse than the larger single country room. In other respects it is better; it has glass windows, a decent chimney, and a trustworthy floor. The single great advantage of the Negro peasant is that he may spend most of his life outside his hovel, in the open fields.

There are four chief causes of these wretched homes: First, long custom born of slavery has assigned such homes to Negroes; white laborers would be offered better accommodations, and might, for that and similar reasons, give better work. Secondly, the Negroes, used to such accommodations, do not as a rule demand better; they do not know what better houses mean. Thirdly, the landlords as a class have not yet come to realize that it is a good business investment to raise the standard of living among labor by slow and judicious methods; that a Negro laborer who demands three rooms and fifty cents a day would give more efficient work and leave a larger profit than a discouraged toiler herding his family in one room and working for thirty cents. Lastly, among such conditions of life there are few incentives to make the laborer become a better farmer. If he is ambitious, he moves to town or tries other labor; as a tenant-farmer his outlook is almost hopeless, and following it as a makeshift, he takes the house that is given him without protest.

In such homes, then, these Negro peasants live. The families are both small and large; there are many single tenants,—widows and bachelors, and remnants of broken groups. The system of labor and the size of the houses both tend to the breaking up of family groups: the grown children go away as contract hands or migrate to town, the sister goes into service; and so one finds many families with hosts of babies, and many newly married couples, but comparatively few families with half-grown and grown sons and daughters. The average size of Negro families has undoubtedly decreased since the war, primarily from economic stress. In Russia over a third of the bridegrooms and over half the brides are under twenty; the same was true of the ante-bellum Negroes. To-day, however, very few of the boys and less than a fifth of the Negro girls under twenty are married. The young men marry between the ages of twenty-five and thirty-five; the young women between twenty and thirty. Such postponement is due to the difficulty of earning sufficient to rear and support a family; and it undoubtedly leads, in the country districts, to sexual immorality. The form of this immorality, however, is very seldom that of prostitution, and less frequently that of illegitimacy than one would imagine. Rather, it takes the form of separation and desertion after a family group has been formed. The number of separated persons is thirty-five to the thousand,—a very large number. It would of course be unfair to compare this number with divorce statistics, for many of these separated women are in reality widowed, were the truth known, and in other cases the separation is not permanent. Nevertheless, here lies the seat of greatest moral danger. There is little or no prostitution among these Negroes, and over three-fourths of the families, as found by house-to-house investigation, deserve to be classed as decent people with considerable regard for female chastity. To be sure, the ideas of the mass would not suit New England, and there are many loose habits and notions. Yet the rate of illegitimacy is undoubtedly lower than in Austria or Italy, and the women as a class are modest. The plague-spot in sexual relations is easy marriage and easy separation. This is no sudden development, nor the fruit of Emancipation. It is the plain heritage from slavery. In those days Sam, with his master's consent, "took up" with Mary. No ceremony was necessary, and in the busy life of the great plantations of the Black Belt it was usually dispensed with. If now the master needed Sam's work in another plantation or in another part of the same plantation, or if he took a notion to sell the slave, Sam's married life with Mary was usually unceremoniously broken, and then it was clearly to the master's interest to have both of them take new mates. This widespread custom of two centuries has not been eradicated in thirty years. To-day Sam's grandson

"takes up" with a woman without license or ceremony; they live together de-
cently and honestly, and are, to all intents and purposes, man and wife.
Sometimes these unions are never broken until death; but in too many cases
family quarrels, a roving spirit, a rival suitor, or perhaps more frequently the
hopeless battle to support a family, lead to separation, and a broken household is the result. The Negro church has done much to stop this practice, and
now most marriage ceremonies are performed by the pastors. Nevertheless,
the evil is still deep seated, and only a general raising of the standard of living will finally cure it.

Looking now at the county black population as a whole, it is fair to characterize it as poor and ignorant. Perhaps ten per cent compose the well-to-do
and the best of the laborers, while at least nine per cent are thoroughly lewd
and vicious. The rest, over eighty per cent, are poor and ignorant, fairly honest and well meaning, plodding, and to a degree shiftless, with some but not
great sexual looseness. Such class lines are by no means fixed; they vary, one
might almost say, with the price of cotton. The degree of ignorance cannot
easily be expressed. We may say, for instance, that nearly two-thirds of them
cannot read or write. This but partially expresses the fact. They are ignorant
of the world about them, of modern economic organization, of the function of
government, of individual worth and possibilities,—of nearly all those things
which slavery in self-defence had to keep them from learning. Much that the
white boy imbibes from his earliest social atmosphere forms the puzzling
problems of the black boy's mature years. America is not another world for
Opportunity to *all* her sons.

It is easy for us to lose ourselves in details in endeavoring to grasp and
comprehend the real condition of a mass of human beings. We often forget
that each unit in the mass is a throbbing human soul. Ignorant it may be, and
poverty stricken, black and curious in limb and ways and thought; and yet it
loves and hates, it toils and tires, it laughs and weeps its bitter tears, and
looks in vague and awful longing at the grim horizon of its life,—all this,
even as you and I. These black thousands are not in reality lazy; they are improvident and careless; they insist on breaking the monotony of toil with a
glimpse at the great town-world on Saturday; they have their loafers and their
rascals; but the great mass of them work continuously and faithfully for a return, and under circumstances that would call forth equal voluntary effort
from few if any other modern laboring class. Over eighty-eight per cent of
them—men, women, and children—are farmers. Indeed, this is almost the
only industry. Most of the children get their schooling after the "crops are
laid by," and very few there are that stay in school after the spring work has
begun. Child-labor is to be found here in some of its worst phases, as foster-
ing ignorance and stunting physical development. With the grown men of the
county there is little variety in work: thirteen hundred are farmers, and two
hundred are laborers, teamsters, etc., including twenty-four artisans, ten merchants, twenty-one preachers, and four teachers. This narrowness of life
reaches its maximum among the women: thirteen hundred and fifty of these
are farm laborers, one hundred are servants and washerwomen, leaving sixty-five housewives, eight teachers, and six seamstresses.

Among this people there is no leisure class. We often forget that in the
United States over half the youth and adults are not in the world earning in-

comes, but are making homes, learning of the world, or resting after the heat of the strife. But here ninety-six per cent are toiling; no one with leisure to turn the bare and cheerless cabin into a home, no old folks to sit beside the fire and hand down traditions of the past; little of careless happy childhood and dreaming youth. The dull monotony of daily toil is broken only by the gayety of the thoughtless and the Saturday trip to town. The toil, like all farm toil, is monotonous, and here there are little machinery and few tools to relieve its burdensome drudgery. But with all this, it is work in the pure open air, and this is something in a day when fresh air is scarce.

The land on the whole is still fertile, despite long abuse. For nine or ten months in succession the crops will come if asked: garden vegetables in April, grain in May, melons in June and July, hay in August, sweet potatoes in September, and cotton from then to Christmas. And yet on two-thirds of the land there is but one crop, and that leaves the toilers in debt. Why is this?

Away down the Baysan road, where the broad flat fields are flanked by great oak forests, is a plantation; many thousands of acres it used to run, here and there, and beyond the great wood. Thirteen hundred human beings here obeyed the call of one,—were his in body, and largely in soul. One of them lives there yet,—a short, stocky man, his dull-brown face seamed and drawn, and his tightly curled hair gray-white. The crops? Just tolerable, he said; just tolerable. Getting on? No—he wasn't getting on at all. Smith of Albany "furnishes" him, and his rent is eight hundred pounds of cotton. Can't make anything at that. Why didn't he buy land! Humph! Takes money to buy land. And he turns away. Free! The most piteous thing amid all the black ruin of war-time, amid the broken fortunes of the masters, the blighted hopes of mothers and maidens, and the fall of an empire,—the most piteous thing amid all this was the black freedman who threw down his hoe because the world called him free. What did such a mockery of freedom mean? Not a cent of money, not an inch of land, not a mouthful of victuals,—not even ownership of the rags on his back. Free! On Saturday, once or twice a month, the old master, before the war, used to dole out bacon and meal to his Negroes. And after the first flush of freedom wore off, and his true helplessness dawned on the freedman, he came back and picked up his hoe, and old master still doled out his bacon and meal. The legal form of service was theoretically far different; in practice, task-work or "cropping" was substituted for daily toil in gangs; and the slave gradually became a metayer, or tenant on shares, in name, but a laborer with indeterminate wages in fact.

Still the price of cotton fell, and gradually the landlords deserted their plantations, and the reign of the merchant began. The merchant of the Black Belt is a contractor, and part despot. His store, which used most frequently to stand at the cross-roads and become the centre of a weekly village, has now moved to town; and thither the Negro tenant follows him. The merchant keeps everything,—clothes and shoes, coffee and sugar, pork and meal, canned and dried goods, wagons and ploughs, seed and fertilizer,—and what he has not in stock he can give you an order for at the store across the way. Here, then, comes the tenant, Sam Scott, after he has contracted with some absent landlord's agent for hiring forty acres of land; he fingers his hat nervously until the merchant finishes his morning chat with Colonel Saunders, and calls out, "Well, Sam, what do you want?" Sam wants him to "furnish" him,—*i.e.,* to advance him food and clothing for the year, and perhaps seed and tools, until his crop is raised and sold. If Sam seems a favorable subject, he and the merchant go to a lawyer, and Sam executes a chattel mortgage on his mule and wagon in return for seed and a week's rations. As soon as the green cotton-leaves appear above the ground, another mortgage is given on the "crop." Every Saturday, or at longer intervals, Sam calls upon the merchant for his "rations"; a family of five usually gets about thirty pounds of fat side-pork and a couple of bushels of cornmeal a month. Besides this, clothing and shoes must be furnished; if Sam or his family is sick, there are orders on the druggist and doctor; if the mule wants shoeing, an order on the blacksmith, etc. If Sam is a hard worker and crops promise well, he is often encouraged to buy more,—sugar, extra clothes, perhaps a buggy. But he is seldom encouraged to save. When cotton rose to ten cents last fall, the shrewd merchants of Dougherty County sold a thousand buggies in one season, mostly to black men.

The security offered for such transactions—a crop and chattel mortgage—may at first seem slight. And, indeed, the merchants tell many a true tale of shiftlessness and cheating; of cotton picked at night, mules disappearing, and tenants absconding. But on the whole the merchant of the Black Belt is the most prosperous man in the section. So skilfully and so closely has he drawn the bonds of the law about the tenant, that the black man has often simply to choose between pauperism and crime; he "waives" all homestead exemptions in his contract; he cannot touch his own mortgaged crop, which the laws put almost in the full control of the land-owner and of the merchant. When the crop is growing the merchant watches it like a hawk; as soon as it is ready for market he takes possession of it, sells it, pays the land-owner his rent, subtracts his bill for supplies, and if, as sometimes happens, there is anything left, he hands it over to the black serf for his Christmas celebration.

The direct result of this system is an all-cotton scheme of agriculture and the continued bankruptcy of the tenant. The currency of the Black Belt is cotton. It is a crop always salable for ready money, not usually subject to great yearly fluctuations in price, and one which the Negroes know how to raise. The landlord therefore demands his rent in cotton, and the merchant will accept mortgages on no other crop. There is no use asking the black tenant, then, to diversify his crops,—he cannot under this system. Moreover, the system is bound to bankrupt the tenant. I remember once meeting a little one-mule wagon on the River road. A young black fellow sat in it driving listlessly, his elbows on his knees. His dark-faced wife sat beside him, stolid, silent.

"Hello!" cried my driver,—he has a most impudent way of addressing these people, though they seem used to it,—"what have you got there?"

"Meat and meal," answered the man, stopping. The meat lay uncovered in the bottom of the wagon,—a great thin side of fat pork covered with salt; the meal was in a white bushel bag.

"What did you pay for that meat?"

"Ten cents a pound." It could have been bought for six or seven cents cash.

"And the meal?"

"Two dollars." One dollar and ten cents is the cash price in town. Here was a man paying five dollars for goods which he could have bought for three dollars cash, and raised for one dollar or one dollar and a half.

Yet it is not wholly his fault. The Negro farmer started behind,—started in debt. This was not his choosing, but the crime of this happy-go-lucky nation which goes blundering along with its Reconstruction tragedies, its Spanish war interludes and Philippine matinees, just as though God really were dead. Once in debt, it is no easy matter for a whole race to emerge.

In the year of low-priced cotton, 1898, out of three hundred tenant families one hundred and seventy-five ended their year's work in debt to the extent of fourteen thousand dollars; fifty cleared nothing, and the remaining seventy-five made a total profit of sixteen hundred dollars. The net indebtedness of the black tenant families of the whole county must have been at least sixty thousand dollars. In a more prosperous year the situation is far better; but on the average the majority of tenants end the year even, or in debt, which means that they work for board and clothes. Such an economic organization is radically wrong. Whose is the blame?

The underlying causes of this situation are complicated but discernible. And one of the chief, outside the carelessness of the nation in letting the slave start with nothing, is the widespread opinion among the merchants and employers of the Black Belt that only by the slavery of debt can the Negro be kept at work. Without doubt, some pressure was necessary at the beginning of the free-labor system to keep the listless and lazy at work; and even to-day the mass of the Negro laborers need stricter guardianship than most Northern laborers. Behind this honest and widespread opinion dishonesty and cheating of the ignorant laborers have a good chance to take refuge. And to all this must be added the obvious fact that a slave ancestry and a system of unrequited toil has not improved the efficiency or temper of the mass of black laborers. Nor is this peculiar to Sambo; it has in history been just as true of John and Hans, of Jacques and Pat, of all ground-down peasantries. Such is the situation of the mass of the Negroes in the Black Belt to-day; and they are thinking about it. Crime, and a cheap and dangerous socialism, are the inevitable results of this pondering. I see now that ragged black man sitting on a log, aimlessly whittling a stick. He muttered to me with the murmur of many ages, when he said: "White man sit down whole year; Nigger work day and night and make crop; Nigger hardly gits bread and meat; white man sittin' down gits all. *It's wrong.*" And what do the better classes of Negroes do to improve their situation? One of two things: if any way possible, they buy land; if not, they migrate to town. Just as centuries ago it was no easy thing for the serf to escape into the freedom of town-life, even so today there are hindrances laid in the way of county laborers. In considerable parts of all the Gulf States, and especially in Mississippi, Louisana, and Arkansas, the Negroes on the plantations in the back-country districts are still held at forced labor practically without wages. Especially is this true in districts where the farmers are composed of the more ignorant class of poor whites, and the Negroes are beyond the reach of schools and intercourse with their advancing fellows. If such a peon should run away, the sheriff, elected by white suffrage, can usually be depended on to catch the fugitive, return him, and ask no questions. If he escape to another county, a charge of petty thieving, easily true, can be depended upon to secure his return. Even if some unduly officious person insist upon a trial, neighborly comity will probably make his conviction sure, and then the labor due the county can easily be bought by the master. Such a system is impossible in the more civilized parts of the South, or near the large towns and cities; but in those vast stretches of land beyond the telegraph and the newspaper the spirit of the Thirteenth Amendment is sadly broken. This represents the lowest economic depths of the black American peasant; and in a study of the rise and condition of the Negro freeholder we must trace his economic progress from the modern serf-dom.

Even in the better-ordered country districts of the South the free move-ment of agricultural laborers is hindered by the migration-agent laws. The "Associated Press" recently informed the world of the arrest of a young white man in Southern Georgia who represented the "Atlantic Naval Supplies Company," and who "was caught in the act of enticing hands from the tur-pentine farm of Mr. John Greer." The crime for which this young man was arrested is taxed five hundred dollars for each county in which the employ-ment agent proposes to gather laborers for work outside the State. Thus the Negroes' ignorance of the labor-market outside his own vicinity is increased rather than diminished by the laws of nearly every Southern State.

Similar to such measures is the unwritten law of the back districts and small towns of the South, that the character of all Negroes unknown to the mass of the community must be vouched for by some white man. This is really a revival of the old Roman idea of the patron under whose protection the new-made freedman was put. In many instances this system has been of great good to the Negro, and very often under the protection and guidance of the former master's family, or other white friends, the freedman progressed in wealth and morality. But the same system has in other cases resulted in the refusal of whole communities to recognize the right of a Negro to change his habitation and to be master of his own fortunes. A black stranger in Baker County, Georgia, for instance, is liable to be stopped anywhere on the public highway and made to state his business to the satisfaction of any white inter-rogator. If he fails to give a suitable answer, or seems too independent or "sassy," he may be arrested or summarily driven away.

Thus it is that in the country districts of the South, by written or unwrit-ten law, peonage, hindrances to the migration of labor, and a system of white patronage exists over large areas. Besides this, the chance for lawless oppres-sion and illegal exactions is vastly greater in the country than in the city, and nearly all the more serious race disturbances of the last decade have arisen from disputes in the county between master and man,—as, for instance, the Sam Hose affair. As a result of such a situation, there arose, first, the Black Belt; and, second, the Migration to Town. The Black Belt was not, as many assumed, a movement toward fields of labor under more genial climatic con-ditions; it was primarily a huddling for self-protection,—a massing of the black population for mutual defence in order to secure the peace and tran-quillity necessary to economic advance. This movement took place between Emancipation and 1880, and only partially accomplished the desired results. The rush to town since 1880 is the counter-movement of men disappointed in the economic opportunities of the Black Belt.

In Dougherty County, Georgia, one can see easily the results of this experiment in huddling for protection. Only ten per cent of the adult population was born in the county, and yet the blacks outnumber the whites four or five to one. There is undoubtedly a security to the blacks in their very numbers, —a personal freedom from arbitrary treatment, which makes hundreds of laborers cling to Dougherty in spite of low wages and economic distress. But a change is coming, and slowly but surely even here the agricultural laborers are drifting to town and leaving the broad acres behind. Why is this? Why do not the Negroes become land-owners, and build up the black landed peasantry, which has for a generation and more been the dream of philanthropist and statesman?

To the car-window sociologist, to the man who seeks to understand and know the South by devoting the few leisure hours of a holiday trip to unravelling the snarl of centuries,—to such men very often the whole trouble with the black field-hand may be summed up by Aunt Ophelia's word, "Shiftless!" They have noted repeatedly scenes like one I saw last summer. We were riding along the highroad to town at the close of a long hot day. A couple of young black fellows passed us in a muleteam, with several bushels of loose corn in the ear. One was driving, listlessly bent forward, his elbows on his knees,—a happy-go-lucky, careless picture of irresponsibility. The other was fast asleep in the bottom of the wagon. As we passed we noticed an ear of corn fall from the wagon. They never saw it,—not they. A rod farther on we noted another ear on the ground; and between that creeping mule and town we counted twenty-six ears of corn. Shiftless? Yes, the personification of shiftlessness. And yet follow those boys: they are not lazy; to-morrow morning they'll be up with the sun; they work hard when they do work, and they work willingly. They have no sordid, selfish, money-getting ways, but rather a fine disdain for mere cash. They'll loaf before your face and work behind your back with good-natured honesty. They'll steal a watermelon, and hand you back your lost purse intact. Their great defect as laborers lies in their lack of incentive to work beyond the mere pleasure of physical exertion. They are careless because they have not found that it pays to be careful; they are improvident because the improvident ones of their acquaintance get on about as well as the provident. Above all, they cannot see why they should take unusual pains to make the white man's land better, or to fatten his mule, or save his corn. On the other hand, the white land-owner argues that any attempt to improve these laborers by increased responsibility, or higher wages, or better homes, or land of their own, would be sure to result in failure. He shows his Northern visitor the scarred and wretched land; the ruined mansions, the worn-out soil and mortgaged acres, and says, This is Negro freedom!

Now it happens that both master and man have just enough argument on their respective sides to make it difficult for them to understand each other. The Negro dimly personifies in the white man all his ills and misfortunes; if he is poor, it is because the white man seizes the fruit of his toil; if he is ignorant, it is because the white man gives him neither time nor facilities to learn; and, indeed, if any misfortune happens to him, it is because of some hidden machinations of "white folks." On the other hand, the masters and the masters' sons have never been able to see why the Negro, instead of settling down to be day-laborers for bread and clothes, are infected with a silly desire to rise in the world, and why they are sulky, dissatisfied, and careless, where their fathers were happy and dumb and faithful. "Why, you niggers have an easier time than I do," said a puzzled Albany merchant to his black customer. "Yes," he replied, "and so does yo' hogs."

Taking, then, the dissatisfied and shiftless field-hand as a starting-point, let us inquire how the black thousands of Dougherty have struggled from him up toward their ideal, and what that ideal is. All social struggle is evidenced by the rise, first of economic, then of social classes, among a homogeneous population. To-day the following economic classes are plainly differentiated among these Negroes.

A "submerged tenth" of croppers, with a few paupers; forty per cent who are metayers and thirty-nine per cent of semi-metayers and wage-laborers. There are left five per cent of money-renters and six per cent of freeholders, —the "Upper Ten" of the land. The croppers are entirely without capital, even in the limited sense of food or money to keep them from seedtime to harvest. All they furnish is their labor; the land-owner furnishes land, stock, tools, seed, and house; and at the end of the year the laborer gets from a third to a half of the crop. Out of his share, however, comes pay and interest for food and clothing advanced him during the year. Thus we have a laborer without capital and without wages, and an employer whose capital is largely his employees' wages. It is an unsatisfactory arrangement, both for hirer and hired, and is usually in vogue on poor land with hard-pressed owners.

Above the croppers come the great mass of the black population who work the land on their own responsibility, paying rent in cotton and supported by the crop-mortgage system. After the war this system was attractive to the freedmen on account of its larger freedom and its possibility for making a surplus. But with the carrying out of the crop-lien system, the deterioration of the land, and the slavery of debt, the position of the metayers has sunk to a dead level of practically unrewarded toil. Formerly all tenants had some capital, and often considerable; but absentee landlordism, rising rack-rent, and falling cotton have stripped them well-nigh of all, and probably not over half of them to-day own their mules. The change from cropper to tenant was accomplished by fixing the rent. If, now, the rent fixed was reasonable, this was an incentive to the tenant to strive. On the other hand, if the rent was too high, or if the land deteriorated, the result was to discourage and check the efforts of the black peasantry. There is no doubt that the latter case is true; that in Dougherty County every economic advantage of the price of cotton in market and of the strivings of the tenant has been taken advantage of by the landlords and merchants, and swallowed up in rent and interest. If cotton rose in price, the rent rose even higher; if cotton fell, the rent remained or followed reluctantly. If the tenant worked hard and raised a large crop, his rent was raised the next year; if that year the crop failed, his corn was confiscated and his mule sold for debt. There were, of course, exceptions to this,—cases of personal kindness and forbearance; but in the vast majority of cases the rule was to extract the uttermost farthing from the mass of the black farm laborers.

The average metayer pays from twenty to thirty per cent of his crop in rent. The result of such rack-rent can only be evil,—abuse and neglect of the soil, deterioration in the character of the laborers, and a widespread sense of injustice. "Wherever the country is poor," cried Arthur Young, "it is in the hands of metayers," and "their condition is more wretched than that of day-laborers." He was talking of Italy a century ago; but he might have been talking of Dougherty County to-day. And especially is that true to-day which he declares was true in France before the Revolution: "The metayers are considered as little better than menial servants, removable at pleasure, and obliged to conform in all things to the will of the landlords." On this low plane half the black population of Dougherty County—perhaps more than half the black millions of this land—are to-day struggling.

A degree above these we may place those laborers who receive money wages for their work. Some receive a house with perhaps a garden-spot; then supplies of food and clothing are advanced, and certain fixed wages are given at the end of the year, varying from thirty to sixty dollars, out of which the supplies must be paid for, with interest. About eighteen per cent of the population belong to this class of semi-metayers, while twenty-two per cent are laborers paid by the month or year, and are either "furnished" by their own savings or perhaps more usually by some merchant who takes his chances of payment. Such laborers receive from thirty-five to fifty cents a day during the working season. They are usually young unmarried persons, some being women; and when they marry they sink to the class of metayers, or, more seldom, become renters.

The renters for fixed money rentals are the first of the emerging classes, and form five per cent of the families. The sole advantage of this small class is their freedom to choose their crops, and the increased responsibility which comes through having money transactions. While some of the renters differ little in condition from the metayers, yet on the whole they are more intelligent and responsible persons, and are the ones who eventually become land-owners. Their better character and greater shrewdness enable them to gain, perhaps to demand, better terms in rents; rented farms, varying from forty to a hundred acres, bear an average rental of about fifty-four dollars a year. The men who conduct such farms do not long remain renters; either they sink to metayers, or with a successful series of harvests rise to be land-owners.

In 1870 the tax-books of Dougherty report no Negroes as landholders. If there were any such at that time,—and there may have been a few,—their land was probably held in the name of some white patron,—a method not uncommon during slavery. In 1875 ownership of land had begun with seven hundred and fifty acres; ten years later this had increased to over sixty-five hundred acres, to nine thousand acres in 1890 and ten thousand in 1900. The total assessed property has in this same period risen from eighty thousand dollars in 1875 to two hundred and forty thousand dollars in 1900. . . .

If all the black land-owners who had ever held land here had kept it or left it in the hands of black men, the Negroes would have owned nearer thirty thousand acres than the fifteen thousand they now hold. And yet these fifteen thousand acres are a creditable showing,—a proof of no little weight of the worth and ability of the Negro people. If they had been given an economic start at Emancipation, if they had been in an enlightened and rich community which really desired their best good, then we might perhaps call such a result small or even insignificant. But for a few thousand poor ignorant field-hands,

in the face of poverty, a falling market, and social stress, to save and capital-
ize two hundred thousand dollars in a generation has meant a tremendous effort. The rise of a nation, the pressing forward of a social class, means a bitter struggle, a hard and soul-sickening battle with the world such as few of
the more favored classes know or appreciate.

Out of the hard economic conditions of this portion of the Black Belt,
only six per cent of the population have succeeded in emerging into peasant
proprietorship; and these are not all firmly fixed, but grow and shrink in
number with the wavering of the cotton-market. Fully ninety-four per cent
have struggled for land and failed, and half of them sit in hopeless serfdom.
For these there is one other avenue of escape toward which they have turned
in increasing numbers, namely, migration to town. A glance at the distribution of land among the black owners curiously reveals this fact. In 1898 the
holdings were as follows: Under forty acres, forty-nine families; forty to two
hundred and fifty acres, seventeen families, two hundred and fifty to one
thousand acres, thirteen families; one thousand or more acres, two families.
Now in 1890 there were forty-four holdings, but only nine of these were
under forty acres. The great increase of holdings, then, has come in the buying of small homesteads near town, where their owners really share in the
town life; this is a part of the rush to town. And for every landowner who
has thus hurried away from the narrow and hard conditions of country life,
how many field-hands, how many tenants, how many ruined renters, have
joined that long procession? Is it not strange compensation? The sin of the
country districts is visited on the town, and the social sores of city life to-day
may, here in Dougherty County, and perhaps in many places near and far,
look for their final healing without the city walls.

JACK LONDON (1876–1916) *What Life Means to Me*

To describe the realities of American working-class life and to show what an American socialist revolution might look like: these are the aims of much of Jack London's fiction. London himself, though, remained to the end of his short life a believer in the same American dream—success by hard work—that he attempts to puncture in the autobiographical essay (1906) below.

London became an active socialist in high school. Over the next ten years— between jobs that took him to Alaskan gold fields, English slums, and a Japanese military prison—he wrote many of the stories, articles and novels that made his reputation as an author and social critic. Yet a close friend remarked of London that "his success was the tragedy of his life" —a judgment that seemed especially legitimate after 1914, when London both defended American counter-revolutionary intervention in Mexico, and refused to condemn World War I, as other socialists had done, as a contest among rival imperialist powers. There seems always to have been a split in London's commitment, between working-class experience and middle-class ambitions. The conflict is perhaps reflected in his curiously mixed style, fundamentally a plain and powerful style, though sometimes overlaid with cloying sentiment.

I was born in the working-class. Early I discovered enthusiasm, ambition, and ideals; and to satisfy these became the problem of my child-life. My environment was crude and rough and raw. I had no outlook, but an uplook rather. My place in society was at the bottom. Here life offered nothing but sordidness and wretchedness, both of the flesh and the spirit; for here flesh and spirit were alike starved and tormented.

Above me towered the colossal edifice of society, and to my mind the only way out was up. Into this edifice I early resolved to climb. Up above, men wore black clothes and boiled shirts, and women dressed in beautiful gowns. Also, there were good things to eat, and there was plenty to eat. This much for the flesh. Then there were the things of the spirit. Up above me, I knew, were unselfishnesses of the spirit, clean and noble thinking, keen intellectual living. I knew all this because I read "Seaside Library" novels, in which, with the exception of the villains and adventuresses, all men and women thought beautiful thoughts, spoke a beautiful tongue, and performed glorious deeds.

In short, as I accepted the rising of the sun, I accepted that up above me was all that was fine and noble and gracious, all that gave decency and dignity to life, all that made life worth living and that remunerated one for his travail and misery.

But it is not particularly easy for one to climb up out of the working-class —especially if he is handicapped by the possession of ideals and illusions. I lived on a ranch in California, and I was hard put to find the ladder whereby to climb. I early inquired the rate of interest on invested money, and worried my child's brain into an understanding of the virtues and excellencies of that remarkable invention of man, compound interest. Further, I ascertained the current rates of wages for workers of all ages, and the cost of living. From all this data I concluded that if I began immediately and worked and saved until I was fifty years of age, I could then stop working and enter into participation in a fair portion of the delights and goodnesses that would then be open to me higher up in society. Of course, I resolutely determined not to marry, while I quite forgot to consider at all that great rock of disaster in the working-class world—sickness.

But the life that was in me demanded more than a meagre existence of scraping and scrimping. Also, at ten years of age, I became a newsboy on the streets of a city, and found myself with a changed uplook. All about me were still the same sordidness and wretchedness, and up above me was still the same paradise waiting to be gained; but the ladder whereby to climb was a different one. It was now the ladder of business. Why save my earnings and invest in government bonds, when, by buying two newspapers for five cents, with a turn of the wrist I could sell them for ten cents and double my capital? The business ladder was the ladder for me, and I had a vision of myself becoming a baldheaded and successful merchant prince.

Alas for visions! When I was sixteen I had already earned the title of "prince." But this title was given me by a gang of cut-throats and thieves, by whom I was called "The Prince of the Oyster Pirates." And at that time I had climbed the first rung of the business ladder. I was a capitalist. I owned a boat and a complete oyster-pirating outfit. I had begun to exploit my fellow-creatures. I had a crew of one man. As captain and owner I took two-thirds of the spoils, and gave the crew one-third, though the crew worked just as hard as I did and risked just as much his life and liberty.

This one rung was the height I climbed up the business ladder. One night I went on a raid amongst the Chinese fishermen. Ropes and nets were worth dollars and cents. It was robbery, I grant, but it was precisely the spirit of capitalism. The capitalist takes away the possessions of his fellow-creatures by means of a rebate, or of a betrayal of trust, or by the purchase of senators and supreme-court judges. I was merely crude. That was the only difference. I used a gun.

But my crew that night was one of those inefficients against whom the capitalist is wont to fulminate, because, forsooth, such inefficients increase expenses and reduce dividends. My crew did both. What of his carelessness he set fire to the big mainsail and totally destroyed it. There weren't any dividends that night, and the Chinese fishermen were richer by the nets and ropes we did not get. I was bankrupt, unable just then to pay sixty-five dollars for a new mainsail. I left my boat at anchor and went off on a bay-pirate boat on a raid up the Sacramento River. While away on this trip, another gang of bay pirates raided my boat. They stole everything, even the anchors; and later on, when I recovered the drifting hulk, I sold it for twenty dollars. I had slipped back the one rung I had climbed, and never again did I attempt the business ladder.

From then on I was mercilessly exploited by other capitalists. I had the muscle, and they made money out of it while I made but a very indifferent living out of it. I was a sailor before the mast, a longshoreman, a roustabout; I worked in canneries, and factories, and laundries; I mowed lawns, and cleaned carpets, and washed windows. And I never got the full product of my toil. I looked at the daughter of the cannery owner, in her carriage, and knew that it was my muscle, in part, that helped drag along that carriage on its rubber tires. I looked at the son of the factory owner, going to college, and knew that it was my muscle that helped, in part, to pay for the wine and good fellowship he enjoyed.

But I did not resent this. It was all in the game. They were the strong. Very well, I was strong. I would carve my way to a place amongst them and make money out of the muscles of other men. I was not afraid of work. I loved hard work. I would pitch in and work harder than ever and eventually become a pillar of society.

And just then, as luck would have it, I found an employer that was of the same mind. I was willing to work, and he was more than willing that I should work. I thought I was learning a trade. In reality, I had displaced two men. I thought he was making an electrician out of me; as a matter of fact, he was making fifty dollars per month out of me. The two men I had displaced had received forty dollars each per month; I was doing the work of both for thirty dollars per month.

This employer worked me nearly to death. A man may love oysters, but too many oysters will disincline him toward that particular diet. And so with me. Too much work sickened me. I did not wish ever to see work again. I fled from work. I became a tramp, begging my way from door to door, wandering over the United States and sweating bloody sweats in slums and prisons.

I had been born in the working-class, and I was now, at the age of eighteen, beneath the point at which I had started. I was down in the cellar of society, down in the subterranean depths of misery about which it is neither nice nor proper to speak. I was in the pit, the abyss, the human cesspool, the shambles and charnel-house of our civilization. This is the part of the edifice of society that society chooses to ignore. Lack of space compels me here to ignore it, and I shall say only that the things I there saw gave me a terrible scare.

I was scared into thinking. I saw the naked simplicities of the complicated civilization in which I lived. Life was a matter of food and shelter. In order to get food and shelter men sold things. The merchant sold shoes, the politician sold his manhood, and the representative of the people, with exceptions, of course, sold his trust; while nearly all sold their honor. Women, too, whether on the street or in the holy bond of wedlock, were prone to sell their flesh. All things were commodities, all people bought and sold. The one commodity that labor had to sell was muscle. The honor of labor had no price in the market-place. Labor had muscle, and muscle alone, to sell.

But there was a difference, a vital difference. Shoes and trust and honor had a way of renewing themselves. They were imperishable stocks. Muscle, on the other hand, did not renew. As the shoe merchant sold shoes, he continued to replenish his stock. But there was no way of replenishing the laborer's stock of muscle. The more he sold of his muscle, the less of it remained to him. It was his one commodity, and each day his stock of it diminished. In the end, if he did not die before, he sold out and put up his shutters. He was a muscle bankrupt, and nothing remained to him but to go down into the cellar of society and perish miserably.

I learned, further, that brain was likewise a commodity. It, too, was different from muscle. A brain seller was only at his prime when he was fifty or sixty years old, and his wares were fetching higher prices than ever. But a laborer was worked out or broken down at forty-five or fifty. I had been in the cellar of society, and I did not like the place as a habitation. The pipes and drains were unsanitary, and the air was bad to breathe. If I could not live on the parlor floor of society, I could, at any rate, have a try at the attic. It was true, the diet there was slim, but the air at least was pure. So I resolved to sell no more muscle, and to become a vender of brains.

Then began a frantic pursuit of knowledge. I returned to California and opened the books. While thus equipping myself to become a brain merchant, it was inevitable that I should delve into sociology. There I found, in a certain class of books, scientifically formulated, the simple sociological concepts I had already worked out for myself. Other and greater minds, before I was born, had worked out all that I had thought and a vast deal more. I discovered that I was a socialist.

The socialists were revolutionists, inasmuch as they struggled to overthrow the society of the present, and out of the material to build the society of the future. I, too, was a socialist and a revolutionist. I joined the groups of working-class and intellectual revolutionists, and for the first time came into intellectual living. Here I found keen-flashing intellects and brilliant wits; for here I met strong and alert-brained, withal horny-handed, members of the working-class; unfrocked preachers too wide in their Christianity for any congregation of Mammon-worshippers; professors broken on the wheel of university subservience to the ruling class and flung out because they were quick with knowledge which they strove to apply to the affairs of mankind.

Here I found, also, warm faith in the human, glowing idealism, sweetnesses of unselfishness, renunciation, and martyrdom—all the splendid, stinging things of the spirit. Here life was clean, noble, and alive. Here life rehabilitated itself, became wonderful and glorious; and I was glad to be alive. I was in touch with great souls who exalted flesh and spirit over dollars and cents, and to whom the thin wail of the starved slum child meant more than all the pomp and circumstance of commercial expansion and world empire. All about me were nobleness of purpose and heroism of effort, and my days and nights were sunshine and starshine, all fire and dew, with before my eyes, ever burning and blazing, the Holy Grail, Christ's own Grail, the warm human, long-suffering and maltreated, but to be rescued and saved at the last.

And I, poor foolish I, deemed all this to be a mere foretaste of the delights of living I should find higher above me in society. I had lost many illusions since the day I read "Seaside Library" novels on the California ranch. I was destined to lose many of the illusions I still retained.

As a brain merchant I was a success. Society opened its portals to me. I entered right in on the parlor floor, and my disillusionment proceeded rapidly. I sat down to dinner with the masters of society, and with the wives and daughters of the masters of society. The women were gowned beautifully, I admit; but to my naïve surprise I discovered that they were of the same clay as all the rest of the women I had known down below in the cellar. "The colonel's lady and Judy O'Grady were sisters under their skins"—and gowns.

It was not this, however, so much as their materialism, that shocked me. It is true, these beautifully gowned, beautiful women prattled sweet little ideals and dear little moralities; but in spite of their prattle the dominant key of the life they lived was materialistic. And they were so sentimentally selfish! They assisted in all kinds of sweet little charities, and informed one of the fact, while all the time the food they ate and the beautiful clothes they wore were bought out of dividends stained with the blood of child labor, and sweated labor, and of prostitution itself. When I mentioned such facts, expecting in my innocence that these sisters of Judy O'Grady would at once strip off their blood-dyed silks and jewels, they became excited and angry, and read me preachments about the lack of thrift, the drink, and the innate depravity that caused all the misery in society's cellar. When I mentioned that I couldn't quite see that it was the lack of thrift, the intemperance, and the depravity of a half-starved child of six that made it work twelve hours every night in a Southern cotton mill, these sisters of Judy O'Grady attacked my private life and called me an "agitator"—as though that, forsooth, settled the argument.

Nor did I fare better with the masters themselves. I had expected to find men who were clean, noble, and alive, whose ideals were clean, noble, and alive. I went about amongst the men who sat in the high places—the preachers, the politicians, the business men, the professors, and the editors. I ate meat with them, drank wine with them, automobiled with them, and studied them. It is true, I found many that were clean and noble; but with rare exceptions, they were not *alive*. I do verily believe I could count the exceptions on the fingers of my two hands. Where they were not alive with rottenness, quick with unclean life, they were merely the unburied dead—clean and noble, like well-preserved mummies, but not alive. In this connection I may especially mentioned the professors I met, the men who live up to that decadent university ideal, "the passionless pursuit of passionless intelligence."

I met men who invoked the name of the Prince of Peace in their diatribes against war, and who put rifles in the hands of Pinkertons [1] with which to shoot down strikers in their own factories. I met men incoherent with indignation at the brutality of prize-fighting, and who, at the same time, were parties to the adulteration of food that killed each year more babies than even red-handed Herod had killed.

I talked in hotels and clubs and homes and Pullmans and steamer-chairs with captains of industry, and marvelled at how little travelled they were in the realm of intellect. On the other hand, I discovered that their intellect, in the business sense, was abnormally developed. Also, I discovered that their morality, where business was concerned, was nil.

---

1. Pinkertons: after Alan Pinkerton, founder of the Pinkerton National Detective Agency, whose men were often hired to break labor strikes.

This delicate, aristocratic-featured gentleman, was a dummy director and a tool of corporations that secretly robbed widows and orphans. This gentleman, who collected fine editions and was an especial patron of literature, paid blackmail to a heavy-jowled, black-browed boss of a municipal machine. This editor, who published patent medicine advertisements and did not dare print the truth in his paper about said patent medicines for fear of losing the advertising, called me a scoundrelly demagogue because I told him that his political economy was antiquated and that his biology was contemporaneous with Pliny.

This senator was the tool and the slave, the little puppet of a gross, uneducated machine boss; so was this governor and this supreme court judge; and all three rode on railroad passes. This man, talking soberly and earnestly about the beauties of idealism and the goodness of God, had just betrayed his comrades in a business deal. This man, a pillar of the church and heavy contributor to foreign missions, worked his shop girls ten hours a day on a starvation wage and thereby directly encouraged prostitution. This man, who endowed chairs in universities, perjured himself in courts of law over a matter of dollars and cents. And this railroad magnate broke his word as a gentleman and a Christian when he granted a secret rebate to one of two captains of industry locked together in a struggle to the death.

It was the same everywhere, crime and betrayal, betrayal and crime—men who were alive, but who were neither clean nor noble, men who were clean and noble but who were not alive. Then there was a great, hopeless mass, neither noble nor alive, but merely clean. It did not sin positively nor deliberately; but it did sin passively and ignorantly by acquiescing in the current immorality and profiting by it. Had it been noble and alive it would not have been ignorant, and it would have refused to share in the profits of betrayal and crime.

I discovered that I did not like to live on the parlor floor of society. Intellectually I was bored. Morally and spiritually I was sickened. I remembered my intellectuals and idealists, my unfrocked preachers, broken professors, and clean-minded, class-conscious workingmen. I remembered my days and nights of sunshine and starshine, where life was all a wild sweet wonder, a spiritual paradise of unselfish adventure and ethical romance. And I saw before me, ever blazing and burning the Holy Grail.

So I went back to the working-class, in which I had been born and where I belonged. I care no longer to climb. The imposing edifice of society above my head holds no delights for me. It is the foundation of the edifice that interests me. There I am content to labor, crowbar in hand, shoulder to shoulder with intellectuals, idealists, and class-conscious workingmen, getting a solid pry now and again and setting the whole edifice rocking. Some day, when we get a few more hands and crowbars to work, we'll topple it over, along with all its rotten life and unburied dead, its monstrous selfishness and sodden materialism. Then we'll cleanse the cellar and build a new habitation for mankind, in which there will be no parlor floor, in which all the rooms will be bright and airy, and where the air that is breathed will be clean, noble, and alive.

Such is my outlook. I look forward to a time when man shall progress upon something worthier and higher than his stomach, when there will be a finer incentive to impel men to action than the incentive of to-day, which is the incentive of the stomach. I retain my belief in the nobility and excellence of the human. I believe that spiritual sweetness and unselfishness will conquer the gross gluttony of to-day. And last of all, my faith is in the working-class. As some Frenchman has said, "The stairway of time is ever echoing with the wooden shoe going up, the polished boot descending."

JOHN MUIR (1838–1914), *Hetch Hetchy Valley,* from *The Yosemite*

The Scots-born explorer, naturalist, and conservationist John Muir first came to "the incomparable Yosemite" in 1868. In his handbook for travelers (1912) he presents a remarkably vivid account of his experiences and observations in the Sierra wilderness. But besides describing the splendor and variety of the American western landscape, much of Muir's writing chronicles the first intrusions upon that landscape by "devotees . . . of the Almighty Dollar." Muir campaigned against the undisciplined disruption of natural ecology and the blind exploitation of natural resources, whose disastrous effects are now visible everywhere. He did so at a time when nature seemed to be an inexhaustible resource, and profit an unquestioned right. Muir's efforts led to the establishment of federal forest reserves and eventually to the National Park System. However, he lost the battle for Hetch Hetchy, which in 1923 was flooded as a reservoir for the city of San Francisco. His defeat indicates the political limitations of the contemporary ecology movement.

Yosemite is so wonderful that we are apt to regard it as an exceptional creation, the only valley of its kind in the world; but Nature is not so poor as to have only one of anything. Several other yosemites have been discovered in the Sierra that occupy the same relative positions on the range and were formed by the same forces in the same kind of granite. One of these, the Hetch Hetchy Valley, is in the Yosemite National Park about twenty miles from Yosemite and is easily accessible to all sorts of travelers by a road and trail that leaves the Big Oak Flat Road at Bronson Meadows a few miles below Crane Flat, and to mountaineers by way of Yosemite Creek basin and the head of the middle fork of the Tuolumne.

It is said to have been discovered by Joseph Screech, a hunter, in 1850, a year before the discovery of the great Yosemite. After my first visit to it in the autumn of 1871, I have always called it the "Tuolumne Yosemite," for it is a wonderfully exact counterpart of the Merced Yosemite, not only in its sublime rocks and waterfalls but in the gardens, groves and meadows of its flowery park-like floor. The floor of Yosemite is about 4000 feet above the sea; the Hetch Hetchy floor about 3700 feet. And as the Merced River flows through Yosemite, so does the Tuolumne through Hetch Hetchy. The walls of both are of gray granite, rise abruptly from the floor, are sculptured in the same style and in both every rock is a glacier monument.

Standing boldly out from the south wall is a strikingly picturesque rock called by the Indians, Kolana, the outermost of a group 2300 feet high, corresponding with the Cathedral Rocks of Yosemite both in relative position and form. On the opposite side of the Valley, facing Kolana, there is a counterpart of the El Capitan that rises sheer and plain to a height of 1800 feet, and over its massive brow flows a stream which makes the most graceful fall I have ever seen. From the edge of the cliff to the top of an earthquake talus [1] it is perfectly free in the air for a thousand feet before it is broken into cascades among talus boulders. It is in all its glory in June, when the snow is melting fast, but fades and vanishes toward the end of summer. The only fall I know with which it may fairly be compared is the Yosemite Bridal Veil; but it excels even that favorite fall both in height and airy-fairy beauty and behavior. Lowlanders are apt to suppose that mountain streams in their wild career over cliffs lose control of themselves and tumble in a noisy chaos of mist and spray. On the contrary, on no part of their travels are they more harmonious and self-controlled. Imagine yourself in Hetch Hetchy on a sunny day in June, standing waist-deep in grass and flowers (as I have often stood), while the great pines sway dreamily with scarcely perceptible motion. Looking northward across the Valley you see a plain, gray granite cliff rising abruptly out of the gardens and groves to a height of 1800 feet, and in front of it Tueeulala's silvery scarf burning with irised sun-fire. In the first white outburst at the head there is abundance of visible energy, but it is speedily hushed and concealed in divine repose, and its tranquil progress to the base of the cliff is like that of a downy feather in a still room. Now observe the fineness and marvelous distinctness of the various sun-illumined fabrics into which the water is woven; they sift and float from form to form down the face of that grand gray rock in so leisurely and unconfused a manner that you can examine their texture, and patterns and tones of color as you would a piece of embroidery held in the hand. Toward the top of the fall you see groups of booming, comet-like masses, their solid, white heads separate, their tails like combed silk interlacing among delicate gray and purple shadows, ever forming and dissolving, worn out by friction in their rush through the air. Most of these vanish a few hundred feet below the summit, changing to varied forms of cloud-like drapery. Near the bottom the width of the fall has increased from about twenty-five feet to a hundred feet. Here it is composed of yet finer tissues, and is still without a trace of disorder—air, water and sunlight woven into stuff that spirits might wear.

So fine a fall might well seem sufficient to glorify any valley; but here, as in Yosemite, Nature seems in nowise moderate, for a short distance to the eastward of Tueeulala booms and thunders the great Hetch Hetchy Fall, Wapama, so near that you have both of them in full view from the same standpoint. It is the counterpart of the Yosemite Fall, but has a much greater volume of water, is about 1700 feet in height, and appears to be nearly vertical, though considerably inclined, and is dashed into huge outbounding bosses of foam on projecting shelves and knobs. No two falls could be more unlike—

---

1. Talus: a pile of fragmented rock detached from a cliff.

Tueeulala out in the open sunshine descending like thistledown; Wapama in a jagged, shadowy gorge roaring and thundering, pounding its way like an earthquake avalanche.

Besides this glorious pair there is a broad, massive fall on the main river a short distance above the head of the Valley. Its position is something like that of the Vernal in Yosemite, and its roar as it plunges into a surging trout-pool may be heard a long way, though it is only about twenty feet high. On Rancheria Creek, a large stream, corresponding in position with the Yosemite Tenaya Creek, there is a chain of cascades joined here and there with swift flashing plumes like the one between the Vernal and Nevada Falls, making magnificient shows as they go their glacier-sculptured way, sliding, leaping, hurrahing, covered with crsip clashing spray made glorious with sifting sunshine. And besides all these a few small streams come over the walls at wide intervals, leaping from ledge to ledge with bird-like song and watering many a hidden cliff-garden and fernery, but they are too unshowy to be noticed in so grand a place.

The correspondence between the Hetch Hetchy walls in their trends, sculpture, physical structure, and general arrangement of the main rock-masses and those of the Yosemite Valley has excited the wondering admiration of every observer. We have seen that the El Capitan and Cathedral Rocks occupy the same relative positions in both valleys; so also do their Yosemite points and North Domes. Again, that part of the Yosemite north wall immediately to the east of the Yosemite Fall has two horizontal benches, about 500 and 1500 feet above the floor, timbered with golden-cup oak. Two benches similarly situated and timbered occur on the same relative portion of the Hetch Hetchy north wall, to the east of Wapama Fall, and on no other. The Yosemite is bounded at the head by the great Half Dome. Hetch Hetchy is bounded in the same way, though its head rock is incomparably less wonderful and sublime in form.

The floor of the Valley is about three and a half miles long, and from a fourth to half a mile wide. The lower portion is mostly a level meadow about a mile long, with the trees restricted to the sides and the river banks, and partially separated from the main, upper, forested portion by a low bar of glacier-polished granite across which the river breaks in rapids.

The principal trees are the yellow and sugar pines, digger pine, incense cedar, Douglas spruce, silver fir, the California and golden-cup oaks, balsam cottonwood, Nuttall's flowering dogwood, alder, maple, laurel, tumion, etc. The most abundant and influential are the great yellow or silver pines like those of Yosemite, the tallest over two hundred feet in height, and the oaks assembled in magnificent groves with massive rugged trunks four to six feet in diameter, and broad, shady, wide-spreading heads. The shrubs forming conspicuous flowery clumps and tangles are manzanita, azalea, spiraea, brier-rose, several species of ceanothus, calycanthus, philadelphus, wild cherry, etc.; with abundance of showy and fragrant herbaceous plants growing about them or out in the open in beds by themselves—lilies, Mariposa tulips, brodiaeas, orchids, iris, spraguea, draperia, collomia, collinsia, castilleja, nemophila, larkspur, columbine, goldenrods, sunflowers, mints of many species, honeysuckle, etc. Many fine ferns dwell here also, especially the beautiful and interesting rock-ferns—pellaea, and cheilanthes of several species—fringing and rosetting dry rock-piles and ledges; woodwardia and asplenium on damp spots with fronds six or seven feet high; the delicate maidenhair in mossy nooks by the falls, and the sturdy, broad-shouldered pteris covering nearly all the dry ground beneath the oaks and pines.

It appears, therefore, that Hetch Hetchy Valley, far from being a plain, common, rock-bound meadow, as many who have not seen it seem to suppose, is a grand landscape garden, one of Nature's rarest and most precious mountain temples. As in Yosemite, the sublime rocks of its walls seem to glow with life, whether leaning back in repose or standing erect in thoughtful attitudes, giving welcome to storms and calms alike, their brows in the sky, their feet set in the groves and gay flowery meadows, while birds, bees, and butterflies help the river and waterfalls to stir all the air into music—things frail and fleeting and types of permanence meeting here and blending, just as they do in Yosemite, to draw her lovers into close and confiding communion with her.

Sad to say, this most precious and sublime feature of the Yosemite National Park, one of the greatest of all our natural resources for the uplifting joy and peace and health of the people, is in danger of being dammed and made into a reservoir to help supply San Francisco with water and light, thus flooding it from wall to wall and burying its gardens and groves one or two hundred feet deep. This grossly destructive commercial scheme has long been planned and urged (though water is pure and abundant can be got from sources outside of the people's park, in a dozen different places), because of the comparative cheapness of the dam and of the territory which it is sought to divert from the great uses to which it was dedicated in the Act of 1890 establishing the Yosemite National Park.

The making of gardens and parks goes on with civilization all over the world, and they increase both in size and number as their value is recognized. Everybody needs beauty as well as bread, places to play in and pray in, where Nature may heal and cheer and give strength to body and soul alike. This natural beauty-hunger is made manifest in the little windowsill gardens of the poor, though perhaps only a geranium slip in a broken cup, as well as in the carefully tended rose and lily gardens of the rich, the thousands of spacious city parks and botanical gardens, and in our magnificent National Parks —the Yellowstone, Yosemite, Sequoia, etc.—Nature's sublime wonderlands, the admiration and joy of the world. Nevertheless, like anything else worth while, from the very beginning, however well guarded, they have always been subject to attack by despoiling gain-seekers and mischief-makers of every degree from Satan to Senators, eagerly trying to make everything immediately and selfishly commercial, with schemes disguised in smug-smiling philanthropy, industriously, sham-piously crying, "Conservation, conservation, panutilization," that man and beast may be fed and the dear Nation made great. Thus long ago a few enterprising merchants utilized the Jerusalem temple as a place of business instead of a place of prayer, changing money, buying and selling cattle and sheep and doves; and earlier still, the first forest reservation, including only one tree, was likewise despoiled. Ever since the establishment of the Yosemite National Park, strife has been going on around its borders and I suppose this will go on as part of the universal battle between right and wrong, however much its boundaries may be shorn, or its wild beauty destroyed.

The first application to the Government by the San Francisco Supervisors for the commercial use of Lake Eleanor and the Hetch Hetchy Valley was made in 1903, and on December 22nd of that year it was denied by the Secretary of the Interior, Mr. Hitchcock, who truthfully said:

Presumably the Yosemite National Park was created such by law because of the natural objects of varying degrees of scenic importance located within its boundaries, inclusive alike of its beautiful small lakes, like Eleanor, and its majestic wonders, like Hetch Hetchy and Yosemite Valley. It is the aggregation of such natural scenic features that makes the Yosemite Park a wonderland which the Congress of the United States sought by law to reserve for all coming time as nearly as practicable in the condition fashioned by the hand of the Creator—a worthy object of National pride and a source of healthful pleasure and rest for the thousands of people who may annually sojourn there during the heated months.

In 1907 when Mr. Garfield became Secretary of the Interior the application was renewed and granted; but under his successor, Mr. Fisher, the matter has been referred to a Commission, which as this volume goes to press still has it under consideration.

The most delightful and wonderful camp-grounds in the Park are its three great valleys—Yosemite, Hetch Hetchy, and Upper Tuolumne; and they are also the most important places with reference to their positions relative to the other great features—the Merced and Tuolumne Canyons, and the High Sierra peaks and glaciers, etc., at the head of the rivers. The main part of the Tuolumne Valley is a spacious flowery lawn four or five miles long, surrounded by magnificent snowy mountains, slightly separated from other beautiful meadows, which together make a series about twelve miles in length, the highest reaching to the feet of Mount Dana, Mount Gibbs, Mount Lyell and Mount McClure. It is about 8500 feet above the sea, and forms the grand central High Sierra camp-ground from which excursions are made to the noble mountains, domes, glaciers, etc.; across the Range to the Mono Lake and volcanoes and down the Tuolumne Canyon to Hetch Hetchy. Should Hetch Hetchy be submerged for a reservoir, as proposed, not only would it be utterly destroyed, but the sublime canyon way to the heart of the High Sierra would be hopelessly blocked and the great camping-ground, as the watershed of a city drinking system, virtually would be closed to the public. So far as I have learned, few of all the thousands who have seen the park and seek rest and peace in it are in favor of this outrageous scheme.

One of my later visits to the Valley was made in the autumn of 1907 with the late William Keith, the artist. The leaf-colors were then ripe, and the great god-like rocks in repose seemed to glow with life. The artist, under their spell, wandered day after day along the river and through the groves and gardens, studying the wonderful scenery; and, after making about forty sketches, declared with enthusiasm that although its walls were less sublime in height, in picturesque beauty and charm Hetch Hetchy surpassed even Yosemite.

That anyone would try to destroy such a place seems incredible; but sad experience shows that there are people good enough and bad enough for anything. The proponents of the dam scheme bring forward a lot of bad arguments to prove that the only righteous thing to do with the people's parks is to destroy them bit by bit as they are able. Their arguments are curiously like those of the devil, devised for the destruction of the first garden—so much of the very best Eden fruit going to waste; so much of the best Tuolumne water and Tuolumne scenery going to waste. Few of their statements are even partly true, and all are misleading.

Thus, Hetch Hetchy, they say, is a "low-lying meadow." On the contrary, it is a high-lying natural landscape garden.

"It is a common minor feature, like thousands of others." On the contrary it is a very uncommon feature; after Yosemite, the rarest and in many ways the most important in the National Park.

"Damming and submerging it 175 feet deep would enhance its beauty by forming a crystal-clear lake." Landscape gardens, places of recreation and worship, are never made beautiful by destroying and burying them. The beautiful sham lake, forsooth, would be only an eyesore, a dismal blot on the landscape, like many others to be seen in the Sierra. For, instead of keeping it at the same level all the year, allowing Nature centuries of time to make new shores, it would, of course, be full only a month or two in the spring, when the snow is melting fast; then it would be gradually drained, exposing the slimy sides of the basin and shallower parts of the bottom, with the gathered drift and waste, death and decay of the upper basins, caught here instead of being swept on to decent natural burial along the banks of the river or in the sea. Thus the Hetch Hetchy dam-lake would be only a rough imitation of a natural lake for a few of the spring months, an open sepulcher for the others.

"Hetch Hetchy water is the purest of all to be found in the Sierra, unpolluted, and forever unpollutable." On the contrary, excepting that of the Merced below Yosemite, it is less pure than that of most of the other Sierra streams, because of the sewerage of campgrounds draining into it, especially of the Big Tuolumne Meadows camp-ground, occupied by hundreds of tourists and mountaineers, with their animals, for months every summer, soon to be followed by thousands from all the world.

These temple destroyers, devotees of ravaging commercialism, seem to have a perfect contempt for Nature, and, instead of lifting their eyes to the God of the mountains, lift them to the Almighty Dollar.

Dam Hetch Hetchy! As well dam for water-tanks the people's cathedrals and churches, for no holier temple has ever been consecrated by the heart of man.

EUGENE VICTOR DEBS (1855–1926), *Speech to the Jury; Speech to the Court*

One of the heros of the American labor movement, Eugene Debs, himself a worker, helped to found both the American Railway Union and the Industrial Workers of the World. As president of the former, he was jailed in 1894 for contempt of court when his union, striking against the Pullman Company of Illinois, was served an injunction. The strike, one of the most famous in American history, was broken by federal troops sent in by President Grover Cleveland against the explicit will of the governor of Illinois. In prison Debs became acquainted with the literature of international socialism and after his release reorganized the A.R.U. into the Social Democratic party, which later became the Socialist party. Several times socialist candidate for president, he polled over 900,000 votes in 1912. In 1918 Debs, like many other socialists, protested America's participation in World War I, and in a speech at Canton, Ohio (June 16, 1918) he denounced imperialist militarism. As a result of that speech he was brought to trial for speaking in violation of the Espionage Act; the two addresses below (September 1918) are direct transcriptions from the trial. Sentenced to ten years in prison, Debs was again nominated his party's candidate for president, and from his cell in Atlanta won nearly a million votes in the 1920 election. He was released by President Harding in 1921.

Debs was always an effective orator, and his style—dramatic, straightforward, often sentimental—was much admired by the working people to whom he spoke.

*

Speech to the Jury

May it please the court, and gentlemen of the jury:

For the first time in my life I appear before a jury in a court of law to answer to an indictment for crime. I am not a lawyer. I know little about court procedure, about the rules of evidence or legal practice. I know only that you gentlemen are to hear the evidence brought against me, that the court is to instruct you in the law, and that you are then to determine by your verdict whether I shall be branded with criminal guilt and be consigned, perhaps, to the end of my life in a felon's cell.

Gentlemen, I do not fear to face you in this hour of accusation, nor do I shrink from the consequences of my utterances or my acts. Standing before you, charged as I am with crime, I can yet look the court in the face, I can look you in the face, I can look the world in the face, for in my conscience, in my soul, there is festering no accusation of guilt. . . .

I am charged in the indictment, first, that I did wilfully cause and attempt to cause or incite insubordination, mutiny, disloyalty and refusal of duty within the military forces of the United States; that I did obstruct and attempt to obstruct the recruiting and enlistment service of the United States. . . .

I am accused further of uttering words intended to procure and incite resistance to the United States and to promote the cause of the imperial German government.

Gentlemen, you have heard the report of my speech at Canton on June 16, and I submit that there is not a word in that speech to warrant the charges set out in the indictment. I admit having delivered the speech. I admit the accuracy of the speech in all of its main features as reported in this proceeding. There were two distinct reports. They vary somewhat but they are agreed upon all of the material statements embodied in that speech.

In what I had to say there my purpose was to educate the people to understand something about the social system in which we live and to prepare them to change this system by perfectly peaceable and orderly means into what I, as a Socialist, conceive to be a real democracy.

From what you heard in the address of counsel for the prosecution, you might naturally infer that I am an advocate of force and violence. It is not true. I have never advocated violence in any form. I always believed in education, in intelligence, in enlightenment, and I have always made my appeal to the reason and to the conscience of the people.

I admit being opposed to the present form of government. I admit being opposed to the present social system. I am doing what little I can, and have been for many years, to bring about a change that shall do away with the rule of the great body of the people by a relatively small class and establish in this country an industrial social democracy.

In the course of the speech that resulted in this indictment, I am charged with having expressed sympathy for Kate Richards O'Hare, for Rose Pastor Stokes, for Ruthenberg, Wagenknecht and Baker. I did express my perfect sympathy with these comrades of mine. I have known them for many years. I have every reason to believe in their integrity, every reason to look upon them with respect, with confidence and with approval.

Kate Richards O'Hare never uttered the words imputed to her in the report. The words are perfectly brutal. She is not capable of using such language. I know that through all of the years of her life she has worked in the interests of the suffering, struggling, poor, that she has consecrated all of her energies, all of her abilities, to their betterment. The same is true of Rose Pastor Stokes. Through all of her life she has been on the side of the oppressed and downtrodden. If she were so inclined she might occupy a place of ease. She might enjoy all of the comforts and leisures of life. Instead of this, she has renounced them all. She has taken her place among the poor, and there she has worked with all of her ability, all of her energy, to make it possible for them to enjoy a little more of the comfort of life.

I said that if these women whom I have known all of these years—that if they were criminals, if they ought to go to the penitentiary, then I too am a criminal, and I too ought to be sent to prison. I have not a word to retract— not one. I uttered the truth. I made no statement in that speech that I am not prepared to prove. If there is a single falsehood in it, it has not been exposed. If there is a single statement in it that will not bear the light of truth, I will retract it. I will make all of the reparation in my power. But if what I said is true, and I believe it is, then whatever fate or fortune may have in store for me I shall preserve inviolate the integrity of my soul and stand by it to the end.

When I said what I did about the three comrades of mine who are in the workhouse at Canton, I had in mind what they had been ever since I have known them in the service of the working class. I had in mind the fact that these three workingmen had just a little while before had their hands cuffed and were strung up in that prison house for eight hours at a time until they fell to the floor fainting from exhaustion. And this because they had refused to do some menial, filthy services that were an insult to their dignity and their manhood.

I have been accused of expressing sympathy for the Bolsheviki of Russia. I plead guilty to the charge. I have read a great deal about the Bolsheviki of Russia that is not true. I happen to know of my own knowledge that they have been grossly misrepresented by the press of this country. Who are these much-maligned revolutionists of Russia? For years they had been the victims of a brutal Czar. They and their antecedents were sent to Siberia, lashed with a knout, if they even dreamed of freedom. At last the hour struck for a great change. The revolution came. The Czar was overthrown and his infamous regime ended. What followed? The common people of Russia came into power, the peasants, the toilers, the soldiers, and they proceeded as best they could to establish a government of the people. . . .

It may be that the much-despised Bolsheviki may fail at last, but let me say to you that they have written a chapter of glorious history. It will stand to their eternal credit. The leaders are now denounced as criminals and outlaws. Let me remind you that there was a time when George Washington, who is now revered as the father of his country, was denounced as a disloyalist, when Sam Adams, who is known to us as the father of the American Revolution, was condemned as an incendiary, and Patrick Henry, who delivered that inspired and inspiring oration, that aroused the colonists, was condemned as a traitor.

They were misunderstood at the time. They stood true to themselves, and they won an immortality of gratitude and glory.

When great changes occur in history, when great principles are involved, as a rule the majority are wrong. The minority are right. In every age there have been a few heroic souls who have been in advance of their time who have been misunderstood, maligned, persecuted, sometimes put to death. Long after their martyrdom monuments were erected to them and garlands were woven for their graves.

I have been accused of having obstructed war. I admit it. Gentlemen, I abhor war. I would oppose the war if I stood alone. When I think of a cold, glittering steel bayonet plunged in the white, quivering flesh of a human being, I recoil with horror. I have often wondered if I could take the life of my fellow man, even to save my own.

Men talk about holy wars. There are none. Let me remind you that it was Benjamin Franklin who said, "There never was a good war or a bad peace."

Napoleon Bonaparte was a high authority upon the subject of war. And when in his last days he was chained to the rock at St. Helena, when he felt the skeleton hand of death reaching for him, he cried out in horror, "War is the trade of savages and barbarians."

I have read some history. I know that it is ruling classes that make war upon one another, and not the people. In all of the history of this world the people have never yet declared a war. Not one. I do not believe that really civilized nations would murder one another. I would refuse to kill a human being on my own account. Why should I at the command of anyone else or at the command of any power on earth?

Twenty centuries ago there was one appeared upon earth we know as the Prince of Peace. He issued a command in which I believe. He said, "Love one another." He did not say, "Kill one another," but "Love one another." He espoused the cause of the suffering poor—just as Rose Pastor Stokes did, just as Kate Richards O'Hare did—and the poor heard him gladly. It was not long before he aroused the ill-will and the hatred of the usurers, the money changers, the profiteers, the high priests, the lawyers, the judges, the merchants, the bankers—in a word, the ruling class. They said of him just what the ruling class says of the Socialist today, "He is preaching dangerous doctrine. He is inciting the common rabble. He is a menace to peace and order." And they had him arraigned, tried, convicted, condemned, and they had his quivering body spiked to the gates of Jerusalem.

This has been the tragic history of the race. In the ancient world Socrates sought to teach some new truths to the people, and they made him drink the fatal hemlock. It has been true all along the track of the ages. The men and women who have been in advance, who have had new ideas, new ideals, who have had the courage to attack the established order of things, have all had to pay the same penalty.

A century and a half ago, when the American colonists were still foreign subjects, and when there were a few men who had faith in the common people and believed that they could rule themselves without a king, in that day to speak against the king was treason. If you read Bancroft or any other standard historian, you will find that a great majority of the colonists believed in the king and actually believed that he had a divine right to rule over them. They had been taught to believe that to say a word against the king, to question his so-called divine right, was sinful. There were ministers opened their Bibles to prove that it was the patriotic duty of the people to loyally serve and support the king. But there were a few men in that day who said, "We don't need a king. We can govern ourselves." And they began an agitation that has been immortalized in history.

Washington, Adams, Paine—these were the rebels of their day. At first they were opposed by the people and denounced by the press. You can remember that it was Franklin who said to his compeers, "We have now to hang together or we'll hang separately bye and bye." And if the Revolution had failed, the revolutionary fathers would have been executed as felons. But it did not fail. Revolutions have a habit of succeeding, when the time comes for them. The revolutionary forefathers were opposed to the form of government in their day. They were denounced, they were condemned. But they had the moral courage to stand erect and defy all the storms of detraction; and that is why they are in history, and that is why the great respectable majority of their day sleep in forgotten graves. The world does not know they ever lived.

At a later time there began another mighty agitation in this country. It was against an institution that was deemed a very respectable one in its time, the institution of chattel slavery. It became all-powerful. It controlled the President, both branches of Congress, the Supreme Court, the press and, to a very large extent, the pulpit. All of the organized forces of society, all the powers of government, upheld chattel slavery in that day. And again a few rebels appeared. One of them was Elijah Lovejoy.[1] Elijah Lovejoy was as much despised in his day as are the leaders of the I. W. W. in our day. Elijah Lovejoy was murdered in cold blood in Alton, Ill., in 1837, simply because he was opposed to chattel slavery—just as I am opposed to wage slavery. When you go down the Mississippi river and look up at Alton, you see a magnificent white shaft erected there in memory of a man who was true to himself and his convictions of right and duty unto death.

It was my good fortune to personally know Wendell Phillips.[2] I heard the story of his persecution, in part at least, from his own eloquent lips just a little while before they were silenced in death.

William Lloyd Garrison, Garrett Smith, Thaddeus Stevens—these leaders of the abolition movement, who were regarded as monsters of depravity, were true to the faith and stood their ground. They are all in history. You are teaching your children to revere their memories, while all of their detractors are in oblivion.

Chattel slavery disappeared. We are not yet free. We are engaged in another mighty agitation today. It is as wide as the world. It is the rise of the toiling and producing masses who are gradually becoming conscious of their interest, their power, as a class, who are organizing industrially and politically, who are slowly but surely developing the economic and political power that is to set them free. They are still in the minority, but they have learned how to wait, and to bide their time.

It is because I happen to be in this minority that I stand in your presence today, charged with crime. It is because I believe as the revolutionary fathers believed in their day, that a change was due in the interests of the people, that the time had come for a better form of government, an improved system, a higher social order, a nobler humanity and a grander civilization. This minority that is so much misunderstood and so bitterly maligned, is in alliance with the forces of evolution, and as certain as I stand before you this after-

1. Elijah Lovejoy (1802–1837): abolitionist editor of the Alton *Observer*.
2. Wendell Phillips (1811–1884): orator, writer, and agitator for such reforms as the enfranchisement of Negroes and women, labor rights, and the abolition of capital punishment.

noon, it is but a question of time until this minority will become the conquering majority and inaugurate the greatest change in all of the history of the world. You may hasten the change; you may retard it; you can no more prevent it than you can prevent the coming of the sunrise on the morrow.

My friend, the assistant prosecutor, doesn't like what I had to say in my speech about internationalism. What is there objectionable to internationalism? If we had internationalism there would be no war. I believe in patriotism. I have never uttered a word against the flag. I love the flag as a symbol of freedom. I object only when that flag is prostituted to base purposes, to sordid ends, by those who, in the name of patriotism, would keep the people in subjection.

I believe, however, in a wider patriotism. Thomas Paine said, "My country is the world. To do good is my religion." Garrison said, "My country is the world and all mankind are my countrymen." That is the essence of internationalism. I believe in it with all of my heart. I believe that nations have been pitted against nations long enough in hatred, in strife, in warfare. I believe there ought to be a bond of unity between all of these nations. I believe that the human race consists of one great family. I love the people of this country, but I don't hate the people of any country on earth—not even the Germans. I refuse to hate a human being because he happens to be born in some other country. Why should I? To me it does not make any difference where he was born or what the color of his skin may be. Like myself he is the image of his creator. He is a human being endowed with the same faculties, he has the same aspirations, he is entitled to the same rights, and I would infinitely rather serve him and love him than hate him and kill him.

We hear a great deal about human brotherhood—a beautiful and inspiring theme. It is preached from a countless number of pulpits. It is vain for us to preach of human brotherhood while we tolerate this social system in which we are a mass of warring units, in which millions of workers have to fight one another for jobs, and millions of business men and professional men have to fight one another for trade, for practice—in which we have individual interests and each is striving to care for himself alone without reference to his fellow men. Human brotherhood is yet to be realized in this world. It never can be under the capitalist-competitive system in which we live.

Yes; I was opposed to the war. I am perfectly willing, on that count, to be branded as a disloyalist, and if it is a crime under the American law punishable by imprisonment for being opposed to human bloodshed, I am perfectly willing to be clothed in the stripes of a convict and to end my days in a prison cell.

If my friends, the attorneys, had known me a little better they might have saved themselves some trouble in procuring evidence to prove certain things against me which I have not the slightest inclination to deny, but rather, upon the other hand, I have a very considerable pride in.

You have heard a great deal about the St. Louis platform.[3] I wasn't at the convention when that platform was adopted, but I don't ask to be excused

---

3. St. Louis platform: in April 1917, a few days after war was declared on Germany, American Socialists met in St. Louis to denounce the imperialist war, to declare their solidarity with the international working class, and to pledge themselves to "continuous, active, and public opposition to the war."

from my responsibility on that account. I voted for its adoption. I believe in its essential principles. There was some of its phrasing that I would have otherwise. I afterwards advocated a restatement. The testimony to the effect that I had refused to repudiate it was true.

At the time that platform was adopted the nation had just entered upon the war and there were millions of people who were not Socialists who were opposed to the United States being precipitated into that war. Time passed; conditions changed. There were certain new developments and I believed there should be a restatement. I have been asked why I did not favor a repudiation of what was said a year before. For the reason that I believed then, as I believe now, that the statement correctly defined the attitude of the Socialist party toward war. That statement, bear in mind, did not apply to the people of this country alone, but to the people of the world. It said, in effect, to the people, especially to the workers, of all countries, "Quit going to war. Stop murdering one another for the profit and glory of ruling classes. Cultivate the arts of peace. Humanize humanity. Civilize civilization." That is the essential spirit and the appeal of the much hated, condemned, St. Louis platform.

Now, the Republican and Democratic parties hold their conventions from time to time. They revise their platforms and their declarations. They do not repudiate previous platforms. Nor is it necessary. With the change of conditions these platforms are outgrown and others take their places. I was not in the convention, but I believe in that platform. I do today. But from the beginning of the war to this day, I have never, by word or act, been guilty of the charges that are embraced in this indictment. If I have criticized, if I have ever condemned, it is because I have believed myself justified in doing so under the laws of the land. I have had precedents for my attitude. This country has been engaged in a number of wars, and every one of them has been opposed, every one of them has been condemned by some of the most eminent men in the country. The war of the Revolution was opposed. The Tory press denounced its leaders as criminals and outlaws. And that is what they were under the divine right of a king to rule men.

The War of 1812 was opposed and condemned; the Mexican War was bitterly condemned by Abraham Lincoln, by Charles Sumner, by Daniel Webster and by Henry Clay. That war took place under the Polk administration. These men denounced the President; they condemned his administration; and they said that the war was a crime against humanity. They were not indicted; they were not tried for crime. They are honored today by all of their countrymen. The war of the Rebellion was opposed and condemned. In 1864 the Democratic party met in convention at Chicago and passed a resolution condemning the war as a failure. What would you say if the Socialist party were to meet in convention today and condemn the present war as a failure? You charge us with being disloyalists and traitors. Were the Democrats of 1864 disloyalists and traitors because they condemned the war as a failure?

I believe in the Constitution of the United States. Isn't it strange that we Socialists stand almost alone today in defending the Constitution of the United States? The revolutionary fathers who had been oppressed under king rule understood that free speech and the free press and the right of free assemblage by the people were the fundamental principles of democratic government. The very first amendment to the Constitution reads: "Congress shall make no law respecting an establishment of religion or prohibiting the free exercise thereof; or abridging the freedom of speech, or of the press; or the right of the people peaceably to assemble, and to petition the government for a redress of grievances." That is perfectly plain English. It can be understood by a child. I believe that the revolutionary fathers meant just what is here stated—that Congress shall make no law abridging the freedom of speech or of the press, or of the right of the people to peaceably assemble, and to petition the government for a redress of grievances.

That is the right that I exercised at Canton on the 16th day of last June; and for the exercise of that right, I now have to answer to this indictment. I believe in the right of free speech, in war as well as in peace. I would not under any circumstances, gag the lips of my bitterest enemy. I would under no circumstances suppress free speech. It is far more dangerous to attempt to gag the people than to allow them to speak freely of what is in their hearts. I do not go as far as Wendell Phillips did. Wendell Phillips said that the glory of free men is that they trample unjust laws under their feet. That is how they repeal them. If a human being submits to having his lips sealed, to be in silence reduced to vassalage, he may have all else, but he is still lacking in all that dignifies and glorifies real manhood.

Now, notwithstanding this fundamental provision in the national law, Socialist meetings have been broken up all over this country. Socialist speakers have been arrested by hundreds and flung into jail, where many of them are lying now. In some cases not even a charge was lodged against them, guilty of no crime except the crime of attempting to exercise the right guaranteed to them by the Constitution of the United States.

I have told you that I am no lawyer, but it seems to me that I know enough to know that if Congress enacts any law that conflicts with this provision in the Constitution, that law is void. If the Espionage Law finally stands, then the Constitution of the United States is dead. If that law is not the negation of every fundamental principle established by the Constitution, then certainly I am unable to read or to understand the English language. . . .

Now, in the course of this proceeding you, gentlemen, have perhaps drawn the inference that I am pro-German, in the sense that I have any sympathy with the imperial government of Germany. My father and mother were born in Alsace. They loved France with a passion that is holy. They understood the meaning of Prussianism, and they hated it with all their hearts. I did not need to be taught to hate Prussian militarism. I knew from them what a hateful, what an oppressive, what a brutalizing thing it was and is. I cannot imagine how any one could suspect that for one moment I could have the slightest sympathy with such a monstrous thing. I have been speaking and writing against it practically all of my life. I know that the Kaiser incarnates all there is of brute force and of murder. And yet I would not, if I had the power, kill the Kaiser. I would do to him what Thomas Paine wanted to do to the king of England. He said, "Destroy the king, save the man."

The thing that the Kaiser embodies and incarnates, called militarism, I would, if I could, wipe from the face of the earth—not only the militarism of Germany, but the militarism of the whole world. I am quite well aware of the fact that the war now deluging the world with blood was precipitated there. Not by the German people, but by the class that rules, oppresses, robs and degrades the German people. President Wilson has repeatedly said that we were not making war on the German people, and yet in war it is the people who are slain, and not the rulers who are responsible for the war.

With every drop in my veins I despise kaiserism, and all that kaiserism expresses and implies. I have sympathy with the suffering, struggling people everywhere. It does not make any difference under what flag they were born, or where they live, I have sympathy with them all. I would, if I could, establish a social system that would embrace them all. It is precisely at this point that we come to realize that there is a reason why the peoples of the various nations are pitted against each other in brutal warfare instead of being united in one all-embracing brotherhood.

War does not come by chance. War is not the result of accident. There is a definite cause for war, especially a modern war. The war that began in Europe can readily be accounted for. For the last forty years, under this international capitalist system, this exploiting system, these various nations of Europe have been preparing for the inevitable. And why? In all these nations the great industries are owned by a relatively small class. They are operated for the profit of that class. And great abundance is produced by the workers; but their wages will only buy back a small part of their product. What is the result? They have a vast surplus on hand; they have got to export it; they have got to find a foreign market for it. As result of this these nations are pitted against each other. They are industrial rivals—competitors. They begin to arm themselves to open, to maintain the market and quickly dispose of their surplus. There is but the one market. All these nations are competitors for it, and sooner or later every war of trade becomes a war of blood.

Now, where there is exploitation there must be some form of militarism to support it. Wherever you find exploitation you find some form of military force. In a smaller way you find it in this country. It was there long before war was declared. For instance, when the miners out in Colorado entered upon a strike about four years ago, the state militia, that is under the control of the Standard Oil Company, marched upon a camp, where the miners and their wives and children were in tents—and, by the way, a report of this strike was issued by the United States Committee on Industrial Relations. When the soldiers approached the camp at Ludlow, where these miners, with their wives and children, were, the miners, to prove that they were patriotic, placed flags above their tents, and when the state militia, that is paid by Rockefeller and controlled by Rockefeller, swooped down upon that camp, the first thing they did was to shoot those United States flags into tatters. Not one of them was indicted or tried because he was a traitor to his country. Pregnant women were killed, and a number of innocent children slain. This in the United States of America—the fruit of exploitation. The miners wanted a little more of what they had been producing. But the Standard Oil Company wasn't rich enough. It insisted that all they were entitled to was just enough to keep them in working order. There is slavery for you. And when at last they protested, when they were tormented by hunger, when they saw their children in tatters, they were shot down as if they had been so many vagabond dogs.

And while I am upon this point let me say just another word. Workingmen who organize, and who sometimes commit overt acts, are very oftentimes condemned by those who have no conception of the conditions under which they live. How many men are there, for instance, who know anything of their own knowledge about how men work in a lumber camp—a logging camp, a turpentine camp? In this report of the United States Commission on Industrial Relations you will find the statement proved that peonage existed in the State of Texas. Out of these conditions springs such a thing as the I. W. W.[4]—when men receive a pittance for their pay, when they work like galley slaves for a wage that barely suffices to keep their protesting souls within their tattered bodies. When they can endure the conditions no longer, and they make some sort of a demonstration, or perhaps commit acts of violence, how quickly are they condemned by those who do not know anything about the conditions under which they work!

Five gentlemen of distinction, among them Professor John Graham Brooks, of Harvard university, said that a word that so fills the world as the I. W. W. must have something in it. It must be investigated. And they did investigate it, each along their own lines, and I wish it were possible for every man and woman in this country to read the result of their investigation. They tell you why and how the I. W. W. was instituted. They tell you, moreover, that the great corporations, such as the Standard Oil Company, such as the Coal Trust, and the Lumber Trust, have, through their agents, committed more crimes against the I. W. W. than the I. W. W. have ever committed against them.

I was asked not long ago if I was in favor of shooting our soldiers in the back. I said, "No, I would not shoot them in the back. I wouldn't shoot them at all. I would not have them shot." Much has been made of a statement that I declared that men were fit for something better than slavery and cannon fodder. I made the statement. I make no attempt to deny it. I meant exactly what I said. Men are fit for something better than slavery and cannon fodder; and the time will come, though I shall not live to see it, when slavery will be wiped from the earth, and when men will marvel that there ever was a time when men who called themselves civilized rushed upon each other like wild beasts and murdered one another, by methods so cruel and barbarous that they defy the power of language to describe. I can hear the shrieks of the soldiers of Europe in my dreams. I have imagination enough to see a battlefield. I can see it strewn with the wrecks of human beings, who but yesterday were in the flush and glory of their young manhood. I can see them at eventide, scattered about in remnants, their limbs torn from their bodies, their eyes gouged out. Yes, I can see them, and I can hear them. I have looked above and beyond this frightful scene. I think of the mothers who are bowed in the shadow of their last great grief—whose hearts are breaking. And I say to myself, "I am going to do the little that lies in my power to wipe from this earth that terrible scourge of war."

If I believed in war I could not be kept out of the first line trenches. I would not be patriotic at long range. I would be honest enough, if I believed in bloodshed, to shed my own. But I do not believe that the shedding of blood bears any actual testimony to patriotism, to love of country, to civiliza-

---

4. I.W.W.: Industrial Workers of the World, a socialist industrial union founded in 1905 by Debs and others.

tion. On the contrary, I believe that warfare, in all of its forms, is an impeachment of our social order, and a rebuke to our much vaunted Christian civilization.

And now, gentlemen of the jury, I am not going to detain you too long. I wish to admit everything that has been said respecting me from this witness chair. I wish to admit everything that has been charged against me except what is embraced in the indictment which I have read to you. I cannot take back a word. I can't repudiate a sentence. I stand before you guilty of having made this speech. I stand before you prepared to accept the consequences of what there is embraced in that speech. I do not know, I cannot tell, what your verdict may be; nor does it matter much, so far as I am concerned.

Gentlemen, I am the smallest part of this trial. I have lived long enough to appreciate my own personal insignificance in relation to a great issue, that involves the welfare of the whole people. What you may choose to do to me will be of small consequence after all. I am not on trial here. There is an infinitely greater issue that is being tried today in this court, though you may not be conscious of it. American institutions are on trial here before a court of American citizens. The future will tell.

And now, your Honor, permit me to return my hearty thanks for your patient consideration. And to you, gentlemen of the jury, for the kindness with which you have listened to me.

My fate is in your hands. I am prepared for the verdict.

*

Speech to the Court

Your Honor, years ago I recognized my kinship with all living beings, and I made up my mind that I was not one bit better than the meanest of earth. I said then, I say now, that while there is a lower class, I am in it; while there is a criminal element, I am of it; while there is a soul in prison, I am not free.

If the law under which I have been convicted is a good law, then there is no reason why sentence should not be pronounced upon me. I listened to all that was said in this court in support and justification of this law, but my mind remains unchanged. I look upon it as a despotic enactment in flagrant conflict with democratic principles and with the spirit of free institutions. . . .

Your Honor, I have stated in this court that I am opposed to the form of our present government; that I am opposed to the social system in which we live; that I believed in the change of both—but by perfectly peaceable and orderly means.

Let me call your attention to the fact this morning that in this system five per cent of our people own and control two-thirds of our wealth; sixty-five per cent of the people, embracing the working class who produce all wealth, have but five per cent to show for it.

Standing here this morning, I recall my boyhood. At fourteen, I went to work in the railroad shops; at sixteen, I was firing a freight engine on a railroad. I remember all the hardships, all the privations, of that early day, and from that time until now, my heart has been with the working class. I could have been in Congress long ago. I have preferred to go to prison. The choice has been deliberately made. I could not have done otherwise. I have no regret.

In the struggle—the unceasing struggle—between the toilers and producers and their exploiters, I have tried, as best I might, to serve those among whom I was born, with whom I expect to share my lot until the end of my days.

I am thinking this morning of the men in the mills and factories; I am thinking of the women who, for a paltry wage, are compelled to work out their lives; of the little children who, in this system, are robbed of their childhood, and in their early tender years, are seized in the remorseless grasp of mammon, and forced into the industrial dungeons, there to feed the machines while they themselves are being starved body and soul. I can see them dwarfed, diseased, stunted, their little lives broken, and their hopes blasted, because in this high noon of our twentieth century civilization money is still so much more important than human life. Gold is god and rules in the affairs of men. The little girls, and there are a million of them in this country—this the most favored land beneath the bending skies, a land in which we have vast areas of rich and fertile soil, material resources in inexhaustible abundance, the most marvelous productive machinery on earth, millions of eager workers ready to apply their labor to that machinery to produce an abundance for every man, woman and child—and if there are still many millions of our people who are the victims of poverty, whose life is a ceaseless struggle all the way from youth to age, until at last death comes to their rescue and stills the aching heart, and lulls the victim to dreamless sleep, it is not the fault of the Almighty, it can't be charged to nature; it is due entirely to an outgrown social system that ought to be abolished not only in the interest of the working class, but in a higher interest of all humanity.

When I think of these little children—the girls that are in the textile mills of all description in the east, in the cotton factories of the south—when I think of them at work in a vitiated atmosphere, when I think of them at work when they ought to be at play or at school, when I think that when they do grow up, if they live long enough to approach the marriage state, they are unfit for it. Their nerves are worn out, their tissue is exhausted, their vitality is spent. They have been fed to industry. Their lives have been coined into gold. Their offspring are born tired. That is why there are so many failures in our modern life.

Your Honor, the five per cent of the people that I have made reference to constitute that element that absolutely rules our country. They privately own all our public necessities. They wear no crowns; they wield no sceptres; they sit upon no thrones; and yet they are our economic masters and our political rulers. They control this government and all of its institutions. They control the courts.

And your Honor, if you will permit me, I wish to make just one correction. It was stated here that I had charged that all federal judges are crooks. The charge is absolutely untrue. I did say that all federal judges are appointed through the influence and power of the capitalistic class and not the working class. If that statement is not true, I am more than willing to retract it.

If the five per cent of our people who own and control all of the sources of wealth, all of the nation's industries, all of the means of our common life, it is they who declare war; it is they who make peace; it is they who control our destiny. And so long as this is true, we can make no just claim to being a democratic government—a self-governing people.

I believe, your Honor, in common with all Socialists, that this nation ought to own and control its industries. I believe, as all Socialists do, that all things that are jointly needed and used ought to be jointly owned—that industry, the basis of life, instead of being the private property of the few and operated for their enrichment, ought to be the common property of all, democratically administered in the interest of all.

John D. Rockefeller has today an income of sixty million dollars a year, five million dollars a month, two hundred thousand dollars a day. He does not produce a penny of it. I make no attack upon Mr. Rockefeller personally. I do not in the least dislike him. If he were in need and it were in my power to serve him, I should serve him as gladly as I would any other human being. I have no quarrel with Mr. Rockefeller personally, nor with any other capitalist. I am simply opposing a social order in which it is possible for one man who does absolutely nothing that is useful to amass a fortune of hundreds of millions of dollars, while millions of men and women who work all of the days of their lives secure barely enough for an existence.

This order of things cannot always endure. I have registered my protest against it. I recognize the feebleness of my effort, but, fortunately, I am not alone. There are multiplied thousands of others who, like myself, have come to realize that before we may truly enjoy the blessings of civilized life, we must reorganize society upon a mutual and cooperative basis; and to this end we have organized a great economic and political movement that spread over the face of all the earth.

There are today upwards of sixty million Socialists, loyal, devoted, adherents to this cause, regardless of nationality, race, creed, color or sex. They are all making common cause. They are all spreading the propaganda of the new social order. They are waiting, watching and working through all the weary hours of the day and night. They are still in the minority. They have learned how to be patient and abide their time. They feel—they know, indeed—that the time is coming, in spite of all opposition, all persecution, when this emancipating gospel will spread among all the peoples, and when this minority will become the triumphant majority and, sweeping into power, inaugurate the greatest change in history.

In that day we will have the universal commonwealth—not the destruction of the nation, but, on the contrary, the harmonious cooperation of every nation with every other nation on earth. In that day war will curse this earth no more.

I have been accused, your Honor, of being an enemy of the soldier. I hope I am laying no flattering unction to my soul when I say that I don't believe the soldier has a more sympathetic friend than I am. If I had my way there would be no soldier. But I realize the sacrifices they are making, your Honor. I can think of them. I can feel for them. I can sympathize with them. That is one of the reasons why I have been doing what little has been in my power to bring about a condition of affairs in this country worthy of the sacrifices they have made and that they are now making in its behalf.

Your Honor, in a local paper yesterday there was some editorial exultation about my prospective imprisonment. I do not resent it in the least. I can understand it perfectly. In the same paper there appears an editorial this morning that has in it a hint of the wrong to which I have been trying to call attention. (Reading) "A senator of the United States receives a salary of $7,500—$45,000 for the six years for which he is elected. One of the candidates for senator from a state adjoining Ohio is reported to have spent through his committee $150,000 to secure the nomination. For advertising he spent $35,000; for printing $30,000; for traveling expenses, $10,000 and the rest in ways known to political managers."

The theory is that public office is as open to a poor man as to a rich man. One may easily imagine, however, how slight a chance one of ordinary resources would have in a contest against this man who was willing to spend more than three times his six years' salary merely to secure a nomination. Were these conditions to hold in every state, the senate would soon become again what it was once held to be—a rich men's club.

Campaign expenditures have been the subject of much restrictive legislation in recent years, but it has not always reached the mark. The authors of primary reform have accomplished some of the things they set out to do, but they have not yet taken the bank roll out of politics.

They never will take it out of politics, they never can take it out of politics, in this system.

Your Honor, I wish to make acknowledgment of my thanks to the counsel for the defense. They have not only defended me with exceptional legal ability, but with a personal attachment and devotion of which I am deeply sensible, and which I can never forget.

Your Honor, I ask no mercy. I plead for no immunity. I realize that finally the right must prevail. I never more clearly comprehended than now the great struggle between the powers of greed on the one hand and upon the other the rising hosts of freedom.

I can see the dawn of a better day of humanity. The people are awakening. In due course of time they will come to their own.

When the mariner, sailing over tropic seas, looks for relief from his weary watch, he turns his eyes toward the southern cross, burning luridly above the tempest-vexed ocean. As the midnight approaches, the southern cross begins to bend, and the whirling worlds change their places, and with starry finger-points the Almighty marks the passage of time upon the dial of the universe, and though no bell may beat the glad tidings, the lookout knows that the midnight is passing—that relief and rest are close at hand.

Let the people take heart and hope everywhere, for the cross is bending, the midnight is passing, and joy cometh with the morning.

> He's true to God who's true to man; wherever wrong is done,
> To the humblest and the weakest, 'neath the all-beholding sun,
> That wrong is also done to us, and they are slaves most base,
> Whose love of right is for themselves and not for all their race.

Your Honor, I thank you, and I thank all of this court for their courtesy and kindness, which I shall remember always.

E. M. FORSTER (1879–1970), *My Wood*

"May no achievement upon an imposing scale be mine," the novelist and critic E. M. Forster once wrote; and in the beautifully worked essay (1926) that follows, Forster's achievement is in miniature. The piece is itself a parable of the effects of private property, though Forster's reliance on such indirect modes as irony, parable, and understatement may suggest his own uncertainty as to the alternatives.
The book to which Forster refers in the opening line is his most successful novel, A Passage to India *(1924).*

A few years ago I wrote a book which dealt in part with the difficulties of the English in India. Feeling that they would have had no difficulties in India themselves, the Americans read the book freely. The more they read it the better it made them feel, and a cheque to the author was the result. I bought a wood with the cheque. It is not a large wood—it contains scarcely any trees, and it is intersected, blast it, by a public footpath. Still, it is the first property that I have owned, so it is right that other people should participate in my shame, and should ask themselves, in accents that will vary in horror, this very important question: What is the effect of property upon the character? Don't let's touch economics; the effect of private ownership upon the community as a whole is another question—a more important question, perhaps, but another one. Let's keep to psychology. If you own things, what's their effect on you? What's the effect on me of my wood?

In the first place, it makes me feel heavy. Property does have this effect. Property produces men of weight, and it was a man of weight who failed to get into the Kingdom of Heaven. He was not wicked, that unfortunate millionaire in the parable, he was only stout; he stuck out in front, not to mention behind, and as he wedged himself this way and that in the crystalline entrance and bruised his well-fed flanks, he saw beneath him a comparatively slim camel passing through the eye of a needle and being woven into the robe of God. The Gospels all through couple stoutness and slowness. They point out what is perfectly obvious, yet seldom realized: that if you have a lot of things you cannot move about a lot, that furniture requires dusting, dusters require servants, servants require insurance stamps, and the whole tangle of them makes you think twice before you accept an invitation to dinner or go for a bathe in the Jordan. Sometimes the Gospels proceed further and say with Tolstoy that property is sinful; they approach the difficult ground of asceticism here, where I cannot follow them. But as to the immediate effects of property on people, they just show straightforward logic. It produces men of weight. Men of weight cannot, by definition, move like the lightning from the East unto the West, and the ascent of a fourteen-stone bishop into a pulpit is thus the exact antithesis of the coming of the Son of Man. My wood makes me feel heavy.

In the second place, it makes me feel it ought to be larger.

The other day I heard a twig snap in it. I was annoyed at first, for I thought that someone was blackberrying, and depreciating the value of the undergrowth. On coming nearer, I saw it was not a man who had trodden on the twig and snapped it, but a bird, and I felt pleased. My bird. The bird was not equally pleased. Ignoring the relation between us, it took fright as soon as it saw the shape of my face, and flew straight over the boundary hedge into a field, the property of Mrs. Henessy, where it sat down with a loud squawk. It had become Mrs. Henessy's bird. Something seemed grossly amiss here, something that would not have occurred had the wood been larger. I could not afford to buy Mrs. Henessy out, I dared not murder her, and limitations of this sort beset me on every side. Ahab did not want that vineyard—he only needed it to round off his property, preparatory to plotting a new curve —and all the land around my wood has become necessary to me in order to round off the wood. A boundary protects. But—poor little thing—the boundary ought in its turn to be protected. Noises on the edge of it. Children throw stones. A little more, and then a little more, until we reach the sea. Happy Canute! Happier Alexander! And after all, why should even the world be the limit of possession? A rocket containing a Union Jack, will, it is hoped, be shortly fired at the moon. Mars. Sirius. Beyond which . . . But these immensities ended by saddening me. I could not suppose that my wood was the destined nucleus of universal dominion—it is so very small and contains no mineral wealth beyond the blackberries. Nor was I comforted when Mrs. Henessy's bird took alarm for the second time and flew clean away from us all, under the belief that it belonged to itself.

In the third place, property makes its owner feel that he ought to do something to it. Yet he isn't sure what. A restlessness comes over him, a vague sense that he has a personality to express—the same sense which, without any vagueness, leads the artist to an act of creation. Sometimes I think I will cut down such trees as remain in the wood, at other times I want to fill up the gaps between them with new trees. Both impulses are pretentious and empty. They are not honest movements towards money-making or beauty. They spring from a foolish desire to express myself and from an inability to enjoy what I have got. Creation, property, enjoyment form a sinister trinity in the human mind. Creation and enjoyment are both very, very good, yet they are often unattainable without a material basis, and at such moments property pushes itself in as a substitute, saying, "Accept me instead —I'm good enough for all three." It is not enough. It is, as Shakespeare said of lust, "The expense of spirit in a waste of shame": it is "Before, a joy proposed; behind, a dream." Yet we don't know how to shun it. It is forced on us by our economic system as the alternative to starvation.It is also forced on us by an internal defect in the soul, by the feeling that in property may lie the germs of self-development and of exquisite or heroic deeds. Our life on earth is, and ought to be, material and carnal. But we have not yet learned to manage our materialism and carnality properly; they are still entangled with the desire for ownership, where (in the words of Dante) "Possession is one with loss."

And this brings us to our fourth and final point: the blackberries.

Blackberries are not plentiful in this meagre grove, but they are easily seen from the public footpath which traverses it, and all too easily gathered. Foxgloves, too—people will pull up the foxgloves, and ladies of an educational tendency even grub for toadstools to show them on the Monday in class. Other ladies, less educated, roll down the bracken in the arms of their gentlemen friends. There is paper, there are tins. Pray, does my wood belong to me or doesn't it? And, if it does, should I not own it best by allowing no one else to walk there? There is a wood near Lyme Regis, also cursed by a public footpath, where the owner has not hesitated on this point. He had built high stone walls each side of the path, and has spanned it by bridges, so that the public circulate like termites while he gorges on the blackberries unseen. He really does own his wood, this able chap. Dives in Hell did pretty well, but the gulf dividing him from Lazarus could be traversed by vision, and nothing traverses it here. And perhaps I shall come to this in time. I shall wall in and fence out until I really taste the sweets of property. Enormously stout, endlessly avaricious, pseudo-creative, intensely selfish, I shall weave upon my forehead the quadruple crown of possession until those nasty Bolshies come and take it off again and thrust me aside into the outer darkness.

MAO TSE-TUNG (1893–   ), *Report on an Investigation of the Peasant Movement in Hunan*

Born in Hunan province of a well-to-do peasant family, educated in Hunan and Peking, Mao Tse-Tung lived from youth amid revolutionary ferment. The Revolution of 1911, which overthrew the ancient Manchu dynasty, was preceded and followed by many unsuccessful revolts and local risings, as was the anti-imperialist, antifeudal insurrection and general strike of 1919 in Peking. When the Communist party of China was founded in 1921 by about a dozen men, including Mao, its policy was to work with the Kuomintang, an already existing revolutionary party. But when in 1927 the Kuomintang leader, Chiang Kai-shek, ordered the massacre of Communist workers in Shanghai, it became obvious how far the older party had moved from revolutionary ideals.

In Hunan, meanwhile, the peasants had taken power into their own hands, through peasant associations that Mao had helped to organize. Convinced that the strength of Chinese revolution lay with the peasants, Mao encouraged the movement and defended it in his Report (March 1927) to the Communist Central Committee. But the Report was tabled, and in May the peasant revolt in Hunan was crushed by Chiang's forces. The civil war that had now begun continued for more than twenty years. The Red Army went underground, organizing peasants and workers, living in the mountains and countryside, waging open and guerrilla warfare under Mao's command. During this period Mao was also chief theoretician of the Chinese revolution and head of the communist governments that had developed in various provinces. By 1949 the Kuomintang could no longer keep up the pretense of power; Chiang withdrew to the island of Taiwan, and on October 1, 1949, the People's Government of China was proclaimed in the ancient imperial city of Peking.

Though it is an early work, the Report displays the characteristic features of Mao's writing: his ironical use of traditional Chinese sayings and stories; his fondness for numerical lists, slogans, and caricatures resembling figures in the classical Chinese drama; his spare but vivid description of events. An excerpt from one of Mao's poems ("The Snow," 1945), gives some idea of his skill:

> *In the north country*
> *A thousand miles are frozen in ice*

And ten thousand miles in eddying snow . . .
Observe: red, clothed in white,
The earth becomes lovely
So that innumerable heroes will court her.

THE IMPORTANCE OF THE
PEASANT PROBLEM

During my recent visit to Hunan I made a first-hand investigation of conditions in the five counties of Hsiangtan, Hsianghsiang, Hengshan, Liling and Changsha. In the thirty-two days from January 4 to February 5, I called together fact-finding conferences in villages and county towns, which were attended by experienced peasants and by comrades working in the peasant movement, and I listened attentively to their reports and collected a great deal of material. Many of the hows and whys of the peasant movement were the exact opposite of what the gentry in Hankow and Changsha are saying. I saw and heard of many strange things of which I had hitherto been unaware. I believe the same is true of many other places, too.

All talk directed against the peasant movement must be speedily set right. All the wrong measures taken by the revolutionary authorities concerning the peasant movement must be speedily changed. Only thus can the future of the revolution be benefited. For the present upsurge of the peasant movement is a colossal event. In a very short time, in China's central, southern and northern provinces, several hundred million peasants will rise like a mighty storm, like a hurricane, a force so swift and violent that no power, however great, will be able to hold it back. They will smash all the trammels that bind them and rush forward along the road to liberation. They will sweep all the imperialists, warlords, corrupt officials, local tyrants and evil gentry into their graves. Every revolutionary party and every revolutionary comrade will be put to the test, to be accepted or rejected as they decide. There are three alternatives. To march at their head and lead them? To trail behind them, gesticulating and criticizing? Or to stand in their way and oppose them? Every Chinese is free to choose, but events will force you to make the choice quickly. . . .

DOWN WITH THE LOCAL TYRANTS AND
EVIL GENTRY! ALL POWER TO THE
PEASANT ASSOCIATIONS!

The main targets of attack by the peasants are the local tyrants, the evil gentry and the lawless landlords, but in passing they also hit out against patriarchal ideas and institutions, against the corrupt officials in the cities and against bad practices and customs in the rural areas. In force and momentum the attack is tempestuous; those who bow before it survive and those who resist perish. As a result, the privileges which the feudal landlords enjoyed for thousands of years are being shattered to pieces. Every bit of the dignity and prestige built up by the landlords is being swept into the dust. With the collapse of the power of the landlords, the peasant associations have now become the sole organs of authority and the popular slogan "All power to the peasant associations" has become a reality. Even trifles such as a quarrel between husband and wife are brought to the peasant association. Nothing can be settled unless someone from the peasant association is present. The association actually dictates all rural affairs, and, quite literally, "whatever it says, goes." Those who are outside the associations can only speak well of them and cannot say anything against them. The local tyrants, evil gentry and lawless landlords have been deprived of all right to speak, and none of them dares even mutter dissent. In the face of the peasant associations' power and pressure, the top local tyrants and evil gentry have fled to Shanghai, those of the second rank to Hankow, those of the third to Changsha and those of the fourth to the county towns, while the fifth rank and the still lesser fry surrender to the peasant associations in the villages.

"Here's ten yuan. Please let me join the peasant association," one of the smaller of the evil gentry will say.

"Ugh! Who wants your filthy money?" the peasants reply.

Many middle and small landlords and rich peasants and even some middle peasants, who were all formerly opposed to the peasant associations, are now vainly seeking admission. Visiting various places, I often came across such people who pleaded with me, "Mr. Committeeman from the provincial capital, please be my sponsor!"

In the Ching Dynasty,[1] the household census compiled by the local authorities consisted of a regular register and "the other" register, the former for honest people and the latter for burglars, bandits and similar undesirables. In some places the peasants now use this method to scare those who formerly opposed the associations. They say, "Put their names down in the other register!"

Afraid of being entered in the other register, such people try various devices to gain admission into the peasant associations, on which their minds are so set that they do not feel safe until their names are entered. But more often than not they are turned down flat, and so they are always on tenterhooks; with the doors of the association barred to them, they are like tramps without a home or, in rural parlance, "mere trash." In short, what was looked down upon four months ago as a "gang of peasants" has now become a most honourable institution. Those who formerly prostrated themselves before the power of the gentry now bow before the power of the peasants. No matter what their identity, all admit that the world since last October is a different one.

"It's Terrible!" or "It's Fine!"

The peasants' revolt disturbed the gentry's sweet dreams. When the news from the countryside reached the cities, it caused immediate uproar among the gentry. Soon after my arrival in Changsha, I met all sorts of people and picked up a good deal of gossip. From the middle social strata upwards to the Kuomintang right-wingers, there was not a single person who did not sum up

---

1. Ching dynasty (1644–1912), established by the Manchu, who conquered China in the seventeenth century.

the whole business in the phrase, "It's terrible!" Under the impact of the views of the "It's terrible!" school then flooding the city, even quite revolutionary-minded people became down-hearted as they pictured the events in the countryside in their mind's eye; and they were unable to deny the word "terrible." Even quite progressive people said, "Though terrible, it is inevitable in a revolution." In short, nobody could altogether deny the word "terrible." But, as already mentioned, the fact is that the great peasant masses have risen to fulfill their historic mission and that the forces of rural democracy have risen to overthrow the forces of rural feudalism. The patriarchal-feudal class of local tyrants, evil gentry and lawless landlords has formed the basis of autocratic government for thousands of years and is the cornerstone of imperialism, warlordism and corrupt officialdom. To overthrow these feudal forces is the real objective of the national revolution. In a few months the peasants have accomplished what Dr. Sun Yat-sen [2] wanted, but failed, to accomplish in the forty years he devoted to the national revolution. This is a marvellous feat never before achieved, not just in forty, but in thousands of years. It's fine. It is not "terrible" at all. It is anything but "terrible." "It's terrible!" is obviously a theory for combating the rise of the peasants in the interests of the landlords; it is obviously a theory of the landlord class for preserving the old order of feudalism and obstructing the establishment of the new order of democracy; it is obviously a counter-revolutionary theory. No revolutionary comrade should echo this nonsense. If your revolutionary viewpoint is firmly established and if you have been to the villages and looked around, you will undoubtedly feel thrilled as never before. Countless thousands of the enslaved—the peasants—are striking down the enemies who battened on their flesh. What the peasants are doing is absolutely right; what they are doing is fine! "It's fine!" is the theory of the peasants and of all other revolutionaries. Every revolutionary comrade should know that the national revolution requires a great change in the countryside. The Revolution of 1911 [3] did not bring about this change, hence its failure. This change is now taking place, and it is an important factor for the completion of the revolution. Every revolutionary comrade must support it, or he will be taking the stand of counter-revolution.

THE QUESTION OF "GOING TOO FAR"

Then there is another section of people who say, "Yes, peasant associations are necessary, but they are going rather too far." This is the opinion of the middle-of-the-roaders. But what is the actual situation? True, the peasants are in a sense "unruly" in the countryside. Supreme in authority, the peasant association allows the landlord no say and sweeps away his prestige. This amounts to striking the landlord down to the dust and keeping him there. The peasants threaten, "We will put you in the other register!" They fine the local tyrants and evil gentry, they demand contributions from them, and they

2. Sun Yat-sen (1866–1925), revolutionary and first president of the Chinese republic in 1911.
3. The Revolution of 1911 overthrew the Manchu or Ching dynasty and made China a republic.

smash their sedan-chairs. People swarm into the houses of local tyrants and evil gentry who are against the peasant association, slaughter their pigs and consume their grain. They even loll for a minute or two on the ivory-inlaid beds belonging to the young ladies in the households of the local tyrants and evil gentry. At the slightest provocation they make arrests, crown the arrested with tall paper hats, and parade them through the villages, saying, "You dirty landlords, now you know who we are!" Doing whatever they like and turning everything upside down, they have created a kind of terror in the countryside. This is what some people call "going too far," or "exceeding the proper limits in righting a wrong," or "really too much."

Such talk may seem plausible, but in fact it is wrong. First, the local tyrants, evil gentry and lawless landlords have themselves driven the peasants to this. For ages they have used their power to tyrannize over the peasants and trample them underfoot; that is why the peasants have reacted so strongly. The most violent revolts and the most serious disorders have invariably occurred in places where the local tyrants, evil gentry and lawless landlords perpetrated the worst outrages. The peasants are clear-sighted. Who is bad and who is not, who is the worst and who is not quite so vicious, who deserves severe punishment and who deserves to be let off lightly—the peasants keep clear accounts, and very seldom has the punishment exceeded the crime. Secondly, a revolution is not a dinner party, or writing an essay, or painting a picture, or doing embroidery; it cannot be so refined, so leisurely and gentle, so temperate, kind, courteous, restrained and magnanimous.[4] A revolution is an insurrection, an act of violence by which one class overthrows another. A rural revolution is a revolution by which the peasantry overthrows the power of the feudal landlord class. Without using the greatest force, the peasants cannot possibly overthrow the deep-rooted authority of the landlords which has lasted for thousands of years. The rural areas need a mighty revolutionary upsurge, for it alone can rouse the people in their millions to become a powerful force. All the actions mentioned here which have been labelled as "going too far" flow from the power of the peasants, which has been called forth by the mighty revolutionary upsurge in the countryside. It was highly necessary for such things to be done in the second period of the peasant movement, the period of revolutionary action. In this period it was necessary to establish the absolute authority of the peasants. It was necessary to forbid malicious criticism of the peasant associations. It was necessary to overthrow the whole authority of the gentry, to strike them to the ground and keep them there. There is revolutionary significance in all the actions which were labelled as "going too far" in this period. To put it bluntly, it is necessary to create terror for a while in every rural area, or otherwise it would be impossible to suppress the activities of the counter-revolutionaries in the countryside or overthrow the authority of the gentry. Proper limits have to be exceeded in order to right a wrong, or else the wrong cannot be righted. Those who talk about the peasants "going too far" seem at first sight to be different from those who say "It's terrible!" as mentioned earlier, but in essence they proceed from the same standpoint and likewise voice a landlord theory that upholds the interests of the privileged classes. Since this theory impedes the

---

4. Refined, etc: these were traditionally said to be the personal virtues of Confucius.

rise of the peasant movement and so disrupts the revolution, we must firmly oppose it. . . .

VANGUARDS OF THE REVOLUTION

Where there are two opposite approaches to things and people, two opposite views emerge. "It's terrible!" and "It's fine!," "riffraff" and "vanguards of the revolution"—here are apt examples.

We said above that the peasants have accomplished a revolutionary task which had been left unaccomplished for many years and have done an important job for the national revolution. But has this great revolutionary task, this important revolutionary work, been performed by all the peasants? No. There are three kinds of peasants, the rich, the middle and the poor peasants. The three live in different circumstances and so have different views about the revolution. . . . An official of the township peasant association (generally one of the "riffraff" type) would walk into the house of a rich peasant, register in hand, and say, "Will you please join the peasant association?" How would the rich peasant answer? A tolerably well-behaved one would say, "Peasant association? I have lived here for decades, tilling my land. I never heard of such a thing before, yet I've managed to live all right. I advise you to give it up!" A really vicious rich peasant would say, "Peasant association! Nonsense! Association for getting your head chopped off! Don't get people into trouble!" Yet, surprisingly enough, the peasant associations have now been established several months, and have even dared to stand up to the gentry. The gentry of the neighbourhood who refused to surrender their opium pipes were arrested by the associations and paraded through the villages. In the county towns, moreover, some big landlords were put to death, like Yen Jung-chiu of Hsiangtan and Yang Chih-tse of Ninghsiang. On the anniversary of the October Revolution, at the time of the anti-British rally and of the great celebrations of the victory of the Northern Expedition, tens of thousands of peasants in every township, holding high their banners, big and small, along with their carrying-poles and hoes, demonstrated in massive, streaming columns. It was only then that the rich peasants began to get perplexed and alarmed. . . .

How about the middle peasants? Theirs is a vacillating attitude. They think that the revolution will not bring them much good. They have rice cooking in their pots and no creditors knocking on their doors at midnight. They, too, judging a thing by whether it ever existed before, knit their brows and think to themselves, "Can the peasant association really last?" "Can the Three People's Principles prevail?" Their conclusion is, "Afraid not!" They imagine it all depends on the will of Heaven and think, "A peasant association? Who knows if Heaven wills it or not?" In the first period, people from the association would call on a middle peasant, register in hand, and say, "Will you please join the peasant association?" The middle peasant would reply, "There's no hurry!" It was not until the second period, when the peasant associations were already exercising great power, that the middle peasants came in. They show up better in the associations than the rich peasants but are not as yet very enthusiastic; they still want to wait and see. It is essential for the peasant associations to get the middle peasants to join and to do a good deal more explanatory work among them.

The poor peasants have always been the main force in the bitter fight in the countryside. They have fought militantly through the two periods of underground work and of open activity. They are the most responsive to Communist Party leadership. They are deadly enemies of the camp of the local tyrants and evil gentry and attack it without the slightest hesitation. "We joined the peasant association long ago," they say to the rich peasants, "why are you still hesitating?" The rich peasants answer mockingly, "What is there to keep you from joining? You people have neither a tile over your heads nor a speck of land under your feet!" It is true the poor peasants are not afraid of losing anything. Many of them really have "neither a tile over their heads nor a speck of land under their feet." What, indeed, is there to keep them from joining the associations? According to the survey of Changsha County, the poor peasants comprise 70 percent, the middle peasants 20 percent, and the landlords and the rich peasants 10 percent of the population in the rural areas. . . . Leadership by the poor peasants is absolutely necessary. Without the poor peasants there would be no revolution. To deny their role is to deny the revolution. To attack them is to attack the revolution. They have never been wrong on the general direction of the revolution. They have discredited the local tyrants and evil gentry. They have beaten down the local tyrants and evil gentry, big and small, and kept them underfoot. Many of their deeds in the period of revolutionary action, which were labelled as "going too far," were in fact the very things the revolution required. Some county governments, county headquarters of the Kuomintang and county peasant associations in Hunan have already made a number of mistakes; some have even sent soldiers to arrest officials of the lower-level associations at the landlords' request. A good many chairmen and committee members of township associations in Hengshan and Hsianghsiang Counties have been thrown in jail. This mistake is very serious and feeds the arrogance of the reactionaries. To judge whether or not it is a mistake, you have only to see how joyful the lawless landlords become and how reactionary sentiments grow, wherever the chairmen or committee members of local peasant associations are arrested. We must combat the counter-revolutionary talk of a "movement of riffraff" and a "movement of lazy peasants" and must be especially careful not to commit the error of helping the local tyrants and evil gentry in their attacks on the poor peasant class. Though a few of the poor peasant leaders undoubtedly did have shortcomings, most of them have changed by now. They themselves are energetically prohibiting gambling and suppressing banditry. Where the peasant association is powerful, gambling has stopped altogether and banditry has vanished. In some places it is literally true that people do not take any articles left by the wayside and that doors are not bolted at night. According to the Hengshan survey, 85 percent of the poor peasant leaders have made great progress and have proved themselves capable and hard-working. Only 15 percent retain some bad habits. The most one can call these is "an unhealthy minority," and we must not echo the local tyrants and evil gentry in undiscriminatingly condemning them as "riffraff." This problem of the "unhealthy minority" can be tackled only under the peasant associations' own slogan of "strengthen discipline," by carrying on propaganda among the masses, by educating the "unhealthy minority," and by tightening the associations' discipline; in no circumstances should soldiers be arbitrarily sent to make such arrests as would damage the prestige of the poor peasants and feed the arrogance of the local tyrants and evil gentry. This point requires particular attention.

FOURTEEN GREAT ACHIEVEMENTS

Most critics of the peasant associations allege that they have done a great many bad things. I have already pointed out that the peasants' attack on the local tyrants and evil gentry is entirely revolutionary behaviour and in no way blameworthy. The peasants have done a great many things, and in order to answer people's criticism we must closely examine all their activities, one by one, to see what they have actually done. I have classified and summed up their activities of the last few months; in all, the peasants under the leadership of the peasant associations have the following fourteen great achievements to their credit.

1. Organizing the Peasants into Peasant Associations

This is the first great achievement of the peasants. In counties like Hsiangtan, Hsianghsiang and Hengshan, nearly all the peasants are organized and there is hardly a remote corner where they are not on the move; these are the best places. In some counties, like Yiyang and Huajung, the bulk of the peasants are organized, with only a small section remaining unorganized; these places are in the second grade. In other counties, like Chengpu and Lingling, while a small section is organized, the bulk of the peasants remain unorganized; these places are in the third grade. . . . According to the figures compiled by the provincial peasant association last November, organizations with a total membership of 1,367,727 have been set up in thirty-seven of the province's seventy-five counties. Of these members about one million were organized during October and November when the power of the associations rose high, while up to September the membership had only been 300,000–400,000. Then came the two months of December and January, and the peasant movement continued its brisk growth. By the end of January the membership must have reached at least two million. As a family generally enters only one name when joining and has an average of five members, the mass following must be about ten million. This astonishing and accelerating rate of expansion explains why the local tyrants, evil gentry and corrupt officials have been isolated, why the public has been amazed at how completely the world has changed since the peasant movement, and why a great revolution has been wrought in the countryside. This is the first great achievement of the peasants under the leadership of their associations.

2. Hitting the Landlords Politically

Once the peasants have their organization, the first thing they do is to smash the political prestige and power of the landlord class, and especially of the local tyrants and evil gentry, that is, to pull down landlord authority and build up peasant authority in rural society. This is a most serious and vital struggle. It is the pivotal struggle in the second period, the period of revolutionary action. Without victory in this struggle, no victory is possible in the economic struggle to reduce rent and interest, to secure land and other means of production, and so on. In many places in Hunan like Hsianghsiang, Hengshan and Hsiangtan Counties, this is of course no problem since the authority of the landlords has been overturned and the peasants constitute the sole authority. But in counties like Liling there are still some places (such as Liling's western and southern districts) where the authority of the landlords seems weaker than that of the peasants but, because the political struggle has not been sharp, is in fact surreptitiously competing with it. In such places it is still too early to say that the peasants have gained political victory; they must wage the political struggle more vigorously until the landlords' authority is completely smashed. All in all, the methods used by the peasants to hit the landlords politically are as follows:

Checking the accounts. More often than not the local tyrants and evil gentry have helped themselves to public money passing through their hands, and their books are not in order. Now the peasants are using the checking of accounts as an occasion to bring down a great many of the local tyrants and evil gentry. In many places committees for checking accounts have been established for the express purpose of settling financial scores with them, and the first sign of such a committee makes them shudder. Campaigns of this kind have been carried out in all the counties where the peasant movement is active; they are important not so much for recovering money as for publicizing the crimes of the local tyrants and evil gentry and for knocking them down from their political and social positions.

Imposing fines. The peasants work out fines for such offences as irregularities revealed by the checking of accounts, past outrages against the peasants, current activities which undermine the peasant associations, violations of the ban on gambling and refusal to surrender opium pipes. This local tyrant must pay so much, that member of the evil gentry so much, the sums ranging from tens to thousands of yuan. Naturally, a man who has been fined by the peasants completely loses face.

Levying contributions. The unscrupulous rich landlords are made to contribute for poor relief, for the organization of cooperatives or peasant credit societies, or for other purposes. Though milder than fines, these contributions are also a form of punishment. To avoid trouble, quite a number of landlords make voluntary contributions to the peasant associations.

Minor protests. When someone harms a peasant association by word or deed and the offence is a minor one, the peasants collect in a crowd and swarm into the offender's house to remonstrate with him. He is usually let off after writing a pledge to "cease and desist," in which he explicitly undertakes to stop defaming the peasant association in the future.

Major demonstrations. A big crowd is rallied to demonstrate against a local tyrant or one of the evil gentry who is an enemy of the association. The demonstrators eat at the offender's house, slaughtering his pigs and consuming his grain as a matter of course. Quite a few such cases have occurred. There was a case recently at Machiaho, Hsiangtan County, where a crowd of fifteen thousand peasants went to the houses of six of the evil gentry and demonstrated; the whole affair lasted four days during which more than 130 pigs were killed and eaten. After such demonstrations, the peasants usually impose fines.

"Crowning" the landlords and parading them through the villages. This sort of thing is very common. A tall paper hat is stuck on the head of one of the local tyrants or evil gentry, bearing the words "Local tyrant so-and-so" or "So-and-so of the evil gentry." He is led by a rope and escorted with big crowds in front and behind. Sometimes brass gongs are beaten and flags waved to attract people's attention. This form of punishment more than any other makes the local tyrants and evil gentry tremble. Anyone who has once been crowned with a tall paper hat loses face altogether and can never again hold up his head. Hence many of the rich prefer being fined to wearing the tall hat. But wear it they must, if the peasants insist. One ingenious township peasant association arrested an obnoxious member of the gentry and announced that he was to be crowned that very day. The man turned blue with fear. Then the association decided not to crown him that day. They argued that if he were crowned right away, he would become case-hardened and no longer afraid, and that it would be better to let him go home and crown him some other day. Not knowing when he would be crowned, the man was in daily suspense, unable to sit down or sleep at ease.

Locking up the landlords in the county jail. This is a heavier punishment than wearing the tall paper hat. A local tyrant or one of the evil gentry is arrested and sent to the county jail; he is locked up and the county magistrate has to try him and punish him. Today the people who are locked up are no longer the same. Formerly it was the gentry who sent peasants to be locked up, now it is the other way round.

"Banishment." The peasants have no desire to banish the most notorious criminals among the local tyrants and evil gentry, but would rather arrest or execute them. Afraid of being arrested or executed, they run away. In counties where the peasant movement is well developed, almost all the important local tyrants and evil gentry have fled, and this amounts to banishment. Among them, the top ones have fled to Shanghai, those of the second rank to Hankow, those of the third to Changsha, and of the fourth to the county towns. Of all the fugitive local tyrants and evil gentry, those who have fled to Shanghai are the safest. Some of those who fled to Hankow, like the three from Huajung, were eventually captured and brought back. Those who fled to Changsha are in still greater danger of being seized at any moment by students in the provincial capital who hail from their counties; I myself saw two captured in Changsha. Those who have taken refuge in the county towns are only of the fourth rank, and the peasantry, having many eyes and ears, can easily track them down. The financial authorities once explained the difficulties encountered by the Hunan Provincial Government in raising money by the fact that the peasants were banishing the well-to-do, which gives some idea of the extent to which the local tyrants and evil gentry are not tolerated in their home villages.

Execution. This is confined to the worst local tyrants and evil gentry and is carried out by the peasants jointly with other sections of the people. For instance, Yang Chih-tse of Ninghsiang, Chou Chia-kan of Yuehyang, and Fu Tao-nan and Sun Po-chu of Huajung were shot by the government authorities at the insistence of the peasants and other sections of the people. In the case of Yen Jung-chiu of Hsiangtan, the peasants and other sections of the people compelled the magistrate to agree to hand him over, and the peasants themselves executed him. Liu Chao of Ninghsiang was killed by the peasants. The execution of Peng Chih-fan of Liling and Chou Tien-chueh and Tsao Yun of Yiyang is pending, subject to the decision of the "special tribunal for trying local tyrants and evil gentry." The execution of one such big landlord reverberates through a whole county and is very effective in eradicating the remaining evils of feudalism. Every county has these major tyrants, some as many as several dozen and others at least a few, and the only effective way of suppressing the reactionaries is to execute at least a few in each county who are guilty of the most heinous crimes. When the local tyrants and evil gentry were at the height of their power, they literally slaughtered peasants without batting an eyelid. Ho Mai-chuan, for ten years head of the defence corps in the town of Hsinkang, Changsha County, was personally responsible for killing almost a thousand poverty-stricken peasants, which he euphemistically described as "executing bandits." In my native county of Hsiangtan, Tang Chun-yen and Lo Shu-lin who headed the defence corps in the town of Yintien have killed more than fifty people and buried four alive in the fourteen years since 1913. Of the more than fifty they murdered, the first two were perfectly innocent beggars. Tang Chun-yen said, "Let me make a start by killing a couple of beggars!" and so these two lives were snuffed out. Such was the cruelty of the local tyrants and evil gentry in former days, such was the White terror they created in the countryside, and now that the peasants have risen and shot a few and created just a little terror in suppressing the counter-revolutionaries, is there any reason for saying they should not do so? *

7. Overthrowing the Clan Authority of the Ancestral Temples and Clan Elders, the Religious Authority of Town and Village Gods, and the Masculine Authority of Husbands

A man in China is usually subjected to the domination of three systems of authority: (1) the state system (political authority), ranging from the national, provincial and county government down to that of the township; (2) the clan system (clan authority), ranging from the central ancestral temple and its branch temples down to the head of the household; and (3) the supernatural system (religious authority), ranging from the King of Hell down to the town and village gods belonging to the nether world, and from the Emperor of Heaven down to all the various gods and spirits belonging to the celestial world. As for women, in addition to being dominated by these three systems of authority, they are also dominated by the men (the authority of the husband). These four authorities—political, clan, religious, and masculine—are the embodiment of the whole feudal-patriarchal system and ideology, and are the four thick ropes binding the Chinese people, particularly the peasants. How the peasants have overthrown the political authority of the landlords in the countryside has been described above. The political authority of the landlords is the backbone of all the other systems of authority. With that overturned, the clan authority, the religious authority and the authority of the

* Great Deeds 3–6 describe economic blows dealt against the landlords, the overthrow of local judicial and political power, and the building of the peasants' armed forces.

husband all begin to totter. Where the peasant association is powerful, the clan elders and administrators of temple funds no longer dare oppress those lower in the clan hierarchy or embezzle clan funds. The worst clan elders and administrators, being local tyrants, have been thrown out. No one any longer dares to practise the cruel corporal and capital punishments that used to be inflicted in the ancestral temples, such as flogging, drowning, and burying alive. The old rule barring women and poor people from the banquets in the ancestral temples has also been broken. The women of Paikuo in Hengshan County gathered in force and swarmed into their ancestral temple, firmly planted their backsides in the seats and joined in the eating and drinking, while the venerable clan bigwigs had willy-nilly to let them do as they pleased. At another place, where poor peasants had been excluded from temple banquets, a group of them flocked in and ate and drank their fill, while the local tyrants and evil gentry and other long-gowned gentlemen all took to their heels in fright.

Everywhere religious authority totters as the peasant movement develops. In many places the peasant associations have taken over the temples of the gods as their offices. Everywhere they advocate the appropriation of temple property in order to start peasant schools and to defray the expenses of the associations, calling it "public revenue from superstition." In Liling County, prohibiting superstitious practices and smashing idols have become quite the vogue. In its northern districts the peasants have prohibited the incense-burning processions to propitiate the god of pestilence. There were many idols in the Taoist temple at Fupoling in Lukou, but when extra room was needed for the district headquarters of the Kuomintang, they were all piled up in a corner, big and small together, and no peasant raised any objection. Since then, sacrifices to the gods, the performance of religious rites, and the offering of sacred lamps have rarely been practised when a death occurs in a family. Because the initiative in this matter was taken by the chairman of the peasant association, Sun Hsiao-shan, he is hated by the local Taoist priests. In the Lungfeng Nunnery in the North Third District, the peasants and primary school teachers chopped up the wooden idols and actually used the wood to cook meat. More than thirty idols in the Tungfu Monastery in the Southern District were burned by the students and peasants together, and only two small images of Lord Pao were snatched up by an old peasant who said, "Don't commit a sin!" In places where the power of the peasants is predominant, only the older peasants and the women still believe in the gods, the younger peasants no longer doing so. Since the latter control the associations, the overthrow of religious authority and the eradication of superstition are going on everywhere.

As to the authority of the husband, this has always been weaker among the poor peasants because, out of economic necessity, their womenfolk have to do more manual labour than the women of the richer classes and therefore have more say and greater power of decision in family matters. With the increasing bankruptcy of the rural economy in recent years, the basis for men's domination over women has already been weakened. With the rise of the peasant movement, the women in many places have now begun to organize rural women's associations; the opportunity has come for them to lift up their heads, and the authority of the husband is getting shakier every day. In a word, the whole feudal-patriarchal system and ideology is tottering with the growth of the peasants' power. At the present time, however, the peasants are concentrating on destroying the landlords' political authority. Wherever it has been wholly destroyed, they are beginning to press their attack in the three other spheres of the clan, the gods, and male domination. But such attacks have only just begun, and there can be no thorough overthrow of all three until the peasants have won complete victory in the economic struggle. Therefore, our present task is to lead the peasants to put their greatest efforts into the political struggle, so that the landlords' authority is entirely overthrown. The economic struggle should follow immediately, so that the land problem and the other economic problems of the poor peasants may be fundamentally solved.

As for the clan system, superstition, and inequality between men and women, their abolition will follow as a natural consequence of victory in the political and economic struggles. If too much of an effort is made, arbitrarily and prematurely, to abolish these things, the local tyrants and evil gentry will seize the pretext to put about such counter-revolutionary propaganda as "the peasant association has no piety towards ancestors," "the peasant association is blasphemous and is destroying religion," and "the peasant association stands for the communization of wives," all for the purpose of undermining the peasant movement. A case in point is the recent events at Hsianghsiang in Hunan and Yanghsin in Hupeh, where the landlords exploited the opposition of some peasants to smashing idols. It is the peasants who made the idols, and when the time comes they will cast the idols aside with their own hands; there is no need for anyone else to do it for them prematurely. The Communist Party's propaganda policy in such matters should be, "Draw the bow without shooting, just indicate the motions." It is for the peasants themselves to cast aside the idols, pull down the temples to the martyred virgins and the arches to the chaste and faithful widows; it is wrong for anybody else to do it for them.

While I was in the countryside, I did some propaganda against superstition among the peasants. I said:

"If you believe in the Eight Characters,[5] you hope for good luck; if you believe in geomancy, you hope to benefit from the location of your ancestral graves. This year within the space of a few months the local tyrants, evil gentry and corrupt officials have all toppled from their pedestals. Is it possible that until a few months ago they all had good luck and enjoyed the benefit of well-sited ancestral graves, while suddenly in the last few months their luck has turned and their ancestral graves have ceased to exert a beneficial influence? The local tyrants and evil gentry jeer at your peasant association and say, 'How odd! Today, the world is a world of committeemen. Look, you can't even go to pass water without bumping into a committeeman!' Quite true, the towns and the villages, the trade unions and the peasant associations, the Kuomintang and the Communist Party, all without exception, have their executive committee members—it is indeed a world of committeemen. But is this due to the Eight Characters and the location of the ancestral

5. Eight Characters: a method of fortune-telling which uses the characters of a person's birthday—two each for the year, month, day and hour. Geomancy, another form of divination, uses the location of the ancestral burial ground.

graves? How strange! The Eight Characters of all the poor wretches in the countryside have suddenly turned auspicious! And their ancestral graves have suddenly started exerting beneficial influences! The gods? Worship them by all means. But if you had only Lord Kuan [6] and the Goddess of Mercy and no peasant association, could you have overthrown the local tyrants and evil gentry? The gods and goddesses are indeed miserable objects. You have worshipped them for centuries, and they have not overthrown a single one of the local tyrants or evil gentry for you! Now you want to have your rent reduced. Let me ask, how will you go about it? Will you believe in the gods or in the peasant association?"

My words made the peasants roar with laughter.

8. Spreading Political Propaganda

Even if ten thousand schools of law and political science had been opened, could they have brought as much political education to the people, men and women, young and old, all the way into the remotest corners of the countryside, as the peasant associations have done in so short a time? I don't think they could. "Down with imperialism!" "Down with the warlords!" "Down with the corrupt officials!" "Down with the local tyrants and evil gentry!"— these political slogans have grown wings, they have found their way to the young, the middle-aged, and the old, to the women and children in countless villages, they have penetrated into their minds and are on their lips. For instance, watch a group of children at play. If one gets angry with another, if he glares, stamps his foot and shakes his fist, you will then immediately hear from the other the shrill cry of "Down with imperialism!"

In the Hsiangtan area, when the children who pasture the cattle get into a fight, one will act as Tang Sheng-chih, and the other as Yeh Kai-hsin; [7] when one is defeated and runs away, with the other chasing him, it is the pursuer who is Tang Sheng-chih and the pursued Yeh Kai-hsin. As to the song "Down with the Imperialist Powers!" of course almost every child in the towns can sing it, and now many village children can sing it too.

Some of the peasants can also recite Dr. Sun Yat-sen's Testament. They pick out the terms "freedom," "equality," "the Three People's Principles," and "unequal treaties" and apply them, if rather crudely, in their daily life. When somebody who looks like one of the gentry encounters a peasant and stands on his dignity, refusing to make way along a pathway, the peasant will say angrily, "Hey, you local tyrant, don't you know the Three People's Principles?" Formerly when the peasants from the vegetable farms on the outskirts of Changsha entered the city to sell their produce, they used to be pushed around by the police. Now they have found a weapon, which is none other than the Three People's Principles. When a policeman strikes or swears at a peasant selling vegetables, the peasant immediately answers back by invoking the Three People's Principles and that shuts the policeman up. Once in Hsiangtan when a district peasant association and a township peasant association could not see eye to eye, the chairman of the township association declared, "Down with the district peasant association's unequal treaties!"

---

6. Kuan: an ancient warrior, worshipped as the god of war.
7. Tang, Yeh: a revolutionary and a reactionary general, respectively.

The spread of political propaganda throughout the rural areas is entirely an achievement of the Communist Party and the peasant associations. Simple slogans, cartoons and speeches have produced such a widespread and speedy effect among the peasants that every one of them seems to have been through a political school. According to the reports of comrades engaged in rural work, political propaganda was very extensive at the time of the three great mass rallies, the anti-British demonstration, the celebration of the October Revolution, and the victory celebration for the Northern Expedition. On these occasions, political propaganda was conducted extensively wherever there were peasant associations, arousing the whole countryside with tremendous effect. From now on care should be taken to use every opportunity gradually to enrich the content and clarify the meaning of those simple slogans.

9. Peasant Bans and Prohibitions

When the peasant associations, under Communist Party leadership, establish their authority in the countryside, the peasants begin to prohibit or restrict the things they dislike. Gaming, gambling, and opium-smoking are the three things that are most strictly forbidden.

Gaming. Where the peasant association is powerful, mahjong, dominoes and card games are completely banned.

The peasant association in the 14th District of Hsianghsiang burned two basketfuls of mahjong sets.

If you go to the countryside, you will find none of these games played; anyone who violates the ban is promptly and strictly punished.

Gambling. Former hardened gamblers are now themselves suppressing gambling; this abuse, too, has been swept away in places where the peasant association is powerful.

Opium-smoking. The prohibition is extremely strict. When the peasant association orders the surrender of opium pipes, no one dares to raise the least objection. In Liling County one of the evil gentry who did not surrender his pipes was arrested and paraded through the villages. . . . Quite a number of venerable fathers of officers in the revolutionary army, old men who were opium-addicts and inseparable from their pipes, have been disarmed by the "emperors" (as the peasants are called derisively by the evil gentry). The "emperors" have banned not only the growing and smoking of opium, but also trafficking in it. A great deal of the opium transported from Kweichow to Kiangsi via the counties of Paoching, Hsianghsiang, Yuhsien and Liling has been intercepted on the way and burned. This has affected government revenues. As a result, out of consideration for the army's need for funds in the Northern Expedition, the provincial peasant association ordered the associations at the lower levels "temporarily to postpone the ban on opium traffic." This, however, has upset and displeased the peasants.

There are many other things besides these three which the peasants have prohibited or restricted, the following being some examples:

The flower drum. Vulgar performances are forbidden in many places.

Sedan-chairs. In many counties, especially Hsianghsiang, there have been cases of smashing sedan-chairs. The peasants, detesting the people who use this conveyance, are always ready to smash the chairs, but the peasant associations forbid them to do so. Association officials tell the peasants, "If you smash the chairs, you only save the rich money and lose the carriers their jobs. Will that not hurt our own people?" Seeing the point, the peasants have worked out a new tactic—considerably to increase the fares charged by the chair-carriers so as to penalize the rich.

Distilling and sugar-making. The use of grain for distilling spirits and making sugar is everywhere prohibited, and the distillers and sugar-refiners are constantly complaining. Distilling is not banned in Futienpu, Hengshan County, but prices are fixed very low, and the wine and spirits dealers, seeing no prospect of profit, have had to stop it.

Pigs. The number of pigs a family can keep is limited, for pigs consume grain.

Chickens and ducks. In Hsianghsiang County the raising of chickens and ducks is prohibited, but the women object. In Hengshan County, each family in Yangtang is allowed to keep only three, and in Futienpu five. In many places the raising of ducks is completely banned, for ducks not only consume grain but also ruin the rice plants and so are worse than chickens.

Feasts. Sumptuous feasts are generally forbidden. In Shaoshan, Hsiangtan County, it has been decided that guests are to be served with only three kinds of animal food, namely, chicken, fish and pork. It is also forbidden to serve bamboo shoots, kelp, and lentil noodles. In Hengshan County it has been resolved that eight dishes and no more may be served at a banquet. Only five dishes are allowed in the East Third District in Liling County, and only three meat and three vegetable dishes in the North Second District, while in the West Third District New Year feasts are forbidden entirely. In Hsianghsiang County, there is a ban on all "egg-cake feasts," which are by no means sumptuous. When a family in the Second District of Hsianghsiang gave an "egg-cake feast" at a son's wedding, the peasants, seeing the ban violated, swarmed into the house and broke up the celebration. In the town of Chiamo, Hsianghsiang County, the people have refrained from eating expensive foods and use only fruit when offering ancestral sacrifices.

Oxen. Oxen are a treasured possession of the peasants. "Slaughter an ox in this life and you will be an ox in the next" has become almost a religious tenet; oxen must never be killed. Before the peasants had power, they could only appeal to religious taboo in opposing the slaughter of cattle and had no means of banning it. Since the rise of the peasant associations their jurisdiction has extended even to the cattle, and they have prohibited the slaughter of cattle in the towns. Of the six butcheries in the county town of Hsiangtan, five are now closed and the remaining one slaughters only enfeebled or disabled animals. The slaughter of cattle is totally prohibited throughout the county of Hengshan. A peasant whose ox broke a leg consulted the peasant association before he dared kill it. When the Chamber of Commerce of Chuchow rashly slaughtered a cow, the peasants came into town and demanded an explanation, and the chamber, besides paying a fine, had to let off firecrackers by way of apology.

Tramps and vagabonds. A resolution passed in Liling County prohibited the drumming of New Year greetings or the chanting of praises to the local deities or the singing of lotus rhymes.[8] Various other counties have similar

---

8. Lotus rhymes: beggars' folk songs.

prohibitions, or these practices have disappeared of themselves, as no one observes them any more. The "beggar-bullies" or "vagabonds" who used to be extremely aggressive now have no alternative but to submit to the peasant associations. In Shaoshan, Hsiangtan County, the vagabonds used to make the temple of the Rain God their regular haunt and feared nobody, but since the rise of the associations they have stolen away. The peasant association in Huti Township in the same county caught three such tramps and made them carry clay for the brick kilns. Resolutions have been passed prohibiting the wasteful customs associated with New Year calls and gifts.

Besides these, many other minor prohibitions have been introduced in various places, such as the Liling prohibitions on incense-burning processions to propitiate the god of pestilence, on buying preserves and fruit for ritual presents, burning ritual paper garments during the Festival of Spirits, and pasting up good-luck posters at the New Year. At Kushui in Hsianghsiang County, there is a prohibition even on smoking water-pipes. In the Second District, letting off firecrackers and ceremonial guns is forbidden, with a fine of 1.20 yuan for the former and 2.40 yuan for the latter. Religious rites for the dead are prohibited in the 7th and 20th Districts. In the 18th District, it is forbidden to make funeral gifts of money. Things like these, which defy enumeration, may be generally called peasant bans and prohibitions.

They are of great significance in two respects. First, they represent a revolt against bad social customs, such as gaming, gambling and opium-smoking. These customs arose out of the rotten political environment of the landlord class and are swept away once its authority is overthrown. Second, the prohibitions are a form of self-defence against exploitation by city merchants; such are the prohibitions on feasts and on buying preserves and fruit for ritual presents. Manufactured goods are extremely dear and agricultural products are extremely cheap, the peasants are impoverished and ruthlessly exploited by the merchants, and they must therefore encourage frugality to protect themselves. As for the ban on sending grain out of the area, it is imposed to prevent the price from rising because the poor peasants have not enough to feed themselves and have to buy grain on the market. The reason for all this is the peasants' poverty and the contradictions between town and country; it is not a matter of their rejecting manufactured goods or trade between town and country in order to uphold the so-called Doctrine of Oriental Culture.[9] To protect themselves economically, the peasants must organize consumers' co-operatives for the collective buying of goods. It is also necessary for the government to help the peasant associations establish credit (loan) co-operatives. If these things were done, the peasants would naturally find it unnecessary to ban the outflow of grain as a method of keeping down the price, nor would they have to prohibit the inflow of certain manufactured goods in economic self-defence.

10. Eliminating Banditry

In my opinion, no ruler in any dynasty from Yu, Tang, Wen and Wu down to the Ching emperors and the presidents of the Republic has ever shown as much prowess in eliminating banditry as have the peasant associations today.

---

9. Oriental Culture: the reactionary rejection of modern scientific civilization in favor of ancient feudal culture and modes of production.

Whenever the peasant associations are powerful, there is not a trace of banditry. Surprisingly enough, in many places even the pilfering of vegetables has disappeared. In other places there are still some pilferers. But in the counties I visited, even including those that were formerly bandit-ridden, there was no trace of bandits. The reasons are: First, the members of the peasant associations are everywhere spread out over the hills and dales, spear or cudgel in hand, ready to go into action in their hundreds, so that the bandits have nowhere to hide. Second, since the rise of the peasant movement the price of grain has dropped—it was six yuan a picul last spring but only two yuan last winter—and the problem of food has become less serious for the people. Third, members of the secret societies have joined the peasant associations, in which they can openly and legally play the hero and vent their grievances, so that there is no further need for the secret "mountain," "lodge," "shrine," and "river" forms of organization. In killing the pigs and sheep of the local tyrants and evil gentry and imposing heavy levies and fines, they have adequate outlets for their feelings against those who oppressed them. Fourth, the armies are recruiting large numbers of soldiers and many of the "unruly" have joined up. Thus the evil of banditry has ended with the rise of the peasant movement. On this point, even the well-to-do approve of the peasant associations. Their comment is, "The peasant associations? Well, to be fair, there is also something to be said for them."

In prohibiting gaming, gambling, and opium-smoking, and in eliminating banditry, the peasant associations have won general approval. . . .

12. The Movement for Education

In China education has always been the exclusive preserve of the landlords, and the peasants have had no access to it. But the landlords' culture is created by the peasants, for its sole source is the peasants' sweat and blood. In China 90 percent of the people have had no education, and of these the overwhelming majority are peasants. The moment the power of the landlords was overthrown in the rural areas, the peasants' movement for education began. See how the peasants who hitherto detested the schools are today zealously setting up evening classes! They always disliked the "foreign-style school." In my student days, when I went back to the village and saw that the peasants were against the "foreign-style school," I, too, used to identify myself with the general run of "foreign-style students and teachers" and stand up for it, feeling that the peasants were somehow wrong. It was not until 1925, when I lived in the countryside for six months and was already a Communist and had acquired the Marxist viewpoint, that I realized I had been wrong and the peasants right. The texts used in the rural primary schools were entirely about urban things and unsuited to rural needs. Besides, the attitude of the primary school teachers towards the peasants was very bad and, far from being helpful to the peasants, they became objects of dislike. Hence the peasants preferred the old-style schools ("Chinese classes," as they called them) to the modern schools (which they called "foreign classes") and the old-style teachers to the ones in the primary schools. Now the peasants are enthusiastically establishing evening classes, which they call peasant schools. Some have already been opened, others are being organized, and on the average there is one school per township. The peasants are very enthusiastic about these schools, and regard them, and only them, as their own. The funds for the evening schools come from the "public revenue from superstition," from ancestral temple funds, and from other idle public funds or property. The county education boards wanted to use this money to establish primary schools, that is, "foreign-style schools" not suited to the needs of the peasants, while the latter wanted to use it for peasant schools, and the outcome of the dispute was that both got some of the money, though there are places where the peasants got it all. The development of the peasant movement has resulted in a rapid rise in their cultural level. Before long tens of thousands of schools will have sprung up in the villages throughout the province; this is quite different from the empty talk about "universal education," which the intelligentsia and the so-called "educationalists" have been bandying back and forth and which after all this time remains an empty phrase.

13. The Cooperative Movement

The peasants really need cooperatives, and especially consumers', marketing and credit cooperatives. When they buy goods, the merchants exploit them; when they sell their farm produce, the merchants cheat them; when they borrow money or rice, they are fleeced by the usurers; and they are eager to find a solution to these three problems. During the fighting in the Yangtse valley last winter, when trade routes were cut and the price of salt went up in Hunan, many peasants organized cooperatives to purchase salt. When the landlords deliberately stopped lending, there were many attempts by the peasants to organize credit agencies, because they needed to borrow money. A major problem is the absence of detailed, standard rules of organization. As these spontaneously organized peasant cooperatives often fail to conform to cooperative principles, the comrades working among the peasants are always eagerly enquiring about "rules and regulations." Given proper guidance, the cooperative movement can spread everywhere along with the growth of the peasant associations.

14. Building Roads and Repairing Embankments

This, too, is one of the achievements of the peasant associations. Before there were peasant associations the roads in the countryside were terrible. Roads cannot be repaired without money, and as the wealthy were unwilling to dip into their purses, the roads were left in a bad state. If there was any road work done at all, it was done as an act of charity; a little money was collected from families "wishing to gain merit in the next world," and a few narrow, skimpily paved roads were built. With the rise of the peasant associations orders have been given specifying the required width—three, five, seven, or ten feet, according to the requirements of the different routes—and each landlord along a road has been ordered to build a section. Once the order is given, who dares to disobey? In a short time many good roads have appeared. This is no work of charity but the result of compulsion, and a little compulsion of this kind is not at all a bad thing. The same is true of the embankments. The ruthless landlords were always out to take what they could from the tenant-peasants and would never spend even a few coppers on embankment repairs; they would leave the ponds to dry up and the tenant-peasants to starve, caring about nothing but the rent. Now that there are peasant associations, the landlords can be bluntly ordered to repair the embankments. When a landlord refuses, the association will tell him politely, "Very well! If you won't do the repairs, you will contribute grain, a *tou* for each work-day." As this is a bad bargain for the landlord, he hastens to do the repairs. Consequently many defective embankments have been turned into good ones.

All the fourteen deeds enumerated above have been accomplished by the peasants under the leadership of the peasant associations. Would the reader please think it over and say whether any of them is bad in its fundamental spirit and revolutionary significance? Only the local tyrants and evil gentry, I think, will call them bad. Curiously enough, it is reported from Nanchang that Chiang Kai-shek, Chang Ching-chiang and other such gentlemen do not altogether approve of the activities of the Hunan peasants. This opinion is shared by Liu Yueh-chih and other right-wing leaders in Hunan, all of whom say, "They have simply gone Red." But where would the national revolution be without this bit of Red? To talk about "arousing the masses of the people" day in and day out and then to be scared to death when the masses do rise—what difference is there between this and Lord Sheh's love of dragons? [10]

----

10. Lord Sheh had his palace decorated with paintings and carvings of dragons. When a live dragon heard of Sheh's admiration and visited him, Sheh was badly frightened.

CHRISTOPHER CAUDWELL (1908–1937), *Liberty: A Study in Bourgeois Illusion,* from *Studies in a Dying Culture*

To the English Marxist critic, Christopher Caudwell, the central paradox of our time is that bourgeois culture, despite its achievements, is in crisis: neither technology nor scholarship nor national prosperity have been able to solve the problems of war, poverty, and crime. "What is the explanation? Either the Devil has come amongst us having great power, or there is a causal explanation for a disease common to economics, science, and art. Why then have not all the psychoanalysts, . . . and bishops who have surveyed the scene, been able to locate a source of infection common to all modern culture? For answer, these people must take to themselves the words of Herzen [the Russian revolutionary writer]: 'We are not the doctor, we are the disease.' " For Caudwell, the explanation was that our culture is dying of a myth—the myth that man is naturally free, that he is at his best when unrestrained by society. This "lie at the heart of contemporary culture" is the theme of Caudwell's best-known work, the Studies in a Dying Culture *(1938), in which he argues that only through society can man be truly liberated.*
Caudwell's commitment to liberty was not limited to his writing. Like many other leftists he went to Spain to fight for the Republican government in the Spanish Civil War (1936–1939) and was killed there at the age of twenty-nine.
The essay below is slightly abridged from the original.

Many will have heard a broadcast by H. G. Wells [1] in which (commenting on the Soviet Union) he described it as a "great experiment which has but half fulfilled its promise," it is still a "land without mental freedom." There are also many essays of Bertrand Russell in which this philosopher explains the importance of liberty, how the enjoyment of liberty is the highest and most important goal of man. Fisher [2] claims that the history of Europe during the last two or three centuries is simply the struggle for liberty. Continually and variously by artists, scientists, and philosophers alike, liberty is thus praised and man's right to enjoy it imperiously asserted.

1. H. G. Wells (1866–1946), English novelist.
2. Fisher, Herbert (1865–1940), English historian.

I agree with this. Liberty does seem to me the most important of all generalised goods—such as justice, beauty, truth—that come so easily to our lips. And yet when freedom is discussed a strange thing is to be noticed. These men—artists, careful of words, scientists, investigators of the entities denoted by words, philosophers, scrupulous about the relations between words and entities—never define precisely what they mean by freedom. They seem to assume that it is quite a clear concept, whose definition everyone would agree about.

Yet who does not know that liberty is a concept about whose nature men have quarrelled perhaps more than about any other? The historic disputes concerning predestination, Karma, Free-Will, Moira, salvation by faith or works, determinism, Fate, Kismet, the categorical imperative, sufficient grace, occasionalism, Divine Providence, punishment and responsibility have all been about the nature of man's freedom of will and action. The Greeks, the Romans, the Buddhists, the Mahomedans, the Catholics, the Jansenists, and the Calvinists, have each had different ideas of liberty. Why, then, do all these bourgeois intellectuals assume that liberty is a clear concept, understood in the same way by all their hearers, and therefore needing no definition? Russell, for example, has spent his life finding a really satisfactory definition of number and even now it is disputed whether he has been successful. I can find in his writings no clear definition of what he means by liberty. Yet most people would have supposed that men are far more in agreement as to what is meant by a number, than what is meant by liberty.

This indefinite use of the words can only mean either that they believe the meaning of the word invariant in history or that they use it in the contemporary bourgeois sense. If they believe the meaning invariant, it is strange that men have disputed so often about freedom. These intellectuals must surely be incapable of such a blunder. They must mean liberty as men in their situation experience it. That is, they must mean by liberty to have no more restrictions imposed on them than they endure at that time. They do not—these Oxford dons or successful writers—want, for example, the restrictions of Fascism, that is quite clear. That would not be liberty. But at present, thank God, they are reasonably free.

Now this conception of liberty is superficial, for not all their countrymen are in the same situation. A, an intellectual with a good education, in possession of a modest income, with not too uncongenial friends, unable to afford a yacht, which he would like, but at least able to go to the winter sports, considers this (more or less) freedom. He would like that yacht, but still—he can write against communism or Fascism or the existing system. Let us for the moment grant that A is free. I propose to analyse this statement more deeply in a moment, and show that it is partial. But let us for the moment grant that A enjoys liberty.

Is B free? B is the sweated non-union shop-assistant of Houndsditch, working seven days of the week. He knows nothing of art, science, or philosophy. He has no culture except a few absurd prejudices, his elementary school education saw to that. He believes in the superiority of the English race, the King's wisdom and loving-kindness to his subjects, the real existence of God, the Devil, Hell, and Sin, and the wickedness of sexual intercourse unless palliated by marriage. His knowledge of world events is derived from the *News of the World,* on other days he has no time to read the papers. He believes that when he dies he will (with luck) enter into eternal bliss. At present, however, his greatest dread is that, by displeasing his employer in some trifle, he may become unemployed.

B's trouble is plainly lack of leisure in which to cultivate freedom. C does not suffer from this. He is an unemployed middle-aged man. He is free for 24 hours a day. He is free to go anywhere—in the streets and parks, and in the Museums. He is allowed to think of anything—the Einstein theory, the Frege definition of classes, or the doctrine of the Immaculate Conception. Regrettably enough, he does none of these things. He quarrels with his wife, who calls him a good-for-nothing waster, and with his children, who because of the Means Test have to pay his rent, and with his former friends, because they can enjoy pleasures he cannot afford. Fortunately he is free to remove himself from existence, and this one afternoon, when his wife is out and there is plenty of money in the gas-meter, he will do.

A is free. Are B and C? I assume that A will reply that B and C are not free. If A asserts that B and C do enjoy real liberty, most of us, without further definition, will know what to think of A's idea of liberty. But a Wells, a Forster, or a Russell would doubtless agree, as vehemently as us, that this is not liberty, but a degrading slavery to environment. He will say that to free B and C we must raise them to A's level, the level, let us say, of the Oxford don. Like the Oxford don, B and C must have leisure and a modest income with which to enjoy the good things and the good ideas of the world.

But how is this to be brought about? Bourgeois social relations are what we have now. No one denies that the dynamic motive of such relations is private profit. Here bourgeois economists and Marxists are agreed. Moreover, if causality has any meaning, and unless we are to throw all scientific method overboard, current economic relations and the unfreedom of B and C must be causally inter-related.

We have, then, bourgeois social relations on the one hand, and these varying degrees of unfreedom—A, B, and C—on the other hand, interconnected as cause and effect. So far, either might be cause, for we have not yet decided whether mental states arise from social relations, or *vice versa.* But as soon as we ask how action is to solve the problem, we see which is primary. It is useless to give B, by means of lectures and picture galleries, opportunity for understanding philosophy or viewing masterpieces of art. He has no time to acquire, before starting work, the taste for them or after starting work the time to gratify it. Nor is C free to enjoy the riches of bourgeois culture as long as his whole existence is clouded by his economic position. It is circumstances that are imprisoning consciousness, not *vice versa.* It is not because B and C are unenlightened that they are members of the working class, but because they are members of the working class, they are unenlightened. And Russell, who writes *In Praise of Idleness,* praises rightly, for he is clever because he is idle and bourgeois, not idle and bourgeois because he is clever.

We now see the cause and effect of the situation. We see that it is not this freedom and unfreedom which produce bourgeois social relations, but that bourgeois social relations alike give rise to these two extremes, the freedom of the idle bourgeois, and the unfreedom of the proletarian worker. It is plain that this effect, if undesirable, can only be changed by changing the cause.

Thus the intellectual is faced with another problem, like that when he had to define more precisely who enjoyed the liberty he regarded as contemporary. Does he wish that there should exist for ever these two states of captivity and freedom, of misery and happiness? Can he enjoy a freedom which is sustained by the same cause as the workers' unfreedom? For if not, he must advance further, and say, "bourgeois social relations must be changed." Change they will, precisely because of this unfreedom they increasingly generate; but to-day the intellectual must decide whether his will will be part of the social forces making for change, or vainly pitted against them.

But how are bourgeois social relations to be changed? Not by a mere effort of the will, for we saw that the mind was made by social relations, not *vice versa*. It is matter, the quantitative foundation of qualitative ideology, that must be changed. It is not enough to argue and convince. Work must be done. The environment must be altered. . . .

Let us, therefore, go deeper, and examine more closely the true nature of bourgeois freedom. Are H. G. Wells, Bertrand Russell, E. M. Forster, you, reader, and I, really free? Do we enjoy even mental freedom? For if we do not enjoy that, we certainly do not enjoy physical freedom.

Bertrand Russell is a philosopher and a mathematician. He takes the method of science seriously, and applies it to various fields of thought. He believes that thoughts are simply special arrangements of matter, even though he calls matter mind-stuff. He agrees that to every psychism corresponds a neurism, that life is a special chemical phenomenon, just as thought is a special biological phenomenon. He is not taken in by the nonsense of entelechies and pure memory.

Why then does he refrain from applying these categories, used everywhere else, to the concept of liberty? In what sense can he believe man to be ever completely free? What meaning can he attach to the word freedom? He rightly detects the idealistic hocus-pocus of smuggling God into science as the Life-Force, entelechy, or the first cause, for the sleight of hand it is. But his liberty is a kind of God; something which he accepts on faith, somehow intervening in the affairs of the universe, and unconnected with causality. Russell's liberty and his philosophy live in different worlds. He has made theology meet science, and seen that theology is a barbarous relic. But he has not performed the last act of integration; he has not asked science's opinion of this belief that the graduate of one of the better universities, with a moderate income, considerable intelligence, and some leisure, is really free.

It is not a question of whether man has in some mysterious fashion free will. For if that were the problem, all men either would or would not have free will, and therefore all men would or would not have liberty. If freedom consists in having free will, and men have free will, we can will as freely under a Fascist, or proletarian, as under a bourgeois Government. But everyone admits that there are degrees of liberty. In what therefore does this difference in liberty consist?

Although liberty does not then depend on free will, it will help us to understand liberty if we consider what is the freedom of the will. Free will consists in this, that man is conscious of the motive that dictates his action. Without this consciousness of antecedent motive, there is no free will. I raise my hand to ward off a blow. The blow dictated my action; none the less, I was conscious that I wanted to ward off the blow; I willed to do so. My will was free; it was an act of my will. There was a cause; but I was conscious of a free volition. And I was conscious of the cause, of the blow.

In sleep a tickling of the soles of the feet actuates the plantar reflex. Such an action we call involuntary. Just as the warding movement was elicited by an outside stimulus, so was the bending of the leg. None the less, we regard the second as unfree, *involuntary*. It was not preceded by a conscious motive. Nor were we conscious of the cause of our action. We thus see that free will exists in so far as we are conscious of an antecedent motive in our mind, regarded as the immediate cause of action. If this motive, or act of will, is itself free, and not forced, we must also be in turn conscious of the antecedent motive that produced it. Free will is not therefore the opposite of causality; it is on the contrary a special and late aspect of causality, it is the *consciousness* of causality. That is why man naturally fits all happenings outside him in a causal frame; because he is conscious of causality in himself. Otherwise it would be a mystery if man, experiencing only uncausality in free will, should assume, as he does, that all other things are linked by causality. If, however, he is only assuming that other objects obey the same laws as he does, both the genesis and success of causality as a cognitive framework for reality are explicable.

Causality and freedom thus are aspects of each other. Freedom is the consciousness of necessity. The universe as a whole is completely free, because that which is not free is determined by something else outside it. But all things are, by definition, contained in the universe, therefore the universe is determined by nothing but itself. But every individual thing in the universe is determined by other things, because the universe is material. This materiality is not "given" in the definition of the universe, but is exactly what science establishes when it explains the world actively and positively.

Thus the only absolute freedom, like the only absolute truth, is the universe itself. But parts of the universe have varying degrees of freedom, according to their degrees of self-determination. In self-determination, the causes are within the thing itself; thus, in the sensation of free will, the antecedent cause of an action is the conscious thought of an individual, and since the action is also that of the individual, we talk of freedom, because there is self-determination. . . .

Man constantly supposes that he is freer than he is. Freudian research has recently shown that events at the level of being—i.e. unconscious physiological events—may give rise to disturbances which usurp conscious functions. In such circumstances a man may not be conscious of the motives of his actions, although he believes he is. He is therefore unfree, for his will's determination arises from events outside consciousness. An example is the neurotic. The neurotic is unfree. He attains freedom by attaining self-determination, that is, by making conscious, motives which before were unconscious. Thus he becomes captain of his soul. I am not now discussing the validity of the various methods by which this knowledge is obtained, or what neurological meaning we are to give to the Freudian symbolism. I agree with this basic assumption of Freudian therapy, that man always obtains more freedom, more self-determination, by a widening of consciousness or, in other words, by an increase of knowledge. In the case of his own mind, man, by obtaining a knowledge of its causality, and the necessity of its functioning, obtains more freedom. Here too freedom is seen to be a special form of determinism, namely, the consciousness of it.

But man cannot simply sit and contemplate his own mind in order to grasp its causality. His body, and likewise his mind, is in constant metabolic relation with the rest of the universe. As a result, when we want to trace any causal mental sequence, in order to be conscious of it, we find it inextricably commingled with events in the outer world. At an early stage we find we must seek freedom in the outer as well as the inner world. We must be conscious, not only of our own laws, but of those of outer reality. Man has always realised that whatever free will may mean it is not will alone, but action also which is involved in liberty. For example, I am immersed in a plaster cast so that I cannot blink an eyelid. None the less, my will is completely free. Am I therefore completely free? Only extremely idealistic philosophers would suggest that I am. A free will is therefore not enough to secure liberty, but our actions also must be unconstrained. Now everyone realises that the outer environment continually constrains our freedom, and that free will is no freedom unless it can act what it wills. It follows that to be really free we must also be able to do what we freely will to do.

But this freedom, too, leads us back to determinism. For we find, and here no philosopher has ever disputed it, that the environment is completely deterministic. That is to say, whatever motion or phenomenon we see, there is always a cause for it, which is itself caused, and so on. And the same causes, in the same circumstances, always secure the same effects. Now an understanding of this iron determinism brings freedom. For the more we understand the causality of the universe, the more we are able to do what we freely will. Our knowledge of the causality of water enables us to build ships and cross the seas; our knowledge of the laws of air enables us to fly; our knowledge of the inevitable behaviour of materials enables us to build houses and bridges; our knowledge of the necessary movements of the planets enables us to construct calendars so that we sow, embark on voyages, and set out to meet each other at the times most conducive to achieving what we will to do. Thus, in the outer world too, determinism is seen to produce freedom, freedom is understood to be a special form of necessity, the *consciousness* of necessity. We see that we attain freedom by our consciousness of the causality of subjective mental phenomena together with our consciousness of the causality of external phenomena. And we are not surprised that the characteristic of the behaviour of objects—causality—is also a characteristic of consciousness, for consciousness itself is only an aspect of an object—the body. The more we gain of this double understanding, the more free we become, possessing both free will and free action. These are not two mutually exclusive things, free will versus determinism—but on the contrary they play into each other's hands.

From this it follows that the animals are less free than men. Creatures of impulse, acting they know not why, subject to all the chances of nature, of other animals, of geographical accidents and climatic change, they are at the mercy of necessity, precisely because they are unconscious of it.

That is not to say they have no freedom, for they possess a degree of freedom. They have some knowledge of the causality of their environment, as is shown by their manipulations of time and space and material—the bird's flight, the hare's leap, the ant's nest. They have some inner self-determination, as is shown by their behaviour. But compared to man, they are unfree.

Implicit in the conception of thinkers like Russell and Forster, that all social relations are restraints on spontaneous liberty, is the assumption that the animal is the only completely free creature. No one constrains the solitary carnivore to do anything. This is of course an ancient fallacy. Rousseau is the famous exponent. Man is born free but is everywhere in chains. Always in the bourgeois mind is this legend of a golden age, of a perfectly good man corrupted by institutions. Unfortunately not only is man not good without institutions, he is not evil either. He is no man at all; he is neither good nor evil; he is an unconscious brute. . . .

Society is a creation by which man attains a fuller measure of freedom than the beasts. It is society and society alone, that differentiates man qualitatively from the beasts. The essential feature of society is economic production. Man, the individual, cannot do what he wants alone. He is unfree alone. Therefore he attains freedom by co-operation with his fellows. Science, by which he becomes conscious of outer reality, is social. Art, by which he becomes conscious of his feelings, is social. Economic production, by which he makes outer reality conform to his feeling, is social, and generates in its interstices science and art.

Thus all the "constraints," "obligations," "inhibitions," and "duties" of society are the very means by which freedom is obtained by men. Liberty is thus the social consciousness of necessity. Liberty is not just necessity, for all reality is united by necessity. Liberty is the consciousness of necessity—in outer reality, in myself, and in the social relations which mediate between outer reality and human selves. The beast is a victim of mere necessity, man is in society conscious and self-determined. Not of course absolutely so, but more so than the beast.

Thus freedom of action, freedom to do what we will, the vital part of liberty, is seen to be secured by the social consciousness of necessity, and to be generated in the process of economic production. The price of liberty is not eternal vigilance, but eternal work.

But what is the relation of society to the other part of liberty, freedom to will? Economic production makes man free to do what he wills, but is he free to will what he will?

We saw that he was only free to do what he willed by attaining the consciousness of outer necessity. It is equally true that he is only free to will what he will by attaining the consciousness of inner necessity. Moreover, these two are not antagonistic, but, as we shall now find, they are one. Consciousness is the result of a specific and highly important form of economic production.

Suppose someone had performed the regrettable experiment of turning Bertrand Russell, at the age of nine months, over to a goat foster-mother, and leaving him to her care, in some remote spot, unvisited by human beings, to grow to manhood. When, say forty years later, men first visited Bertrand Russell, would they find him with the manuscripts of the *Analysis of Mind* and the *Analysis of Matter* in his hands? Would they even find him in possession of his definition of number, as the class of all classes? No. In contradiction to his present state, his behaviour would be both illogical and impolite.

It looks, therefore, as if Russell, as we know and value him, is primarily a social product. Russell is a philosopher and not an animal because he was taught not only manners, but language, and so given access to the social wisdom of ages of effort. Language filled his head with ideas, showed him what to observe, taught him logic, put all other men's wisdom at his disposal, and awoke in him affectively the elementary decencies of society—morality, justice, and liberty. Russell's consciousness, like that of all useful social objects, was a creation. It is Russell's consciousness that is distinctively him, that is what we value in him, as compared to an anthropoid ape. Society made him, just as it makes a hat.

It goes without saying that Russell's "natural gifts" (or, as we say more strictly, his genotype) were of importance to the outcome. But that is only to say that the material conditions the finished product. Society is well aware that it cannot make a silk purse out of a sow's ear or, except in special circumstances, a don out of a cretin. But it is also aware that out of iron ore you can make rocks, bridges, ships, or micrometers, and, out of that plastic material, man's genotype, you can make Aztecs, ancient Egyptians, Athenians, Prussians, proletarians, parsons, or public schoolboys.

It also goes almost without saying that a man is not a hat. He is a unique social product, the original of Butler's fantasy of machines that gave birth to machines. He himself is one of those machines. The essential truth about man, as compared with hats, is that he is not a hat, but the man who wears it. And the essential truth about this fashioning process of man by society, is that the fashioning is primarily of his consciousness, a process that does not take place with anything else. Now it is precisely because society elaborates his consciousness, that man, although a social product like a hat, is capable of free will, whereas a hat, being unconscious, is not capable of free will. The coming-to-be of a man, his "growing up," is society fashioning *itself,* a group of consciousnesses, themselves made by previous consciousnesses, making another. So the torch of liberty is handed on, and burns still brighter. But it is in living that man's consciousness takes its distinctive stamp, and living is simply entering into social relations.

But, it will be urged, man—the individual—sees the world for himself alone—mountains, sky, and sea. Alone in his study he reflects on fate and death. True. But mountains and sea have a meaning to him, precisely because he is articulate-speaking, because he has a socially-moulded consciousness. Death, fate, and sea are highly-evolved social concepts. Each individual contributes a little to altering and elaborating them, but how small a contribution compared to the immense pressure of the past! Language, science, and art are all simply the results of man's uniting with his fellows socially to learn about himself and outer reality, in order to impose his desires upon it. Both knowledge and effort are only possible in co-operation, and both are made necessary by man's struggles to be freer.

Thus man's inner freedom, the conscious will, acting towards conscious ends, is a product of society; it is an economic product. It is the most refined of the products society achieves in its search for freedom. . . . Man, as society advances, has a consciousness composed less and less of unmodified instinct, more and more of socially-fashioned knowledge and emotion. Man understands more and more clearly the necessities of his own being and of outer reality. He becomes increasingly more free.

The illusion that our minds are free to the extent that, like the beasts, we are unconscious of the causality of our mental states, is just what secures our unfreedom. Bourgeois society to-day clearly exhibits in practice this truth, which we have established by analysis in theory. The bourgeois believes that liberty consists in absence of social organisation; that liberty is a negative quality, a deprivation of existing obstacles to it; and not a positive quality, the reward of endeavour and wisdom. This belief is itself the outcome of bourgeois social relations. As a result of it, the bourgeois intellectual is unconscious of the causality that makes his consciousness what it is. Like the neurotic who refuses to believe that his compulsion is the result of a certain unconscious complex, the bourgeois refuses to believe that his conception of liberty as a mere deprivation of social restraints arises from bourgeois social relations themselves, and that it is just this illusion which is constraining him on every side. He refuses to see that his own limited liberty; the captivity of the worker, and all the contradictions of developing bourgeois relations— pacifism, fascism, war, hate, cruelty, disease—are bound in one net of causality, that each is influenced by each, and that therefore it is fallacious to suppose a simple effort of the will of the free man, without knowledge of the causes, will banish fascism, war, and slumps. Because of his basic fallacy, this type of intellectual always tries to cure positive social evils, such as wars, by negative individual actions, such as non-co-operation, passive resistance or conscientious objection. This is because he cannot rid himself of the assumption that the individual is free. But we have shown that the individual is never free. He can only attain freedom by social co-operation. He can only do what he wants by using social forces. If, therefore, he wishes to stop poverty, war, and misery, he must do it, not by passive resistance, but by using social relations. But in order to use social relations he must understand them. He must become conscious of the laws of society, just as, if he wants to lever up a stone, he must know the laws of levers.

Once the bourgeois intellectual can see that society is the only instrument of freedom, he has advanced a step farther along the road to freedom. But until then he is unfree. True he is a logician, he understands the causality of nature, Einstein's theories, all the splendid apparatus of social discovery, but he still believes in a magic world of social relations divorced from these theories, in which only the god of bourgeois liberty rules. This is proved, not only in his theory, in the way his doctrine of liberty is accepted like a theological dogma, and never made to square with all his philosophic and scientific knowledge; but it is also proved in action, when the bourgeois intellectual is powerless to stop the development of increasing unfreedom in bourgeois society. All the compulsions of militancy, fascism, and economic distress harry contemporary society, and all he can oppose to them is individualistic action, conscientious objection and passive resistance. This is bound to be the case if he is unfree. Like a man who believes he can walk upon the water and drowns in it, the bourgeois intellectual asserts a measure of freedom that does not in fact exist, and is therefore unfree mentally and physically. Who cannot see iron compulsion stalking through the bourgeois world today? We are free when we can do what we will. Society is an instrument of freedom in so far as it secures what men want. The members of bourgeois society, all of them, worker, capitalist, and capitalist-intellectual, want an increase in material wealth, happiness, freedom from strife, from danger of death, security. But bourgeois society to-day produces a decrease in material wealth and also creates unemployment, unhappiness, strife, insecurity, constant war. Therefore all who live in bourgeois society—democratic, Fascist or Rooseveltian—are unfree, for bourgeois society is not giving them what they desire. The fact that they have, or have not, votes or "freedom of speech" does not alter, in any way, their unfreedom.

Why does not bourgeois society fulfil the wants of its members? Because it does not understand the laws of economic production—it is unorganised and unplanned. It is unconscious of the necessities of economic production, and, because of that, cannot make economic production fulfil its desires. Why is it unconscious of the necessities of economic production? Because, for historical reasons, it believes that economic production is best when each man is left free to produce for himself what seems to him most profitable to produce. In other words, it believes that freedom is secured by the lack of social organisation of the individual in the function of society, economic production. As we saw, this individual freedom through unconsciousness is a delusion. Unconscious, deluded bourgeois society is therefore unfree. Even Russell is unfree; and in the next war, as in the last, will be put in gaol.[3]

This very unfreedom—expressed as individualism—in the basic function of society, ultimately generates every form of external constraint. The bourgeois revolutionary asserted a fallacious liberty—that man was born good and was everywhere in chains, that institutions made him bad. It turned out that this liberty he claimed was individualism in private production. This revealed its fallacious nature as a freedom by appearing at once as a restraint. For it could only be secured, it was only a name, for unrestricted right to own the means of production, which is in itself a restriction on those who are thus alienated from their livelihood. Obviously, what I own absolutely my neighbour is restricted from touching.

All social relations based on duty and privilege were changed by the bourgeois revolution into exclusive and forcible rights to ownership of cash. I produce for my individual self, for profit. Necessarily, therefore, I produce for the market, not for use. I work for cash, not from duty to my lord or retainer. My duties to the State could all now be compounded for cash. All my obligations of contract, whether of marriage or social organisation, could be compounded for cash. Cash appeared as the only obligation between men and men, who were otherwise apparently completely free—free master, free labourer, free producer, free consumer, free markets, free trade, free entrepreneur, the free flow of capital from hand to hand and land to land. And even man's obligations to cash appeared an obligation of cash to him, to be absolutely owned by him.

This dissolution of social obligations could be justified if man was free in himself, and if, doing what seemed best for him, for his own good and profit, he would in fact get what he desired, and so secure freedom. It was a return

---

3. Gaol: Russell was imprisoned briefly for his pacifist opposition to Britain's participation in World War I. Caudwell's prediction was not fulfilled, as Russell left England during World War II.

to the apparent liberty of the jungle, where each beast struggles only for himself, and owes no obligations to anyone. But this liberty, as we saw, is an illusion. The beast is less free than man. The desires of the jungle cancel each other out, and no one gets exactly what he wants. No beast is free.

This fallacy at once revealed itself as a fallacy in the following way. Complete freedom to own property meant that society found itself divided into haves and have-nots, like the beasts in the jungle. The have-nots, each trying to do what was best for him in the given circumstances, according to the bourgeois doctrine of liberty, would have forcibly seized the property from the haves. But this would have been complete anarchy, and though anarchy, according to bourgeois theory, is complete liberty, in practice the bourgeois speedily sees that to live in the jungle is not to be free. Property is the basis of his mode of living. In such circumstances social production could not be carried on, and society would dissolve, man return to savagery, and freedom altogether perish. Thus the bourgeois contradicted his theory in practice from the start. The State took its distinctive modern form as the enforcement of bourgeois rights by coercion. Police, standing army and laws were all brought into being to protect the haves from the "free" desires of the have-nots. Bourgeois liberty at once gives rise to bourgeois coercion, to prisons, armies, contracts, to all the sticky and restraining apparatus of the law, to all the ideology and education centred round the sanctity of private property, to all the bourgeois commandments. Thus bourgeois liberty was built on a lie, bound to reveal in time its contradictions.

Among the have-nots, bourgeois freedom gave rise to fresh coercions. The free labourer, owning nothing, was free to sell his labour in any market. But this became a form of slavery worse, in its unrestricted form, than chattel slavery, a horror that Government Blue Books describing pre-Factory Act conditions make vivid for all their arid phraseology. They show how unrestricted factory industrialisation made beasts of men, women, and children, how they died of old age in their thirties, how they rose early in the morning exhausted to work and knocked off late at night only to sink exhausted to sleep, how the children were aged by work before they had ceased to be infants. Made worse than a slave—for he was still free to be unemployed—the labourer fought for freedom by enforcing social restraints on his employers. Banding with others in trade unions, he began the long fight that gave rise to the various Factory Acts, wage agreements, and all the elaborate social legislation which to-day coerces the bourgeois employer.

And, after all this, even the bourgeois himself is not free. The unrestricted following of his illusion of liberty enslaves him. His creed demands unrestricted competition, and this, because it is unrestricted, works as wildly and blindly as the weather. It makes him as unfree, as much at the mercy of a not understood chance, as a cork bobbing on the waves. So he too seeks freedom in restraint—industry is increasingly sheltered by amalgamations, rings, tariffs, price agreements, "unfair competition" clauses, subsidies, and Government protection for the exploitation of Colonial areas. Bourgeois liberty makes overt its self-contradictions by becoming monopoly.

Here is the secret paradox of bourgeois development and decline. The bourgeois abandoned feudal relations in the name of a liberty which he visualised as freedom from social restraints. Such a liberty would have led to savagery. But in fact the liberty he claimed—"unrestricted" private property

—really involved restraint, that is, it gave rise to complex forms of social organisation, which were more many-sided, more incessant, and more all-pervading, than feudal restraints. Thus the cash relation, which he conceived as putting an end to all social restraints, and thus giving him liberty, did give him a larger measure of liberty than in feudalism, but in the opposite way to his expectations, by imposing far more complex organisations than those of feudal civilisation. All the elaborate forms of bourgeois contracts, market organisation, industrial structure, national States, trade unions, tariffs, Imperialism, and bureaucratic democratic government, the iron pressure of the consumer and the labour market, the dole, subsidy, bounties—all these multifarious forms of social organisation—were brought into being by a class that demanded the dissolution of social organisation. And the fact that bourgeois civilisation obtained a greater measure of control over its environment than feudal—and was that much freer—is precisely because all these complex social organisations were brought into being—but brought blindly.

Blindly brought into being; that is the source of the ultimate unfreedom of bourgeois civilisation. Because it is not conscious of the fact that private ownership of the means of production, unrestricted competition, and the cash nexus of their natures, involve various forms of restraint—alienation from property, captivity to slump and war, unemployment and misery—bourgeois society is unable to control itself. The various forms of social organisation it has blindly erected, as an animal tunnelling for gold might throw up great mounds of earth, are all haphazard and not understood. It believes that to become conscious of them fully, to manipulate them consciously for the ends of the will, is to be an advocate of determinism, to kill liberty, to bring into birth the bee-hive state. For still, in spite of all the havoc the bourgeois sees around him, he believes that only the beast is free, and that to be subject to all the winds of chance, at the mercy of wars and slumps and social strife, is to be free.

Any definition of liberty is humbug that does not mean this: liberty to do what one wants. A people is free whose members have liberty to do what they want—to get the goods they desire and avoid the ills they hate. What do men want? They want to be happy, and not to be starved or despised or deprived of the decencies of life. They want to be secure, and friendly with their fellows, and not conscripted to slaughter and be slaughtered. They want to marry, and beget children, and help, not oppress each other. Who is free who cannot do these things, even if he has a vote, and free speech? Who then is free in bourgeois society, for not a few men but millions are forced by circumstances to be unemployed, and miserable, and despised, and unable to enjoy the decencies of life? Millions are forced to go out and be slaughtered, or to kill, and to oppress each other. Millions are forced to strive with their fellows for a few glittering prizes, and to be deprived of marriage, and a home, and children, because society cannot afford them these things. Millions and millions of men are not free. These are the elements of liberty, and it is insane—until these are achieved—for a limited class to believe it can secure the subtleties of liberty. Only when these necessities are achieved, can man rise higher and, by the practice of art and science, learn more clearly what he wants, and what he can get; having only then passed from the sphere of necessity to that of freedom.

Each step to higher consciousness is made actively with struggle and difficulty. It is man's natural but fatal error to suppose that the path of liberty is easy, that is a mere negative, a relaxation, the elimination of an obstacle in his path. But it is more than that. True freedom must be created as strenuously as we make the instruments of freedom, tools and machines. It must be wrested out of the heart of reality, including the inner reality of man's mind.

That is why all lovers of liberty, who have understood the nature of freedom, and escaped from the ignorant categories of bourgeois thought, turn to Communism. For that is simply what Communism is, the attainment of more liberty than bourgeois society can reach. Communism has as its basis the understanding of the causality of society, so that all the unfreedom involved in bourgeois society, the enslavement of the have-nots by the haves, and the slavery of both haves and have-nots to wars, slumps, depression and superstition, may be ended. To be conscious of the laws of dead matter: that is something; but it is not enough. Communism seizes hold of a higher degree of self-determination, to rescue man from war, starvation, hate, and coercion, by becoming conscious of the causality of society. It is Communism that makes free will real to man, by making society conscious of itself. To change reality we must understand its laws. If we *wish* to move a stone, we *must* apply the leverage in the proper place. If we *wish* to change bourgeois social relations into communist, we *must* follow a certain path. The have-nots, the proletariat, must take over the means of production from the haves, the bourgeoisie, and since, as we saw, these two freedoms are incompatible, restraint, in the form of the coercive state, must remain in being as long as the bourgeoisie try to get back their former property. But, unlike the former situation, this stage is only temporary. This stage is what is known as the dictatorship of the proletariat, the necessary step from the dictatorship of the bourgeoisie— which is what the bourgeois state is—to the classless state, which is what Communism is. And as Russia shows, even in the dictatorship of the proletariat, before the classless State has come into being, man is already freer. He can avoid unemployment, and competition with his fellows, and poverty. He can marry and beget children, and achieve the decencies of life. He is not asked to oppress his fellows.

To the worker, subject to unemployment, starved in the midst of plenty, this path eventually becomes plain. Despite the assurances of the bourgeoisie that in a democratic or national State he is completely free, he revolts. And who, in those days, will stand by his side? Will the bourgeoisie, themselves pinched and disfranchised by the growing concentration of capital, discouraged, pessimistic, harried into war and oppression by "forces beyond control," and yet still demanding liberty? On the answer to that question, which each individual bourgeois must make, sooner or later, will depend whether he strives in those days to make men free or to keep them in chains. And this too depends on whether he has understood the nature of liberty. The class to whom capitalism means liberty steadily contracts, but those once of that class who are now enslaved to war, and imperialism and poverty, still cling to that bourgeois interpretation of liberty that has abundantly proved its falsehood. They can only escape and become free by understanding the active nature of liberty, and by becoming conscious of the path they must follow to attain it.

Their will is not free as long as they will liberty but produce unfreedom. It is only free when they will communism and produce liberty.

This good, liberty, contains all good. Not only at the simple level of current material wants, but where all men's aspirations bud, freedom is the same goal, pursued in the same way. Science is the means by which man learns what he can do, and therefore it explores the necessity of outer reality. Art is the means by which man learns what he wants to do, and therefore it explores the essence of the human heart. And bourgeoisdom, shutting its eyes to beauty, turning its back on science, only follows its stupidity to the end. It crucifies liberty upon a cross of gold, and if you ask in whose name it does this, it replies, "In the name of personal freedom."

LEON TROTSKY (1879–1940),
Their Morals and Ours

Both before and after the Russian Revolution of 1917, much of Trotsky's life was spent in exile. At nineteen he was deported to Siberia for having secretly organized factory workers; he escaped to London where, with Lenin and other political exiles, he worked for the revolution at home. The events of 1905 brought him back to Russia as a leader of the Petersburg Workers' Soviet. This first Russian revolution created a constitutional monarchy with little sympathy for communists. The Soviet was dissolved, and Trotsky, sentenced in 1907 to Siberia, again escaped, this time to Vienna, then to Switzerland and France. Expelled from France in 1916, he found asylum in the United States, where he worked as a journalist and lecturer in New York. With the outbreak of the second revolution in February 1917, Trotsky returned to Russia and in October led the third revolution, which brought the communists to power. In Lenin's government he was Commissar for Foreign Affairs and then Commissar of War.

After the death of Lenin in 1924, the conflict that had developed within the party as to the methods and future of communism became an open struggle, with Trotsky and Joseph Stalin as chief antagonists. This struggle was to dominate the rest of Trotsky's life. It motivated the essay below (1938), which protests the tendency of bourgeois liberals to lump all communists together and to condemn communism itself for the brutalities of Stalin's regime. In 1929 Trotsky was deported to Turkey, and during the next few years was denied permanent asylum in nearly every European country. Finally he was admitted to Mexico, where he continued to analyze Stalin's policies until in 1940 an agent of Stalin assassinated him with an iceaxe.

Always a prolific writer, Trotsky is acknowledged to be the outstanding stylist and orator of the Russian Revolution, as well as one of its major theoreticians. His intellectual breadth, trenchant irony and sarcasm, analytical power, and commitment to the revolution are as evident in the present essay as in the rest of his work. In its examination of the nature of moral law, the piece provides an extended commentary on Blake's aphorism from "The Marriage of Heaven and Hell": "One law for the lion and ox is oppression."

During an epoch of triumphant reaction, Messrs. Democrats, Social Democrats, Anarchists, and other representatives of the "Left" camp begin to exude double their usual amount of moral effluvia, similar to persons who perspire doubly in fear. Paraphrasing the Ten Commandments or the Sermon on the Mount, these moralists address themselves not so much to triumphant reaction as to those revolutionists suffering under its persecution, who with their "excesses" and "amoral" principles, "provoke" reaction and give it moral justification. Moreover they prescribe a simple but certain means of avoiding reaction: it is necessary only to strive and morally to regenerate oneself. Free samples of moral perfection for those desirous are furnished by all the interested editorial offices.

The class basis of this false and pompous sermon is—the intellectual petty bourgeoisie. The political basis—their impotence and confusion in the face of approaching reaction. The psychological basis—their effort at overcoming the feeling of their own inferiority through masquerading in the beard of a prophet.

A moralizing philistine's favorite method is the lumping of reaction's conduct with that of revolution. He achieves success in this device through recourse to formal analogies. To him Czarism and Bolshevism are twins. Twins are likewise discovered in fascism and communism. An inventory is compiled of the common features in Catholicism—or more specifically, Jesuitism— and Bolshevism. Hitler and Mussolini, utilizing from their side exactly the same method, disclose that liberalism, democracy, and Bolshevism represent merely different manifestations of one and the same evil. The conception that Stalinism and Trotskyism are "essentially" one and the same now enjoys the joint approval of liberals, democrats, devout Catholics, idealists, pragmatists, and anarchists. If the Stalinists are unable to adhere to this "People's Front," then it is only because they are accidentally occupied with the extermination of Trotskyists.

The fundamental feature of these *rapprochements* and similitudes lies in their completely ignoring the material foundation of the various currents, that is, their class nature and by that token their objective historical role. Instead they evaluate and classify different currents according to some external and secondary manifestation, most often according to their relation to one or another abstract principle which for the given classifier has a special professional value. Thus to the Roman pope, Freemasons and Darwinists, Marxists and anarchists are twins because all of them sacrilegiously deny the Immaculate Conception. To Hitler, liberalism and Marxism are twins because they ignore "blood and honor." To a democrat, fascism and Bolshevism are twins because they do not bow before universal suffrage. And so forth.

Undoubtedly the currents grouped above have certain common features. But the gist of the matter lies in the fact that the evolution of mankind exhausts itself neither by universal suffrage, nor by "blood and honor," nor by the dogma of the Immaculate Conception. The historical process signifies primarily the class struggle; moreover, different classes in the name of different aims may in certain instances utilize similar means. Essentially it cannot be otherwise. Armies in combat are always more or less symmetrical; were there nothing in common in their methods of struggle they could not inflict blows upon each other.

If an ignorant peasant or shopkeeper, understanding neither the origin nor the sense of the struggle between the proletariat and the bourgeoisie, discovers himself between the two fires, he will consider both belligerent camps with equal hatred. And who are all these democratic moralists? Ideologists of intermediate layers who have fallen, or are in fear of falling, between the two fires. The chief traits of the prophets of this type are alienism to great historical movements, a hardened conservative mentality, smug narrowness, and a most primitive political cowardice. More than anything, moralists wish that history should leave them in peace with their petty books, little magazines, subscribers, common sense, and moral copybooks. But history does not leave them in peace. It cuffs them now from the left, now from the right. Clearly —revolution and reaction, Czarism and Bolshevism, communism and fascism, Stalinism and Trotskyism—are all twins. Whoever doubts this may feel the symmetrical skull bumps upon both the right and left sides of these very moralists.

The most popular and most imposing accusation directed against Bolshevik "amoralism" bases itself on the so-called Jesuitical maxim of Bolshevism: "The end justifies the means." From this it is not difficult to reach the further conclusion: since the Trotskyists, like all Bolsheviks (or Marxists) do not recognize the principles of morality, there is, consequently, no "principled" difference between Trotskyism and Stalinism. Q.E.D. . . .

Should we care to take Messrs. Unmaskers seriously, then first of all we would ask them: what are your own moral principles? Here is a question which will scarcely receive an answer. Let us admit for the moment that neither personal nor social ends can justify the means. Then it is evidently necessary to seek criteria outside of historical society and those ends which arise in its development. But where? If not on earth, then in the heavens. In divine revelation popes long ago discovered faultless moral criteria. Petty secular popes speak about eternal moral truths without naming their original source. However, we are justified in concluding: since these truths are eternal, they should have existed not only before the appearance of half-monkey-half-man upon the earth but before the evolution of the solar system. Whence then did they arise? The theory of external morals can in nowise survive without God.

Moralists of the Anglo-Saxon type, in so far as they do not confine themselves to rationalist utilitarianism, the ethics of bourgeois bookkeeping, appear to be conscious or unconscious students of Viscount Shaftesbury, who —at the beginning of the eighteenth century!—deduced moral judgments from a special "moral sense," supposedly once and for all given to man. Supra-class morality inevitably leads to the acknowledgment of a special substance, of a "moral sense," "conscience," some kind of absolute which is nothing more than the philosophic-cowardly pseudonym for God. Independent of "ends," that is, of society, morality, whether we deduce it from eternal truths or from the "nature of man," proves in the end to be a form of "natural theology." Heaven remains the only fortified position for military operations against dialectic materialism. . . .

Whoever does not care to return to Moses, Christ or Mohammed; whoever is not satisfied with eclectic hodge-podges must acknowledge that morality is a product of social development; that there is nothing invariable about it; that it serves social interests; that these interests are contradictory; that morality more than any other form of ideology has a class character.

But do not elementary moral precepts exist, worked out in the development of mankind as an integral element necessary for the life of every collective body? Undoubtedly such precepts exist, but the extent of their action is extremely limited and unstable. Norms "obligatory upon all" become the less forceful the sharper the character assumed by the class struggle. The highest pitch of the class struggle is civil war which explodes into mid-air all moral ties between the hostile classes.

Under "normal" conditions a "normal" man observes the commandment: "Thou shalt not kill!" But if he murders under exceptional conditions for self-defense, the judge condones his action. If he falls victim to a murderer, the court will kill the murderer. The necessity of the court's action, like that of the self-defense, flows from antagonistic interests. So far as the state is concerned, in peaceful times it limits itself to individual cases of legalized murder so that in time of war it may transform the "obligatory" commandment, "Thou shalt not kill!" into its opposite. The most "humane" governments, which in peaceful times "detest" war, proclaim during war that the highest duty of their armies is the extermination of the greatest possible number of people.

The so-called "generally recognized" moral precepts preserve an essentially algebraic, that is, an indeterminate character. They merely express the fact that man, in his individual conduct, is bound by certain common norms that flow from his being a member of society. The highest generalization of these norms is the "categorical imperative" of Kant. But in spite of the fact that it occupies a high position upon the philosophic Olympus, this imperative does not embody anything categorical, because it embodies nothing concrete. It is a shell without content.

This vacuity in the norms obligatory upon all arises from the fact that in all decisive questions people feel their class membership considerably more profoundly and more directly than their membership in "society." The norms of "obligatory" morality are in reality charged with class, that is, antagonistic content. The moral norm becomes the more categorical the less it is "obligatory" upon all. The solidarity of workers, especially of strikers or barricade fighters, is incomparably more "categorical" than human solidarity in general.

The bourgeoisie, which far surpasses the proletariat in the completeness and irreconcilability of its class consciousness, is vitally interested in imposing *its* moral philosophy upon the exploited masses. It is exactly for this purpose that the concrete norms of the bourgeois catechism are concealed under moral abstractions patronized by religion, philosophy, or that hybrid which is called "common sense." The appeal to abstract norms is not a disinterested philosophic mistake but a necessary element in the mechanics of class deception. The exposure of this deceit which retains the tradition of thousands of years is the first duty of a proletarian revolutionist.

In order to guarantee the triumph of their interests in big questions, the ruling classes are constrained to make concessions on secondary questions, naturally only so long as these concessions are reconciled in the bookkeeping. During the epoch of capitalistic upsurge, especially in the last few decades before the World War, these concessions, at least in relation to the top layers of the proletariat, were of a completely genuine nature. Industry at that time expanded almost uninterruptedly. The prosperity of the civilized nations— partially, too, that of the toiling masses—increased. Democracy appeared solid. Workers' organizations grew. At the same time reformist tendencies deepened. The relations between the classes softened, at least outwardly. Thus certain elementary moral precepts in social relations were established along with the norms of democracy and the habits of class collaboration. The impression was created of an evermore free, more just, and more humane society. The rising line of progress seemed infinite to "common sense."

Instead, however, war broke out with a train of convulsions, crises, catastrophes, epidemics, and bestiality. The economic life of mankind landed in an impasse. The class antagonisms became sharp and naked. The safety valves of democracy began to explode one after the other. The elementary moral precepts seemed more fragile than the democratic institutions and reformist illusions. Mendacity, slander, bribery, venality, coercion, murder, grew to unprecedented dimensions. To a stunned simpleton all these vexations seem a temporary result of war. Actually they are manifestations of imperialist decline. The decay of capitalism denotes the decay of contemporary society with its right and its morals. . . .

Let us note in justice that the most sincere and at the same time the most limited petty-bourgeois moralists still live even today in the idealized memories of yesterday and hope for its return. They do not understand that morality is a function of the class struggle; that democratic morality corresponds to the epoch of liberal and progressive capitalism; that the sharpening of the class struggle, in passing through its latest phase, definitively and irrevocably destroyed this morality; that in its place came the morality of fascism on one side, on the other the morality of proletarian revolution.

Democracy and "generally recognized" morality are not the only victims of imperialism. The third suffering martyr is "universal" common sense. This lowest form of the intellect is not only necessary under all conditions but under certain conditions is also sufficient. Common sense's basic capital consists of the elementary conclusions of universal experience: not to put one's fingers in fire, whenever possible to proceed along a straight line, not to tease vicious dogs . . . and so forth and so on. Under a stable social milieu common sense is sufficient for bargaining, healing, writing articles, leading trade unions, voting in parliament, marrying, and reproducing the race. But when that same common sense attempts to go beyond its valid limits into the arena of more complex generalizations, it is exposed as just a clot of prejudices of a definite class and a definite epoch. No more than a simple capitalist crisis brings common sense to an impasse; and before such catastrophes as revolution, counterrevolution, and war, common sense proves a perfect fool. In order to realize the catastrophic transgressions against the "normal" course of events higher qualities of intellect are necessary, philosophically expressed as yet only by dialectic materialism. . . .

Russia took the greatest leap in history, a leap in which the most progressive forces of the country found their expression. Now in the current reaction, the sweep of which is proportionate to the sweep of the revolution, backwardness is taking its revenge. Stalinism embodies this reaction. The barbarism of old Russian history upon new social bases seems yet more disgusting since it is constrained to conceal itself in hypocrisy unprecedented in history.

The liberals and the social democrats of the West, who were constrained by the Russian Revolution into doubt about their rotted ideas, now experienced a fresh influx of courage. The moral gangrene of the Soviet bureaucracy seemed to them the rehabilitation of liberalism. Stereotyped copybooks are drawn out into the light: "every dictatorship contains the seeds of its own degeneration"; "only democracy guarantees the development of personality"; and so forth. The contrasting of democracy and dictatorship, including in the given case a condemnation of socialism in favor of the bourgeois regime, stuns one from the point of view of theory by its illiterateness and unscrupulousness. The Stalinist pollution, a historical reality, is counterpoised to democracy—a supra-historical abstraction. But democracy also possesses a history in which there is no lack of pollution. In order to characterize Soviet bureaucracy we have borrowed the names of "Thermidor" and "bonapartism" from the history of bourgeois democracy [1] because—let this be known to the retarded liberal doctrinaires—*democracy came into the world not at all through the democratic road*. Only a vulgar mentality can satisfy itself by chewing on the theme that bonapartism was the "natural offspring" of jacobinism, the historical punishment for infringing upon democracy, and so on. Without the Jacobin retribution upon feudalism, bourgeois democracy would have been absolutely unthinkable. Contrasting the concrete historical stages of jacobinism, Thermidor, bonapartism to the idealized abstraction of "democracy" is as vicious as contrasting the pains of childbirth to a living infant.

Stalinism in turn is not an abstraction of "dictatorship," but an immense bureaucratic reaction against the proletarian dictatorship in a backward and isolated country. The October revolution abolished privileges, waged war against social inequality, replaced the bureaucracy with self-government of the toilers, abolished secret diplomacy, strove to render all social relationships completely transparent. Stalinism re-established the most offensive forms of privileges, imbued inequality with a provocative character, strangled mass self-activity under police absolutism, transformed administration into a monopoly of the Kremlin oligarchy and regenerated the fetishism of power in forms that absolute monarchy dared not dream of.

Social reaction in all forms is constrained to mask its real aims. The sharper the transition from revolution to reaction, the more the reaction is dependent upon the traditions of revolution, that is, the greater its fear of the masses—the more is it forced to resort to mendacity and frame-up in the struggle against the representatives of the revolution. Stalinist frame-ups are not a fruit of Bolshevik "amoralism"; no, like all important events in history, they are a product of the concrete social struggle, and the most perfidious and severest of all at that: the struggle of a new aristocracy against the masses that raised it to power.

Verily boundless intellectual and moral obtuseness is required to identify the reactionary police morality of Stalinism with the revolutionary morality of the Bolsheviks. Lenin's party has long ceased to exist—it was shattered between inner difficulties and world imperialism. In its place rose the Stalin-

---

1. The history of bourgeois democracy: that is, from the French Revolution of 1789. Jacobins were the more radical among the revolutionaries, who instituted the "reign of terror" to suppress counter-revolutionary activity. During Thermidor (July; eleventh month of the revolutionary calendar), 1794, the terror ended and Jacobinism was suppressed. The way was prepared for the dictatorship of Napoleon Bonaparte.

ist bureaucracy, the transmissive mechanism of imperialism. The bureaucracy substituted class collaboration for the class struggle on the world arena, social patriotism for internationalism. In order to adapt the ruling party to the tasks of reaction, the bureaucracy "renewed" its composition through executing revolutionists and recruiting careerists.

Every reaction regenerates, nourishes and strengthens those elements of the historical past which the revolution struck but which it could not vanquish. The methods of Stalinism bring to the highest tension, to culmination, and at the same time to absurdity all those methods of untruth, brutality, and baseness which constitute the mechanics of control in every class society including also that of democracy. Stalinism is a single clot of all monstrosities of the historical State, its most malicious caricature and disgusting grimace. When the representatives of old society puritanically counterpoise a sterilized democratic abstraction to the gangrene of Stalinism, we can with full justice recommend to them, as to all of old society, that they fall enamored of themselves in the warped mirror of Soviet Thermidor. True, the GPU [2] far surpasses all other regimes in the nakedness of its crimes. But this flows from the immense amplitude of events shaking Russia under the influence of world imperialist demoralization.

Among the liberals and radicals there are not a few individuals who have assimilated the methods of the materialist interpretation of events and who consider themselves Marxists. This does not hinder them, however, from remaining bourgeois journalists, professors or politicians. A Bolshevik is inconceivable, of course, without the materialist method, in the sphere of morality too. But this method serves him not solely for the interpretation of events but rather for the creation of a revolutionary party of the proletariat. It is impossible to accomplish this task without complete independence from the bourgeoisie and their morality. . . .

A revolutionary Marxist cannot begin to approach his historical mission without having broken morally from bourgeois public opinion and its agencies in the proletariat. For this, moral courage of a different caliber is required than that of opening wide one's mouth at meetings and yelling, "Down with Hitler!" "Down with Franco!" It is precisely this resolute, completely-thought-out, inflexible rupture of the Bolsheviks from conservative moral philosophy not only of the big but of the petty bourgeoisie which mortally terrorizes democratic phrasemongers, drawing-room prophets and lobbying heroes. From this are derived their complaints about the "amoralism" of the Bolsheviks. . . .

Civil war is the most severe of all forms of war. It is unthinkable not only without violence against tertiary figures but, under contemporary technique, without murdering old men, old women and children. Must one be reminded of Spain? [3] The only possible answer of the "friends" of republican Spain sounds like this: civil war is better than fascist slavery. But this completely correct answer merely signifies that the *end* (democracy or socialism) justifies,

---

2. GPU: Stalin's secret police system.

3. Spain: the Spanish Civil War (1936–1939) between an elected republican government and an insurgent coalition of army officers, monarchists, clerks, and large property-owners, ended in the defeat of the loyalist republican forces and the establishment of Franco's fascist dictatorship.

under certain conditions, such *means* as violence and murder. Not to speak about lies! Without lies war would be as unimaginable as a machine without oil. In order to safeguard even the session of the *Cortes* (February 1, 1938) from Fascist bombs the Barcelona government several times deliberately deceived journalists and their own population. Could it have acted in any other way? Whoever accepts the end—victory over Franco—must accept the means—civil war with its wake of horrors and crimes.

Nevertheless, lying and violence "in themselves" warrant condemnation? Of course, even as does the class society which generates them. A society without social contradictions will naturally be a society without lies and violence. However there is no way of building a bridge to that society save by revolutionary, that is, violent, means. The revolution itself is a product of class society and of necessity bears its traits. From the point of view of "eternal truths" revolution is of course "antimoral." But this merely means that idealist morality is counterrevolutionary, that is, in the service of the exploiters.

"Civil war," will perhaps respond the philosopher caught unawares, "is however a sad exception. But in peaceful times a healthy socialist movement should manage without violence and lying." Such an answer however represents nothing less than a pathetic evasion. There is no impervious demarcation between "peaceful" class struggle and revolution. Every strike embodies in an unexpanded form all the elements of civil war. Each side strives to impress the opponent with an exaggerated representation of its resoluteness to struggle and its material resources. Through their press, agents, and spies the capitalists labor to frighten and demoralize the strikers. From their side, the workers' pickets, where persuasion does not avail, are compelled to resort to force. Thus "lying and worse" are an inseparable part of the class struggle even in its most elementary form. It remains to be added that the very conception of *truth* and *lie* was born of social contradictions.

Stalin arrests and shoots the children of his opponents after these opponents have themselves been executed under false accusations. With the help of the institution of family hostages Stalin compels those Soviet diplomats to return from abroad who permitted themselves an expression of doubt upon the infallibility of Yagoda or Yezhov.[4] The moralists of *Neuer Weg* [5] consider it necessary and timely to remind us on this occasion of the fact that Trotsky in 1919 "also" introduced a law upon hostages. But here it becomes necessary to quote literally:

The detention of innocent relatives by Stalin is disgusting barbarism. But it remains a barbarism as well when it was dictated by Trotsky (1919).

Here is the idealistic moralist in all his beauty! His criteria are as false as the norms of bourgeois democracy—in both cases *parity* is supposed where in actuality there is not even a trace of it.

We will not insist here upon the fact that the Decree of 1919 led scarcely to even one execution of relatives of those commanders whose perfidy not

---

4. Yagoda, Yezhov: directors of the GPU and of the purge trials of 1934–1939. Yagoda himself was convicted in 1938 of conspiracy against Stalin.

5. *Neuer Weg* (*The New Road*): a newspaper published by German socialist emigrés.

only caused the loss of innumerable human lives but threatened the revolution itself with direct annihilation. The question in the end does not concern that. If the revolution had displayed less superfluous generosity from the very beginning, hundreds of thousands of lives would have been saved. Thus or otherwise I carry full responsibility for the Decree of 1919. It was a necessary measure in the struggle against the oppressors. Only in the historical content of the struggle lies the justification of the decree as in general the justification of the whole civil war which, too, can be called, not without foundation, "disgusting barbarism."

We leave to some Emil Ludwig [6] or his ilk the drawing of Abraham Lincoln's portrait with rosy little wings. Lincoln's significance lies in his not hesitating before the most severe means once they were found to be necessary in achieving a great historic aim posed by the development of a young nation. The question lies not even in which of the warring camps caused or itself suffered the greatest number of victims. History has different yardsticks for the cruelty of the Northerners and the cruelty of the Southerners in the Civil War. A slaveowner who through cunning and violence shackles a slave in chains, and a slave who through cunning or violence breaks the chains—let not the contemptible eunuchs tell us that they are equals before a court of morality! . . .

When the October revolution was defending itself against the united forces of imperialism on a five thousand mile front, the workers of the whole world followed the course of the struggle with such ardent sympathy that in their forums it was extremely risky to indict the "disgusting barbarism" of the institution of hostages. Complete degeneration of the Soviet state and the triumph of reaction in a number of countries was necessary before the moralists crawled out of their crevices—to aid Stalin. If it is true that the repressions safeguarding the privileges of the new aristocracy have the same moral value as the revolutionary measures of the liberating struggle, then Stalin is completely justified, if—if the proletarian revolution is not completely condemned.

Seeking examples of immorality in the events of the Russian Civil War, Messrs. Moralists find themselves at the same time constrained to close their eyes to the fact that the Spanish Revolution also produced an institution of hostages, at least during that period when it was a genuine revolution of the masses. If the indicters dare not attack the Spanish workers for their "disgusting barbarism," it is only because the ground of the Pyrennean peninsula is still too hot for them. It is considerably more convenient to return to 1919. This is already history, the old men have forgotten and the young ones have not yet learned. For the same reason Pharisees of various hues return to Kronstadt and Makhno with such obstinacy—here exists a free outlet for moral effluvia!

It is impossible not to agree with the moralists that history chooses grievous pathways. But what type of conclusion for practical activity is to be drawn from this? Leo Tolstoy recommended that we ignore the social conventions and perfect ourselves. Mahatma Gandhi advises that we drink goat's

---

6. Emil Ludwig: German biographer, noted for his glowingly dramatic, but sometimes unreliable, portraits of great men.

milk. Alas, the "revolutionary" moralists of *Neuer Weg* did not drift far from these recipes. "We should free ourselves," they preach, "from those morals of the Kaffirs to whom only what the enemy does is wrong." Excellent advice! "We should free ourselves. . . ." Tolstoy recommended in addition that we free ourselves from the sins of the flesh. However, statistics fail to confirm the success of his recommendation. Our centrist manikins have succeeded in elevating themselves to supra-class morality in a class society. But almost two thousand years have passed since it was stated: "Love your enemies." "Offer also the other cheek. . . ." However, even the holy Roman father so far has not "freed himself" from hatred against his enemies. Truly, Satan, the enemy of mankind, is powerful!

To apply different criteria to the actions of the exploiters and the exploited signifies, according to these pitiful manikins, standing on the level of the "morals of the Kaffirs." First of all such a contemptuous reference to the Kaffirs is hardly proper from the pen of "socialists." Are the morals of the Kaffirs really so bad? Here is what the *Encyclopaedia Britannica* says upon the subject:

> In their social and political relations they display great tact and intelligence; they are remarkably brave, warlike, and hospitable, and were honest and truthful until through contact with the whites they became suspicious, revengeful and thievish, besides acquiring most European vices.

It is impossible not to arrive at the conclusion that white missionaries, preachers of eternal morals, participated in the corruption of the Kaffirs.

If we should tell the toiler-Kaffir how the workers arose in a part of our planet and caught their exploiters unawares, he would be very pleased. On the other hand, he would be chagrined to discover that the oppressors had succeeded in deceiving the oppressed. A Kaffir who has not been demoralized to the marrow of his bones by missionaries will never apply one and the same abstract moral norm to the oppressors and the oppressed. Yet he will easily comprehend an explanation that it is the function of these abstract norms to prevent the oppressed from arising against their oppressors.

What an instructive coincidence: in order to slander the Bolsheviks, the missionaries of *Neuer Weg* were compelled at the same time to slander the Kaffirs; moreover, in both cases, the slander follows the line of the official bourgeois lie: against revolutionists and against the colored races. No, we prefer the Kaffirs to all missionaries, both spiritual and secular! . . .

The Russian "Social Revolutionaries" were always the most moral individuals: essentially they were composed of ethics alone. This did not prevent them, however, at the time of revolution from deceiving the Russian peasants. In the Parisian organ of Kerensky, that very ethical socialist who was the forerunner of Stalin in manufacturing spurious accusations against the Bolsheviks, another old "Social Revolutionary," Zenzinov, writes:

> Lenin, as is known, taught that for the sake of gaining the desired ends communists can, and sometimes must, "resort to all sorts of devices, maneuvers and subterfuge." [*New Russia,* February 17, 1938, p. 3]

From this they draw the ritualistic conclusion: Stalinism is the natural offspring of Leninism.

Unfortunately, the ethical indicter is not even capable of quoting honestly. Lenin said:

It is necessary to be able . . . to resort to all sorts of devices, maneuvers, and illegal methods, to evasion and subterfuge, *in order to penetrate into the trade unions, to remain in them, and to carry on communist work in them at all costs.*

The necessity for evasion and maneuvers, according to Lenin's explanation, is called forth by the fact that the reformist bureaucracy, betraying the workers to capital, baits revolutionists, persecutes them, and even resorts to turning the bourgeois police upon them. "Maneuvers" and "subterfuge" are in this case only methods of valid self-defense against the perfidious reformist bureaucracy.

The party of this very Zenzinov once carried on illegal work against Czarism, and later—against the Bolsheviks. In both cases it resorted to craftiness, evasion, false passports, and other forms of "subterfuge." All these *means* were considered not only "ethical" but also heroic, because they corresponded to political *aims* of the petty bourgeoisie. But the situation changes at once when proletarian revolutionists are forced to resort to conspirative measures against the petty bourgeois democracy. The key to the morality of these gentlemen has, as we see, a class character!

The "amoralist" Lenin openly, in the press, gives advice concerning military craftiness against perfidious leaders. And the moralist Zenzinov maliciously chops both ends from the quotation in order to deceive the reader: the ethical indicter is proved as usual a petty swindler. Not for nothing was Lenin fond of repeating: it is very difficult to meet a conscientious adversary!

A worker who does not conceal the "truth" about the strikers' plans from the capitalists is simply a betrayer deserving contempt and boycott. The soldier who discloses the "truth" to the enemy is punished as a spy. Kerensky tried to lay at the Bolsheviks' door the accusation of having disclosed the "truth" to Ludendorff's staff. It appears that even the "holy truth" is not an end in itself. More imperious criteria which, as analysis demonstrates, carry a class character, rule over it.

The life and death struggle is unthinkable without military craftiness, in other words, without lying and deceit. May the German proletariat then not deceive Hitler's police? Or perhaps Soviet Bolsheviks have an "immoral" attitude when they deceive the GPU? Every pious bourgeois applauds the cleverness of police who succeed through craftiness in seizing a dangerous gangster. Is military craftiness really permissible when the question concerns the overthrow of the gangsters of imperialism?

Norman Thomas [7] speaks about "that strange communist amorality in which nothing matters but the party and its power" (*Socialist Call,* March 12, 1938, p. 5). Moreover, Thomas throws into one heap the present Comintern, that is, the conspiracy of the Kremlin bureaucracy against the working class, with the Bolshevik party, which represented a conspiracy of the advanced workers against the bourgeoisie. This thoroughly dishonest juxtaposition has

---

7. Norman Thomas (1884–1968), American pastor, pacifist, and leader of the Socialist party. He often ran for president on the Socialist ticket, advocating evolutionary, not revolutionary, socialism.

already been sufficiently exposed above. Stalinism merely screens itself under the cult of the party; actually it destroys the party, and tramples it in filth. It is true, however, that to a Bolshevik the party is everything. The drawing-room socialist, Thomas, is surprised by and rejects a similar relationship between a revolutionist and revolution because he himself is only a bourgeois with a socialist "ideal." In the eyes of Thomas and his kind the party is only a secondary instrument for electoral combinations and other similar uses, no more. His personal life, interests, ties, moral criteria exist outside the party. With hostile astonishment he looks down upon the Bolshevik to whom the party is a weapon for the revolutionary reconstruction of society, including also its morality. To a revolutionary Marxist there can be no contradiction between personal morality and the interests of the party, since the party embodies in his consciousness the very highest tasks and aims of mankind. It is naïve to imagine that Thomas has a higher understanding of morality than the Marxists. He merely has a base conception of the party.

"All that arises is worthy of perishing," says the dialectician, Goethe. The destruction of the Bolshevik party—an episode in world reaction—does not, however, disparage its worldwide historical significance. In the period of its revolutionary ascendance, that is, when it actually represented the proletarian vanguard, it was the most honest party in history. Wherever it could, of course, it deceived the class enemies; on the other hand it told the toilers the truth, the whole truth, and nothing but the truth. Only thanks to this did it succeed in winning their trust to a degree never before achieved by any other party in the world.

The clerks of the ruling classes call the organizers of this party "amoralists." In the eyes of conscious workers this accusation carries a complimentary character. It signifies: Lenin refused to recognize moral norms established by slaveowners for their slaves and never observed by the slaveowners themselves; he called upon the proletariat to extend the class struggle into the moral sphere too. Whoever fawns before precepts established by the enemy will never vanquish that enemy!

The "amoralism" of Lenin, that is, his rejection of supraclass morals, did not hinder him from remaining faithful to one and the same ideal throughout his whole life; from devoting his whole being to the cause of the oppressed; from displaying the highest conscientiousness in the sphere of ideas and the highest fearlessness in the sphere of action, from maintaining an attitude untainted by the least superiority to an "ordinary" worker, to a defenseless woman, to a child. Does it not seem that "amoralism" in the given case is only a pseudonym for higher human morality?

A means can be justified only by its end. But the end in its turn needs to be justified. From the Marxist point of view, which expresses the historical interests of the proletariat, the end is justified if it leads to increasing the power of man over nature and to the abolition of the power of man over man.

"We are to understand then that in achieving this end anything is permissible?" sarcastically demands the philistine, demonstrating that he understood nothing. That is permissible, we answer, which *really* leads to the liberation of mankind. Since this end can be achieved only through revolution, the liberating morality of the proletariat of necessity is endowed with a revolutionary character. It irreconcilably counteracts not only religious dogma but every kind of idealistic fetish, these philosophic gendarmes of the ruling class. It deduces a rule of conduct from the laws of the development of society, thus primarily from the class struggle, this law of all laws.

"Just the same," the moralist continues to insist, "does it mean that in the class struggle against capitalists all means are permissible: lying, frame-up, betrayal, murder, and so on?" Permissible and obligatory are those and only those means, we answer, which unite the revolutionary proletariat, fill their hearts with irreconcilable hostility to oppression, teach them contempt for official morality and its democratic echoers, imbue them with consciousness of their own historic mission, raise their courage and spirit of self-sacrifice in the struggle. Precisely from this it flows that *not* all means are permissible. When we say that the end justifies the means, then for us the conclusion follows that the great revolutionary end spurns those base means and ways which set one part of the working class against other parts, or attempt to make the masses happy without their participation; or lower the faith of the masses in themselves and their organization, replacing it by worship for the "leaders." Primarily and irreconcilably, revolutionary morality rejects servility in relation to the bourgeoisie and haughtiness in relation to the toilers, that is, those characteristics in which petty-bourgeois pedants and moralists are thoroughly steeped.

These criteria do not, of course, give a ready answer to the question as to what is permissible and what is not permissible in each separate case. There can be no such automatic answers. Problems of revolutionary morality are fused with the problems of revolutionary strategy and tactics. The living experience of the movement under the clarification of theory provides the correct answer to these problems.

Dialectic materialism does not know dualism between means and end. The end flows naturally from the historical movement. Organically the means are subordinated to the end. The immediate end becomes the means for a further end. In his play, *Franz von Sickingen,* Ferdinand Lassalle [8] puts the following words into the mouth of one of the heroes:

> . . . *Show not the* goal
> *But show also the* path. *So closely interwoven*
> *Are path and goal that each with other*
> *Ever changes, and other* paths *forthwith*
> *Another* goal *set up.*

Lassalle's lines are not at all perfect. Still worse is the fact that in practical politics Lassalle himself diverged from the above expressed precept—it is sufficient to recall that he went as far as secret agreements with Bismarck! [9] But the dialectic interdependence between means and end is expressed entirely correctly in the above-quoted sentences. Seeds of wheat must be sown in order to yield an ear of wheat.

---

8. Ferdinand Lassalle (1825–1864): founder of the first workingmen's party in Germany.

9. Bismarck: Otto von Bismarck (1815–1898), reactionary Prussian statesman responsible for antisocialist laws in Germany.

Is individual terror, for example, permissible or impermissible from the point of view of "pure morals"? In this abstract form the question does not exist at all for us. Conservative Swiss bourgeois even now render official praise to the terrorist William Tell. Our sympathies are fully on the side of Irish, Russian, Polish, or Hindu terrorists in their struggle against national and political oppression. The assassinated Kirov, a rude satrap, does not call forth any sympathy. Our relation to the assassin remains neutral only because we know not what motives guided him. If it became known that Nikolayev acted as a conscious avenger of workers' rights trampled upon by Kirov, our sympathies would be fully on the side of the assassin. However, not the question of subjective motives but that of objective expediency has for us the decisive significance. Are the given means really capable of leading to the goal? In relation to individual terror, both theory and experience bear witness that such is not the case. To the terrorist we say: it is impossible to replace the masses; only in the mass movement can you find expedient expression for your heroism. However, under conditions of civil war, the assassination of individual oppressors ceases to be an act of individual terror. If, we shall say, a revolutionist bombed General Franco and his staff into the air, it would hardly evoke moral indignation even from the democratic eunuchs. Under the conditions of civil war a similar act would be politically completely expedient. Thus, even in the sharpest question—murder of man by man—moral absolutes prove futile. Moral evaluations, together with political ones, flow from the inner needs of struggle.

The liberation of the workers can come only through the workers themselves. There is, therefore, no greater crime than deceiving the masses, palming off defeats as victories and friends as enemies, bribing workers' leaders, fabricating legends, staging false trials—in a word, doing what the Stalinists do. These means can serve only one end: lengthening the domination of a clique already condemned by history. But they cannot serve to liberate the masses. That is why the Fourth International leads against Stalinism a life and death struggle.

The masses, of course, are not at all impeccable. Idealization of the masses is foreign to us. We have seen them under different conditions, at different stages and, in addition, in the biggest political shocks. We have observed their strong and weak sides. Their strong side—resoluteness, self-sacrifice, heroism—has always found its clearest expression in times of revolutionary upsurge. During this period the Bolsheviks headed the masses. Afterward a different historical chapter loomed when the weak side of the oppressed came to the forefront: heterogeneity, insufficiency of culture, narrowness of world outlook. The masses tired of the tension, became disillusioned, lost faith in themselves—and cleared the road for the new aristocracy. In this epoch the Bolsheviks ("Trotskyists") found themselves isolated from the masses. Practically we went through two such big historic cycles: 1897–1905, years of flood tide; 1907–1913, years of the ebb; 1917–1923, a period of upsurge unprecedented in history; and finally, a new period of reaction which has not ended even today. In these immense events the "Trotskyists" learned the rhythm of history, that is, the dialectics of the class struggle. They also learned, it seems, and to a certain degree successfully, how to subordinate their subjective plans and programs to this objective rhythm. The learned not to fall into despair over the fact that the laws of history do not depend upon their individual tastes and are not subordinated to their own moral criteria. They learned to subordinate their individual desires to the laws of history. They learned not to become frightened by the most powerful enemies, if their power is in contradiction to the needs of historical development. They know how to swim against the stream in the deep conviction that the new historic flood will carry them to the other shore. Not all will reach that shore, many will drown. But to participate in this movement with open eyes and with an intense will—only this can give the highest moral satisfaction to a thinking being!

P.S.—I wrote these lines during those days when my son [10] struggled, unknown to me, with death. I dedicate to his memory this small work which, I hope, would have met with his approval—Leon Sedov was a genuine revolutionist, and despised the Pharisees.

---

10. My son: Trotsky's elder son, Leon Sedov, was his father's closest assistant, though he remained in Paris while Trotsky went to Mexico. On February 16, 1938, at the age of thirty-two, Sedov died mysteriously in a Paris hospital after a successful operation for appendicitis. Circumstantial evidence suggests that he was poisoned by an agent of the GPU.

HO CHI MINH (1890–1969),
Declaration of Independence of the Democratic Republic of Viet-Nam; Address to the Frenchmen in Indochina.

"France has milked it for one hundred years," said President Roosevelt in 1944; "the people of Indochina are entitled to something better than that." For nearly a century the Vietnamese had fought French colonialism, and when Japan invaded Viet-Nam during World War II, they fought the Japanese as well. The collapse of Japan in 1945 encouraged the French to reestablish themselves in Viet-Nam; driven out after the disastrous battle of Dien Bien Phu in 1954, they were soon replaced by Americans.

With Japan's defeat, the communist independence movement (Viet Minh) led by Ho Chi Minh was able openly to assert its influence over much of the country; independence was formally proclaimed, with Ho as president. Most of Ho's writing consists of short newspaper articles, speeches, and propaganda pieces; the two documents below are dated respectively September and October 1945. Their rhetoric, deliberately modelled on that of the American and French revolutions, is intended to evoke the sympathy of a worldwide audience—including the American government, whose intervention in Viet-Nam Ho hoped to forestall. Ho's rhetorical purpose is to expose the difference between the stated ideals and the practice of bourgeois nations, between commitment to a revolutionary past and commitment to a revolutionary future. But other pieces in this volume—by Patrick Henry, Frederick Douglass, W. E. B. du Bois, Christopher Caudwell, Robert Jungk, and others—suggest that the intentions of bourgeois society are not, after all, very far from its practice. Since that is the case, Ho's use of bourgeois revolutionary rhetoric becomes a questionable technique.

*

Declaration of Independence
of the Democratic Republic
of Viet-Nam

All men are created equal; they are endowed by their Creator with certain unalienable Rights; among these are Life, Liberty, and the pursuit of Happiness.

This immortal statement was made in the Declaration of Independence of the United States of America in 1776. In a broader sense, this means: All the peoples on the earth are equal from birth, all the peoples have a right to live, to be happy and free.

The Declaration of the French Revolution made in 1791 on the Rights of Man and the Citizen also states: "All men are born free and with equal rights, and must always remain free and have equal rights."

Those are undeniable truths.

Nevertheless, for more than eighty years, the French imperialists, abusing the standard of Liberty, Equality, and Fraternity, have violated our Fatherland and oppressed our fellow citizens. They have acted contrary to the ideals of humanity and justice.

In the field of politics, they have deprived our people of every democratic liberty.

They have enforced inhuman laws; they have set up three distinct political regimes in the North, the Center, and the South of Viet-Nam in order to wreck our national unity and prevent our people from being united.

They have built more prisons than schools. They have mercilessly slain our patriots; they have drowned our uprisings in rivers of blood.

They have fettered public opinion; they have practiced obscurantism against our people.

To weaken our race they have forced us to use opium and alcohol.[1]

In the field of economics, they have fleeced us to the backbone, impoverished our people and devastated our land.

They have robbed us of our rice fields, our mines, our forests, and our raw materials. They have monopolized the issuing of bank notes and the export trade.

They have invented numerous unjustifiable taxes and reduced our people, especially our peasantry, to a state of extreme poverty.

They have hampered the prospering of our national bourgeoisie; they have mercilessly exploited our workers.

In the autumn of 1940, when the Japanese fascists violated Indochina's territory to establish new bases in their fight against the Allies, the French imperialists went down on their bended knees and handed over our country to them.

Thus, from that date, our people were subjected to the double yoke of the French and the Japanese. Their sufferings and miseries increased. The result was that, from the end of last year to the beginning of this year, from Quang Tri Province to the North of Viet-Nam, more than two million of our fellow citizens died from starvation. On March 9 [1945], the French troops were disarmed by the Japanese. The French colonialists either fled or surrendered, showing that not only were they incapable of "protecting" us, but that, in the span of five years, they had twice sold our country to the Japanese.

On several occasions before March 9, the Viet Minh League urged the French to ally themselves with it against the Japanese. Instead of agreeing to this proposal, the French colonialists so intensified their terrorist activities

---

1. Alcohol: since the alcohol monopoly was held by the colonial administration, they encouraged the establishment of opium and alcohol houses, and even imposed minimum sales quotas for alcohol in certain areas.

against the Viet Minh members that before fleeing they massacred a great number of our political prisoners detained at Yen Bay and Cao Bang.

Notwithstanding all this, our fellow citizens have always manifested toward the French a tolerant and humane attitude. Even after the Japanese *Putsch* of March, 1945, the Viet Minh League helped many Frenchmen to cross the frontier, rescued some of them from Japanese jails, and protected French lives and property.

From the autumn of 1940, our country had in fact ceased to be a French colony and had become a Japanese possession.

After the Japanese had surrendered to the Allies, our whole people rose to regain our national sovereignty and to found the Democratic Republic of Viet-Nam.

The truth is that we have wrested our independence from the Japanese and not from the French.

The French have fled, the Japanese have capitulated, Emperor Bao Dai has abdicated. Our people have broken the chains which for nearly a century have fettered them and have won independence for the Fatherland. Our people at the same time have overthrown the monarchic regime that has reigned supreme for dozens of centuries. In its place has been established the present Democratic Republic.

For these reasons, we, members of the Provisional Government, representing the whole Vietnamese people, declare that from now on we break off all relations of a colonial character with France; we repeal all the international obligation that France has so far subscribed to on behalf of Viet-Nam, and we abolish all the special rights the French have unlawfully acquired in our Fatherland.

The whole Vietnamese people, animated by a common purpose, are determined to fight to the bitter end against any attempt by the French colonialists to reconquer their country.

We are convinced that the Allied nations, which at Teheran and San Francisco[2] have acknowledged the principles of self-determination and equality of nations, will not refuse to acknowledge the independence of Viet-Nam.

A people who have courageously opposed French domination for more than eighty years, a people who have fought side by side with the Allies against the fascists during these last years, such a people must be free and independent.

For these reasons, we, members of the Provisional Government of the Democratic Republic of Viet-Nam, solemnly declare to the world that Viet-Nam has the right to be a free and independent country—and in fact it is so already. The entire Vietnamese people are determined to mobilize all their physical and mental strength, to sacrifice their lives and property in order to safeguard their independence and liberty.

---

2. Teheran and San Francisco: sites of great-power conferences in 1943 and 1945 respectively; the latter established the United Nations.

*

Address to the Frenchmen in Indochina

I want to address a few words to you not as President of the Democratic Republic of Viet-Nam, but as a sincere friend of the honest Frenchmen.

You love France and want it to be independent. You love your compatriots and want them to be free. Your patriotism is a glory to you because it is mankind's highest ideal.

But we also have a right to love our fatherland and want it to be independent, have we not? We also have a right to love our compatriots and want them to be free, have we not? What you consider as your ideal must be ours too.

We neither dislike nor hate the French people. On the contrary, we respect them as a great people who were the first to propagate the lofty ideals of liberty, equality, and fraternity and have greatly contributed to culture, science, and civilization.

Our struggle is not directed against France, nor is it directed against honest Frenchmen, but we are fighting the cruel domination of French colonialism in Indochina. You will understand to what extent this colonialism has misused the reputation of France and imposed upon us disastrous calamities: forced labor, *corvées,*[1] salt tax, compulsory consumption of opium and alcohol, heavy taxes, complete absence of freedom, incessant terrorism, moral and material sufferings, and ruthless exploitation. Ask yourselves who has benefited by making us suffer in such a way. Is it France and the French people? No, France does not become richer from colonialist exploitation, and it is not due to the absence of this exploitation that it will become poorer. On the contrary, expenditure for the colonies is another burden loaded upon the French people's shoulders.

Do the French planters and industrialists in Indochina profit? Before you give an answer, I want you to put yourselves in our situation for a moment. What would you do if foreigners came and imposed on you an endless string of plagues and sufferings? I strongly believe that you would struggle to the last against this domination. Then why do you want us shamefully to accept French domination?

You have also known that this domination profits neither France nor the French people. It only enriches the few colonialist sharks and blemishes France's reputation.

Some people say that it is to save face that France is trying to cling to Indochina.

The recognition of Viet-Nam's independence will not lower France's prestige, but will heighten it before the world and history. This gesture will show to the world at large, and particularly to the Vietnamese, that today's France is completely different from the old imperialist France. It will win the respect

---

1. *Corvées:* obligatory services to landlords or rulers.

of all peoples and the love of the Vietnamese who now, as always, want nothing else than to see their Fatherland independent.

Frenchmen in Indochina! Don't you think that mankind's blood has been shed too much? Don't you think that peace, a genuine peace built on justice and democratic ideals must be a substitute for war, that freedom, equality, and fraternity must be realized in all countries with no discrimination between nationalities and races?

We do not fear death, because we want to live. Like you, we want to live free, not to be trampled underfoot and strangled. Hence, we have made a distinction between good Frenchmen and bad ones.

I repeat that we are struggling for our independence, we are struggling against domination and not against honest Frenchmen.

At present the French colonialists have started their offensive against us in the South. They have begun to kill so many of our compatriots, committed arson and sacking. We are obliged to fight these invaders in order to safeguard our families and Fatherland.

However, everywhere in Viet-Nam the lives and property of the Frenchmen are being protected and will continue to be protected, provided they are content to live quietly and do not cause trouble.

I solemnly guarantee that the Frenchmen who earn their living honestly and live quietly will always be treated by us as friends and brothers. We are a people advocating peace and respecting others' interests and freedom.

Frenchmen in Indochina! It is now up to you to show that you are worthy children of the glorious heroes who formerly struggled for freedom, equality, and fraternity.

MARSHALL MCLUHAN (1911–   ), *Know-How* and *Looking Up to My Son,* from *The Mechanical Bride: Folklore of Industrial Man*

The condition to which the Canadian scholar and critic Marshall McLuhan addresses himself in The Mechanical Bride *(1951) is one of "public helplessness"; for as McLuhan notes in his preface, "Ours is the first age in which many thousands of the best-trained individual minds have made it a full-time business to get inside the collective public mind. . . . Today the tyrant rules not by club or fist, but, disguised as a market researcher, he shepherds his flocks in the ways of utility and comfort." Advertising is not simply a way of alerting the public to certain products, or even of persuading the public to buy. It functions both as folklore and as propaganda, representing "a world of social myths or forms," and reinforcing the values on which capitalist society rests.*

The book, a series of short essays, analyzes the means by which various ads manipulate the reader; in this sense it is a study of social rhetoric. The first piece below—about the effect of mechanical technology on our moral sense and on our self-image—gives another dimension to the problem raised in Jungk's essay on the atomic scientists. The second concerns the influence of a competitive economy on family relations, and may be contrasted with Pelletier's description of childhood in an Indian village.

Terse and ironic, McLuhan's prose mixes scholarly and vernacular styles, often within a single sentence: creating a verbal jolt to remind one that the author's purpose is to "arrest the maelstrom" for contemplation.

*

Know-How

As the ad [1] implies, know-how is at once a technical and a moral sphere. It is a duty for a woman to love her husband and also to love that soap that will make her husband love her. It is a duty to be glamorous, cheerful, efficient, and, so far as possible, to run the home like an automatic factory. This ad also draws attention to the tendency of the modern housewife, after a premar-

---

1. The ad:—for an "Automagic Gladiron"—says: "How to iron shirts without hating your husband! . . . You'll love him and your Gladiron when you sit and iron shirts in 4½ minutes."

ital spell in the business world, to embrace marriage and children but not housework. Emotionally, she repudiates physical tasks with the same conviction that she pursues hygiene. And so the ad promises her a means of doing physical work without hating the husband who has trapped her into household drudgery.

To purchase gadgets that relieve this drudgery and thus promote domestic affection is, therefore, a duty, too. And so it is that not only labor-saving appliances but food and nylons ("your legs owe it to their audience") are consumed and promoted with moral fervor.

But gadgets and gimmicks did not begin as physical objects, nor are they only to be understood as such today. Benjamin Franklin, protean prototype and professor of know-how, is equally celebrated for both his material and psychological technology. In his *Autobiography,* still a central feature of Yankee moral structure, he tells, for example, how he hit upon a system of moral bookkeeping which would enable any man to achieve perfection in several months. The trick is to select only one fault at a time for deletion, and by concentration and persistence the moral slate will soon be clean. Related to this system was his discovery of various techniques for winning friends and influencing people which are still as serviceable as ever.

Some of the contents of the summer issue of *Woman's Life,* 1947, which are listed on the back cover as follows, illustrate Ben Franklin's know-how mentality very well: "How To Hold a Man," "Eight Ways To Ruin a Compliment," "How Are Your Home Manners?" "Ways To Meet New Men." "Plan Your Charm," "If You Want To Be in Movies," and so on through the know-how hall of mirrors. On the other side of the cover is advertised a book by Louis E. Bisch, *How To Get Rid of "Nerves,"* which lists such chapters as "How To Avoid Nerves When Married," "How To Avoid Boredom," "How To Make Your Wishes Come True."

Books on how to relax would seem just about to cancel out books on how to build up nervous tension for success drive.

A recent book by Ira Wallach, entitled *How To Be Deliriously Happy,* provides know-how for the whole range of success drives, recommending that if you are in debt, go deeper. If you think you are inferior, look at yourself in a mirror bordered with eagles. Say to yourself you are taller than Napoleon. Which all adds up to the simple formula implicit in all formulas for living and success philosophy: "Love that strait jacket."

Locked in one of these mechanical strait jackets, a man may feel safe and strong, but he can exercise very little of his human character or dignity. And it is possible to understand this passion for mechanical strait jackets today by considering it in relation to similar human behavior in totally diverse circumstances. In his *Hero With a Thousand Faces,* Joseph Campbell compares our modern dilemma with that of primitive men:

For the primitive hunting peoples of those remotest human milleniums when the sabertooth tiger, the mammoth and the lesser presences of the animal kingdom were the primary manifestations of what was alien—the source at once of danger and of sustenance—the great human problem was to become linked psychologically to the task of sharing the wilderness with these beings. An unconscious identification took place, and this was finally rendered conscious in the half-human, half-animal, figures of the totem-ancestors . . . through acts of literal imitation

. . . an effective annihilation of the human ego was accomplished and society achieved a cohesive organization.

It is precisely the same annihilation of the human ego that we are witnessing today. Only, whereas men in those ages of terror got into animal strait jackets, we are unconsciously doing the same *vis à vis* the machine. And our ads and entertainment provide insight into the totem images we are daily contriving in order to express this process. But technology is an abstract tyrant that carries its ravages into deeper recesses of the psyche than did the sabertooth tiger or the grizzly bear.

Concentration on technique and abstract system began for the Western world, says Werner Sombart in his *Quintessence of Capitalism,* with the rise of scholastic method in theology in the twelfth century. The monks were also the first begetters of methods of abstract finance, and the clockwork order of their communal lives gave to the tradesmen of the growing towns the great example of systematic time economy. The puritan both retained the scholastic method in theology and gave it expression in the precision and austerity of his secular existence. So that it is scarcely fantastic to say that a great modern business is a secular adaptation of some of the most striking features of medieval scholastic culture. Confronted with the clockwork precision of scholastic method, Lewis Mumford could think only of the mechanical parallel of a smoothly working textile plant. The object of this systematic process is now production and finance rather than God. And evangelical zeal is now centered in the department of sales and distribution rather than in preaching. But the scientific structure and moral patterns of the monastic discipline are still intact, so that anybody seeking to understand or modify the religious intensity of modern technology and business has to look closely into these antecedents.

The know-how of the twelfth century was dedicated to an all-inclusive knowledge of human and divine ends. The secularizing of this system has meant the adaptation of techniques not for knowledge but for use. Instead of an intelligible map of man and creation, modern technology offers immediate comfort and profit. But it is still paradoxically permeated with a medieval spirit of religious intensity and moral duty, which causes much conflict of mind and confusion of purpose in producers and consumers alike. So that the Marxists urge that technology be finally cut loose from religion as a means of resolving these conflicts; but this is merely to repudiate the parent while idolizing the offspring. More common and hopeful is the effort to modify the social and individual effects of technology by stressing concepts of social biology, as Lewis Mumford and others do. But in this conception there is the dubious assumption that the organic is the opposite of the mechanical. Professor Norbert Wiener, maker of mechanical brains, asserts that, since all organic characteristics can now be mechanically produced, the old rivalry between mechanism and vitalism is finished. After all, the Greek word "organic" meant "machine" to them. And Samuel Butler in *Erewhon* pointed out how very biological modern machines had become: "The stoker is almost as much a cook for his engine as our own cooks for ourselves." And as a result of our obsessional care for these objects, he goes on, they daily acquire "more of that self-regulating, self-acting power which will be better than any intellect." Consequently we have now arrived near the day of the automatic factory, when we shall find it as natural for an unaided factory to produce cars as for the liver to secrete bile or the plant to put forth leaves.

Fortune (November, 1949) offers "A Key to the Automatic Factory" in pointing out that "the computers that direct guns might also direct machines." How persistently the face of murderous violence associates itself with know-how! It is hard to say why the public target of such a factory should be any happier than the recipient of a bomb or shell. And it has long been plain that the executives of production and selling have been thinking in military terms, smashing public resistance with carefully planned barrages followed by shock troops of salesmen to mop up the pockets. It will take more than a change of vocabulary to eradicate this lethal aspect of know-how, for it is not easily separated from its origins or its uses. The public may smile at the suggestion that it need be perturbed at being the target for a barrage of corn flakes or light bulbs. But this industrial ammunition has the character of exploding in the brain cortex and making its impact on the emotional structure of all society.

The symbolist esthetic theory of the late nineteenth century seems to offer an even better conception than social biology for resolving the human problems created by technology. This theory leads to a conception of orchestrating human arts, interests, and pursuits rather than fusing them in a functional biological unit, as even with Giedion and Mumford. Orchestration permits discontinuity and endless variety without the universal imposition of any one social or economic system. It is a conception inherent not only in symbolist art but in quantum and relativity physics. Unlike Newtonian physics, it can entertain a harmony that is not unilateral, monistic, or tyrannical. It is neither progressive nor reactionary but embraces all previous actualizations of human excellence while welcoming the new in a simultaneous present. . . .

Standing on the threshold of the technological era, Jonathan Swift wrote a prophetic account of its human dangers in the third book of *Gulliver's Travels*. At the same time, John Locke, godfather of the American Constitution, pointed out that the dangers of know-how lie in the ease with which it distracts us from the obvious: "He that was sharp-sighted enough to see the configuration of the minute particles of the spring of a clock, and observe on what its elasticity depends, would discover something very admirable; but if eyes so framed could not at a distance see what o'clock it was, their owner would not be benefited by their acuteness."

Anybody who turns his scrutiny on the typical behavior of men absorbed in the dream of technology will find himself making that point over and over again. Know-how is so eager and powerful an ally of human needs that it is not easily controlled or kept in a subordinate role, even when directed by spectacular wisdom. Harnessed merely to a variety of blind appetites for power and success, it draws us swiftly into that labyrinth at the end of which waits the minotaur. So it is in this period of passionate acceleration that the world of the machines begins to assume the threatening and unfriendly countenance of an inhuman wilderness even less manageable than that which once confronted prehistoric man. Reason is then swiftly subdued by panic desires to acquire protective coloration. As terrified men once got ritually and psychologically into animal skins, so we already have gone far to assume and to propagate the behavior mechanisms of the machines that frighten and overpower us.

Much hope, however, still emerges from those parts of the scene where rational self-awareness and reasonable programs of self-restraint can be cultivated. Combatants merely infect one another. But the friendly dialogue of rational beings can also be as catching as it is civilizing.

*

Looking Up to My Son

The ad agencies, at least, are never likely to underestimate the power of a woman. Dip into the daytime serial world and you will find the dissatisfaction and anxiety experienced by millions of women who live isolated lives from 8:00 A.M. till 6:00 P.M. They look up to their sons or live for their children because they are unable to find any meaning or satisfaction in the present. In small towns a man often goes home to lunch and spends very little time getting to and from work. In rural society men are within shout of home most of the time, and mother and children are daily witnesses and even assistants of their labors. Even in big cities a few decades ago it was common for home and shop to be closely connected, while in the London of Charles Lamb not only work but the rural countryside could be reached on foot in a few minutes. Under these conditions not only were father, mother, and children often united during the day, but they were close to an intimately known community.

In these circumstances most of our current marital problems and child-rearing headaches did not exist. And today Le Corbusier, Lewis Mumford, and Siegfried Giedion alike have shown how we may by a reasonable distribution of modern power and by town and country planning enjoy all these lost advantages without sacrifice of any new gains.

The present ad [1] is already a bit old-fashioned because in the past five years mothers have been taught to ask themselves anxiously not "Did I give my baby the right capsules?" but "Did I give my baby an Oedipus complex?" Otherwise the pattern of maternal concentration on the child as a substitute for an absentee father and a defaulting community life remains unchanged.

If Dad is the downtown quarterback whose work is a remote abstraction to his family, and if that work requires endless pep and smiles and an outpouring of psychological energies in narrow and rigid patterns of cheerful confidence, he is likely to remain a little on the adolescent side of maturity. He will tend to be a bore to a woman who has another pattern of existence which includes much leisure to brood on the margin of the full flow of commercial life. Mom begins to "dream of looking up to my son," a son different from his father, a son who will be a much bigger and tougher quarterback. Our ad reads:

I will help him grow in stature . . . by giving him care which will add inches to his height, help him form straight, sturdy limbs, build a back as erect as a great tree, and develop a mighty chest. This dream I will make come true!

---

1. The present ad: the ad—for a particular brand of cod-liver oil—shows a mother holding her baby. Copy begins, "I dream of looking up to my son. I see him one day as a man of stature, a new-world man towering free and confident in an untroubled generation."

The ad then goes into the familiar routine of treating the body as a factory for producing statistically ascertainable results which will justify the maternal dream.

The most disconcerting fact is the dream itself. It is a dream of aggression geared to an impersonal business community. And it is a dream which, as is shown in other exhibits, isolates business success from every other social quality.

Pictorially, the ad links the most lofty sentiments of motherly devotion and sacrifice to a dream that is unconsciously crude and base. This helps to explain how it occurs that refined and idealistic women in our world are so often the mothers of ruthless men who enslave themselves to the low drudgery of avarice or who live in thrice-heated furnaces of passion for dubious distinction. The objectives of a commercial society, when filtered through the medium of maternal idealism, acquire a lethal intensity. For women don't invent the goals of society. They interpret them to their children. In her *Male and Female,* Dr. Mead explores the American paradox of "conditional love," showing from many points of view the emotional structuring which results, especially in boys and men, from affection that is tendered or withdrawn as a reward or penalty, at first for eating and toilet habits, later for assertiveness at school and in business. In this prevalent situation a child or adult merits love only when he is successful. The present ad is that entire drama in capsule form. But the drama is not of recent origin, as Dr. Mead is aware.

The mother pictured here, anxiously and expectantly poised over her child, has been taught to regard the child not as spiritually masculine but as a sexually neutral bundle of potential energy which vocational training will gear to high achievement. Her first job, however, is to pump the maximal number of vitamins and calories into this little chemical factory. And the child soon learns to regard itself as primed for success both by food and facts. The food will insure the big chest and athletic prowess; the facts will answer the sixty-four-dollar questions. Every child today is thus a potential genius, promise-crammed.

The ultimate absurdity of this attitude gets frequent expression in those dog-food ads which exhort us to "nourish every inch of him with old horse if you want to have more fun with him." The ad men for the canned-horse industry have found no better way to sell their product than to parody the ads of the kiddie-food industry.

If it were possible to define success in a great number of ways, a success drive might not be destructive. If there were as many recognized kinds of success as there are temperaments, tastes, skills, and degrees of knowledge, a society dedicated to success might yet develop very great harmony amid variety and richness of experience and insight. As Whitehead put it in *Adventures of Ideas:*

The vigour of civilized societies is preserved by the widespread sense that high aims are worthwhile. . . . All strong interests easily become impersonal, the love of a good job well done. There is a sense of harmony about such an accomplishment, the Peace brought by something worthwhile. Such personal gratification arises from an aim beyond personality.

But in an industrial world, which measures success in terms of consumption goods, the result of a personal and private success obsession is to exclude most of the varieties of human temperament and talent from the overcrowded race to the narrow goal. Poverty, rather than richness, of experience and expression is the result. And bitterness rather than quiet self-possession is the state of mind of these not qualified for the narrow goals set up by technological and executive pursuits.

For the failures there is also the sense that they have forfeited the parental and wifely affection which was conditionally tendered during their period of "promise." But even for the successful there is often the sense of paying too much for a success which, after all, does little to satisfy their deeper human qualities or which easily palls on the daily domestic audience. Not to have lived according to the dictates of one's own reason but to have sought, even successfully, goals alien to oneself is no recipe for happiness.

The baby boy in the ad will grow up to say in a thousand different ways: "Look, Mom, I'm dancing! I owe it all to you, Mom!" Every act of his life will be directed to an audience from which he will expect sympathy and approval. Even the epileptic contortions of a Danny Kaye or a Betty Hutton are a popular dramatic expression of these social attitudes and expectations, which were even more vividly rendered by Al Jolson on his knees singing "Mammy." Less obviously, the same insatiable craving for audience approval appears in Clifton Webb's satiric portrayal of the virtuoso of unexpected accomplishments: "They laughed when I took up the vaulting pole," or "when I entered the delivery room," or "when I picked up the conductor's baton." Even if he should be a conqueror who has crushed many other lives, he will still expect sympathy and approval. Dale Carnegie based his *How To Win Friends and Influence People* on the premise that since the typical gangster regards himself as a misunderstood public benefactor, how much more does the respectable businessman require truckloads of adulation to keep him in good humor. Dale Carnegie's jackal strategy is to advise each of us to be an approving mom to the toughies of the world of action so that they will pay and pay to keep us near them. Just keep looking up to these tousled sons with wonder and admiration in your eyes. In all they do, let them know that "mother would approve."

Because the present ad, with its hook-up between mother love, vitamins, and personal ambition, is very centrally located in the dynamics of our culture, it would be possible to relate it legitimately to much more of our world. For it is of the nature of human life to have a consistency of some sort, conscious or unconscious, rational or irrational. It is here assumed that there is some point in bringing as much as possible of our lives within the harmonic scheme of a critically conscious and reasonable order.

ROLAND BARTHES (1915–   ), *Political Modes of Writing* from *Writing Degree Zero*

In Writing Degree Zero, *the French literary and linguistic scholar Roland Barthes discusses the "third dimension of Form": that component in writing which is neither content nor style, but which concerns the writer's relation to history and to society at large. This component Barthes calls the "Ethic of language"; it involves "the choice of a human attitude, the affirmation of a certain Good," and it is in terms of its Ethic that Barthes analyzes some types of political writing. His remarks on the character of bourgeois revolutionary prose may be tested against the pieces by Patrick Henry and Thomas Paine; those on Marxist writing are relevant in varying degrees to several Marxist essays in the volume, though it is debatable whether Barthes' conclusion is justified: that "any political mode of writing can only uphold a police world." His analysis of Marxist writing also suggests a certain affinity between the communist world view and that of such apocalyptic revolutionaries as the Taborites and Gerrard Winstanley.*
Barthes' work, intended for a limited community of academic intellectuals, displays a style that is compressed, abstract, and occasionally obscure.

All modes of writing have in common the fact of being "closed" and thus different from spoken language. Writing is in no way an instrument for communication, it is not an open route through which there passes only the intention to speak. A whole disorder flows through speech and gives it this self-devouring momentum which keeps it in a perpetually suspended state. Conversely, writing is a hardened language which is self-contained and is in no way meant to deliver to its own duration a mobile series of approximations. It is on the contrary meant to impose, thanks to the shadow cast by its system of signs, the image of a speech which had a structure even before it came into existence. What makes writing the opposite of speech is that the former always *appears* symbolical, introverted, ostensibly turned towards an occult side of language, whereas the second is nothing but a flow of empty signs, the movement of which alone is significant. The whole of speech is epitomized in this expendability of words, in this froth ceaselessly swept onwards, and speech is found only where language self-evidently functions like a devouring process which swallows only the moving crest of the words. Writing, on the contrary, is always rooted in something beyond language, it develops like a seed, not like a line, it manifests an essence and holds the threat of a secret, it is an anti-communication, it is intimidating. All writing will therefore contain the ambiguity of an object which is both language and coercion: there exists fundamentally in writing a "circumstance" foreign to language, there is, as it were, the weight of a gaze conveying an intention which is no longer linguistic. This gaze may well express a passion of language, as in literary modes of writing; it may also express the threat of retribution, as in political ones: writing is then meant to unite at a single stroke the reality of the acts and the ideality of the ends. This is why power, or the shadow cast by power, always ends in creating an axiological writing, in which the distance which usually separates fact from value disappears within the very space of the word, which is given at once as description and as judgment. The word becomes an alibi, that is, an elsewhere and a justification. This, which is true of the literary modes of writing, in which the unity of the signs is ceaselessly fascinated by zones of infra- or ultra-language, is even truer of the political ones, in which the alibi stemming from language is at the same time intimidation and glorification: for it is power or conflict which produce the purest types of writing.

We shall see later that classical writing was a ceremonial which manifested the implantation of the writer into a particular political society, and that to speak like Vaugelas [1] meant in the first place to be connected with the exercise of power. The Revolution did not modify the norms of this writing, since its force of thinkers remained, all things considered, the same, having merely passed from intellectual to political power; but the exceptional conditions of the struggle nevertheless brought about, within the great Form of classicism, a revolutionary mode of writing proper, defined not by its structure (which was more conventional than ever) but by its closed character and by its counterpart, since the use of language was then linked, as never before in history, to the Blood which had been shed. The Revolutionaries had no reason to wish to alter classical writing; they were in no way aware of questioning the nature of man, still less his language, and an "instrument" they had inherited from Voltaire, Rousseau or Vauvenargues could not appear to them as compromised. It was the singularity of the historical circumstances which produced the identity of the revolutionary mode of writing. Baudelaire spoke somewhere of the "grandiloquent truth of gestures on life's great occasions." The Revolution was in the highest degree one of those great occasions when truth, through the bloodshed that it costs, becomes so weighty that its expression demands the very forms of theatrical amplification. Revolutionary writing was the one and only grand gesture commensurate with the daily presence of the guillotine. What today appears turgid was then no more than life-size. This writing, which bears all the signs of inflation, was an exact writing: never was language more incredible, yet never was it less spurious. This grandiloquence was not only form modelled on drama; it was also the awareness of it. Without this extravagant pose, typical of all the great revolutionaries, which enabled Guadet, the Girondin, when arrested at Saint-Emilion, to declare without looking ridiculous, since he was about to die: "Yes, I am Guadet. Executioner, do your duty. Go take my head to the tyrants of my

---

1. Claude de Vaugelas (1585–1650): French grammarian, whose *Remarques sur la langue française* became a standard for cultured usage.

country. It has always turned them pale; once severed, it will turn them paler still," the Revolution could not have been this mythical event which made History fruitful, along with all future ideas on revolution. Revolutionary writing was so to speak the entelechy of the revolutionary legend: it struck fear into men's hearts and imposed upon them a citizen's sacrament of Bloodshed.

Marxist writing is of a different order. Here the closed character of the form does not derive from rhetorical amplification or from grandiloquence in delivery, but from a lexicon as specialized and as functional as a technical vocabulary; even metaphors are here severely codified. French revolutionary writing always proclaimed a right founded on bloodshed or moral justification, whereas from the very start Marxist writing is presented as the language of knowledge. Here, writing is univocal, because it is meant to maintain the cohesion of a Nature; it is the lexical identity of this writing which allows it to impose a stability in its explanations and a permanence in its method; it is only in the light of its whole linguistic system that Marxism is perceived in all its political implications. Marxist writing is as much given to understatement as revolutionary writing is to grandiloquence, since each word is no longer anything but a narrow reference to the set of principles which tacitly underlie it. For instance, the word "imply," frequently encountered in Marxist writing, does not there have its neutral dictionary meaning; it always refers to a precise historical process, and is like an algebraical sign representing a whole bracketed set of previous postulates.

Being linked to action, Marxist writing has rapidly become, in fact, a language expressing value-judgments. This character, already visible in Marx, whose writing however remains in general explanatory, has come to pervade writing completely in the era of triumphant Stalinism. Certain outwardly similar notions, for which a neutral vocabulary would not seek a dual designation, are evaluatively parted from each other, so that each element gravitates towards a different noun: for instance, "cosmopolitanism" is the negative of "internationalism" (already in Marx). In the Stalinist world, in which *definition,* that is to say the separation between Good and Evil, becomes the sole content of all language, there are no more words without values attached to them, so that finally the function of writing is to cut out one stage of a process: there is no more lapse of time between naming and judging, and the closed character of language is perfected, since in the last analysis it is a value which is given as explanation of another value. For instance, it may be alleged that such and such a criminal has engaged in activities harmful to the interests of the state; which boils down to saying that a criminal is someone who commits a crime. We see that this is in fact a tautology, a device constantly used in Stalinist writing. For the latter no longer aims at founding a Marxist version of the facts, or a revolutionary rationale of actions, but at presenting reality in a prejudged form, thus imposing a reading which involves immediate condemnation: the objective content of the word "deviationist" puts it into a penological category. If two deviationists band together, they become "fractionists," which does not involve an objectively different crime, but an increase in the sentence imposed. One can enumerate a properly Marxist writing (that of Marx and Lenin) and a writing of triumphant

Stalinism; there certainly is as well a Trotskyist writing and a tactical writing, for instance that of the French Communist party with its substitution of "people," then of "plain folk," for "working class," and the wilful ambiguity of terms like "democracy," "freedom," "peace," etc.

There is no doubt at all that each regime has its own writing, no history of which has yet been written. Since writing is the spectacular commitment of language, it contains at one and the same time, thanks to a valuable ambiguity, the reality and the appearance of power, what it is, and what it would like to be thought to be: a history of political modes of writing would therefore be the best of social phenomenologies. For instance, the French Restoration evolved a class writing by means of which repression was immediately given as a condemnation spontaneously arising from classical "Nature": workers claiming rights were always "troublemakers," strike-breakers were "good workmen," and the subservience of judges became, in this language, the "paternal vigilance of magistrates" (it is thanks to a similar procedure that Gaullism today calls Communists "separatists"). We see that here the function of writing is to maintain a clear conscience and that its mission is fraudulently to identify the original fact with its remotest subsequent transformation by bolstering up the justification of actions with the additional guarantee of its own reality. This fact about writing is, by the way, typical of all authoritarian regimes; it is what might be called police-state writing: we know, for example, that the content of the word "Order" always indicates repression.

The spreading influence of political and social facts into the literary field of consciousness has produced a new type of scriptor, halfway between the party member and the writer, deriving from the former an ideal image of committed man, and from the latter the notion that a written work is an act. Thus while the intellectual supersedes the writer, there appears in periodicals and in essays a militant mode of writing entirely freed from stylistic considerations, and which is, so to speak, a professional language signifying "presence." In this mode of writing, nuances abound. Nobody will deny that there is such a thing, for instance, as a writing typical of *Esprit* or of *Les Temps Modernes*.[2] What these intellectual modes of writing have in common, is that in them language, instead of being a privileged area, tends to become the sufficient sign of commitment. To come to adopt a closed sphere of language under the pressure of all those who do not speak it, is to proclaim one's act of choosing, if not necessarily one's agreement with that choice. Writing here resembles the signature one affixes at the foot of a collective proclamation one has not written oneself. So that to adopt a mode of writing—or, even better, to make it one's own—means to save oneself all the preliminaries of a choice, and to make it quite clear that one takes for granted the reasons for such a choice. Any intellectual writing is therefore the first of the "leaps of the intellect." Whereas an ideally free language never could function as a sign of my own person and would give no information whatsoever about my his-

2. *Esprit* and *Les Temps Modernes* are two prominent monthlies, the first Left-wing Catholic and the second directed by J.-P. Sartre. [Barthes' footnote.]

tory and my freedom, the writing to which I entrust myself already exists entirely as an institution; it reveals my past and my choice, it gives me a history, it blazons forth my situation, it commits me without my having to declare the fact. Form thus becomes more than ever an autonomous object, meant to signify a property which is collective and protected, and this object is a trouble-saving device: it functions as an economy signal whereby the scriptor constantly imposes his conversion without ever revealing how it came about.

This duplicity of today's intellectual modes of writing is emphasized by the fact that in spite of the efforts made in our time, it has proved impossible successfully to liquidate Literature entirely: it still constitutes a verbal horizon commanding respect. The intellectual is still only an incompletely transformed writer, and unless he scuttles himself and becomes for ever a militant who no longer writes (some have done so, and are therefore forgotten), he cannot but come back to the fascination of former modes of writing, transmitted through Literature as an instrument intact but obsolete. These intellectual modes of writing are therefore unstable, they remain literary to the extent that they are powerless, and are political only through their obsession with commitment. In short, we are still dealing with ethical modes of writing, in which the conscience of the scriptor (one no longer ventures to call him a writer) finds the comforting image of collective salvation.

But just as, in the present state of History, any political mode of writing can only uphold a police world, so any intellectual mode of writing can only give rise to a para-literature, which no longer dares to speak its name. Both are therefore in a complete blind alley, they can lead only to complicity or impotence, which means, in either case, to alienation.

ROBERT JUNGK (1913–　　　), *For They Know Not What They Do* from *Brighter Than a Thousand Suns*

In the introduction to Brighter Than A Thousand Suns *(1956), the German historian and journalist Robert Jungk writes that "no novel could be as revealing, as penetrating, or as exciting as a factual account of the atomic scientists' tragedy based on their own stories and on documents." That tragedy—the collective abandonment of conscience which led to the atomic bombing of Hiroshima and Nagasaki in August 1945—Jungk recounts in his book, which combines the methods of historiography and the novel. Although the book is entirely factual, Jungk's moral judgment is clear throughout, not only in explicit statements but also in his selection of material and in the symbolic value he attaches to weather, place names, and the "terrible fates" of some who were associated with the bomb. Open to question is Jungk's implicit suggestion of retributive justice, and also the statement of the chapter title itself. Jungk's techniques for molding the reader's response may be compared and contrasted with those of Thucydides, Plutarch, and Froissart; though for Jungk, narrative itself is the most persuasive rhetoric.*

Never was the pace at Los Alamos fiercer than after the capitulation of the Third Reich. "Our husbands worked almost incessantly," Eleanor Jette, the wife of a leading atomic scientist, remembers. She was a sort of local celebrity on account of her authorship of the sketches regularly performed on New Year's Eve in which the difficulties of life on the mesa and the peculiarities of certain of its prominent inhabitants were good-naturedly satirized.

But in June and July 1945 even she lost her sense of humour. It seemed the weather had conspired to frustrate the bomb builders. For weeks not a drop of rain fell. A dry, hot wind blew from the desert over the settlement. The grass withered. Foliage and pine needles dried up on the trees. Now and then the sky darkened and lightning flickered in the distance over the Sangre de Cristo Mountains. But the clouds did not open. Forest fires started on a number of occasions close to the town of laboratories. It was feared that the wind would carry sparks to the residential quarters, office buildings, and workshops. They were still all timber constructed and would easily catch fire. But if this happened the only water available for extinguishing purposes was Ashley Pond, a small pool in the centre of the settlement. The supply system did not now even suffice for the most necessary personal ablutions with this precious liquid. "We brushed our teeth with Coca-Cola," says a hospital nurse. "To cap it all some cases of chicken-pox chose this particular moment to break out among the schoolchildren. It became more important than ever for all the children to be able to wash as often as possible and that was just when there was a shortage of water."

A directive from Groves required the first bomb to be ready for testing by the middle of July and the second to be available for war purposes in August. Philip Morrison states: "I can personally testify that a date in the neighbourhood of the 10th of August was the mysterious deadline which we, who were working daily on the job of finishing the bomb, had to observe at all costs, irrespective of money troubles or the mass of development work still to come."

The rush of business, the heat, and the scarcity of water combined to make everyone irritable. Mrs. Jette reports: "One day, as I was passing an old acquaintance, I quite innocently said 'Good morning!' He instantly turned upon me in a fury, exclaiming: 'What's so *good* about the morning?' "

During this final stage of the construction of the atom bomb two young physicists . . . became particularly conspicuous. They were the exceptionally tall Californian Luis W. Alvarez and the skinny Louis Slotin, born in Canada of Russian parents who had fled there from the pogroms. Both these scientists were "war babies" who had first come to be experts at their trade by doing war work and achieved their first big results in arms laboratories. In their eyes the "new power" was neither so wonderful nor so terrible as it seemed to the veterans with whom they worked. They had not, therefore, much sympathy with the doubts that afflicted their seniors in these last few months.

Alvarez, the son of a well-known surgeon at the Mayo clinic, had come to Los Alamos rather late, after distinguishing himself in the secret radar laboratory attached to the Massachusetts Institute of Technology. He had made some important discoveries there, including the invention of a bomb-aiming device and the ground-control approach system now in use at practically all airfields. On the Hill at Los Alamos he and his still younger research team had succeeded in constructing the complex release mechanism of the bomb, accurate to one-millionth of a second.

The testing of this apparatus, so far as it could be done in the laboratory, was regarded as one of the most dangerous jobs in Los Alamos. It was undertaken in narrow, isolated canyons at a considerable distance from the mesa on which the residential quarters and workshops had been built. After Alvarez had completed to his satisfaction, in the spring of 1945, the first development model of this bomb release and tried it out, he handed over production of the final model to Dr Bainbridge, the Technical Director, and asked Oppenheimer for a new assignment, preferably close to the front line.

At the end of May 1945 Alvarez and his team were sent to the air base on the island of Tinian in the Pacific, from which almost daily raids with ordinary explosive and incendiary bombs were carried out against Japan. He developed there, while awaiting his first definite employment of the atom bomb, a measuring device to be dropped at the same time as the bomb. It was designed for transmission by radio signal to the bombing aircraft of information on the strength of the shock waves released by the new weapon.

Meanwhile Slotin had been busy testing the interior mechanism of the experimental bomb. It consisted of two hemispheres which would come together at the moment of release, thereby enabling the uranium they contained to unite in a "critical mass." The determination of this critical size—referred to simply as "crit" in the Los Alamos jargon—had been one of the chief problems studied by the theoretical department. But the quantity of uranium required, the scattering angle and range of the neutrons to be emitted by the chain reaction, the speed at which the two hemispheres would have to collide, and a whole series of other data could be only approximately estimated. If absolute precision and certainty were to be attained, it could only be by way of experiment in every case. Such experiments were assigned to the group in the charge of Frisch, the discoverer of fission, who had been brought to Los Alamos from England. Slotin was one of the members of this group. He was in the habit of experimenting without taking any special protective measures. His only instruments were two screwdrivers, by means of which he allowed the two hemispheres to slide towards each other on a rod, while he watched them with incessant concentration. His object was to do no more than just reach the critical point, the very first step in the chain reaction, which would immediately stop the moment he parted the spheres again. If he passed the point or was not quite quick enough in breaking contact, the mass might become supercritical and produce a nuclear explosion. Frisch himself had once nearly lost his life during one of these experiments at Los Alamos.

Slotin knew, of course, by how narrow a margin his chief had escaped death. But the daring young scientist thoroughly enjoyed risking his life in this way. He called it "twisting the dragon's tail." Ever since his earliest youth he had gone in search of fighting, excitement, and adventure. He had volunteered for service in the Spanish civil war, more for the sake of the thrill of it than on political grounds. He had often been in extreme danger as an anti-aircraft gunner in that war. As soon as the Second World War broke out he immediately joined the Royal Air Force. But in spite of distinguished service in active conflict he was obliged to resign shortly afterwards, when it was discovered that at his medical examination he had managed to conceal the fact that he was near-sighted.

On the way home from Europe to his native city of Winnipeg in Canada Slotin met an acquaintance in Chicago who convinced him that in view of his high scientific qualifications—he had won a prize for biophysics while a student at King's College in London—he could do more for the war effort in a laboratory than in a fighter aircraft. He had therefore found employment first as a biochemist and then as a member of the group which constructed the big cyclotron in the Metallurgical Laboratory of the Manhattan Project. The young man was popular with everyone. Nothing in life seemed to interest him so passionately as his work, to which he devoted himself day and night.

After working at Oak Ridge with Wigner on the development of new types of reactor, Slotin eventually arrived in Los Alamos. He had hoped to be transferred with Alvarez to Tinian at the beginning of 1945, in order to undertake the assembly there of the explosive heart of the first atom bomb to be used in the war. But as he was a Canadian citizen the security authorities were bound by the regulations to refuse his application. By way of consolation he was given the task of mounting the internal mechanism of the Alamogordo experimental bomb and handing it over officially to the Army on behalf of the Laboratory. A copy of the document sent to him certifying the delivery to the Army of the nuclear component of the first complete atom bomb was thenceforward the principal exhibit in his collection of diplomas, boxing trophies, and letters of appreciation of his services.

On 21 May 1946, not quite a year later, Slotin was carrying out an experiment, similar to those he had so often successfully performed in the past. It was connected with the preparation of the second atom-bomb test, to be performed in the waters of the South Sea atoll of Bikini. Suddenly his screwdriver slipped. The hemispheres came too close together and the material became critical. The whole room was instantly filled with a dazzling, bluish glare. Slotin, instead of ducking and thereby possibly saving himself, tore the two hemispheres apart with his hands and thus interrupted the chain reaction. By this action he saved the lives of the seven other persons in the room. He had realized at once that he himself would be bound to succumb to the effects of the excessive radiation dose which he had absorbed. But he did not lose his self-control for a moment. He told his colleagues to go and stand exactly where they had been at the instant of the disaster. He then drew on the blackboard, with his own hand, an accurate sketch of their relative positions, so that the doctors could ascertain the degree of radiation to which each of those present had been exposed.

As he was sitting with Al Graves, the scientist who, except himself, had been most severely infected by the radiation, waiting at the roadside for the car which had been ordered to take them to the hospital, he said quietly to his companion: "You'll come through all right. But I haven't the faintest chance myself." It was only too true. Nine days later the man who had experimentally determined the critical mass for the first atom bomb died in terrible agony.

The recording card of the neutron counter had been left behind in Slotin's laboratory. It showed a thin red line which rose steadily till it stopped abruptly at the instant of the catastrophe. The radiation had become so strong at that moment that the delicate instrument could no longer register it. The scientist charged with ascertaining from the available data what had happened, as a matter of physics, after Slotin's hand had slipped, was Klaus Fuchs.

Strange to say, a terrible fate was also in store for the complement of the cruiser *Indianapolis,* which took to Tinian the greater part of the explosive heart of the first atom bomb destined for use against Japan. Only three men aboard the vessel, the fastest in the American fleet, had any idea what she was carrying. The rest simply supposed that there must be something very important in the big wooden case which had been hoisted aboard, with every precaution, on the morning of 16 July shortly before the ship put to sea. During the voyage from San Francisco to Tinian very special security measures were taken for defence against hostile submarines. Everyone heaved a sigh of relief when the *Indianapolis,* after unloading her secret cargo at Tinian, stood for the offing. But before the cruiser had reached her second port of call she was struck, at five minutes past midnight on 30 July, by a torpedo. Owing to a series of unfortunate circumstances news of the sinking did not reach naval headquarters for another four days. Signals from another ship were wrongly taken to be routine reports from the *Indianapolis* of her position and owing to one more misunderstanding she was not reported as overdue at Leyte harbour. Therefore, salvage units arrived too late at the scene of the disaster, and of the ship's 1,196 men, only 316 were rescued.

Some days before the first test of the bomb it was an open secret in Alamogordo, even among the wives and children of the Los Alamos scientists, that some particularly important and exciting event was in preparation. The test was referred to under the code name "Trinity." No clear explanation has hitherto been forthcoming as to why this blasphemous expression was employed, above all in such a connexion. One probability is that it was taken from the name of a turquoise mine near Los Alamos, which had been laid under a curse and therefore abandoned by the superstitious Indians. Another guess supposes that it was chosen because at that time the first three atom bombs were approaching completion, and that the code name was derived simply and solely from the existence of that hellish trinity.

The main topic of conversation among the atomic scientists working at Los Alamos naturally turned on the question, "Will the 'gadget' "—the word "bomb" was discreetly avoided—"go off or not?" The majority believed that the theoretical hypotheses would be proved right. But the possibility of failure had always to be taken into account. Alvarez, constructor of the trigger of the bomb, had often enough told over-confident colleagues how in 1943, when his invention for blind landing had been demonstrated to the military authorities, it had failed no less than four times before it eventually worked.

The question whether the first complete atom bomb would be a "dud" or a success, or, as they said at Los Alamos, a "girl" or a "boy," aroused such intense interest that it became the pretext for a charming little game with horror. Lothar W. Nordheim, an atomic physicist who had once been a member of the old guard of Göttingen, relates: "The scientists at Los Alamos had a betting pool before the first test of 16 July 1945 on the size of the burst. But most estimates were too low by far except for one or two wild guesses."

The only estimate that was nearly correct came from Oppenheimer's friend Robert Serber, who had not been in Los Alamos for some time. When he was asked at a later date why he of all people should have been so nearly right in his forecast, he replied: "It was really only out of politeness. I thought that as a guest I ought to name a flatteringly high figure."

On Thursday the 12th and Friday the 13th of July 1945 the components of the interior explosive mechanism of the experimental bomb left Los Alamos by the "back door," along a secret road built during the war. They were transported from "Site S," where they had been assembled, to the experimental area known as the *Jornada del Muerto* (Death Tract) near the village of Oscuro (which means "dark"). Here, in the middle of the desert, a tall frame of iron scaffolding had been put up to hold the bomb. Because of the many thunderstorms experienced during the month it was decided not to place the bomb in position until the last possible moment. A bomb of about equal size, filled with ordinary explosive, had been strung up on the scaffolding a few days before to test the conditions. It had been struck by lightning, and had gone off with a loud bang.

The central portion of the bomb was fitted to it in an old farmhouse under the direction of Dr Robert Bacher, head of the Bomb Physics Division at Los Alamos. General Farrell, Groves's deputy, writes in this connexion: "During final preliminary assembly a bad few minutes developed when the assembly of an important section of the bomb was delayed. The entire unit was machine-tooled to the finest measurement. The insertion was partially completed when it apparently wedged tightly and would go no farther. Dr Bacher, however, was undismayed and reassured the group that time would solve the problem. In three minutes' time Dr Bacher's statement was verified and basic assembly was completed without further incident."

Those of the atomic scientists who had not left Los Alamos a week earlier to carry out final preparations held themselves in readiness for departure at any moment. They had with them provisions and also, at the express order of those in charge of the experiment, a snake-bite kit. On 14 and 15 July heavy thunderstorms, accompanied by great quantities of hail, broke over Los Alamos. The participants in the experiment, many of whom then learned for the first time the precise aim and object of the work they had been doing, were addressed by Hans Bethe, head of the Theoretical Division, in the biggest of the community halls, ordinarily used for movies. Bethe's speech ended with the words: "Human calculation indicates that the experiment must succeed. But will Nature act in conformity with our calculations?" The audience then boarded buses camouflaged with paint and set off on the four hours' journey to the experimental area.

By two o'clock in the morning all those taking part in the experiment were in their places. They were assembled in the Base Camp, some ten miles from Point Zero where there stood the high scaffolding on which the new, still untested weapon had been placed—the bomb on which they had been working for the last two years and had now finally brought to completion. They tried on the dark glasses with which they had been provided and smeared their faces, by artificial light, with anti-sunburn cream. They could hear dance music from the loudspeakers distributed throughout the area. From time to time the music was interrupted by news of the progress of the preparations. It had been arranged that the shot should take place at 4 a.m. But the bad weather rendered a postponement necessary.

At the control point, slightly over five and a half miles from the scaffolding, Oppenheimer and Groves conferred about whether the test should be put off altogether. Groves reports: "During most of the time we were strolling about in the dark, outside the control building, looking up at the stars. We kept assuring each other that either one or both of the two stars visible had grown brighter." After consultation with the meteorological experts it was eventually decided to explode the experimental bomb at 5.30 a.m.

At ten minutes past five Oppenheimer's deputy, the atomic physicist Saul K. Allison, one of the twenty people in the control room, began to send out time signals. At about the same time Groves, who had by then left the control point and returned to the Base Camp, something over four miles farther back, was giving the scientific personnel waiting at the Camp their last instructions. They were to put on their sunglasses and lie down on their faces with their heads turned away. For it was considered practically certain that anyone who tried to observe the flames with the naked eye would be blinded.

During the ensuing period of waiting, which seemed an eternity, hardly a word was spoken. Everyone was giving free play to his thoughts. But so far as those who have been asked can remember, these thoughts were not apocalyptic. Most of the people concerned, it appears, were trying to work out how long it would be before they could shift their uncomfortable position and obtain some kind of view of the spectacle awaited. Fermi, experimental-minded as ever, was holding scraps of paper, with which he meant to gauge the air pressure and thereby estimate the strength of the explosion the moment it occurred. Frisch was intent on memorizing the phenomenon as precisely as possible, without allowing either excitement or preconceived notions to interfere with his faculties of perception. Groves was wondering for the hundredth time whether he had taken every possible step to ensure rapid evacuation in the case of a disaster. Oppenheimer oscillated between fears that the experiment would fail and fears that it would succeed.

Then everything happened faster than it could be understood. No one saw the first flash of the atomic fire itself. It was only possible to see its dazzling white reflection in the sky and on the hills. Those who then ventured to turn their heads perceived a bright ball of flame, growing steadily larger and larger. "Good God, I believe that the long-haired boys have lost control!" a senior officer shouted. Carson Mark, one of the most brilliant members of the Theoretical Division, actually thought—though his intelligence told him the thing was impossible—that the ball of fire would never stop growing till it had enveloped all heaven and earth. At that moment everyone forgot what he had intended to do.

Groves writes: "Some of the men in their excitement, having had three years to get ready for it, at the last minute forgot those welders' helmets and stumbled out of the cars where they were sitting. They were distinctly blinded for two to three seconds. In that time they lost the view of what they had been waiting for over three years to see."

People were transfixed with fright at the power of the explosion. Oppenheimer was clinging to one of the uprights in the control room. A passage from the *Bhagavad Gītā,* the sacred epic of the Hindus, flashed into his mind.

> *If the radiance of a thousand suns*
> *were to burst into the sky,*
> *that would be like*
> *the splendour of the Mighty One—*

Yet, when the sinister and gigantic cloud rose up in the far distance over Point Zero, he was reminded of another line from the same source:

> *I am become Death, the shatterer of worlds.*

Sri Krishna, the Exalted One, lord of the fate of mortals, had uttered the phrase. But Robert Oppenheimer was only a man, into whose hands a mighty, a far too mighty, instrument of power had been given.

It is a striking fact that none of those present reacted to the phenomenon as professionally as he had supposed he would. They all, even those—who constituted the majority—ordinarily without religious faith or even any inclination thereto, recounted their experiences in words derived from the linguistic fields of myth and theology. General Farrell, for example, states:

The whole country was lighted by a searing light with an intensity many times that of the midday sun. . . . . Thirty seconds after the explosion came, first, the air blast pressing hard against the people and things, to be followed almost immediately by the strong, sustained, awesome roar which warned of doomsday and made us feel that we puny things were blasphemous to dare tamper with the forces heretofore reserved to the Almighty. Words are inadequate tools for the job of acquainting those not present with the physical, mental, and psychological effects. It had to be witnessed to be realized.

Even so cool and matter-of-fact a person as Enrico Fermi received a profound shock, in spite of the retort he had made to all the objections of his colleagues to the bomb during the discussions of the past few weeks. He had always said: "Don't bother me with your conscientious scruples! After all, the thing's superb physics!" Never before had he allowed anyone else to drive his car. But on this occasion he confessed that he did not feel capable of sitting at the wheel and asked a friend to take it for him on the road back to Los Alamos. He told his wife, the morning after his return, that it had seemed to him as if the car were jumping from curve to curve, skipping the straight stretches in between.

It appears that General Groves was the first to regain his composure. He consoled one of the scientists who rushed up to him almost in tears, announcing that the unexpectedly powerful explosion had destroyed all his observation and measuring instruments, with the words: "Well, if the instruments couldn't stand it, the bang must certainly have been a pretty big one. And that, after all, was what we most wanted to know." To General Farrell he remarked: "The war's over. One or two of those things, and Japan will be finished."

The general public was, for the time being, told nothing about this first world-shaking atomic explosion. Dwellers near the experimental area up to a distance of some 125 miles had seen an unusually bright light in the sky about 5.30 a.m. But they were put on the wrong scent by the head of the Manhattan District press agency, Jim Moynahan, who sent the false information that a munitions depot had blown up in the Alamogordo region. He added that no lives had been lost.

On the other hand the security authorities, when they tried to restrict knowledge of the successful test to those who had taken part in it, failed once more in their object. Within a few days the scientists' whispering campaign had carried the news to all the Manhattan Project laboratories. Harrison Brown, one of the younger men on research at Oak Ridge, recalls: "We knew about the fireball, the mushroom cloud, the intense heat. Following Alamogordo many of us signed a petition urging that the atomic bomb should not be used against Japan without prior demonstration and opportunity to surrender. And we urged that the government start immediately to study the possibility of securing international control of the new weapon."

The petition mentioned by Brown had been drafted by Szilard, who, after the failure of his efforts at the White House and the negative results of the Franck Report, had decided to lead a last forlorn hope. His idea was to collect the greatest possible number of signatures from participants in the Manhattan Project protesting against the use of the bomb. When a copy of the petition came into the hands of the director of the Oak Ridge laboratory he at once informed Groves of the movement. It would have been difficult for the General to forbid the men on research to sign the document. He therefore hit on a different method of stopping its further circulation. Szilard's petition was declared "secret." And the law stated that secret papers could only be taken from one place to another under military guard. Thus all Groves had to do was to decree: "Unfortunately, we cannot spare any troops for the protection of this document. Until we can do so it must be kept locked up."

In Chicago the men working in the Metallurgical Laboratory were growing more and more restless. John A. Simpson, a young physicist who took a particularly active part in the efforts to prevent the bomb being dropped, states: "In June an extensive panel discussion was held within the Laboratory by several of the younger scientists, covering subjects ranging from the ways of using the bomb to international controls. Following these discussions the military officials refused to permit more than three people to enter into discussions on the problem at Laboratory meetings. The scientists then resorted to the fantastic technique of holding meetings in a small room, where a succession of about twenty people would, one at a time, enter to discuss these problems with a panel of two or three scientists selected for the evening."

Excitement ran so high in Chicago that eventually the Director, A. H. Compton, had a vote taken, through his deputy, Farrington Daniels, who put the following questions:

Which of the following procedures comes closest to your choice as the way in which any new weapon that we might develop should be used in the Japanese war?

(1) Use them in the manner that is from the military point of view most effective in bringing about prompt Japanese surrender at minimum cost to our own armed forces (23 votes, i.e. 15 per cent).

(2) Give a military demonstration in Japan, to be followed by a renewed opportunity for surrender before full use of the weapon (69 votes, i.e. 46 per cent).

(3) Give an experimental demonstration in this country with representatives of Japan present followed by a new opportunity for surrender before full use of weapon (39 votes, i.e. 26 per cent).

(4) Withhold military use of the weapons but make public experimental demonstration of their effectiveness (16 votes, i.e. 11 per cent).

(5) Maintain as secret as possible all developments of our new weapons and refrain from using them in this war (3 votes, i.e. 2 per cent).

Unfortunately the voting, in which 150 persons participated, took place without any previous debate. Consequently, the greatest number of votes, 69, were cast for the second alternative, suggesting a military demonstration in Japan. But after the first two bombs had been dropped on the centre of the town of Hiroshima and on Nagasaki most of the 69 voters explained that they had taken a "military demonstration in Japan" to mean an attack on purely military objectives, not on targets occupied also, in fact mainly, by civilians.

It will be noted from the above summary that, compared with alternative (2), 39 votes were cast for experimental demonstration in the United States, 23 for leaving the military authorities a free hand, 16 for a public demonstration without military use of the bomb, and 3 for keeping the whole affair secret and not employing the bomb in the current war.

Szilard had obtained the signatures of 67 prominent scientists before Groves had been able to stop further circulation of the petition. Szilard then sent his appeal direct to President Truman. But he only succeeded, by this procedure, in having the matter again referred to the body by which it had twice previously been held up, viz. the Interim Committee charged with advising the President in this fateful question. The most influential members of that committee in this matter were the four atomic physicists whose task it was to facilitate, as professional experts, the form that advice should take. These were Oppenheimer, Fermi, Compton, and Lawrence. For the third time within two months they had the opportunity to throw the weight of their authoritative opinion into the scale. Those who opposed the dropping of the bomb on Japan had good grounds for believing that the four scientists would now, after the Alamogordo test, revise their former judgement. For prior to 16 July no one had known whether and if so with what effect the new weapon would explode. But now all calculations had been exceeded ten and twenty times over. The participants in the experiment no longer spoke of the bomb and its effects as a "firecracker" but as a "shattering experience." Surely so great a shock would induce the committee to plead, at this eleventh hour, for a remission of the death sentence passed upon the prospective victims of the first atomic bombardment ever planned.

The argument which had carried most weight in the informal debates preceding the employment of the bomb was the consideration that although the new weapon would undoubtedly entail the sacrifice of very many human lives, on the other hand it might well prevent even greater destruction of life and property on both sides if it really should bring about an immediate end to the war. Ever since May the American public had remained deeply affected by reports of the exceptionally bloody fighting for the island of Okinawa. Although the Japanese knew that Germany had been defeated and that their own position was now hopeless, they continued to defend themselves with incredible obstinacy and contempt of death. More Americans had been killed or severely wounded on Okinawa alone than during the whole campaign for the reconquest of the Philippines. This fact gave rise to the fear that an invasion of Japan would cost hundreds of thousands of human lives on both sides.

When the four professional experts of the scientific panel set themselves once more to study the crucial problem of employment of the atomic bomb, the following question, Compton recalls, was submitted to them: "Can we think of any other means of ending the war quickly?"

But the dilemma represented by the alternatives of dropping the bomb or allowing the war to go on indefinitely did not, as we know today, correspond with the true nature of the situation. It was based, in exactly the same way as the earlier alternatives—"Either we build an atom bomb or Hitler will do it first"—on a false estimation of the plans and resources of the enemy.

The intelligence services of both the Army and the Navy of the United States were in fact at this date already convinced that the final downfall of Japan could only be a question of a few more weeks. Alfred MacCormack, Military Intelligence Director for the Pacific Theatre of War, recollects that "we had such complete control of the air over Japan that we knew when and from what port every ship would put to sea. The Japanese had no longer enough food in stock and their fuel reserves were practically exhausted. We had begun a secret process of mining all their harbours, which was steadily isolating them from the rest of the world. If we had brought this operation to its logical conclusion the destruction of Japan's cities with incendiary and other bombs would have been quite unnecessary. But General Norstad declared, at Washington, that this blockading action was a cowardly proceeding unworthy of the Air Force. It was therefore discontinued."

The surrender of Japan could not only have been achieved by intensification of the blockade. The chances of bringing it about by clever diplomacy were even more favourable. For Japan was at that time more than ripe for capitulation. The country was to a great extent willing to capitulate. At the end of April Fujimura, the Japanese Naval Attaché in the Third Reich, who had gone to Berne when Germany collapsed, was introduced by Dr Friedrich Hack, an anti-Nazi German, to three close colleagues of Allen Dulles, resident in the Swiss capital as chief of the American intelligence organization, the O.S.S. Fujimura told them he was ready to bring pressure to bear on his government with a view to inducing it to accept American capitulation terms. Almost at the same time the Military Attaché, General Okamoto, acting independently, approached the Dulles organization, through the International Settlements Bank at Basle, with a similar proposal. But both these plans came to nothing, as Washington did not wish to commit itself to a precise statement of terms and Tokyo gave no support whatever to the efforts of the two Japanese in Switzerland.

But another attempt made by Japan for the earliest possible restoration of peace might have been taken more seriously. At the suggestion of the Japanese Emperor a movement was initiated to end the war with the United States through the Soviet Union. The first steps toward that goal were taken 12 July—the very day on which the first consignment of components for the Alamogordo test of the atom bomb left Los Alamos. But the Russians had little interest in bringing the war to an end before they themselves entered it against Japan as had been determined at Yalta in the previous February. They accordingly at first did all they could to avoid consultation with the Japanese emissaries. When Ambassador Sato was at last given a hearing, the Russians only passed on Tokyo's proposals to the Americans after intentional delay, making light of their importance.

Washington, however, had long known of these manoeuvres, for the Americans had deciphered the Japanese secret code. They had been reading, ever since the middle of July, the urgent instructions sent by radio to Sato in Moscow by Prime Minister Tojo, as well as the replies of the Ambassador. Among other messages they had read the words: "Japan is defeated. We must face that fact and act accordingly."

But Truman, instead of exploiting diplomatically these significant indications of Japanese weakness, issued a proclamation on 26 July at the Potsdam Conference, which was bound to make it difficult for the Japanese to capitulate without "losing face" in the process. The President had at that date already been informed by General Groves, in an impressive report, that the experiment at Alamogordo had succeeded beyond all expectations. The American historian Robert J. C. Butow, who has made a comparative study from both American and Japanese sources of the events that preceded the collapse of Japan, is of the opinion that at this period the war could very well have been brought rapidly to an end by diplomatic measures, for example by conveying the conditions laid down in the Potsdam proclamation to Prince

Konoye—who had already been given the widest possible plenipotentiary powers by the Emperor—by the discreet use of political channels instead of broadcasting them to the entire world.

Butow writes: "Had the Allies given the Prince a week of grace in which to obtain his Government's support for acceptance of the proposals, the war might have ended towards the latter part of July or the very beginning of the month of August, without the atomic bomb and without Soviet participation in the conflict." [1]

But probably the main reason why the American government remained blind to the possibility of such measures was the knowledge that it possessed the atomic bomb. Instead of patiently undoing the knot it appeared more convenient to cut it with a slash or two of the shining new weapon.

It would no doubt have required considerable courage on the part of the responsible politicians and strategists concerned to renounce employment of the bomb for the time being. For they could not help fearing that the entire Manhattan Project, which had hitherto swallowed up nearly two billions of dollars, might perhaps be described, after the war, as a senseless waste of money. In that case the praise and fame they might otherwise expect would turn to mockery and censure.

President Truman, in his memoirs, writes that his "yes" decided the issue of the dropping of the bomb. On this passage General Groves remarked to the author: "Truman did not so much say 'yes' as not say 'no.' It would indeed have taken a lot of nerve to say 'no' at that time."

If even the President of the United States did not dare to change gear, any such action was far less to be expected of the four atomic experts of the scientific panel, who had never hitherto offered any serious resistance to the plans of their superiors. They felt themselves caught in a vast machinery and they certainly were inadequately informed as to the true political and strategic situation. [2] If at that time they had had the moral strength to protest on purely humane grounds against the dropping of the bomb, their attitude would no doubt have deeply impressed the President, the Cabinet, and the generals. Once more the four atomic scientists "only did their duty."

The hopes of those who opposed the use of the bomb were revived for a moment longer when they heard that Oppenheimer was closeted with General Groves at a specially arranged meeting. In reality, however, the scientist, in seeking this interview with Groves shortly before the bomb was dropped, merely desired in the first place to convince his companion that it would soon be time to think of constructing less primitive atomic weapons. Thus the sum of a thousand individual acts of an intensely conscientious character led eventually to an act of collective abandonment of conscience, horrifying in its magnitude.

---

1. See Robert J. Butow, *Japan's Decision to Surrender,* Hoover Library Publication No. 24, Stanford University Press, 1954, pp. 133–5. [Jungk's note.]

2. General Groves states that he, too, had not been told of the Japanese peace feelers. The State Department, on the other hand, though it knew every detail of the action taken by Tokyo in this connexion, had been given not the slightest warning of the imminent use of the new weapon. [Jungk's note.]

ERNESTO CHÉ GUEVARA (1928–1967), *Camilo*

When Columbus discovered Cuba in 1492, he called it "the most beautiful
land human eyes have ever seen." The island remained a Spanish colony
for four centuries, despite attempts by other nations to acquire it, including
a group of American diplomats who in 1854 tried to buy Cuba for use as
a slave state. In 1899 Cuba won independence from Spain, but fell under
the protection of the United States, which reserved the right to intervene in
Cuban internal affairs. The United States used that "right" several times in
order to suppress revolts against unpopular regimes.
Spanish colonists had made Cuba a one-crop economy—sugar—based on the
large plantation or latifundia, *a system that was retained when the Spanish*
were replaced by American absentee landlords and investors in the enor-
mously profitable sugar industry. Rural Cubans, however, lived in poverty,
squalor, ignorance, and disease; this, together with the corruption and bru-
tality of dictator Fulgencio Batista, generated popular support for the revo-
lutionary movement launched by the young lawyer Fidel Castro and his
guerrillas. On New Years' Day, 1959, Batista fled Cuba and his forces sur-
rendered to the rebel army.
Ché Guevara, born and trained as a doctor in Argentina, had been Castro's
chief lieutenant; in the new government he was president of the national
bank and then minister of industry. Camilo Cienfuegos, another of Castro's
top commanders, disappeared in 1959 en route by plane from Camaguey
to Havana. Ché's eulogy (1964), both reminiscence and propaganda, de-
scribes the making of a hero: like the archetypal hero, Camilo arrives un-
known from an unknown past; he becomes "an artist of the revolution"
and then disappears as mysteriously as he came. A year after the piece was
written, Guevara left Cuba to work for revolution in Bolivia, where in
1967 he was captured and killed by the Bolivian army. Largely through
the efforts of American and European commercial media, Ché has become
the kind of popular hero that he makes of Camilo—a process in which, as
in the piece itself, one observes the drama of the self supplanting revolu-
tionary ideology.

Memory is a way of reviving the past, the dead. To remember Camilo is to
remember things which are past or dead, and yet Camilo is a living part of
the Cuban Revolution, immortal by his very nature. I would like simply to
give our comrades of the Rebel Army an idea of who this invincible guerrilla
fighter was. I am able to do so, since, from the sad hours of the first setback

at Alegría de Pío on, we were always together; and it is my duty to do so, because, far more than a comrade in arms, in joys and victories, Camilo was a
real brother.

I never got to know him in Mexico, as he joined us at the last minute. He
had come from the United States without any previous recommendation, and
we didn't have any confidence in him—or in anyone else, in fact—in those
risky days. He came on the *Granma*,[1] just one among the eighty-two who
crossed the sea at the mercy of the elements to carry out a feat that was to
shake the entire continent. I realized what he was like before I actually got to
know him through hearing a characteristic exclamation of his during the disastrous battle of Alegría de Pío.[2]

I was wounded, stretched out in a clearing, next to a comrade covered
with blood who was firing his last rounds, ready to die fighting. I heard someone cry weakly: "We're lost. Let's surrender." And a clear voice from somewhere among the men shouted in reply: "Nobody surrenders here!"—
followed by a four-letter word.

The battle ended, we survived, and I went on breathing, thanks to the help
of Comrade Almeida. Five of us wandered around the steep cliffs near Cabo
Cruz. One clear moonlit night we came upon three other comrades sleeping
peacefully, without any fear of the soldiers. We jumped them, believing them
to be enemies. Nothing happened, but the incident served later as a standing
joke between us: the fact that I was among those who had caught them by
surprise, and the fact that it was I who had to raise the white flag so that they
would not shoot us, mistaking us for Batista soldiers.

And so then there were eight of us. Camilo was hungry and wanted to eat;
he didn't care what or where, he simply wanted to eat. This led to some serious disagreements with him, because he continually wanted to approach
bohíos [peasant huts] to ask for food. Twice, for having followed the advice
of "the hungry ones," we nearly fell into the hands of enemy soldiers who
had killed dozens of our comrades. On the ninth day "the hungry ones" won
out, and we approached a *bohío,* ate, and all got sick. And among the sickest
was, naturally, Camilo, who, like a hungry lion, had gulped down an entire
kid.

During that period I was more a medic than a soldier. I put Camilo on a
special diet and ordered him to stay behind in the *bohío,* where he would receive proper attention. That trouble passed, and we were together again, and
the days lengthened into weeks and months during which many comrades
were killed. Camilo showed his mettle, earning the rank of lieutenant of the
vanguard of our one and only beloved column, which would later be called
the José Martí[3] Column No. 1, under Fidel's personal command.

Almeida and Raúl were captains; Camilo, lieutenant of the vanguard;
Efigenio Ameijeiras, leader of the rear guard; Ramiro Valdés, lieutenant in
one of Raúl's platoons; and Calixto, soldier in another platoon. In other
words, all our forces were born there, where I was the group's lieutenant

---

1. *Granma:* the yacht on which Castro, Guevara, and other rebels returned from
Mexico to begin guerrilla war in December 1956.
2. Alegría de Pío: a sugar plantation where, on December 5, the invaders suffered
their first war casualties.
3. José Martí: Cuban writer, poet, and leader of the movement for independence
from Spain.

medic. Later, following the battle of Uvero, I was given the rank of captain, and, a few days later, the rank of major and the command of a column.

One day Camilo was made captain of the column that I commanded, the Fourth Column. We bore that number to deceive the enemy, as actually there were only two. And it was there that Camilo began his career of exploits, and it was with untiring effort and extraordinary zeal that, time and again, he hunted down enemy soldiers. Once he shot a soldier of the enemy's scouting party at such close range that he caught the man's rifle before it even hit the ground. Another time he planned to let the first of the enemy soldiers go by until he was abreast of our troop, and then open flank fire. The ambush never materialized, because someone in our group got nervous and opened fire before the enemy got close enough. By then Camilo was "Camilo, Lord of the Vanguard," a real guerrilla fighter who was able to assert his individuality through his own colorful way of fighting.

I recall my anxiety during the second attack on Pino del Agua, when Fidel ordered me to stay with him and gave Camilo the responsibility of attacking one of the enemy's flanks. The idea was simple. Camilo was to attack and take one end of the enemy camp and then surround it. The firing started, and he and his men took the sentry post and continued advancing, entering the settlement, killing or taking prisoner every soldier in their path. The town was taken house by house until finally the enemy organized its resistance and the barrage of bullets began to take its toll among our ranks. Valuable comrades, among them Noda and Capote, lost their lives in this battle.

An enemy machine gunner advanced, surrounded by his men, but at a given moment he found himself amidst a veritable storm of gunfire. The machine gunner's assistants were killed, and the soldier manning the gun dropped it and fled. It was dawn. The attack had begun at night. Camilo hurled himself across the machine gun to seize and defend it, and was shot twice. A bullet pierced his left thigh, and another hit him in the abdomen. He got away, and his comrades carried him. We were two kilometers away, with the enemy between us. We could hear machine-gun bursts and shouting: "There goes Camilo's gun!" "That's Camilo firing!" and *vivas* for Batista. We all thought Camilo had been killed. Later we praised his luck that the bullet had entered and left his abdomen without hitting his intestines or any vital organ.

Then came the fateful day of April 9, and Camilo, the trailblazer, went to the Oriente plains and became a legend, striking terror into the heart of the enemy forces mobilized in the Bayamo area. Once he was surrounded by 600 men, and there were only twenty in the rebel force. They resisted an entire day against an enemy advance that included two tanks, and at night they made a spectacular escape.

Later came the offensive and, in the face of imminent danger and the concentration of forces, Camilo was called, as he was the man Fidel trusted to leave in his place when he went to a specific front. Then came the marvelous story of the invasion and his chain of victories on the plains of Las Villas—a difficult feat, as the terrain afforded little natural protection. These actions were magnificent for their audacity, and at the same time one could already see Camilo's political attitude, his decision regarding political problems, his strength and his faith in the people.

Camilo was happy, down to earth, and a joker. I remember that in the

Sierra a peasant, one of our great, magnificent, anonymous heroes, had been nicknamed by Camilo, who accompanied this with a dirty gesture. One day the peasant came to see me as head of the column, complaining that he shouldn't be insulted and that he was no ventriloquist. As I didn't understand, I went to speak with Camilo so that he could explain the man's strange attitude. What happened was that Camilo had looked at the man with an air of disrespect and called him a ventriloquist, and, as the peasant didn't know what a ventriloquist was, he was terribly offended.

Camilo had a little alcohol burner, and he used to cook cats and offer them as a delicacy to new recruits who joined us. It was one of the many tests of the Sierra, and more than one failed this preliminary "examination" when he refused to eat the proffered cat. Camilo was a man of anecdotes, a million anecdotes. They were a part of his nature. His appreciation of people and his ability to get along with them were a part of his personality. These qualities, which today we sometimes forget or overlook, were present in all his actions, something precious that few men can attain. It is true, as Fidel has said, that he had no great amount of book learning, but he had the natural intelligence of the people who had chosen him from among thousands to place him in that privileged place earned by his audacity, his tenacity, his intelligence and devotion. Camilo was uncompromisingly loyal to two things, and with the same results: He had unlimited loyalty and devotion to Fidel and the people. Fidel and the people march together, and Camilo's devotion was projected toward them both.

Who killed Camilo? Who killed the man who, in the lives of others like him, lives on in the people? Such men do not die so long as the people do not authorize it. The enemy killed him, killed him because they wanted him to die, because there are no completely safe airplanes, because pilots are not able to acquire all the necessary experience, because he was overloaded with work and had to be in Havana as quickly as possible. He was killed by his drive.

Camilo did not measure danger. He utilized it as a game, he played with it, he courted it, he attracted and handled it and, with his guerrilla's mentality, a mere cloud could not detain or deflect him from the line he was following. It happened at a time everyone knew him, admired and loved him; it could have happened before, and then his story would have been known merely as that of a guerrilla captain. There will be many Camilos, as Fidel has said; and there have been Camilos, I can add—Camilos who died before completing the magnificent work he had managed to complete, thus entering the pages of history. Camilo and the other Camilos—the ones who fell early and those still to come—are the index of the people's strength; they are the most complete expression of the heights that can be reached by a nation fighting to defend its purest ideals and with complete faith in the fulfillment of its noblest goals.

There is too much to be said to allow me to put his essence into a lifeless mold, which would be equivalent to killing him. It is better to leave it like this, in general descriptive terms, without spelling out in black and white his socio-economic ideology, which was not precisely defined. But we must always bear in mind that there was never a man—not even before the revolution—comparable to Camilo: a complete revolutionary, a man of the people, an artist of the revolution, sprung from the heart of the Cuban nation. His mind was incapable of the slightest slackening or disappointment. He is an object of daily remembrance; he is the one who did this or that, something by Camilo; he who left his distinct and indelible imprint on the Cuban Revolution, who is present among those who fell early in their revolutionary careers and those heroes who are yet to come.

In his constant and eternal rebirth, Camilo is the image of the people.

MALCOLM X (1925–1965),
The Ballot or the Bullet

In his Autobiography *(1964), Malcolm X wrote, "It has always been my belief that I will die by violence. I have done all that I can to be prepared." The belief was correct: Malcolm was assassinated on February 21, 1965, as he was about to address a large meeting in the Audubon Ballroom, New York.*

Born in Omaha, Nebraska, Malcolm Little was converted in prison to the Nation of Islam (Black Muslims), a nationalist, separatist and antiwhite organization. He became a national spokesman for the Muslims, but broke with them in March 1964 to form the Organization for Afro-American Unity. Two extended trips to Africa and the Middle East confirmed his rejection of Black Muslim ideology, for in a world of multicolored Muslims Malcolm perceived that " 'white man,' as commonly used, means complexion only secondarily; primarily it described attitudes and actions. In America, 'white man' meant specific attitudes and actions toward the black man, and toward all other non-white men." Shortly before his death, Malcolm stated in various interviews that he no longer believed in a separate black state, that blacks must have political understanding in order to act effectively, and that the black movement in America is not simply racial but is part of "a global rebellion of the oppressed against the oppressor, the exploited against the exploiter."

Unlike Frederick Douglass and W. E. B. duBois, Malcolm X makes no attempt to imitate the rhetoric of educated white people; his primary audience, unlike theirs, was not middle-class white America but the black ghetto of his own roots; his purpose was less to explain the black man's condition than to change it. That background, that audience, and that purpose are evident in the speech below, given in Cleveland in April 1964.

Mr. Moderator, Brother Lomax, brothers and sisters, friends and enemies: I just can't believe everyone in here is a friend and I don't want to leave anybody out. The question tonight, as I understand it, is "The Negro Revolt, and Where Do We Go From Here?" or "What Next?" In my little humble way of understanding it, it points toward either the ballot or the bullet.

Before we try and explain what is meant by the ballot or the bullet, I would like to clarify something concerning myself. I'm still a Muslim, my religion is still Islam. That's my personal belief. Just as Adam Clayton Powell is a Christian minister who heads the Abyssinian Baptist Church in New

York, but at the same time takes part in the political struggles to try and bring about rights to the black people in this country; and Dr. Martin Luther King is a Christian minister down in Atlanta, Georgia, who heads another organization fighting for the civil rights of black people in this country; and Rev. Galamison, I guess you've heard of him, is another Christian minister in New York who has been deeply involved in the school boycotts to eliminate segregated education; well, I myself am a minister, not a Christian minister, but a Muslim minister; and I believe in action on all fronts by whatever means necessary.

Although I'm still a Muslim, I'm not here tonight to discuss my religion. I'm not here to try and change your religion. I'm not here to argue or discuss anything that we differ about, because it's time for us to submerge our differences and realize that it is best for us to first see that we have the same problem, a common problem—a problem that will make you catch hell whether you're a Baptist, or a Methodist, or a Muslim, or a nationalist. Whether you're educated or illiterate, whether you live on the boulevard or in the alley, you're going to catch hell just like I am. We're all in the same boat and we all are going to catch the same hell from the same man. He just happens to be a white man. All of us have suffered here, in this country, political oppression at the hands of the white man, economic exploitation at the hands of the white man, and social degradation at the hands of the white man.

Now in speaking like this, it doesn't mean that we're anti-white, but it does mean we're anti-exploitation, we're anti-degradation, we're anti-oppression. And if the white man doesn't want us to be anti-him, let him stop oppressing and exploiting and degrading us. Whether we are Christians or Muslims or nationalists or agnostics or atheists, we must first learn to forget our differences. If we have differences, let us differ in the closet; when we come out in front, let us not have anything to argue about until we get finished arguing with the man. If the late President Kennedy could get together with Khrushchev and exchange some wheat, we certainly have more in common with each other than Kennedy and Khrushchev had with each other.

If we don't do something real soon, I think you'll have to agree that we're going to be forced either to use the ballot or the bullet. It's one or the other in 1964. It isn't that time is running out—time has run out! 1964 threatens to be the most explosive year America has ever witnessed. The most explosive year. Why? It's also a political year. It's the year when all of the white politicians will be back in the so-called Negro community jiving you and me for some votes. The year when all of the white political crooks will be right back in your and my community with their false promises, building up our hopes for a letdown, with their trickery and their treachery, with their false promises which they don't intend to keep. As they nourish these dissatisfactions, it can only lead to one thing, an explosion; and now we have the type of black man on the scene in America today—I'm sorry, Brother Lomax—who just doesn't intend to turn the other cheek any longer.

Don't let anybody tell you anything about the odds are against you. If they draft you, they send you to Korea and make you face 800 million Chinese. If you can be brave over there, you can be brave right here. These odds aren't as great as those odds. And if you fight here, you will at least know what you're fighting for.

I'm not a politician, not even a student of politics; in fact, I'm not a student of much of anything. I'm not a Democrat, I'm not a Republican, and I don't even consider myself an American. If you and I were Americans, there'd be no problem. Those Hunkies that just got off the boat, they're already Americans; Polacks are already Americans; the Italian refugees are already Americans. Everything that came out of Europe, every blue-eyed thing, is already an American. And as long as you and I have been over here, we aren't Americans yet.

Well, I am one who doesn't believe in deluding myself. I'm not going to sit at your table and watch you eat, with nothing on my plate, and call myself a diner. Sitting at the table doesn't make you a diner, unless you eat some of what's on that plate. Being here in America doesn't make you an American. Being born here in America doesn't make you an American. Why, if birth made you American, you wouldn't need any legislation, you wouldn't need any amendments to the Constitution, you wouldn't be faced with civil-rights filibustering in Washington, D. C., right now. They don't have to pass civil-rights legislation to make a Polack an American.

No, I'm not an American. I'm one of the 22 million black people who are the victims of Americanism. One of the 22 million black people who are the victims of democracy, nothing but disguised hypocrisy. So, I'm not standing here speaking to you as an American, or a patriot, or a flag-saluter, or a flag-waver—no, not I. I'm speaking as a victim of this American system. And I see America through the eyes of the victim. I don't see any American dream; I see an American nightmare.

These 22 million victims are waking up. Their eyes are coming open. They're beginning to see what they used to only look at. They're becoming politically mature. They are realizing that there are new political trends from coast to coast. As they see these new political trends, it's possible for them to see that every time there's an election the races are so close that they have to have a recount. They had to recount in Massachusetts to see who was going to be governor, it was so close. It was the same way in Rhode Island, in Minnesota, and in many other parts of the country. And the same with Kennedy and Nixon when they ran for president. It was so close they had to count all over again. Well, what does this mean? It means that when white people are evenly divided, and black people have a bloc of votes of their own, it is left up to them to determine who's going to sit in the White House and who's going to be in the dog house.

It was the black man's vote that put the present administration in Washington, D. C. Your vote, your dumb vote, your ignorant vote, your wasted vote put in an administration in Washington, D. C., that has seen fit to pass every kind of legislation imaginable, saving you until last, then filibustering on top of that. And your and my leaders have the audacity to run around clapping their hands and talk about how much progress we're making. And what a good president we have. If he wasn't good in Texas, he sure can't be good in Washington, D. C. Because Texas is a lynch state. It is in the same breath as Mississippi, no different; only they lynch you in Texas with a Texas accent and lynch you in Mississippi with a Mississippi accent. And these Negro leaders have the audacity to go and have some coffee in the White House with a Texan, a Southern cracker—that's all he is—and then come out and tell you and me that he's going to be better for us because, since he's from the South, he knows how to deal with the Southerners. What kind of logic is that? Let Eastland be president, he's from the South too. He should be better able to deal with them than Johnson.

In this present administration they have in the House of Representatives 257 Democrats to only 177 Republicans. They control two-thirds of the House vote. Why can't they pass something that will help you and me? In the Senate, there are 67 senators who are of the Democratic Party. Only 33 of them are Republicans. Why, the Democrats have got the government sewed up, and you're the one who sewed it up for them. And what have they given you for it? Four years in office, and just now getting around to some civil-rights legislation. Just now, after everything else is gone, out of the way, they're going to sit down now and play with you all summer long—the same old giant con game that they call filibuster. All those are in cahoots together. Don't you ever think they're not in cahoots together, for the man that is heading the civil-rights filibuster is a man from Georgia named Richard Russell. When Johnson became president, the first man he asked for when he got back to Washington, D. C., was "Dicky"—that's how tight they are. That's his boy, that's his pal, that's his buddy. But they're playing that old con game. One of them makes believe he's for you, and he's got it fixed where the other one is so tight against you, he never has to keep his promise.

So it's time in 1964 to wake up. And when you see them coming up with that kind of conspiracy, let them know your eyes are open. And let them know you got something else that's wide open too. It's got to be the ballot or the bullet. The ballot or the bullet. If you're afraid to use an expression like that, you should get on out of the country, you should get back in the cotton patch, you should get back in the alley. They get all the Negro vote, and after they get it, the Negro gets nothing in return. All they did when they got to Washington was give a few big Negroes big jobs. Those big Negroes didn't need big jobs, they already had jobs. That's camouflage, that's trickery, that's treachery, window-dressing. I'm not trying to knock out the Democrats for the Republicans, we'll get to them in a minute. But it is true—you put the Democrats first and the Democrats put you last.

Look at it the way it is. What alibis do they use, since they control Congress and the Senate? What alibi do they use when you and I ask, "Well, when are you going to keep your promise?" They blame the Dixiecrats. What is a Dixiecrat? A Democrat. A Dixiecrat is nothing but a Democrat in disguise. The titular head of the Democrats is also the head of the Dixiecrats, because the Dixiecrats are a part of the Democratic Party. The Democrats have never kicked the Dixiecrats out of the party. The Dixiecrats bolted themselves once, but the Democrats didn't put them out. Imagine, these low-down Southern segregationists put the Northern Democrats down. But the Northern Democrats have never put the Dixiecrats down. No, look at that thing the way it is. They have got a con game going on, a political con game, and you and I are in the middle. It's time for you and me to wake up and start looking at it like it is, and trying to understand it like it is; and then we can deal with it like it is.

The Dixiecrats in Washington, D. C., control the key committees that run the government. The only reason the Dixiecrats control these committees is because they have seniority. The only reason they have seniority is because they come from states where Negroes can't vote. This is not even a government that's based on democracy. It is not a government that is made up of representatives of the people. Half of the people in the South can't even vote. Eastland is not even supposed to be in Washington. Half of the senators and congressmen who occupy these key positions in Washington, D. C., are there illegally, are there unconstitutionally.

I was in Washington, D. C., a week ago Thursday, when they were debating whether or not they should let the bill come onto the floor. And in the back of the room where the Senate meets, there's a huge map of the United States, and on that map it shows the location of Negroes throughout the country. And it shows that the Southern section of the country, the states that are most heavily concentrated with Negroes, are the ones that have senators and congressmen standing up filibustering and doing all other kinds of trickery to keep the Negro from being able to vote. This is pitiful. But it's not pitiful for us any longer; it's actually pitiful for the white man, because soon now, as the Negro awakens a little more and sees the vise that he's in, sees the bag that he's in, sees the real game that he's in, then the Negro's going to develop a new tactic.

These senators and congressmen actually violate the constitutional amendments that guarantee the people of that particular state or county the right to vote. And the Constitution itself has within it the machinery to expel any representative from a state where the voting rights of the people are violated. You don't even need new legislation. Any person in Congress right now, who is there from a state or a district where the voting rights of the people are violated, that particular person should be expelled from Congress. And when you expel him, you've removed one of the obstacles in the path of any real meaningful legislation in this country. In fact, when you expel them, you don't need new legislation, because they will be replaced by black representatives from counties and districts where the black man is in the majority, not in the minority.

If the black man in these Southern states had his full voting rights, the key Dixiecrats in Washington, D. C., which means the key Democrats in Washington, D. C., would lose their seats. The Democratic Party itself would lose its power. It would cease to be powerful as a party. When you see the amount of power that would be lost by the Democratic Party if it were to lose the Dixiecrat wing, or branch, or element, you can see where it's against the interests of the Democrats to give voting rights to Negroes in states where the Democrats have been in complete power and authority ever since the Civil War. You just can't belong to that party without analyzing it.

I say again, I'm not anti-Democrat, I'm not anti-Republican, I'm not anti-anything. I'm just questioning their sincerity, and some of the strategy that they've been using on our people by promising them promises that they don't intend to keep. When you keep the Democrats in power, you're keeping the Dixiecrats in power. I doubt that my good Brother Lomax will deny that. A vote for a Democrat is a vote for a Dixiecrat. That's why, in 1964, it's time now for you and me to become more politically mature and realize what the ballot is for; what we're supposed to get when we cast a ballot; and that if we don't cast a ballot, it's going to end up in a situation where we're going to have to cast a bullet. It's either a ballot or a bullet.

In the North, they do it a different way. They have a system that's known as gerrymandering, whatever that means. It means when Negroes become too heavily concentrated in a certain area, and begin to gain too much political power, the white man comes along and changes the district lines. You may say, "Why do you keep saying white man?" Because it's the white man who does it. I haven't ever seen any Negro changing any lines. They don't let him get near the line. It's the white man who does this. And usually, it's the white man who grins at you the most, and pats you on the back, and is supposed to be your friend. He may be friendly, but he's not your friend.

So, what I'm trying to impress upon you, in essence, is this: You and I in America are faced not with a segregationist conspiracy, we're faced with a government conspiracy. Everyone who's filibustering is a senator—that's the government. Everyone who's finagling in Washington, D. C., is a congressman—that's the government. You don't have anybody putting blocks in your path but people who are a part of the government. The same government that you go abroad to fight for and die for is the government that is in a conspiracy to deprive you of your voting rights, deprive you of your economic opportunities, deprive you of decent housing, deprive you of decent education. You don't need to go to the employer alone, it is the government itself, the government of America, that is responsible for the oppression and exploitation and degradation of black people in this country. And you should drop it in their lap. This government has failed the Negro. This so-called democracy has failed the Negro. And all these white liberals have definitely failed the Negro.

So, where do we go from here? First, we need some friends. We need some new allies. The entire civil-rights struggle needs a new interpretation, a broader interpretation. We need to look at this civil-rights thing from another angle—from the inside as well as from the outside. To those of us whose philosophy is black nationalism, the only way you can get involved in the civil-rights struggle is give it a new interpretation. That old interpretation excluded us. It kept us out. So, we're giving a new interpretation to the civil-rights struggle, an interpretation that will enable us to come into it, take part in it. And these handkerchief-heads who have been dillydallying and pussyfooting and compromising—we don't intend to let them pussyfoot and dillydally and compromise any longer.

How can you thank a man for giving you what's already yours? How then can you thank him for giving you only part of what's already yours? You haven't even made progress, if what's being given to you, you should have had already. That's not progress. And I love my Brother Lomax, the way he pointed out we're right back where we were in 1954. We're not even as far up as we were in 1954. We're behind where we were in 1954. There's more segregation now than there was in 1954. There's more racial animosity, more racial hatred, more racial violence today in 1964, than there was in 1954. Where is the progress?

And now you're facing a situation where the young Negro's coming up. They don't want to hear that "turn-the-other-cheek" stuff, no. In Jacksonville, those were teenagers, they were throwing Molotov cocktails. Negroes have never done that before. But it shows you there's a new deal coming in. There's new thinking coming in. There's new strategy coming in. It'll be Molotov cocktails this month, hand grenades next month, and something else next month. It'll be ballots, or it'll be bullets. It'll be liberty, or it will be death. The only difference about this kind of death—it'll be reciprocal. You know what is meant by "reciprocal"? That's one of Brother Lomax's words, I stole it from him. I don't usually deal with those big words because I don't usually deal with big people. I deal with small people. I find you can get a whole lot of small people and whip hell out of a whole lot of big people. They haven't got anything to lose, and they've got everything to gain. And they'll let you know in a minute: "It takes two to tango; when I go, you go."

The black nationalists, those whose philosophy is black nationalism, in bringing about this new interpretation of the entire meaning of civil rights, look upon it as meaning, as Brother Lomax has pointed out, equality of opportunity. Well, we're justified in seeking civil rights, if it means equality of opportunity, because all we're doing there is trying to collect for our investment. Our mothers and fathers invested sweat and blood. Three hundred and ten years we worked in this country without a dime in return—I mean without a *dime* in return. You let the white man walk around here talking about how rich this country is, but you never stop to think how it got rich so quick. It got rich because you made it rich.

You take the people who are in this audience right now. They're poor, we're all poor as individuals. Our weekly salary individually amounts to hardly anything. But if you take the salary of everyone in here collectively it'll fill up a whole lot of baskets. It's a lot of wealth. If you can collect the wages of just these people right here for a year, you'll be rich—richer than rich. When you look at it like that, think how rich Uncle Sam had to become, not with this handful, but millions of black people. Your and my mother and father, who didn't work an eight-hour shift, but worked from "can't see" in the morning until "can't see" at night, and worked for nothing, making the white man rich, making Uncle Sam rich.

This is our investment. This is our contribution—our blood. Not only did we give of our free labor, we gave of our blood. Every time he had a call to arms, we were the first ones in uniform. We died on every battlefield the white man had. We have made a greater sacrifice than anybody who's standing up in America today. We have made a greater contribution and have collected less. Civil rights, for those of us whose philosophy is black nationalism, means: "Give it to us now. Don't wait for next year. Give it to us yesterday, and that's not fast enough."

I might stop right here to point out one thing. Whenever you're going after something that belongs to you, anyone who's depriving you of the right to have it is a criminal. Understand that. Whenever you are going after something that is yours, you are within your legal rights to lay claim to it. And anyone who puts forth any effort to deprive you of that which is yours, is breaking the law, is a criminal. And this was pointed out by the Supreme Court decision. It outlawed segregation. Which means segregation is against the law. Which means a segregationist is breaking the law. A segregationist is a criminal. You can't label him as anything other than that. And when you demonstrate against segregation, the law is on your side. The Supreme Court is on your side.

Now, who is it that opposes you in carrying out the law? The police department itself. With police dogs and clubs. Whenever you demonstrate against segregation, whether it is segregated education, segregated housing, or anything else, the law is on your side, and anyone who stands in the way is not the law any longer. They are breaking the law, they are not representatives of the law. Any time you demonstrate against segregation and a man has the audacity to put a police dog on you, kill that dog, kill him, I'm telling you, kill that dog. I say it, if they put me in jail tomorrow, kill—that—dog. Then you'll put a stop to it. Now, if these white people in here don't want to see that kind of action, get down and tell the mayor to tell the police department to pull the dogs in. That's all you have to do. If you don't do it, someone else will.

If you don't take this kind of stand, your little children will grow up and look at you and think "shame." If you don't take an uncompromising stand —I don't mean go out and get violent; but at the same time you should never be nonviolent unless you run into some nonviolence. I'm nonviolent with those who are nonviolent with me. But when you drop that violence on me, then you've made me go insane, and I'm not responsible for what I do. And that's the way every Negro should get. Any time you know you're within the law, within your legal rights, within your moral rights, in accord with justice, then die for what you believe in. But don't die alone. Let your dying be reciprocal. This is what is meant by equality. What's good for the goose is good for the gander.

When we begin to get in this area, we need new friends, we need new allies. We need to expand the civil-rights struggle to a higher level—to the level of human rights. Whenever you are in a civil-rights struggle, whether you know it or not, you are confining yourself to the jurisdiction of Uncle Sam. No one from the outside world can speak out in your behalf as long as your struggle is a civil-rights struggle. Civil rights comes within the domestic affairs of this country. All of our African brothers and our Asian brothers and our Latin-American brothers cannot open their mouths and interfere in the domestic affairs of the United States. And as long as it's civil rights, this comes under the jurisdiction of Uncle Sam.

But the United Nations has what's known as the charter of human rights, it has a committee that deals in human rights. You may wonder why all of the atrocities that have been committed in Africa and in Hungary and in Asia and in Latin America are brought before the UN, and the Negro problem is never brought before the UN. This is part of the conspiracy. This old, tricky, blue-eyed liberal who is supposed to be your and my friend, supposed to be in our corner, supposed to be subsidizing our struggle, and supposed to be acting in the capacity of an adviser, never tells you anything about human rights. They keep you wrapped up in civil rights. And you spend so much time barking up the civil-rights tree, you don't even know there's a human-rights tree on the same floor.

When you expand the civil-rights struggle to the level of human rights, you can then take the case of the black man in this country before the nations in the UN. You can take it before the General Assembly. You can take Uncle Sam before a world court. But the only level you can do it on is the level of human rights. Civil rights keeps you under his restrictions, under his jurisdiction. Civil rights keeps you in his pocket. Civil rights means you're asking Uncle Sam to treat you right. Human rights are something you were born with. Human rights are your God-given rights. Human rights are the rights that are recognized by all nations of this earth. And any time any one violates your human rights, you can take them to the world court. Uncle Sam's hands are dripping with blood, dripping with the blood of the black man in this country. He's the earth's number-one hypocrite. He has the audacity—yes, he has—imagine him posing as the leader of the free world. The free world!—and you over here singing "We Shall Overcome." Expand the civil-rights struggle to the level of human rights, take it into the United Nations, where our African brothers can throw their weight on our side, where our Asian brothers can throw their weight on our side, where our Latin-American brothers can throw their weight on our side, and where 800 million Chinamen are sitting there waiting to throw their weight on our side.

Let the world know how bloody his hands are. Let the world know the hypocrisy that's practiced over here. Let it be the ballot or the bullet. Let him know that it must be the ballot or the bullet.

When you take your case to Washington, D. C., you're taking it to the criminal who's responsible; it's like running from the wolf to the fox. They're all in cahoots together. They all work political chicanery and make you look like a chump before the eyes of the world. Here you are walking around in America, getting ready to be drafted and sent abroad, like a tin soldier, and when you get over there, people ask you what are you fighting for, and you have to stick your tongue in your cheek. No, take Uncle Sam to court, take him before the world.

By ballot I only mean freedom. Don't you know—I disagree with Lomax on this issue—that the ballot is more important than the dollar? Can I prove it? Yes. Look in the UN. There are poor nations in the UN; yet those poor nations can get together with their voting power and keep the rich nations from making a move. They have one nation—one vote, everyone has an equal vote. And when those brothers from Asia, and Africa and the darker parts of this earth get together, their voting power is sufficient to hold Sam in check. Or Russia in check. Or some other section of the earth in check. So, the ballot is most important.

Right now, in this country, if you and I, 22 million African-Americans—that's what we are—Africans who are in America. You're nothing but Africans. Nothing but Africans. In fact, you'd get farther calling yourself African instead of Negro. Africans don't catch hell. You're the only one catching hell. They don't have to pass civil-rights bills for Africans. An African can go anywhere he wants right now. All you've got to do is tie your head up. That's right, go anywhere you want. Just stop being a Negro. Change your name to Hoogagagooba. That'll show you how silly the white man is. You're dealing with a silly man. A friend of mine who's very dark put a turban on his head and went into a restaurant in Atlanta before they called themselves desegregated. He went into a white restaurant, he sat down, they served him, and he said, "What would happen if a Negro came in here?" And there he's sitting, black as night, but because he had his head wrapped up the waitress looked back at him and says, "Why, there wouldn't no nigger dare come in here."

So, you're dealing with a man whose bias and prejudice are making him lose his mind, his intelligence, every day. He's frightened. He looks around and sees what's taking place on this earth, and he sees that the pendulum of time is swinging in your direction. The dark people are waking up. They're losing their fear of the white man. No place where he's fighting right now is he winning. Everywhere he's fighting, he's fighting someone your and my complexion. And they're beating him. He can't win any more. He's won his last battle. He failed to win the Korean War. He couldn't win it. He had to sign a truce. That's a loss. Any time Uncle Sam, with all his machinery for warfare, is held to a draw by some rice-eaters, he's lost the battle. He had to sign a truce. America's not supposed to sign a truce. She's supposed to be bad. But she's not bad any more. She's bad as long as she can use her hydrogen bomb, but she can't use hers for fear Russia might use hers. Russia can't use hers, for fear that Sam might use his. So, both of them are weaponless. They can't use the weapon because each's weapon nullifies the other's. So the only place where action can take place is on the ground. And the white man can't win another war fighting on the ground. Those days are over. The black man knows it, the brown man knows it, the red man knows it, and the yellow man knows it. So they engage him in guerrilla warfare. That's not his style. You've got to have heart to be a guerrilla warrior, and he hasn't got any heart. I'm telling you now.

I just want to give you a little briefing on guerrilla warfare because, before you know it, before you know it—It takes heart to be a guerrilla warrior because you're on your own. In conventional warfare you have tanks and a whole lot of other people with you to back you up, planes over your head and all that kind of stuff. But a guerrilla is on his own. All you have is a rifle, some sneakers and a bowl of rice, and that's all you need—and a lot of heart. The Japanese on some of those islands in the Pacific, when the American soldiers landed, one Japanese sometimes could hold the whole army off. He'd just wait until the sun went down, and when the sun went down they were all equal. He would take his little blade and slip from bush to bush, and from American to American. The white soldiers couldn't cope with that. Whenever you see a white soldier that fought in the Pacific, he has the shakes, he has a nervous condition, because they scared him to death.

The same thing happened to the French up in French Indochina. People who just a few years previously were rice farmers got together and ran the heavily-mechanized French army out of Indochina. You don't need it— modern warfare today won't work. This is the day of the guerrilla. They did the same thing in Algeria. Algerians, who were nothing but Bedouins, took a rifle and sneaked off to the hills, and de Gaulle and all of his highfalutin' war machinery couldn't defeat those guerrillas. Nowhere on this earth does the white man win in a guerrilla warfare. It's not his speed. Just as guerrilla warfare is prevailing in Asia and in parts of Africa and in parts of Latin America, you've got to be mighty naive, or you've got to play the black man cheap, if you don't think someday he's going to wake up and find that it's got to be the ballot or the bullet.

I would like to say, in closing, a few things concerning the Muslim Mosque, Inc., which we established recently in New York City. It's true we're Muslims and our religion is Islam, but we don't mix our religion with our politics and our economics and our social and civil activities—not any more. We keep our religion in our mosque. After our religious services are over, then as Muslims we become involved in political action, economic action and social and civic action. We become involved with anybody, any-where, any time and in any manner that's designed to eliminate the evils, the political, economic and social evils that are afflicting the people of our community.

The political philosophy of black nationalism means that the black man should control the politics and the politicians in his own community; no more. The black man in the black community has to be re-educated into the science of politics so he will know what politics is supposed to bring him in return. Don't be throwing out any ballots. A ballot is like a bullet. You don't throw your ballots until you see a target, and if that target is not within your reach, keep your ballot in your pocket. The political philosophy of black nationalism is being taught in the Christian church. It's being taught in the NAACP. It's being taught in CORE meetings. It's being taught in SNCC [Student Nonviolent Coordinating Committee] meetings. It's being taught in Muslim meetings. It's being taught where nothing but atheists and agnostics come together. It's being taught everywhere. Black people are fed up with the dillydallying, pussyfooting, compromising approach that we've been using to-ward getting our freedom. We want freedom *now,* but we're not going to get it saying "We Shall Overcome." We've got to fight until we overcome.

The economic philosophy of black nationalism is pure and simple. It only means that we should control the economy of our community. Why should white people be running all the stores in our community? Why should white people be running the banks of our community? Why should the economy of our community be in the hands of the white man? Why? If a black man can't move his store into a white community, you tell me why a white man should move his store into a black community. The philosophy of black nationalism involves a re-education program in the black community in regards to economics. Our people have to be made to see that any time you take your dollar out of your community and spend it in a community where you don't live, the community where you live will get poorer and poorer, and the community where you spend your money will get richer and richer. Then you wonder why where you live is always a ghetto or a slum area. And where you and I are concerned, not only do we lose it when we spend it out of the community, but the white man has got all our stores in the community tied up; so that though we spend it in the community, at sundown the man who runs the store takes it over across town somewhere. He's got us in a vise.

So the economic philosophy of black nationalism means in every church, in every civic organization, in every fraternal order, it's time now for our people to become conscious of the importance of controlling the economy of our community. If we own the stores, if we operate the businesses, if we try and establish some industry in our own community, then we're developing to the position where we are creating employment for our own kind. Once you gain control of the economy of your own community, then you don't have to picket and boycott and beg some cracker downtown for a job in his business.

The social philosophy of black nationalism only means that we have to get together and remove the evils, the vices, alcoholism, drug addiction, and other evils that are destroying the moral fiber of our community. We our-selves have to lift the level of our community, the standard of our community to a higher level, make our own society beautiful so that we will be satisfied in our own social circles and won't be running around here trying to knock our way into a social circle where we're not wanted.

So I say, in spreading a gospel such as black nationalism, it is not designed to make the black man re-evaluate the white man—you know him already—but to make the black man re-evaluate himself. Don't change the white man's mind—you can't change his mind, and that whole thing about appealing to the moral conscience of America—America's conscience is bankrupt. She lost all conscience a long time ago. Uncle Sam has no conscience. They don't know what morals are. They don't try and eliminate an evil because it's evil, or because it's illegal, or because it's immoral; they eliminate it only when it threatens their existence. So you're wasting your time appealing to the moral conscience of a bankrupt man like Uncle Sam. If he had a conscience, he'd straighten this thing out with no more pressure being put upon him. So it is not necessary to change the white man's mind. We have to change our own mind. You can't change his mind about us. We've got to change our own minds about each other. We have to see each other with new eyes. We have to see each other as brothers and sisters. We have to come together with warmth so we can develop unity and harmony that's necessary to get this problem solved ourselves. How can we do this? How can we avoid jealousy? How can we avoid the suspicion and the divisions that exist in the community? I'll tell you how.

I have watched how Billy Graham comes into a city, spreading what he calls the gospel of Christ, which is only white nationalism. That's what he is. Billy Graham is a white nationalist; I'm a black nationalist. But since it's the natural tendency for leaders to be jealous and look upon a powerful figure like Graham with suspicion and envy, how is it possible for him to come into a city and get all the cooperation of the church leaders? Don't think because they're church leaders that they don't have weaknesses that make them envious and jealous—no, everybody's got it. It's not an accident that when they want to choose a cardinal [as Pope] over there in Rome, they get in a closet so you can't hear them cussing and fighting and carrying on.

Billy Graham comes in preaching the gospel of Christ, he evangelizes the gospel, he stirs everybody up, but he never tries to start a church. If he came in trying to start a church, all the churches would be against him. So, he just comes in talking about Christ and tells everybody who gets Christ to go to any church where Christ is; and in this way the church cooperates with him. So we're going to take a page from his book.

Our gospel is black nationalism. We're not trying to threaten the existence of any organization, but we're spreading the gospel of black nationalism. Anywhere there's a church that is also preaching and practicing the gospel of black nationalism, join that church. If the NAACP is preaching and practicing the gospel of black nationalism, join the NAACP. If CORE is spreading and practicing the gospel of black nationalism, join CORE. Join any organization that has a gospel that's for the uplift of the black man. And when you get into it and see them pussyfooting or compromising, pull out of it because that's not black nationalism. We'll find another one.

And in this manner, the organizations will increase in number and in quantity and in quality, and by August, it is then our intention to have a black nationalist convention which will consist of delegates from all over the country who are interested in the political, economic and social philosophy of black nationalism. After these delegates convene, we will hold a seminar, we will hold discussions, we will listen to everyone. We want to hear new ideas and new solutions and new answers. And at that time, if we see fit then to form a black nationalist party, we'll form a black nationalist party. If it's necessary to form a black nationalist army, we'll form a black nationalist army. It'll be the ballot or the bullet. It'll be liberty or it'll be death.

It's time for you and me to stop sitting in this country, letting some cracker senators, Northern crackers and Southern crackers, sit there in Washington, D. C., and come to a conclusion in their mind that you and I are supposed to have civil rights. There's no white man going to tell me anything about *my* rights. Brothers and sisters, always remember, if it doesn't take senators and congressmen and presidential proclamations to give freedom to the white man, it is not necessary for legislation or proclamation or Supreme Court decisions to give freedom to the black man. You let that white man know, if this is a country of freedom, let it be a country of freedom; and if it's not a country of freedom, change it.

We will work with anybody, anywhere, at any time, who is genuinely interested in tackling the problem head-on, nonviolently as long as the enemy is nonviolent, but violent when the enemy gets violent. We'll work with you on the voter-registration drive, we'll work with you on rent strikes, we'll work with you on school boycotts—I don't believe in any kind of integration; I'm not even worried about it because I know you're not going to get it anyway; you're not going to get it because you're afraid to die; you've got to be ready to die if you try and force yourself on the white man, because he'll get just as violent as those crackers in Mississippi, right here in Cleveland. But we will still work with you on the school boycotts because we're against a segregated school system. A segrated school system produces children who, when they graduate, graduate with crippled minds. But this does not mean that a school is segregated because it's all black. A segregated school means a school that is controlled by people who have no real interest in it whatsoever.

Let me explain what I mean. A segregated district or community is a community in which people live, but outsiders control the politics and the economy of that community. They never refer to the white section as a segregated community. It's the all-Negro section that's a segregated community. Why? The white man controls his own school, his own bank, his own economy, his own politics, his own everything, his own community—but he also controls yours. When you're under someone else's control, you're segregated. They'll always give you the lowest or the worst that there is to offer, but it doesn't mean you're segregated just because you have your own. You've got to *control* your own. Just like the white man has control of his, you need to control yours.

You know the best way to get rid of segregation? The white man is more afraid of separation than he is of integration. Segregation means that he puts you away from him, but not far enough for you to be out of his jurisdiction; separation means you're gone. And the white man will integrate faster than he'll let you separate. So we will work with you against the segregated school system because it's criminal, because it is absolutely destructive, in every way imaginable, to the minds of the children who have to be exposed to that type of crippling education.

Last but not least, I must say this concerning the great controversy over rifles and shotguns. The only thing that I've ever said is that in areas where the government has proven itself either unwilling or unable to defend the lives and the property of Negroes, it's time for Negroes to defend themselves. Article number two of the constitutional amendments provides you and me the right to own a rifle or a shotgun. It is constitutionally legal to own a shotgun or a rifle. This doesn't mean you're going to get a rifle and form battalions and go out looking for white folks, although you'd be within your rights —I mean, you'd be justified; but that would be illegal and we don't do anything illegal. If the white man doesn't want the black man buying rifles and shotguns, then let the government do its job. That's all. And don't let the white man come to you and ask you what you think about what Malcolm says —why, you old Uncle Tom. He would never ask you if he thought you were going to say, "Amen!" No, he is making a Tom out of you.

So, this doesn't mean forming rifle clubs and going out looking for people, but it is time, in 1964, if you are a man, to let that man know. If he's not going to do his job in running the government and providing you and me with the protection that our taxes are supposed to be for, since he spends all those billions for his defense budget, he certainly can't begrudge you and me spending $12 or $15 for a single-shot, or double-action. I hope you understand. Don't go out shooting people, but any time, brothers and sisters, and especially the men in this audience—some of you wearing Congressional Medals of Honor, with shoulders this wide, chests this big, muscles that big —any time you and I sit around and read where they bomb a church and murder in cold blood, not some grownups, but four little girls while they were praying to the same god the white man taught them to pray to, and you and I see the government go down and can't find who did it.

Why, this man—he can find Eichmann hiding down Argentina somewhere. Let two or three American soldiers, who are minding somebody else's business way over in South Vietnam, get killed, and he'll send battleships, sticking his nose in their business. He wanted to send troops down to Cuba and make them have what he calls free elections—this old cracker who doesn't have free elections in his own country. No, if you never see me another time in your life, if I die in the morning, I'll die saying one thing: the ballot or the bullet, the ballot or the bullet.

If a Negro in 1964 has to sit around and wait for some cracker senator to filibuster when it comes to the rights of black people, why, you and I should hang our heads in shame. You talk about a march on Washington in 1963, you haven't seen anything. There's some more going down in '64. And this time they're not going like they went last year. They're not going singing "We Shall Overcome." They're not going with white friends. They're not going with placards already painted for them. They're not going with round-trip tickets. They're going with one-way tickets.

And if they don't want that non-nonviolent army going down there, tell them to bring the filibuster to a halt. The black nationalists aren't going to wait. Lyndon B. Johnson is the head of the Democratic Party. If he's for civil rights, let him go into the Senate next week and declare himself. Let him go in there right now and declare himself. Let him go in there and denounce the Southern branch of his party. Let him go in there right now and take a moral stand—right now, not later. Tell him, don't wait until election time. If he

waits too long, brothers and sisters, he will be responsible for letting a condition develop in this country which will create a climate that will bring seeds
up out of the ground with vegetation on the end of them looking like something these people never dreamed of. In 1964, it's the ballot or the bullet.
Thank you.

R. D. LAING (1927–   ),
Violence and Love

"Alienation as our present destiny," writes the Scots-born psychoanalyst R. D. Laing, "is achieved only by outrageous violence perpetrated by human beings on human beings." Various forms of violence have been described in this volume by writers as diverse as Jonathan Swift and Karl Marx, Jack London and Robert Jungk, Mary Wollstonecraft and Malcolm X. Laing's purpose in the essay below (1965) is to consider violence committed in daily life through the cultivation of a false consciousness which cripples our senses, our moral convictions, and our imagination. It is a process that Laing calls "the mystification of experience," for it teaches us to mistrust our truest perceptions. In Laing's piece one recognizes the intellectual tradition also represented in Blake's "The Marriage of Heaven and Hell"; seeing the insanity of adjusting to an insane world, both of them dare us to be sane. Most certainly on the side of the Blakeian Devils, Laing writes with the intensity of infernal vision.

From the moment of birth, when the stone-age baby first confronts its twentieth-century mother, the baby is subjected to forces of outrageous violence, called love, as its mother and father have been, and their parents and their parents before them. These forces are mainly concerned with destroying most of the baby's potentialities. This enterprise is on the whole successful. By the time the new human being is fifteen or so, we are left with a being like ourselves, a half-crazed creature, more or less adjusted to a mad world. This is normality in our present age.

Love and violence, properly speaking, are polar opposites. Love lets its object be, but with affection and concern. Violence attempts to constrain its object's freedom, to force it to act in the way we desire, with ultimate indifference to its object's own existence or destiny.

My theme is that we are effectively destroying ourselves by violence masquerading as love.

Let us suppose that we live in two worlds, an inner world and an outer world. What I refer to as the inner world is not located in space "inside" the body or the mind; rather, it is an accepted way of talking which will serve our present purpose well enough, as long as we do not take the distinction between inner and outer too literally. By inner, I refer to our personal idiom for experiencing our bodies, other people, the animate and inanimate world:

imagination, dreams, fantasy, and beyond that to reaches of experience that, once more for want of a better word I shall call spiritual.

I shall restate a frequently reiterated assertion about modern man, that is, about ourselves: in gaining control of the outer world, we have largely lost touch with the inner world. We have become strangers to our own experience, we are alienated from ourselves.

The average man over twenty-five—allow me this fiction—is almost totally estranged from inner experiences. He has little awareness of the body as a subjective event. He has little capacity of imagination. He has usually totally forgotten his whole world of experience before the age of seven. He may remember none of his dreams, or perhaps only one repetitive childhood nightmare. The mode of experience which psychoanalysts call fantasy is even more remote from his consciousness, and is usually totally unknown; he may even be incredulous that there is such a thing. And immediate experience, in contrast to belief or faith, of a spiritual realm, of demons, spirits, Powers, Dominions, Principalities, Seraphim and Cherubim, the Light, is even more remote. As domains of experience become more remote it requires greater and greater open-mindedness even to conceive of their existence.

Many people do not believe that every night they enter a realm of experience during sleep, in which they forget their dreams when they awake. Even some psychoanalysts do not believe that fantasy is an ever-present corporeal experience that underpins all others, and as for spiritual experience, even many of those who are fully aware of fantasy believe that fantasy is the furthest that experience goes under "normal" circumstances. Beyond that is simply the realm of the pathological, hallucinations, phantasmagoric mirages, delusions.

This state of affairs represents an almost unbelievable devastation of our experience. This devastation is the work of violence that has been perpetrated on each of us, and by each of us on ourselves. Much of this violence is subsumed under the name of love.

I am a specialist, God help me, in events in inner space and time, in those experiences that are fairly inaccurately described as thoughts, images, reveries, memories, dreams, visions, hallucinations, dreams of memories, memories of dreams, memories of visions, dreams of hallucinations, refractions of refractions of refractions of that original Alpha and Omega of experience and reality, that Reality on whose repression, denial, splitting, projection, falsification, and general desecration and profanation our civilization as much as on anything is based.

When our inner world begins to be rediscovered, small wonder that what we come upon is a shambles. I refer to ourselves. Bodies half-dead: genitals dissociated from genitals. Without inner unity, with just enough sense of continuity to clutch at identity, that current idolatry. We live equally out of our bodies, and out of our minds.

When, to use Heidegger's phrase, "the Dreadful has already happened," we can hardly expect other than that the Thing will echo externally the destruction already wrought internally. Concerned as I am with this inner world, observing day in and day out its devastation, I ask why has this happened?

One cause of this internal destruction is that we are endowed with a capacity to act inwardly on our experience of ourselves, others, and the world, as well as to act outwardly through behavior itself on the external world.

We act inwardly on our experience at the behest of others, just as we learn to behave in compliance to them. We are taught what to experience and what not to experience, as we are taught what movements to make and what sounds to emit. A child of two is already a moral mover and moral talker and moral experiencer. He already moves the "right" way, makes the "right" noises, and knows what he should feel and what he should not feel. His movements have become stereometric types, enabling the anthropologist to identify the child's national, even his regional characteristics through his rhythm and style. As he is taught to move in specific ways, out of the whole range of possible movements, so he is taught to experience, out of the whole range of possible experience.

The family is usually the first instrument for what is called socialization, that is, getting each new recruit to the human race to behave and experience in substantially the same way as those who have already gotten here. We are all fallen Sons of Prophecy, who have learned to die in the Spirit and be reborn in the flesh. This is known also as selling one's birthright for a mess of pottage.

I have some difficulty in being precise here, because I cannot give examples either from my consulting-room or my own research at this moment. But I shall cite some examples from Jules Henry, professor of anthropology and sociology at Washington University, in his study of the American school system:[1]

> The observer is just entering her fifth-grade classroom for the observation period. The teacher says, "Which one of you nice polite boys would like to take [the observer's] coat and hang it up?" From the waving hands, it would seem that all would like to claim the honor. The teacher chooses one child, who takes the observer's coat. . . . The teacher conducted the arithmetic lessons mostly by asking, "Who would like to tell the answer to the next problem?" This question was followed by the usual large and agitated forest of hands, with apparently much competition to answer.

> What strikes us here is the precision with which the teacher was able to mobilize the potentialities in the boys for the proper social behavior, and the speed with which they responded. The large number of waving hands proves that most of the boys have already become absurd; but they have no choice. Suppose they sat there frozen? . . .

> A skilled teacher sets up many situations in such a way that a *negative attitude can be construed only as treason*. The function of questions like, "Which one of you nice polite boys would like to take [the observer's] coat and hang it up?" is to bind the children into absurdity—to compel them to acknowledge that absurdity is existence, to acknowledge that it is better to exist absurd than not to exist at all. The reader will have observed that the question is not put, "Who *has* the answer to the next problem?" but, "Who *would like to tell* it?" What at one time in our culture was phrased as a challenge in skill in arithmetic, becomes an invitation to group participation. The essential issue is *that nothing is but what it is made to be by the alchemy of the system.*

> In a society where competition for the basic cultural goods is a pivot of action, people cannot be taught to love one another. It thus becomes necessary for the school to teach children how to hate, and without appearing to do so, for our culture cannot tolerate the idea that babes should hate each other.

1. "American Schoolrooms: Learning the Nightmare," *Columbia University Forum,* 6, no. 2 (Spring 1963): 24–30, which is a condensation of Chapter Eight of J. Henry, *Culture Against Man* (New York: Random House, 1963). [Laing's note.]

Here is another example given by Henry:

Boris had trouble reducing 12/16 to the lowest terms, and could only get as far as 6/8. The teacher asked him quietly if that was as far as he could reduce it. She suggested he "think." Much heaving up and down and waving of hands by other children, all frantic to correct him. Boris pretty unhappy, probably mentally paralyzed. The teacher, quiet, patient, ignores the others and concentrates with look and voice on Boris. After a minute or two she turns to the class and says, "Well, who can tell Boris what the number is?" A forest of hands appears, and the teacher calls Peggy. Peggy says that four may be divided into the numerator and the denominator.

Henry comments:

Boris's failure has made it possible for Peggy to succeed; his misery is the occasion for her rejoicing. This is a standard condition of the contemporary American elementary school. To a Zuni, Hopi, or Dakota Indian, Peggy's performance would seem cruel beyond belief, for competition, the wringing of success from somebody's failure, is a form of torture foreign to those noncompetitive cultures.
Looked at from Boris's point of view, the nightmare at the blackboard was, perhaps, a lesson in controlling himself so that he would not fly shrieking from the room under enormous public pressure. Such experiences force every man reared in our culture, over and over again, night in, night out, even at the pinnacle of success, to dream not of success, but of failure. In school the external nightmare is internalized for life. Boris was not learning arithmetic only; he was learning the *essential nightmare also. To be successful in our culture one must learn to dream of failure.*

It is Henry's contention that education in practice has never been an instrument to free the mind and the spirit of man, but to bind them. We think we want creative children, but what do we want them to create?

If all through school the young were provoked to question the Ten Commandments, the sanctity of revealed religion, the foundations of patriotism, the profit motive, the two-party system, monogamy, the laws of incest, and so on. . . . [*Ibid.*, p. 25]

—there would be such creativity that society would not know where to turn. Children do not easily give up their innate imagination, curiosity, and dreaminess. You have to love them to get them to do that. Love is the path through permissiveness to discipline.
What school must do is to induce children to want to think the way the school wants them to think. "What we see," in the American kindergarten and early schooling process, Henry says, "is the pathetic surrender of babies" (*ibid.*, p. 26). You will, I trust, recognize the principles whether they are applied later on or sooner, in the school or in the home.
Just the fact that this is "American" enables one to see it, because it is possibly that bit different. It is the most difficult thing in the world to see this sort of thing in our own culture.
What Henry describes in American schools is a strategy that I have observed frequently in British families studied by my colleagues and myself. I have called this strategy *mystification,* taking the concept from the description given by Karl Marx of the way the exploiting class seeks to bemuse the ex-

ploited by representing forms of exploitation as forms of benevolence, so that the exploited are induced to feel grateful for their victimization, and mad or wrong to try to reverse the state of affairs.

Let me present an example that may serve further to epitomize what I have in mind:

A child is playing noisily in the evening; his mother is tired and wants him to go to bed. A straight statement would be:

"I am tired. I want you to go to bed," or:
"Go to bed, because I say so," or:
"Go to bed, because it's your bedtime."

A mystifying way to induce the child to go to bed would be:

"I'm sure you feel tired, darling, and want to go to bed now, don't you?"

Mystification occurs here in different respects. What is ostensibly a statement about how the child feels ("you are tired") is really a command: "Go to bed." The child is told how he feels (he may or may not feel or be tired), and what he is told he feels is what mother feels herself. If we suppose he does not feel tired he may contradict his mother's statement. He may then become liable to a further mystifying ploy such as:

"Mother knows best," or:
"Don't be cheeky."

The essence of mystification is that violence is defined as love. Genuine conflict is thereby avoided, for if conflict does occur it breaks in terms that are already subverted. It is claimed, for instance, that when one is really being spontaneous one is being selfish and ungrateful, and so on.

The result of our adjustment to our society is that having been tricked out of our minds, that is to say, out of our personal world of experience, out of that unique meaning with which potentially we may endow the external world, we have been simultaneously conned into the illusion that we are separate "skin-encapsulated egos." Having at one and the same time lost our *selves,* and developed the illusion that we are autonomous *egos,* we are expected to comply by inner consent with external constraints, to an almost unbelievable extent.

The others have installed themselves in our hearts, and we call them ourselves. Each person, not being himself either to others or to himself, just as others are not themselves to themselves or to us, neither recognizes himself in the other, nor the other in himself. Hence being at least a double absence, haunted by the ghost of his own murdered self, no wonder modern man is addicted to other persons, and the more time he spends with others, the more lonely he becomes.

There is a further twist of the tourniquet. For now, love becomes a further alienation, a further act of violence. My need is a need to be needed, my longing is a longing to be longed for. I act now to install what I take to be myself in what I take to be the other person's heart. Proust wrote:

How have we the courage to wish to live, how can we make a movement to preserve ourselves from death, in a world where love is provoked by a lie and consists solely in the need of having our sufferings appeased by whatever being has made us suffer.

But no one makes us suffer. The violence we perpetrate and have done to ourselves, the recriminations, reconciliations, the ecstasies and the agonies of a love affair, are based on the socially conditioned illusion that two actual persons are in relationship. Under the circumstances, this is a dangerous state of hallucination and delusion, a mishmash of fantasy, exploding and imploding, of broken hearts, reparation and revenge.

Yet within all this, I do not preclude the occasions when, most lost, the lovers may discover each other, moments when recognition does occur, when hell can turn to heaven and come down to earth, when this crazy distraction can become joy and celebration.

But my theme has been violence masquerading as love. Once the fissure into self and ego, inner and outer, good and bad occurs, all else is an infernal dance of false dualities. It has always been recognized that if you split Being down the middle, if you insist on grabbing *this* without *that,* if you cling to the good without the bad, denying the one for the other, what happens is that the dissociated evil impulse, now evil in a double sense, returns to permeate and possess the good and turn it into itself.

When the great Tao is lost, spring forth benevolence and righteousness.

When wisdom and sagacity arise, there are great hypocrites.

When family relations are no longer harmonious, we have filial children and devoted parents.

When a nation is in confusion and disorder, patriots are recognized.

We must be very careful of our selective blindness. The Germans reared children in the 'thirties who regarded it as their duty to exterminate the Jews, adore their leader, to kill and die for the Fatherland. The majority of my own generation did not or do not regard it as stark raving mad to feel it better to be dead than Red. None of us, I take it, has lost too many hours' sleep over the threat of imminent annihilation of the human race and our own responsibility for this state of affairs.

In the last fifty years, we human beings have slaughtered by our own hands something like seventy million of our own species. We all live under constant threat of our total annihilation. We seem to seek death and destruction as much as life and happiness. We are driven, it seems, to kill and be killed as we are to live and let live. Only by the most outrageous violation of ourselves have we achieved our capacity to live in relative adjustment to a civilization apparently driven to its own destruction. Perhaps to a limited extent we can undo what has been done to us, and what we have done to ourselves. Perhaps men and women were born to love one another, simply and genuinely, rather than to this travesty that we can call love. If we can stop destroying ourselves we may stop destroying others. We have to begin by admitting and even accepting our violence, rather than blindly destroying ourselves with it, and therewith we have to realize that we are as deeply afraid to live and to love as we are to die.

WILFRED PELLETIER,
Childhood in an Indian Village

A Canadian Odawa Indian, Wilfred Pelletier grew up on Wikwemikong Reserve, Ontario. He has been director of the Canadian National Indian Council and is now with the Institute for Indian Studies at Rochdale College, Toronto. Although his description (1969) of the Indian community cannot serve as a political model for the future of Western industrial society, it does analyze some effects of domestic colonialism, and offers some insight into the forms of social relation that are possible in a noncompetitive society. Pelletier's experience of family life especially, and of the role of children in Odawa society, provides a polar contrast to the American and British norm described by McLuhan and Laing.

Going back as far as I can remember as a child in an Indian community, I had no sense of knowing about the other people around me except that we were all somehow equal; the class structure in the community was horizontal. There was only one class. Nobody was interested in getting on top of anybody else.

You could see it in our games. Nobody organized them. There weren't any competitive sports. But we were involved in lots of activity (I was not like I am now; I was in pretty good shape at that time) and we were organized, but not in the sense that there were ways of finding out who had won and who had lost. We played ball like everyone else, but no one kept score. In fact, you would stay up at bat until you hit the ball. If somebody happened to walk by on the street, an old guy, we'd tease him and bug him to come over and try to hit the ball, and he would come over and he'd swing away. If they threw us out on first, we'd stay on first anyway. We ran to second, and they would throw us out there, and sometimes we'd get thrown out all the way around.

We had a number of other games we used to play. There was one where we used to try and hit each other between two lines with a ball. It didn't really make any difference if you got hit or whether you stayed in the centre and tried to hit the other guy or not. But it was very, very difficult to hit these guys. I remember standing between these two lines, and all of a sudden the guys would take off, and you could be two or three feet from them, and you would have to throw the ball at them, and you just couldn't hit those guys. They were really terrific.

It was later on in life that I began to realize that what we were really doing was *playing*. Very much like animals play. When you observe the bear, the adult, the male and female are always playing with the cubs. The otters do the same thing. None of the kind of play we had was really structured and organized. That came after the recreation directors from the outside world came in and told us that we had a problem in the community, that we were not organized, and they were going to introduce some.

They introduced them all right, and the tremendous competitiveness that went with them. It's not as bad on Manitoulin Island, where I'm from, as it is a lot of other places where competitiveness is rolling in. I'm glad I can remember that as a kid I was able to become involved with a community with others and nobody was competing. Even if we did formally compete in the games we did, no one was a winner though someone may have won. It was only the moment. If you beat someone by pulling a bow and arrow and shooting the arrow further, it only meant that you shot the arrow further at that moment. That's all it lasted. It didn't mean you were better in any way whatsoever. It just meant that at that particular time the arrow went further; maybe it was just the way you let the bow go. These kinds of things are very important to me and that is why I am talking about them and, probably, exploring while I'm talking, now. When I get the opportunity to listen to myself the odd time I try to explore those kinds of things that I can remember as a child.

One of the very important things was the relationship we had with our families. We didn't always live at home. We lived wherever we happened to be at that particular time when it got dark. If you were two or three miles away from home, then that is where you slept. People would feed you even if they didn't know who you were. We'd spend an evening, perhaps, with an old couple, and they would tell us stories. Most of these stories were legends, and they were told to us mostly in the winter-time. In the summer people would generally take us out and we would do a number of things which in some way would allow us to learn about life and what it was all about: that is, by talking about some particular person and demonstrating what that person did. At no time, in all the years I spent there, do I ever remember anyone teaching us anything.

I have been to numerous communities across Canada and I still do not find where Indians teach. All young children were allowed to grow, to develop, to learn. They didn't teach you that this was mommy, daddy, desk, ash-tray, house, etc. We learned about these things by listening to the words adults spoke, what they said when they were talking, and built our own kind of relationship with the article. If you observe your children now you will see a child turn a chair over, cover it with a blanket and use it for a house. He can relate many ways to a chair. As we get older we have only one relationship and that is to stick our rear ends on that chair. It's for no other purpose, and, in fact, we tell our kids that that is what it is, and it belongs in a corner and don't move it out of there.

These things I remember very well. We were brought up to have a different relationship to a house and to all the things that surrounded us. That is, the values that adults placed on things in the community did not necessarily carry over into their child and lead him to place the same values on them.

Children discovered the values of these things on their own, and developed their own particular relationship to them.

This is very closely related to the religion of the community, which centred entirely on man. One of the practiced ethics of the community was non-interference. No one interfered with us, and this way of living still exists today. If you go to an Indian home the kids don't come up and bug you while you are talking to someone else. They might come and stand by you quietly, just as an adult might. If you observe Indians someplace, they will stand quietly, and only when they are acknowledged, will they speak. If they get into a group session, they will act the same way. They will sit and listen to people talk, and when they get the opportunity they will speak, but they won't cut you off or interfere. There are some who do this now, but not very many. Most of them will just wait. The whole background in the educational system was that of observing and feeling. This is how they learned.

It was a very different kind of learning situation that we were in as children. In fact, all of the things we did related to our way of life. Everything had to fit into the whole; we didn't learn things in parts. As an example: if we watched someone running an outboard motor, we would learn everything that was involved in working that motor. If someone taught someone here to do that, after he was finished he might add a safety program on top of it. This would be an additional thing. The way Indians learned it, they built in a safety program while they were learning through their observations and because their very lives depended on their doing it right.

And just as we didn't separate our learning from our way of life, we didn't separate our work from it either. The older women, for example, who used to work all day at whatever—tanning hides, etc., didn't really think of it as work. It was a way of life. That's the real difference between the kind of society we have now where we equate these kinds of things with work and yet will go out and play sports and enjoy it and the kind of society I'm talking about. Here we go and work and use maybe half or a quarter of the energy we spend playing sports, but we call it work and we feel differently about it altogether. These are the kinds of differences that exist. Indian people who had a way of life and who felt it was their way of life didn't call it work. It was part of the way they provided for their families; and they "worked" very hard.

One of the reasons, of course, why they didn't call it "work" was that they didn't have any foremen. As I mentioned before, there wasn't any kind of a vertical structure in the community. In these communities what existed was a sharing of power. In spite of what everybody says, we really didn't have chiefs, that is, people who were bosses. We had medicine men, who were wise men. The rest were leaders in particular ways. They weren't leaders as we look at them today. It was a different kind of leadership in that the person who was leader had special abilities, say in fishing or hunting. He took the leadership that day, and then discarded the leadership when he was finished with the job. He had power only for the time he wanted to do something. That power came in all forms of all the things he did in the community, so that he used power only for the things he wanted to do, and then he immediately shed it so that someone else could pick it up and it could change hands several times in the community in a day or a week or whatever.

Only in times of war and disaster was a vertical structure used. The war chief would designate various jobs to various people and use that vertical structure. This was only in times of danger. Otherwise, it was horizontal. My grandfather one time told me this, although it didn't sink in until just a few years ago, that to have power is destructive. You'll be destructive if you have power because if people don't join you, then you will destroy them. I forgot this and dug around for power and began to lose friends. I was making decisions for people even with the background I have. Now I have such a problem fighting this thing off, because people are always putting me in a position where I have power. They say I am director of the Institute of Indian Studies. This is not true. I'm just at Rochdale College. Where I am everyone makes up their own minds in terms of what they want to do, and they do those things, and if I can be of assistance, then I assist. I've got my own thing that I hope to do. One of the things that I'm interested in is the kind of lives that the young Indian people now at Rochdale live—what is happening to them in the city.

The city has special problems for them as it had for me. For many of them were raised in Indian homes, where the attitude is that no child ever should be rejected. In an Indian home, if a child's face is dirty or his diaper is wet, he is picked up by anyone. The mother or father or whoever comes into the house. He is never rejected. And they don't stick children in cribs, where they can only look in one direction—up. The child generally sits or stands (often tied in), so he can relate to the world in all directions. And children are fed whenever they are hungry. They are never allowed to be in want. Whatever is wanted is given to them. If a child wants to play with something, it is always placed in his hand. No one would think of putting a rattle slightly out of reach, so he would try to grab it and be aggressive. No one would think of feeding the baby only at set times. What follows this approach in terms of attitudes and way of life is immense. The child's nature is very strongly influenced in the first four or five years. The children become very non-competitive. They have no need to compete.

The whole situation changes, however, when they go out into the world, where the attitudes and values are totally different. A world, further, in which their values are not acceptable. Where for many of us as children we were not even permitted to speak our own language. Of course, we still tried to speak our own language, but we were punished for it. Four or five years ago they were still stripping the kids of their clothes up around Kenora and beating them for speaking their own language. It is probably still happening in many other institutions today. I was punished several times for speaking Indian not only on the school grounds but off the school grounds and on the street, and I lived across from the school. Almost in front of my own door my first language was forbidden me, and yet when I went into the house my parents spoke Indian.

Our language is so important to us as a people. Our language and our language structure related to our whole way of life. How beautiful that picture language is where they only tell you the beginning and the end, and you fill in everything, and they allow you to feel how you want to feel. Here we manipulate and twist things around and get you to hate a guy. The Indian doesn't do that. He'll just say that some guy got into an accident, and he won't give you any details. From there on you just explore as far as you want to. You'll say: "What happened?", and he'll tell you a little more. "Did he go through the windshield?" "Yep!" He only answers questions. All of the in-between you fill in for yourself as you see it. We are losing that feeling when we lose our language at school. We are taught English, not Indian, as our first language. And that changes our relationship with our parents. All of a sudden we begin saying to our parents "you're stupid." We have begun to equate literacy with learning, and this is the first step down. It is we who are going down and not our parents, and because of that separation we are going down lower and lower on the rung because it is we who are rejecting our parents; they are not rejecting us. The parents know that, but they are unable to do anything about it. And we take on the values, and the history of somebody else.

And part of the reason our parents say so little is that that's their way. They don't teach like white people; they let their children make their own decisions. The closest they ever got to formal teaching was to tell us stories. Let me give you an example. We had been out picking blueberries one time, and while sitting around this guy told us this story. The idea was that he wanted to get us to wash up—to wash our feet because we had been tramping through this brush all day long. He talked about a warrior who really had a beautiful body. He was very well built, and he used to grease himself and take care of his body. One day this warrior was out, and he ran into a group of other people whom he had never seen before. They started to chase him. He had no problem because he was in such good shape. He was fooling around and playing with them because he was such a good runner. He ran over hills and over rocks, teasing them. Then he ran into another group. The first group gave up the chase. But now he had to run away from this other group, and he was fooling around doing the same thing with them. All of a sudden he ran into a third group. He ran real hard and all of a sudden he fell. He tried to get up and he couldn't. He spoke to his feet and said "What's wrong with you? I'm going to get killed if you don't get up and get going." They said: "That's alright. You can comb your hair and grease your body and look after your legs and arms but you never did anything for us. You never washed us or cleaned us or greased us or nothing." He promised to take better care of the feet if they would get up and run, and so they did.

This is one of the stories we were told, and we went up and washed our feet right away and then went to bed. Maybe this happens among other ethnic groups, I don't know, but this is the kind of learning we had. I will never forget the kinds of things we learned, because to me it all belongs to me. It isn't something that someone says is so; it's mine. I'd want to go hunting, and the guys would know I couldn't get across the stream because it was flooded, but they wouldn't say anything. They'd let me go, and I'd tell them I'd see them later where the rocks are, and they'd say O.K. knowing all this time I couldn't get through. But they wouldn't tell me that. They'd let me experience it. And I'm grateful to these people for allowing me to have this kind of exploration/learning situation. Secondly, of course, the fact is that maybe I could have gotten across where they couldn't, discovered something different, a method that was new. I think this kind of learning situation is one of the really important things that Indians have today and which could contribute to the society we have today. That is, a learning situation *for people,* instead of teaching or information giving.

All these things—the various ways Indian life differed from that in our present society—I didn't learn until after I left the reserve community later on in life. Then I could understand how very differently structured the two communities are. While it didn't have a vertical structure, our community was very highly structured. So highly structured that there wasn't anything that could happen that somebody could almost immediately, in some way, solve, whatever problem arose. Without any given signals or the appearance of any communication whatsoever (there were no telephones) the most complex social action used to happen. If somebody died in that community, nobody ever said we should dig a grave. The grave was dug, the box was made, everything was set up . . . the one who baked pies baked pies. Everyone did something in that community, and if you tried to find out who organized it, you couldn't.

It's exactly the same way today. You cannot find out who organizes these things. In 1964 Prime Minister Pearson came up to the reserve. We had a cocktail party in the hall, and at the same time there was a big buffet organized for him. This was organized by a woman from Toronto. She went up there and set this whole thing up. He had been coming there every year. This was his riding. Every year they turned out a beautiful meal for him, and he never knew who to thank because it was just all of a sudden there; it was done. The people just got together. There was no foreman or boss. There was no vertical structure, and it just happened. You should have been there in '64. It was chaotic. There were no knives, no deserts, nobody had cut up the heads of lettuce that were all over, because this woman came there and gave orders, and the people wouldn't do anything until she told them what to do. She got so busy that she couldn't tell everybody what to do, and she had four or five turkeys all over the town in different people's ovens, and that's where they sat. They had to go and tell the women to bring the turkeys down because they wouldn't do it on their own. There was someone in charge. Had there not been anyone in charge it would have gone off fine. It was a real mess. This is the difference. Here you organize, and you know those kinds of structures, and they mean something to you. You instinctively behave in certain ways to those things.

But it's more than that too. As I see it, organization comes out of a need for immediate order—say in war. When it develops this way so that people say let's organize, and they get together and create a vertical structure, and place somebody up at the top and then it becomes a power group, and from there on it filters on down until after a while you have somebody running that organization, two or three people or maybe eventually just one, and all the rest of the people get suppressed, pushed down, and held down by that very thing they formally sought. You give power to someone and suppress others.

I don't know if a different kind of structural organization can exist today. I know some people are trying to make a different one—some people in Rochdale College and I suspect in many places where people are getting together and trying to live communally. I remember as a child a different kind of organization existing, and I have come to call it now "community consciousness." That community can exist and function and solve all its problems without any kinds of signals, like a school of fish. All of a sudden you see them move; they shift altogether. That is exactly the way most Indian communities function. And yet we have the Department of Indian Affairs coming and telling us we have no organization. The local priest or minister will come and tell us we have to be organized. The Recreation Department will come along and say there's no organization in this community. And when they come it's like shooting a goose in a flock of geese. When you hit him you disrupt the pattern. So every time somebody comes into the community they disrupt the pattern. Every time you remove a resource person from the community you disrupt the pattern. You break it up, and they have to re-organize. But in a lot of communities this is very hard to do, and some of them have been too hurt to make it. Indian resource people begin to drop out of sight and white organizers take over, making it even more difficult for Indian people to function. I know that in one community where there are 740 people (about two-thirds of them children) there are 18 organizations. There are 3 churches that all have 2 or 3 organizations, and there is also a community development officer who has a number of organizations behind him, and they are in such conflict that the community cannot function. It's just sitting there, with people at each other's throats. The people who come in can't understand that if a guy is sitting under a tree and doing nothing but observing the stars or the clouds in the daytime or the birds flying, he is running through a recreational pattern and at the same time he is learning. These are all parts of a whole. Most Indian people deal with wholeness. It is much different than the way we deal with things where we segment them and deal with them only in parts.

It is also very difficult to know what to do now—now that the organizers have come in. The dependency is so great and government and outside resources have created this dependency. They have removed most of the human resource and certainly all the economic base from most Indian communities and there is very little left. Yet the Indian relationship to that dependency is much different from ours in this society. Indians may receive welfare, but most of them feel it is a right. They don't look down on people who are on welfare. Drawing welfare doesn't change the nature of the person. In the same way, if they walk into a room that is messy they don't say the woman is sloppy. They say the room is sloppy. A lot of them don't paint their houses. That is because they don't have the same relationship to that house that we in this society do. Clothes don't make the man. Relationships are built on something that is not materialistic. The same thing applies to money. If you observe your children when they have money, they want to get rid of it right away. How long do children stay mad at one another? A moment. All of these behaviour patterns that you observe in children are very much related to adult Indians. Your history books say that when the white men first came here they noted that the Indians were very child-like. That is very true in many ways. But if you look at it, how beautiful to be child-like and yet be mature. Here we say that you mustn't show feelings. I don't agree with that. If a man can cry, then he has feelings. Indians cry all the time. We get together and sing songs, and we cry in these songs. But this society is very machine-like, and so we begin to act like machines and then we become machines.

Because of this approach Indians don't really want to fight for their rights. They really don't want to get into the society at all. In this way they are probably different from the black people on this continent who are a much larger group, and have no choice but to fight for their rights. When they get these rights, what they are doing in essence is moving into society. When they do get in, they might make the changes they want in terms of their cultural background or how they look at things, or whatever, and these changes may give them the freedom to practice or do those things they want to do.

But the Indians have fundamentally rejected society as it now is. The Indians are expert at making all programs that the Indian Affairs Branch has ever come up with a failure by withdrawing. The Indians embrace everything that comes into a community. If you want to build a church, that's fine. We'll help you build that church, etc. Then once they see that they can't relate to that church in any way, they withdraw and the thing falls apart. If you want to build a road, they'll help you build one, with the result that some reserves have roads running all over the place, but nobody uses them. The Branch has a history of complete failure. The Indians have always rejected it. We have a society here where we must win. For everything you do you must end up fighting—fighting for your rights, good against evil, war against poverty, the fight for peace. The whole base of the western culture has an enemy concept. What would happen if you remove the enemy? How then do you defeat somebody who is on your side? I suspect that if you remove the enemy the culture might collapse. The Indian can't fight on your terms. For a start he doesn't even have the numbers, much less the inclination. So he withdraws. And he pays a certain price. He suffers poverty in many ways.

But maybe the future is with the Indian. Marshall McLuhan says that the only people living in the 21st century are the Indians, the Eskimos, some French people and the Japanese. All the rest, because they deal with history, live in the 19th century because they deal with the past and not the present. The pan-Indian movement, with the Native American Church, recognizes this and there are various Indian cultures that are moving closer and closer together. It's a spontaneous thing that just happened. It's just growing and there isn't anyone who is heading it up. It's a movement. And it's made me much more hopeful.

BIBLIOGRAPHY

The bibliography follows the sequence of material in the volume.

AMOS, THUCYDIDES, PLUTARCH, FLORUS

Lindblom, J. *Prophecy in Ancient Israel.* Philadelphia, 1962.
Mays, James L. *Amos: A Commentary.* Philadelphia, 1969.
Hammond, N. G. L. *A History of Greece to 322 B.C.* Oxford, 1959.
Warman, M. S. *From Pericles to Cleophon: A Source Book and Reader in Athenian Politics.* London, 1954.
Athenian Studies Presented to William Scott Ferguson. Cambridge, Mass., 1940.
Seager, Robin, ed. *The Crisis of the Roman Republic: Studies in Political and Social History.* New York, 1969.
Plutarch's Lives, trans. Bernadotte Perrin. London, 1914–1926.

HERESY, BALL, FROISSART

Auerbach, Erich. *Literary Language and Its Public in Late Latin Antiquity and in the Middle Ages.* New York, 1965.
Pirenne, Henri. *Economic and Social History of Medieval Europe.* London, 1936.
Leff, Gordon. *Heresy in the Later Middle Ages.* Manchester, 1967.
Throop, Palmer A. *Criticism of the Crusade: A Study of Opinion and Crusade Propaganda.* Amsterdam, 1940.
Hilton, Rodney and Fagan, H. *The English Rising of 1381.* London, 1950.

TÁBORITES, MÜNTZER

Cohn, Norman. *The Pursuit of the Millenium.* London, 1957.
Kaminsky, Howard. *A History of the Hussite Revolution.* Berkeley, 1967.
Macek, Josef. *The Hussite Movement in Bohemia.* Prague, 1958.
Spinka, Matthew. *John Hus: A Biography.* Princeton, 1968.
Williams, George Huntston. *The Radical Reformation.* Philadelphia, 1962.
Engels, Frederick. *The Peasant War in Germany.* New York, 1926.
Kautsky, Karl. *Communism in Central Europe in the Time of the Reformation.* London, 1897, New York, 1959.

MILTON, WINSTANLEY, SWIFT

Milton, John, *The Works of John Milton,* 2 vols. Edited by Frank A. Patterson. New York, 1940.
Prall, Stuart E., ed. *The Puritan Revolution: A Documentary History.* New York, 1968.
Hill, Christopher. *Puritanism and Revolution.* London, 1958.
Wolfe, Don M. *Milton in the Puritan Revolution.* New York, 1941.

Weber, Max. *The Protestant Ethic and the Spirit of Capitalism.* London, 1930.
Swift, Jonathan. *Prose Works of Jonathan Swift,* 14 vols. Edited by Herbert Davis. Oxford, 1939, New York, 1964–1968.
Ferguson, Oliver Watkins. *Jonathan Swift and Ireland.* Urbana, 1962.
Gipson, Lawrence H. *The British Empire before the American Revolution.* New York, 1958.

HENRY, PAINE, BLAKE, WOLLSTONECRAFT, SHELLEY

Beard, Charles A. *An Economic Interpretation of the Constitution of the United States.* New York, 1913.
Paine, Thomas, *Complete Writings of Thomas Paine.* Edited by Philip S. Foner. New York, 1945.
Lefebvre, Georges. *The Coming of the French Revolution, 1789.* New York, 1947.
Blake, William, *The Poetry and Prose of William Blake.* Edited by David V. Erdman. New York, 1965.
Erdman, David V. *Blake, Prophet Against Empire.* Princeton, 1954.
Shelley, Percy Bysshe, *Complete Works of Percy Bysshe Shelley.* Edited by R. Ingpen and Walter E. Peck. 10 vols., New York, 1926–1930; reprint edition, Staten Island, N.Y., 1965.
Brailsford, Henry Noel. *Shelley, Godwin, and Their Circle.* New York, 1913.
Cameron, Kenneth Neill. *The Young Shelley: Genesis of a Radical.* New York, 1950.

CARLYLE, MARX, ENGELS

Carlyle, Thomas, *The Works of Thomas Carlyle.* 30 vols. Edited by H. D. Traill. New York, 1896–1901, 1969.
Houghton, Walter E. *The Victorian Frame of Mind, 1830–1870.* New Haven, 1957.
DuVeau, Georges. *1848, the Making of a Revolution.* New York, 1967.
Thompson, E. P. *The Making of the English Working Class.* New York, 1963.
Hammond, J. L. and Hammond, Barbara. *The Town Labourer.* London, 1917.
Berlin, Isaiah. *Karl Marx, His Life and Environment.* London, 1939.
Garaudy, Roger. *Karl Marx: The Evolution of His Thought.* New York, 1967.
Lenin, V. I. *Marx, Engels, Marxism: A Collection of Articles.* New York, 1935.

DOUGLASS, THOREAU

Thoreau, Henry David, *The Writings of Henry David Thoreau,* 20 vols. New York, 1906.
Stampp, Kenneth. *The Peculiar Institution.* New York, 1956.
Elkins, Stanley. *Slavery.* Chicago, 1959.
Aptheker, Herbert. *American Negro Slave Revolts.* New York, 1943.
Duberman, Martin B., ed. *The Antislavery Vanguard: New Essays on the Abolitionists.* Princeton, 1965.
Marx, Karl and Engels, Frederick. *The Civil War in the United States.* New York, 1937.

MORRIS, KROPOTKIN

Morris, William, *Collected Works of William Morris.* 24 vols. Edited by May Morris. New York, 1910–1915, 1966.
Thompson, E. P. *William Morris: Romantic to Revolutionary.* London, 1955.
Adams, Henry. *Mont-Saint-Michel and Chartres.* Boston, 1905.
Klingender, F. D. *Art and the Industrial Revolution.* London, 1947.
Plekhanov, George. *Anarchism and Socialism.* Chicago, 1908.
Krimerman, Leonard I. and Perry, Lewis, ed. *Patterns of Anarchy: A Collection of Writings on the Anarchist Tradition.* New York, 1966.

STANTON

Stanton, Elizabeth Cady. *History of Woman Suffrage.* New York, 1881.
Kraditor, Aileen S. *Ideas of the Woman Suffrage Movement, 1890–1920.* New York, 1965.
Friedan, Betty. *The Feminine Mystique.* New York, 1963.
Bird, Carolyn. *Born Female: The High Cost of Keeping Women Down.* New York, 1968.
Engels, Frederick. *The Origin of the Family, Private Property, and the State.* New York, 1942.

DUBOIS, LONDON, DEBS

Herskovits, Melville J. *The Myth of the Negro Past.* New York, 1941.
Myrdal, Gunnar. *An American Dilemma: The Negro Problem and Modern Democracy.* New York, 1944.
Debs, His Life, Writings, and Speeches. Girard, Kansas, 1908.
Boyle, Robert O. and Morais, Herbert. *Labor's Untold Story.* New York, 1955.

MAO, TROTSKY, CAUDWELL

Mao Tse-Tung. *Selected Works of Mao Tse-Tung.* Peking, 1965.
Strong, Anna Louise. *China's Millions: The Revolutionary Struggles from 1927 to 1935.* New York, 1935.
Burchett, Wilfred G. *China's Feet Unbound.* Melbourne, 1952.
Hinton, William. *Fanshen: A Documentary of Revolution in a Chinese Village.* New York, 1966.
Deutscher, Isaac. *The Prophet Armed. Trotsky: 1879–1921.* New York, 1954.
———. *The Prophet Unarmed. Trotsky: 1921–1929.* New York, 1959.
———. *The Prophet Outcast. Trotsky: 1929–1940.* New York, 1963.
Orwell, George. *Homage to Catalonia.* London, 1938.

MCLUHAN, BARTHES, JUNGK

Mills, C. Wright. *The Power Elite.* New York, 1956.
Marcuse, Herbert. *One-Dimensional Man.* Boston, 1964.
Caudwell, Christopher. *Illusion and Reality: A Study of the Sources of Poetry.* London, 1937.
Fischer, Ernst. *The Necessity of Art.* Baltimore, 1963.
Trotsky, Leon. *Literature and Revolution.* New York, 1925.
Mao Tse-Tung. *Talks at the Yenan Forum on Literature and Art.* In *Selected Works,* vol. III. Peking, 1967.
Hersey, John. *Hiroshima.* New York, 1946.
Alperovitz, Gar. *Atomic Diplomacy: Hiroshima and Potsdam.* New York, 1965.

HO, GUEVARA, MALCOLM X

Lacouture, Jean. *Vietnam: Between Two Truces.* New York, 1966.
Raskin, Marcus G. and Fall, Bernard B., ed. *The Viet-Nam Reader.* New York, 1965.
Schell, Jonathan. *The Village of Ben Suc.* New York, 1967.
Zinn, Howard. *Vietnam: the Logic of Withdrawal.* Boston, 1967.
Zeitlin, Maurice and Scheer, Robert. *Cuba: Tragedy in Our Hemisphere.* New York, 1963.

James, Daniel, ed. *The Complete Bolivian Diaries of Ché Guevara and Other Captured Documents*. New York, 1968.
The Autobiography of Malcolm X. New York, 1964.

LAING, PELLETIER
Laing, R. D. *The Politics of Experience*. New York, 1967.
Szasz, Thomas. *Law, Liberty and Psychiatry*. New York, 1963.
Goodman, Paul. *Growing Up Absurd*. New York, 1960.
Ariès, Philippe. *Centuries of Childhood: A Social History of Family Life*. London, 1962.

INDEX

Abolition movement, 157, 173, 176, 177, 242
Adams, Samuel, 240, 241
"Admonition to Peace," 51, 106
Adventures of Ideas, 314
advertising, as social propaganda, 309; and woman's role, 309–310, 313–315
Alexis, Saint, 30
alienation, 320, 353, 354
Alison, William Pulteney, 133, 138
Allison, Saul K., 326
Alvarez, Luis W., 322, 323, 325
American Railway Union, 238
American Revolution, 85, 101–106, 240, 241–242, 244
Amos, 7
Analysis of Matter, 281
Analysis of Mind, 281
anarchists, views on law and authority, 187–197
Anthony, Susan B., 200
Anti-Slavery Convention, World's, 198–199
anti-war protests, 238–248, 250–251
Arnold, Matthew, 129
art, 202, 288; and medieval industry, 208–211; symbolist esthetic theory, 312
atheism, 129–131, 138
Athens-Melos dialogue, 11–17
atomic bomb, construction and testing of, 321–328; and Japanese peace feelers, 331–332; opposition to use of, 328–330; used against Japan, 329, 331
atomic bombing, morality of, 321, 332
authority, law and, 187–197
Autobiography of Benjamin Franklin, 310
Autobiography of Malcolm X, 338
automation, 311; as violence, 312

Bacher, Robert F., 325, 326
Ball, John, 34–35, 36–38, 41–44, 46–47
Barthes, Roland, 316
Bastille, taking of, 107–108, 110
Batista, Fulgencio, 333
Baudelaire, Charles P., 317
Bernard of Fontcaude, 24–25, 32
Bethe, Hans, 326
Bisch, Louis E., 310
Black Belt farm-laborers, 213–224
Black Muslims, 338, 347
Black nationalism, "ballot-or-bullet" speech, 338–352; philosophy of, 348–349; on segregation, 344–345, 350
Blake, William, 113, 120
Bohemia, Hussite uprising, 48–50, 60n
Bolsheviks, 240; moral values of, 289–303
Bonaparte, Napoleon, 241, 294
bourgeoisie, 132, 154, 155, 226, 227, 277, 287; definition of, 141n, development of, 141–142; objections to communism, 150–154; and proletariat, 141–149
Brighter Than a Thousand Suns, 321
brotherhood of man concept, 36, 74, 243, 246, 248
Brown, Harrison, 328
Brown, John, 157–172
Burke, Edmund, 101, 106–107, 108, 110, 111, 112, 120, 195
Butler, Samuel, 311
Butow, Robert J. C., 331–332

Campbell, Joseph, 310
capital, 145, 149, 150, 151, 152, 154; definition of, 142n
capitalist system, 132, 243, 248, 249–250, 287, 293
capitalists *see* bourgeoisie
Carlyle, Thomas, 132
Carnegie, Dale, 315